ESSENTIAL ESSAYS
VOLUME 2

Stuart Hall: Selected Writings

A Series Edited by Catherine Hall and Bill Schwarz

ESSENTIAL ESSAYS

Identity and
Diaspora

VOLUME 2 | Stuart Hall

Edited by
David Morley

DUKE UNIVERSITY PRESS | DURHAM AND LONDON | 2019

Library of Congress Cataloging-in-Publication Data
Names: Hall, Stuart, [date] author. | Morley, David, [date] editor.
Title: Essential essays / Stuart Hall ; edited by David Morley.
Other titles: Foundations of cultural studies. | Identity and diaspora.
Description: Durham : Duke University Press, 2018. | Series: Stuart Hall,
    selected writings | Includes bibliographical references and index.
Identifiers: LCCN 2018022953 (print)
LCCN 2018049804 (ebook)
ISBN 9781478002413 (v. 1 ; ebook)
ISBN 9781478002710 (v. 2 ; ebook)
ISBN 9781478000747 (v. 1 ; hardcover ; alk. paper)
ISBN 1478000740 (v. 1 ; hardcover ; alk. paper)
ISBN 9781478000938 (v. 1 ; pbk. ; alk. paper)
ISBN 1478000937 (v. 1 ; pbk. ; alk. paper)
ISBN 9781478001287 (v. 2 ; hardcover ; alk. paper)
ISBN 1478001283 (v. 2 ; hardcover ; alk. paper)
ISBN 9781478001638 (v. 2 ; pbk. ; alk. paper)
ISBN 1478001631 (v. 2 ; pbk. ; alk. paper)
Subjects: LCSH: Sociology. | Culture.
Classification: LCC HM585 (ebook) | LCC HM585 .H34 2018 (print) |
    DDC 301—dc23
LC record available at https://lccn.loc.gov/2018022953

Cover art: Dawoud Bey, *Stuart McPhail Hall, 9 May 1998*, diptych
portrait (detail). Collection of the National Portrait Gallery, London.
© Dawoud Bey. Courtesy of the artist.

CONTENTS

The essays published here represent a number of Stuart Hall's better-known reflections on intellectual life and politics, which, for many of us, still live in the mind. They derive from a long period, over many years. Each is written with verve and a sense of urgency. They are, properly, *essays*—conceived for the moment. They have a life of their own, having shaped to varying degrees the intellectual landscape that remains our own. On these terms, they should be judged.

They were seldom conceived principally as contributions to academic thought, even while their academic impact proved significant. The overriding imperative was to clarify thought on the matter in hand and to suggest a route through the quandaries that, at the time, prevailed. In such circumstances, in Hall's mind the conventions required of academic writing weren't paramount. These mattered, of course, but they didn't preoccupy him. Many of the essays published here began life as talks which, when it was decided they should appear in print, were only retrospectively supplied with the academic apparatus of bibliographies and citations. As talks, or even as essays to be published, this bibliographic labor was often conducted after the event, on the run. This has led us to the conclusion that the production of a uniform text is not possible. What can be done has been done. But the retrospective reconstruction of complete bibliographic referencing is now beyond our reach.

This explains the variety of bibliographic systems that compose the volume as well as the variations in presentation. Meanwhile, in the body of the essays small additions and clarifications occur. Certain minor interpolations have been supplied to explain matters that might otherwise escape contemporary readers, and references from the original publication to companion articles, in journals or books, have been deleted. A small handful of obvious errors has been corrected, misprints dispatched, and the occasional refinement in punctuation has been introduced. But otherwise, the essays presented here remain as they were when they first entered public life.

Catherine Hall
Bill Schwarz
Series Editors

ACKNOWLEDGMENTS

Thanks to Les Back, Kuan-Hsing Chen, and David Scott for agreeing to the republication of their interviews with Stuart Hall. The editor is grateful to Leanne Benford, Vana Goblot, Christian Høgsbjerg, and James Taylor for their help with the script, and to Nick Beech for letting me draw from his indispensable bibliography. Bill Schwarz is owed much more than gratitude, as without all his help the book would simply not exist. We owe more than we can say to Ken Wissoker, who with intellectual insight, labor, and goodwill has brought the Stuart Hall: Selected Writings series to life. Thanks as well to the team at Duke, particularly Elizabeth Ault and Christi Stanforth.

From the Edge of Empire to the Diaspora in the Metropolis

Stuart Hall was born in Kingston, Jamaica, in 1932 into an aspirant middle-class brown Jamaican family. He was always conscious of the overbearing complexity of what he later came to call the "pigmentocracy" of Jamaican society. Skin color was a crucial issue—he was conscious of being known as the blackest member of his own family, and his mother's censorious reaction to his sister's attempt to build a relationship with a boyfriend who was considered to be "too black" created a familial crisis that remained vivid in Stuart's mind throughout his life. All of that, as he explained at various points, made him feel that he had to escape the Caribbean if he was to survive. Having received a classically British formal education at a prestigious institution—Jamaica College in Kingston—he duly won a Rhodes Scholarship, which enabled him to escape from Jamaica, and arrived at Oxford University in 1951 to study English literature.[1]

His accounts of the initial train ride, following his arrival, through the English countryside en route to Oxford stressed how very much at home he felt in many ways—being thoroughly familiar with the English landscape from the novels of Thomas Hardy. However, at Oxford he soon realized that although he could easily study English culture on the page, he could never completely "belong" there, being so fundamentally formed by the colonial experience of Jamaica. He was, he came to realize, simply one member of a particular generation of postwar migrants—starting with those who arrived in the UK on the ship the *Empire Windrush* in 1948—and who, he said, he knew constituted his prime subject, ever since he met them coming out of Paddington Station, off the boat trains. To that extent, he was part of a massive demographic and cultural change in the composition of the population of Britain, and in some ways he always remained, in part, an "outsider," a familiar stranger in a liminal position with a fundamentally migrant/diasporic perspective on the culture of the country in which he lived most of his life. His subjectivity was formed not only on the edges of the British empire but on the edges of the West itself.

Having rapidly involved himself with left-wing politics while at Oxford, becoming a key figure in the emergence of what became known as the "New Left," he also (as he put it) found himself "dragged into Marxism backwards"— simultaneously opposed to the Soviet tanks in Budapest and to the Anglo-French paratroopers dispatched to the Suez Canal. In the crucial (and for Stuart, politically formative) moment of 1956, when those crises in Hungary and Egypt shook the foundations of both of the Cold War empires, he and his fellow "postcolonials" found it necessary (rather in the spirit of the Non-Aligned Movement of the time) to begin deconstructing the Eurocentric prejudices of the very Marxism to which they had initially been attracted. Only thus could they address the questions at stake in the emerging post-imperial politics of the era, as movements for national independence grew in strength everywhere.

By the mid-1950s, many of Stuart's cohort of fellow migrant students were beginning to look toward a "return" to their countries of origin, in order to participate in and help shape their emerging postcolonial movements— and in Stuart's case, evidently, the particular temptation was to return to Caribbean politics in order to pursue these issues. However, for a variety of reasons, both to do with his own sense of discomfort with the culture of Jamaica, Stuart decided to stay in the UK.[2] At the same time, he moved out of the academic environment at Oxford, abandoning his proposed DPhil in order to pursue the politics of the various New Left projects in which he was involved and that were then based in London. He was, at this time, involved with the *Universities and Left Review* and its associated Partisan Coffee House and book clubs as well as with the formation of the *New Left Review*, of which he became the editor. This was also the beginning of his long career as a public, campaigning intellectual, not only in relation to matters of Marxism and class politics but also through his involvement in the Campaign for Nuclear Disarmament (in which context he met his future wife, Catherine, on a CND protest march in 1964).

Throughout this time, he supported himself by teaching what was then called "liberal studies" in a secondary school in a poor area of South London— and that work focused on the emerging areas of popular culture. He was, in fact, teaching what would nowadays be called media studies. In this endeavor, Stuart brought the skills in literary analysis that he had developed at Oxford to bear on defining the new media of the day (cinema and, later, television), working in conjunction with a new generation of teachers and scholars attracted to the British Film Institute, especially Paddy Whannel, with whom he wrote *The Popular Arts* in 1964.

This work brought him to the attention of Richard Hoggart, whose *The Uses of Literacy* had been published to considerable acclaim in 1957, and who had subsequently been invited by the University of Birmingham to set up what became the Centre for Contemporary Cultural Studies (CCCS) there in 1964. Hoggart invited Stuart to join him as the Centre's first research fellow that same year, and Stuart and his family moved to Birmingham, where they stayed until 1979.

Stuart gradually took over directorship of CCCS from Hoggart from the late 1960s onward—initially on a de facto basis, as Hoggart spent an increasing amount of his time working in Paris with UNESCO—then becoming full-time director in 1969. The story of the development of what retrospectively became internationally famous as "The Birmingham School" under Stuart's intellectual leadership has been widely rehearsed, and the interested reader can easily consult a whole range of sources.[3]

From Birmingham to the Open University and Rivington Place

The first installment of this pair of volumes devoted to Stuart's *Essential Essays* focuses principally on the development of his work during the initial period of his involvement with the New Left, and then through his time at CCCS. During this period, Stuart's approach, while initially much influenced by dialogues with the work of Richard Hoggart, Raymond Williams, and Edward Thompson, gradually moved away from that left-wing "culturalist" perspective—and from the more fundamentalist forms of Marxism espoused by some parts of the New Left.[4] This transition occurred at CCCS through a series of paradigm-shifting intellectual encounters both with revisionist forms of Marxism (especially Althusser, Poulantzas, and, most importantly, Gramsci), structural anthropology and linguistics (Lévi-Strauss, Saussure), semiology (Barthes and Veron), and later with psychoanalytic theory (both Freud and Lacan), deconstruction, and new forms of historical work based around discourse analysis of a variety of types (Foucault, Derrida).

Besides the hothouse development of these academic and analytical perspectives, the work of the CCCS was also awash with the political conflicts of the 1970s and 1980s, as first feminism, gay, and, later, queer politics, and then antiracism and the politics of identity, and the intersections of race, ethnicity, and gender all created moments of intellectual crisis within CCCS.[5] If all these contentious—and deeply conflictual—debates were, of course, the very lifeblood of what made CCCS an increasingly powerful intellectual influence in Britain and, as time went on, internationally, they were nonetheless personally exhausting for Stuart. In 1980 he left CCCS and moved to the Open University, with the ambition of taking the new forms of Cultural Studies that had been developed at CCCS to a wider educational audience. He was then able to address these new constituencies through the many courses on media, popular culture, and identity, which he developed and ran during his years there, until his retirement in 1997.

As has been noted in the introductory materials in volume 1 and as can be seen in the materials collected in the subsequent parts of this volume, Stuart's so-called retirement became an extremely productive period. During the 1980s and 1990s Stuart had developed a large body of theoretical work on questions of race and ethnicity, diaspora and identity—the key elements of which are represented in this volume. Having done so, in his retirement he then became heavily involved in active forms of support for a variety of black arts initiatives, principally in the fields of film and photography, leading, ultimately, to the development of the Rivington Place Arts Centre, set up to promote cultural diversity in the visual arts, which opened in London in 2007 and of which Stuart was the first chairman.

However, at this stage, having offered these skeletal facts about Stuart's life and work, it is important to note here that Stuart himself was always resistant to mere autobiography. Thus, even when his work took an autobiographical turn in the mid-1980s, as he more directly confronted questions raised by the politics of identity, the biographical dimension, which he then added in to his writing, is not to be taken at face value. When in his speech at the Illinois conference on Cultural Studies in 1990 he chose to recount his own experience of Cultural Studies and of CCCS itself, he explained carefully that in speaking autobiographically he did so not in order to seize "the authority of authenticity" but rather to properly situate himself in relation to the historical circumstances in which he had lived and worked—and thus to carefully delimit any generalizations that might otherwise be drawn from his specific experiences.[6] Later, in telling his own family story, as he does in the interview with Kuan-Hsing Chen (chapter 6), he renders his experiential account of discovering his own blackness in tandem with its own theorization—in coming to understand what it means to be part of the peripheral, displaced, and marginalized diaspora. In doing so, he implicitly follows the Irish poet Patrick Kavanagh in treating the self as not so much an unquestioned ground of knowledge or revelation but rather as only an illustration of wider themes.

In all these contexts, Stuart is careful to recognize that identity is always something constructed in discourse rather than some given sociological or biological essence that preexists representation. In general terms, his exploration of these issues is perhaps best explicated in his essay "The Work of Representation," where he explores the significance of the contribution of Foucauldian (and other) forms of discourse analysis.[7] He is also very clear about the extent that identity, far from being a matter of self-creation, is, rather, best understood as something constructed in and through a dialogic process—in which individuals attempt to develop a sense of their identity in (sometimes conflictual) interaction with identities thrust upon them by others. Thus, elsewhere, Stuart talks about how "at different times in my 30 years in England, I have been hailed or interpellated as 'coloured,' 'West Indian,' 'Negro,' . . . 'immigrant' . . . sometimes abusively, sometimes in a friendly manner, sometimes ambiguously."[8] Here we see Stuart also implicitly connecting Volosinov's perspective on the political significance of struggles over the multi-accentuality of the sign (whether in matters of class, race, or ethnicity) with more contemporary approaches to recent struggles over the resignification of markers of identity such as "black," "gay," or "queer."[9]

Questions of Publication and Periodization

The conclusion of this (heavily condensed) story of the earlier parts of Stuart's life and work also brings us to a formal point of juncture, at which it is perhaps worth rehearsing the logic according to which these two volumes have been constructed and, indeed, how they have been divided. When dealing with someone for whom the bibliography of their published work over their lifetime runs to more than sixty-five pages, with an output covering a vast array of different fields, the task of selecting a mere twenty-three of the essays, which are then deemed to constitute the "essential" ones, has been a daunting one. The long and complex process of selection of the materials has been rehearsed in the introduction to volume 1.[10]

The key editorial task has been to try to square the circle of making the selection comprehensive enough to represent the full range of Stuart's interests and achievements while restricting it to an overall length that made it manageable as a publishable project. The material in the two volumes combined runs to approximately 300,000 words—which was clearly beyond the manageable contents for a single book. The key decision was then how best to divide the materials between the two volumes. The main organizing principle adopted, for heuristic reasons, has been a chronological one. Volume 1 concentrates, on the whole, on the products of the earlier parts of Stuart's career, and volume 2 focuses on the later work. As can be seen both from the titles of the two volumes (*Foundations of Cultural Studies* and *Identity and Diaspora*) and from the headings of the different parts of each volume, that earlier work concentrates, overall, on discussions of the constituent parts and defining approaches of Cultural Studies, on questions of cultural theory and methodology, and on the difficulties of developing interdisciplinary perspectives. Its empirical foci tend, in general, to be on questions of class and culture, and concerns with media, ideology, and representation. Central to Stuart's work during that period was the development of a nonessentialist form of "Marxism without guarantees," which enabled him, working from a theoretical base developed from his encounter with Althusser and Gramsci, to produce a conjuncturalist form of political analysis and intervention. This is represented most prominently in Stuart's massively influential analysis of the emerging forms of authoritarian populism—and specifically of Thatcherism—which came to dominate British politics from the 1980s onward. The two most emblematic products of this period of Stuart's work are represented in part IV of volume 1, in the form of "The Great Moving Right Show" and the retrospective account of the gestation and production of what subsequently became the canonical book *Policing the Crisis*.

As can readily be seen by looking at both the title of this volume and the headings of its parts, in his later work Stuart more often took as his explicit topic questions of race, ethnicity, and identity, and, to that extent, the essays in this volume can be seen to display a shift in the focus of his analytical attention. However, while it has proved heuristically useful to adopt this distinction, I must immediately declare it to only be operating here "under erasure" and not to be a distinction that should be taken at face value. In the first place, Stuart's anti-essentialist analysis of race and ethnicity is only made possible on the basis of the theoretical anti-essentialism previously produced in relation to his analysis of class; moreover, as we shall see, questions of race and ethnicity had long informed his earlier work, even when not highlighted as the ostensible topic under discussion.

Interweaving the Intellectual Threads: Articulating Class, Race, and Diaspora

In the 1997 interview with David Scott (included here as chapter 8), the question is posed as to the extent to which Stuart should be understood to be a specifically Caribbean intellectual.[11] Scott observes there that the question of race is sometimes understood to have only taken a central place in Stuart's work starting in the mid-1980s. Politely as ever, Stuart firmly demurs at this formulation, observing that although he understands why people might say this, "in fact, it's not quite true, you know." He goes on to point out not only that he was producing empirically based and policy-related work on race and immigration in Britain from the 1950s onward but that he was also addressing these matters in theoretical terms in essays from the late 1970s such as "Race, Articulation, and Societies Structured in Dominance" (volume 1, chapter 6) and "Pluralism, Race and Class in Caribbean Society"—although some part of that work was circulated though the channels of UNESCO's Division of Human Rights rather than being visible within the academic Cultural Studies.[12]

However, the point is a complex one because as Scott himself notes elsewhere, Stuart had written about West Indian literature when he first came to England in the 1950s, and then published early studies of immigrant culture, such as *The Young Englanders* in 1967.[13] Stuart also insists here on the autobiographical context of his early involvement in these issues. Thus, he points out that as part of the New Left he also had a strong practical involvement in the early stages of antiracist politics in the UK, following the Notting Hill race riots of the mid-1950s, and explains that his interests in the Caribbean and questions of race never left him, even if they were not always the most prominent and visible parts of his work. Similarly, his later work in an essay titled "The West and the Rest" (chapter 5) needs to be considered in the context of the fact that, right from the moment of 1956, Stuart entered the New

Left as part of a cosmopolitan group of Third World students "from Surinam, from Egypt, the Sudan" who were all fundamentally decentered from the dominant Eurocentric narratives of race, whiteness, and empire.

The autobiographical dimension is also central to explaining the seeming conundrum, referred to earlier, that Scott poses as to why, for instance, Stuart was not conspicuously visible as a Caribbean intellectual in the early 1960s. In response, Stuart explains that this was not only because of his earlier decision not to return after Oxford but because, psychically, he continued to feel "blocked" by the cultural trauma he experienced as part of his Jamaican upbringing, which had made him feel he had to leave—and, indeed, to then stay away. As he explains, it was not until the 1970s, when Jamaica was beginning to recognize itself as a black society, speaking patois and listening to reggae, under the Africanizing influence of Rastafarianism, that he felt that there was a space there in which he could begin to work.

As he notes, through the late 1970s and early 1980s, he continued to produce work on race, principally under the auspices of the UNESCO Division of Human Rights. At the same time, as he explains, if he had taken little explicit involvement in writing about the geographical Caribbean, nonetheless substantial parts of its population had evidently followed him to England, as migrants—and, in their wake, questions of race had become increasingly central to British politics. As he notes, CCCS had been involved in research projects on black crime and later "mugging," starting in the early 1970s (see volume 1, chapters 12 and 13). Later, the CCCS Race and Politics Group, involving influential figures such as Paul Gilroy, Erroll Lawrence, Hazel V. Carby, and Pratibha Parmar, among others, produced the pathbreaking volume *The Empire Strikes Back*.[14] This was central to the development of new theorizations of race, ethnicity, and diaspora, while later, in 1987, Paul Gilroy published his widely influential *There Ain't No Black in the Union Jack*.[15]

In putting together the two volumes that constitute this overall project, my principal concern throughout has been to demonstrate the continuities and links between the different phases and aspects of Stuart's work. In this context, I am very conscious of how, in so many ways, it has long circled around the mutual imbrication of structures of class, race, ethnicity, gender, culture, and politics. Very frequently in these essays, although only one of those factors is given the declared central focus of attention, the articulation of that one with the other issues in play is central to the analysis. I would argue that the capacity to deal with the ensuing complexities of those multidimensional perspectives is constitutive of Stuart's particular approach.

Thus, even when he is ostensibly talking about class, he is always doing so from a diasporic perspective—because that experience was fundamental to his whole approach, as he explains in different essays in both these volumes.

I have indicated earlier (see my general introduction to the first volume) a number of instances of Stuart's early engagement with these issues in the broader context of questions of colonialism, empire, and immigration, written at different times, from the 1950s onward. Then, from the early 1970s, in the initial iterations of what became the now canonical *Policing the Crisis*, questions of race (and, specifically, images of black criminality) were central to his analysis of the emerging forms of authoritarian populism that came to dominate British politics over the subsequent decades.

In attempting to represent the full breadth of Stuart's approach, and in an attempt to build a bridging perspective, editorially, into these two volumes, the greatest part of that burden is carried by the essay titled "Race, Articulation, and Societies Structured in Dominance" from 1980 (volume 1, chapter 6) and the paired essay from 1986 titled "Gramsci's Relevance for the Study of Race and Ethnicity," which functions as the prologue to this volume, setting the conceptual framework for much of what follows here. In the case of the first of those two essays, we see that as early as 1980, Stuart was painstakingly working his way through a critique of a variety of attempts to theorize the structure of apartheid in South Africa, as a way to create the development of a methodology that would allow him to understand the articulation of questions of race and class.

In "Race, Articulation, and Societies Structured in Dominance," Stuart outlines the logic of how the theoretical developments first outlined in his critique of classical Marxism can also be applied to the study of what he calls here "racially structured social formations." He takes the analyses of the "test-case" situation of apartheid-era South Africa produced by Harold Wolpe and John Rex as a key point of reference, interrogating them for what lessons they can offer us in developing an analysis that would be capable of articulating questions of race and class without reducing either to an essentialist or epiphenomenal status. The exposition there offers an initial formulation of the arguments that then appear in more developed form in chapter 1 of this volume. However, the earlier formulation is particularly worthy of attention because it clearly shows the intellectual roots of his later development of a nonessentialist politics of black subjectivity and of "new ethnicities." These roots lie, as this chapter shows, in the critique of both the monocausal forms of explanation developed by "teleological Marxism" and of the descriptive (rather than properly analytic) approaches favored by various forms of sociological pluralism.

His central intention in that argument is to develop a mode of analysis that avoids attributing to race a singular, unitary, and transhistorical character, which is presumed to assert itself in the same way everywhere, just as he simultaneously refuses to treat "His Majesty the Economy" as ultimately determining of everything else. For him, the question is how to recognize the "tendential" forms of pressure and articulation that one structural factor in a social formation exercises on another. In all this, the South African case (at a point at which the system of apartheid was beginning to crack but had not yet broken down) was particularly germane and offered an exemplary instance of how these issues would need to be worked through.

At a metatheoretical level, the focus on apartheid helps clarify the *differentia specifica* of the South African case. The peculiarity of its deviations from the classical capitalist path of development helps demonstrate that the society cannot be understood simply in terms of classical Marxism's concept of the class struggle but also requires attention to the particular forms of what John Rex calls "the race war" engendered by colonial conquest. While the racial dynamics cannot be understood without reference to its economic structure, economics provides only the necessary—rather than the sufficient—conditions, if we are to understand the specific forms of social relations developed in South Africa.

As Stuart notes, this approach alerts us to the importance of refusing classical Marxism's Euro-centeredness "based as it is on extrapolating to other social formations forms of development peculiar to—and illegitimately generalised from—European cases." Here we see the roots of Stuart's later analysis of the specificities of racial and ethnic dynamics in colonial and postcolonial societies, in the Caribbean and elsewhere—which are also indicated here both in his references to Ernesto Laclau's critique of Andre Gunder Frank's ahistorical Marxism and to the important work of Eugene Genovese on the "troublesome case" of plantation slavery.

In a way that then links directly to Althusser's work on the "relative autonomy" of the different levels of a social formation, in which matters of politics, law, culture, and ideology can themselves have determining effects, Stuart insists that we also see here the importance of "the specific . . . form in which underpaid labour surplus is pumped out of direct producers," as Marx formulates it.[16] At a more fundamental level, this point is derived directly from Stuart's commentary on Marx's methodology, in his "Notes on the 1857 Introduction to the *Grundrisse*." In this commentary, which is central to Stuart's work, he is at pains to reject the notion of any abstract mode of analysis that fails to attend to the historical specificity of a particular social formation, as it has developed in empirically given circumstances. He is not interested in any all-encompassing "general model" of how the capitalist mode of production determines everything about a social formation. Rather, he is concerned with how the economic, political, legal, and ideological dimensions of a society come to form what he calls, following Althusser, a "complex unity, structured in dominance," where what needs to be understood is how its different elements are articulated together. This was crucial to Stuart's thought, and it was via Althusser's rejection of the Hegelian model of a society as an expressive totality, determined by a single (economic or other) cause, that he was able to develop a more flexible mode of Marxism, mobilizing the concepts of relative autonomy, displacement, dislocation, condensation, and overdetermination. Here, as in "Gramsci's Relevance to the Study of Race and Ethnicity" alongside Althusser, Gramsci is credited with making a fundamental contribution to the development of a nonreductionist form of Marxism, and in his case, one that more specifically escapes the Eurocentrism of much of classical Marxism, precisely because of its attention to the (internal and external) colonial dimensions of the Italian situation.

What then becomes clear in the final part of the race/articulation chapter is how readily the critique of essentialist forms of Marxism can be transposed to the analysis of questions of race and ethnicity. Here, Stuart rejects analyses that invoke a common/universal structure of racism as a general feature of human societies. Rather, his declared aim is to develop an analysis of the historically specific forms of racism and its effects, and of the different ways in which racist ideologies have operated in specific historical and empirical conjunctures. Thus, in working through these theoretical and methodological questions as carefully as this chapter does, it makes a major contribution to our understanding of the articulation (to use his own terminology) of Stuart's analyses of class structures with his analyses of race and ethnicity.

Ending at the Beginning

If the narrative of Stuart's intellectual development is sometimes told as one in which his involvement in matters of globalization and diaspora is only seen to come at a late stage of his career, nothing could, in fact, be further from the truth. As indicated earlier, it was among a set of ex-colonial intellectuals, many of them from outside Britain, that Stuart was first engaged in the genesis of the New Left of the 1950s.[17] That itself was a crucial point in decentering what is sometimes regarded as the essential "Britishness" both of the New Left and (later) of Cultural Studies itself. Moreover, as John Akomfrah has recently pointed out, the focus on questions of diaspora, migration, and creolization in Stuart's later work, far from being a sudden disavowal of his Marxism in favor of some modish form of identity politics, is prefigured in some of his earliest work.[18] This is well exemplified in Akomfrah's own film *The Unfinished Conversation*, where, as early as 1964, Stuart can be heard on the soundtrack of a BBC radio "Home Service" documentary program titled "A Generation of Strangers" worrying about the phenomenon of Britain producing, among its new migrant families, "young black people who . . . he fears, will discover, as they move into adulthood . . . whatever their capacities and potential, that they are nonetheless defined within British society by the colour of their skin."[19]

We find Stuart there rehearsing many of the themes concerning race and ethnicity that will also figure in his later work. To this extent, as Akomfrah argues, for Stuart "questions pertaining to race were always already in place from the very beginning," and race marked a constituting space from which Cultural Studies developed. Thus, while at a later point, the analysis of those issues in *Policing the Crisis* became the most "visible tip of the iceberg of race," the issue was always already "floating in the sea of cultural studies."[20] Nonetheless, in his later life, Stuart was increasingly preoccupied with questions of identity and subjectivity, especially concerning those on the racialized margins of the former colonizing nations. After his retirement from the Open University, his growing involvement in the Black Arts movement gave him a new lease of intellectual life, and he became chair both of the Institute of International Visual Arts (inIVA) and of the Association of Black Photographers, Autograph (ABP), and organized their successful joint bid for grant funding. This then provided the possibility to create a secure institutional home for both of them—at the purpose-built Rivington Place Arts Centre in East London, which opened in 2007.[21] In some quarters, this engagement with aesthetic matters in the Black Arts movement was treated as a new (or even a surprising) development. However, as he explains in the interview with Les Back (chapter 9), in many ways this took him back to his early interest in documentary photography.[22] Moreover, as made clear in an interview with Colin MacCabe in 2007, as far as he was concerned, he had been involved in arguments about aesthetics for almost fifty years, ever since writing *The Popular Arts* with Paddy Whannel. These aspects of Stuart's later work are happily now continued by his ex-colleagues at inIVA and Autograph ABP at Rivington Place.

Thus my introduction to the essays in this volume ends here by emphasizing the close connections between the endings and the beginnings of Stuart's work, stressing, once again, the continuities that underlie its changing foci and emphases. Further detailed commentary on the particular chapters in the following parts of the book—"Deconstructing Identities: The Politics of Anti-Essentialism," "The Postcolonial and the Diasporic," and on the more informal discourses of the interviews with David Scott and Les Back—are offered in the separate introductions to parts II, III, and IV of this volume. Beyond this, the epilogue brings matters to a (provisional) conclusion by reproducing the edited transcript of a talk that Stuart originally delivered extempore at a conference in Jamaica in 2007 titled "The Thought of Stuart Hall"—thus giving Stuart himself the last words on all these matters.

NOTES

1 The basic information about Stuart Hall's life, his career, and the development of his work is outlined at more length in the introduction to Stuart Hall, *The Essential Essays, Volume 1: The Foundations of Cultural Studies*, to which the interested reader is invited to refer. For anyone without access to that information, its outlines are briefly restated here. Anyone wanting a richer and fuller account of the relationship between Stuart's life circumstances and the development of his work should consult the magisterial account offered in Stuart Hall, *Familiar Stranger: A Life between Two Islands* (London: Penguin, 2017).

2 On the question of Stuart as a specifically "Caribbean" intellectual, see the interview with David Scott (ch. 8, this volume).

3 These sources include Dennis Dworkin, *Cultural Materialism in Post-War Britain: History the New Left and the Origins of Cultural Studies* (Durham, NC: Duke University Press, 1997); Michael Green, "The Centre for Contemporary Cultural Studies," in *Re-Reading English*, ed. Peter Widdowson (London: Methuen, 1982); Geoff Eley, "Stuart Hall 1932–2014," *History Workshop Journal*, no. 79 (2015): 303–320; and Graeme Turner, *British Cultural Studies* (London: Routledge, 2000).

4 See Stuart's own generous assessment of his debt to Hoggart in Hall, *The Essential Essays, Volume 1*, ch. 1.

5 Charlotte Brunsdon, "A Thief in the Night: Stories of Feminism in the 1970s and CCCS," in *Stuart Hall: Critical Dialogues in Cultural Studies*, ed. David Morley and Kuan-Hsing Chen (London: Routledge, 1996).

6 See his comments on these issues in the talk given at the Illinois conference on Cultural Studies in Hall, *The Essential Essays, Volume 1*, ch. 3.

7 Stuart Hall, "The Work of Representation," in *Representation: Cultural Representations and Signifying Practices*, ed. Stuart Hall (London: Sage/Open University, 1997).

8 Stuart Hall, "Signification, Representation and Ideology: Althusser and the Poststructuralist Debates," *Critical Studies in Mass Communication* 2, no. 2 (1985): 108.

9 V. N. Volosinov, *Marxism and the Philosophy of Language* (New York: Academic Press, 1973); Judith Butler, *Gender Trouble* (New York: Routledge, 1990), and *Giving an Account of Oneself* (New York: Fordham University Press, 2005); Judith Butler, Ernesto Laclau, and Slavoj Žižek, *Contingency, Hegemony, Universality* (London: Verso, 2000).

10 In order to avoid misunderstanding, it is also worth noting here the rather evident, if unavoidable, irony of using the word "essential" in the titles of these volumes, which represent the work of a scholar who was, above all, an anti-essentialist.

11 See also the discussion of this question in the epilogue to this volume.

12 Stuart Hall, "Pluralism, Race and Class in Caribbean Society," in *Race and Class in Postcolonial Society* (Paris: UNESCO, 1978).

13 David Scott, *The Voice of Stuart Hall: Intimations of an Ethics of Receptive Generosity* (Durham, NC: Duke University Press, 2017).

14 Centre for Contemporary Cultural Studies, *The Empire Strikes Back: Race and Racism in 70s Britain* (London: Hutchinson, 1982).

15 Important titles in this thread of work inspired by the new approaches to questions of race developed at CCCS include Paul Gilroy, *There Ain't No Black in the Union Jack* (London: Hutchinson, 1987); Kobena Mercer and Isaac Julien, "Introduction: De Margin and De Centre," *Screen* 29, no. 4 (1988): 2–12; and Paul Gilroy, *The Black Atlantic: Modernity and Double Consciousness* (London: Verso, 1993). The following year saw the publication of Kobena Mercer, *Welcome to the Jungle* (London: Routledge, 1994). Paul Gilroy's *After Empire: Melancholia or Convivial Culture* (London: Routledge) was published in 2004, and in 2011 there appeared *Black Britain: A Photographic History* (London: Saqi), jointly authored by Paul Gilroy and Stuart Hall. Most recently, Mercer has edited a volume presenting the Du Bois lectures that Stuart delivered at Harvard University in 1994 titled *The Fateful Triangle: Race, Ethnicity, Nation* (Cambridge, MA: Harvard University Press, 2017).

16 Stuart's analysis here follows Barrington Moore Jr.'s approach to the crucial function of political and legal forms for extracting surplus value from labor, in explaining the historical development of different forms of dictatorship and democracy: *The Social Origins of Dictatorship and Democracy* (London: Peregrine, 1969). Barrington Moore's analysis itself shares some qualities with the "harder" form of Rex's distinctive "left Weberianism," of which Stuart speaks approvingly in that chapter.

17 In reminiscing about that experience, Stuart once observed that among that group, Perry Anderson was probably the only British person, and that, anyway, he was partly Irish.

18 John Akomfrah, "The Partisan's Prophecy," in *Stuart Hall: Conversations, Projects and Legacies*, ed. Julian Henriques and David Morley (London: Goldsmiths Press, 2018).

19 "A Generation of Strangers," radio broadcast on BBC "Home Service," August 23, 1964. See also Stuart Hall, *The Young Englanders* (London: National Committee of Commonwealth Immigrants, 1967); "Black Britons" (part 1), *Community* 1, no. 2 (1970): 3–5; "Black Britons" (part 2), *Community* 1, no. 3 (1970): 12–16; and "Our Neighbours from the West Indies," shown on Granada TV in 1971.

20 Akomfrah, "The Partisan's Prophecy," 5–6.

21 The securing of this funding, in which Stuart played a leading role, was an enormously significant achievement, as this was the first publicly funded new-build international arts gallery to open in London since the Hayward Gallery forty years earlier.

22 As outlined in his essays "The Social Eye of Picture Post," *Working Papers in Cultural Studies*, no. 2 (1972): 71–120, and "The Determinations of News Photographs," *Working Papers in Cultural Studies*, no. 3 (1972): 53–87.

PART I

PROLOGUE

Class, Race, and Ethnicity

In this chapter, written in 1986, we see Stuart further developing the analysis originally begun in writings such as "Race, Articulation, and Societies Structured in Dominance" (1980; volume 1, chapter 6), building on his critique there of essentialism and specifying rather more exactly how Gramsci's own anti-essentialist forms of conjuncturalist analysis of politics can be deployed in the service of developing anti-essentialist forms of understanding of the politics of race, ethnicity, and identity. There is a strong continuity between the conjunctural analysis of class structures offered in these earlier writings—which are at pains to avoid reducing political and ideological issues to mere reflections of the economy—and the analysis in the chapters that Stuart develops in the essays in the following parts of this volume, in which he critiques the equally inadequate notion of an essential black subject. Thus, in his introduction to Stuart's Du Bois lectures, Kobena Mercer astutely points to the extent to which his earlier, sociologically oriented work on race and ethnicity "provides the architectonic grounding" for the more discursive approaches to these questions displayed in his later work.[1] However, he also rightly points out that Hall's appropriation of the decentered subjectivity of poststructuralism is what enables him to then move to a perspective which grants a fuller, constitutive role to questions of culture, discourse, and subjectivity in the formation of all modes of identity.[2]

The issue here is not simply analytical but also political. As Mercer observes, it is the "possibility of breaking with oppressive regimes of racial meaning . . . at stake in the polysemic agency of difference, which makes discourse the medium in which historically subordinated subjects can . . . activate resistance." Putting the point less abstractly, he explains that in his work on "new ethnicities" and identities Stuart turns his attention to the resignification of the term "black" within antiracist politics by Afro-Caribbeans and Asians in the UK in the 1970s and shows how this discursively transformational act provided the ground of resistance and was "the generative source from which political rupture and social change [was] born."[3]

In order to specify what it is exactly that we can learn from Gramsci's mode of analysis and how it can be used in the study of racism, race, and ethnicity, Stuart first offers a systematic exposition of his methodology that synthesizes many of his passing comments elsewhere. He begins by clarifying the status of Gramsci's work, not as any kind of general theory or social science in the abstract sense but rather as an attempt to apply some of Marx's central concepts to new historical conditions in a genuinely open-ended spirit.[4] To this extent, Gramsci supplies Stuart with a model for using theory to illuminate particular situations and a methodology for disinterring concrete historical analyses from one situation and transplanting them effectively so as to illuminate another. In all of this, just as in his "Notes on Marx's '1857 Introduction' to the *Grundrisse*," Stuart insists on the importance of attending to the intermediate levels of determination necessary to transform abstract concepts to a point where they are adequate to the analysis of concrete empirical circumstances. He notes that there are certain parallels between Gramsci's experience of Sardinia's colonial relationship to the Italian mainland (which gives Gramsci his understanding of the specific relation of the underdeveloped poor South of Italy to the industrialized and modernized North) and contemporary questions of postcolonialism and ethnic division that face us today. It is Gramsci's distinctive theoretical perspective, his methodology, and the problematic within which it operates that Stuart holds up as exemplary.[5]

Gramsci also offers a principled rejection of any form of economic reductionism that would presume the existence of objective historical laws with automatic consequences in the manner of scientific positivism. It is this that allows him to conceptualize the theoretical space in which to substitute for simplistic teleologies of inevitable sequences of events with guaranteed outcomes what Stuart calls the "conditional tense" of the analysis of relations of force in unstable equilibria. In this, it is the relative autonomy that Gramsci grants to political and cultural factors—with a determining effectivity of their own, in the war of position conducted around the state and civil society—that is critical. This is what allows him to link explicitly political issues of ideology to the question of the lived forms of popular culture. In doing so, he recognizes the contradictory nature of consciousness and of common sense itself. The recognition of this degree of discursive fluidity and provisionality then allows Stuart to make the analogy between the inadequacy of any conception of a pregiven, class-conscious, unified proletarian revolutionary subject and, similarly, any model of a predetermined antiracist black consciousness. In the end, he argues, what we can derive from a Gramscian perspective is a concrete analysis not of racism in general but of specific historical racisms, as they are constituted in particular sociocultural circumstances.[6]

NOTES

1 Kobena Mercer, "Introduction," *The Fateful Triangle: Race, Ethnicity, Nation* (Cambridge, MA: Harvard University Press, 2017), 9.

2 This is articulated in Stuart's discussion of the "great decenterings" of modernity in chapter 2, this volume.

3 Mercer, "Introduction," 17–18.

4 In a similar spirit, in his "Anecdotes of Mr Keuner," Bertolt Brecht presents the story of a potential voter who explains to the canvassers at his door that he would be more likely to vote for a politician who was able to offer some questions for open-ended debate, rather than one who offers only preestablished answers: Bertolt Brecht, *Stories of Mr Keuner*, trans. Martin Chalmers (San Francisco: City Lights, 2001).

5 On this, see also Stuart Hall, Gregor McLennan, and Robert Lumley, "Politics and Ideology: Gramsci," in *On Ideology*, ed. Centre for Contemporary Cultural Studies (London: Hutchinson, 1978).

6 This is a theme to which Stuart returns in his interview with Les Back in ch. 9, this volume.

CHAPTER 1

Gramsci's Relevance for the Study of Race and Ethnicity

I.

The aim of this collection of essays is to facilitate "a more sophisticated examination of the hitherto poorly elucidated phenomenon of racism and to examine the adequacy of the theoretical formulations, paradigms and interpretive schemes in the social and human sciences . . . with respect to intolerance and racism and in relation to the complexity of problems they pose." This general rubric enables me to situate more precisely the kind of contribution which a study of Gramsci's work can make to the larger enterprise.[1] In my view, Gramsci's work does *not* offer a *general* social science which can be applied to the analysis of social phenomena across a wide comparative range of historical societies. His potential contribution is more limited. It remains, for all that, of seminal importance. His work is, precisely, of a "sophisticating" kind. He works, broadly, within the Marxist paradigm. However, he has extensively revised, renovated, and sophisticated many aspects of that theoretical framework to make it more relevant to contemporary social relations in the twentieth century. His work therefore has a direct bearing on the question of the "adequacy" of existing social theories, since it is precisely in the direction of "complexifying existing theories and problems" that his most important theoretical contribution is to be found. These points require further clarification before a substantive résumé and assessment of Gramsci's theoretical contribution can be offered.

Gramsci was not a "general theorist." Indeed, he did not practice as an academic or scholarly theorist of any kind. From beginning to end, he was and remained a political intellectual and a socialist activist on the Italian political scene. His "theoretical" writing was developed out of this more organic engagement with his own society and times and was always intended to serve, not an abstract academic purpose, but the aim of "informing political practice." It is therefore essential not to mistake the level of application at which Gramsci's concepts operate. He saw himself as, principally, working within the broad parameters of historical materialism, as outlined by the tradition of Marxist scholarship defined by the work of Marx and Engels and, in the early decades of the twentieth century, by such figures as Lenin, Luxemburg, Trotsky, Labriola, Togliatti, etc. (I cite those names to indicate Gramsci's frame of reference within Marxist thought, not his precise position in relation to those particular figures—to establish the latter is a more complicated issue). This means that his theoretical contribution has, always, to be *read* with the understanding that it is operating on, broadly, Marxist terrain. That is to say, Marxism provides the general limits within which Gramsci's developments, refinements, revisions, advances, further thoughts, new concepts, and original formulations all operate. However, Gramsci was never a "Marxist" in either a doctrinal, orthodox, or "religious" sense. He understood that the general framework of Marx's theory had to be constantly developed theoretically; applied to new historical conditions; related to developments in society which Marx and Engels could not possibly have foreseen; and expanded and refined by the addition of new concepts.

Gramsci's work thus represents neither a "footnote" to the already-completed edifice of orthodox Marxism nor a ritual evocation of orthodoxy which is circular in the sense of producing "truths" which are already well known. Gramsci practices a genuinely "open" Marxism, which develops many of the insights of Marxist theory in the direction of new questions and conditions. Above all, his work brings into play concepts which classical Marxism did not provide but without which Marxist theory *cannot* adequately explain the complex social phenomena which we encounter in the modern world. It is essential to understand these points if we are to situate Gramsci's work against the background of existing "theoretical formulations, paradigms and interpretive schemes in the social and human sciences."

Not only is Gramsci's work not a *general* work of social science, of the status of, say, the work of such "founding fathers" as Max Weber or Émile Durkheim; it also does not anywhere appear in that recognizable, general, synthesizing form. The main body of Gramsci's theoretical ideas are scattered throughout his occasional essays and polemical writing—he was an active and prolific political journalist—and, of course, in the great collection of *Prison Notebooks*, which Gramsci wrote without benefit of access to libraries or other reference books, either during his enforced leisure in Mussolini's prison after his arrest (1926–1933) or after his release, but when he was already terminally ill (1933–1937). This fragmentary body of writing, including the *Notebooks* (the *Quaderni del carcere*), is mainly to be found now in the Istituto Gramsci in Rome, where a definitive critical edition of his work is still in the course of completion for publication.[2]

Not only are the writings scattered; they are often fragmentary in form rather than sustained and "finished" pieces of writing. Gramsci was often writing—as in the *Prison Notebooks*—under the most unfavorable circumstances: for example, under the watchful eye of the prison censor and without any other books from which to refresh his memory. Given these circumstances, the *Notebooks* represent a remarkable intellectual feat. Nevertheless, the "costs" of his having to produce them in this way, of never being able to go back to them with time for critical reflection, were considerable. The *Notebooks* are what they say—*notes*—shorter or more extended but not woven into a sustained discourse or coherent text. Some of his most complex arguments are displaced from the main text into long footnotes. Some passages have been reformulated, but with little guidance as to which of the extant versions Gramsci regarded as the more "definitive" text.

As if these aspects of "fragmentariness" do not present us with formidable enough difficulties, Gramsci's work may appear fragmentary in another, even deeper sense. He was constantly using "theory" to illuminate concrete historical cases or political questions—or thinking large concepts in terms of their application to concrete and specific situations. Consequently, Gramsci's work often appears almost *too* concrete: too historically specific, too delimited in its references, too "descriptively" analytic, too time- and context-bound. His most illuminating ideas and formulations are typically of this conjunctural kind. To make more general use of them, they have to be delicately disinterred from their concrete and specific historical embeddedness and transplanted into new soil with considerable care and patience.

Some critics have assumed that Gramsci's concepts operate at this level of concreteness only because he did not have the time or inclination to raise them to a higher level of conceptual generality—the exalted level at which "theoretical ideas" are supposed to function. Thus both Althusser and

Poulantzas have proposed at different times "theorizing" Gramsci's insufficiently theorized texts. This view seems to me mistaken. Here, it is essential to understand, from the epistemological viewpoint, that concepts can operate at very different *levels of abstraction* and are often consciously intended to do so. The important point is not to "misread" one level of abstraction for another. We expose ourselves to serious error when we attempt to "read off" concepts which were designed to operate at a high level of abstraction as if they automatically produced the same theoretical effects when translated to another, more concrete, "lower" level of operation. In general, Gramsci's concepts were quite explicitly designed to operate at the lower levels of historical concreteness. He was not aiming "higher"—and missing his theoretical target! Rather we have to understand this level of historico-concrete descriptiveness in terms of Gramsci's relation to Marxism.

Gramsci remained a "Marxist," as I have said, in the sense that he developed his ideas within the general framework of Marx's theory: that is, taking for granted concepts like "the capitalist mode of production," the "forces and relations of production," etc. These concepts were pitched by Marx at the most general level of abstraction. That is to say, they are concepts which enable us to grasp and understand the broad processes which organize and structure the capitalist mode of production when reduced to its bare essentials, and at *any* stage or moment of its historical development. The concepts are "epochal" in their range and reference. However, Gramsci understood that as soon as these concepts have to be applied to specific historical social formations, to particular societies at specific stages in the development of capitalism, the theorist is required to move from the level of "mode of production" to a lower, more concrete level of application. This "move" requires not simply more detailed historical specification, but—as Marx himself argued—the application of new concepts and further levels of determination in addition to those pertaining to simple exploitative relations between capital and labor, since the latter serve to specify "the capitalist mode" only at the highest level of reference. Marx himself, in his most elaborated methodological text (his "1857 Introduction" to the *Grundrisse*), envisaged the "production of the concrete in thought" as taking place through a succession of analytic approximations, each adding further levels of determination to the necessarily skeletal and abstract concepts formed at the highest level of analytic abstraction. Marx argued that we could only "think the concrete" through these successive levels of abstraction. That was because the concrete, in reality, consisted of "many determinations"—which, of course, the levels of abstraction we use to think about it with must approximate, in thought. (On these questions of Marxist epistemology, see Hall, "Marx's Notes on Method," *Working Papers in Cultural Studies* 6 [1977].)

That is why, as Gramsci moves from the general terrain of Marx's mature concepts (as outlined, for example, in *Capital*) to specific historical conjunctures, he can still continue to "work within" their field of reference. But when he turns to discuss in detail, say, the *Italian* political situation in the 1930s, or changes in the complexity of the class democracies of "the West" after imperialism and the advent of mass democracy, or the specific differences between "eastern" and "western" social formations in Europe, or the type of politics capable of resisting the emerging forces of fascism, or the new forms of politics set in motion by developments in the modern capitalist state, he understands the necessity to adapt, develop, and *supplement* Marx's concepts with new and original ones. First, because Marx concentrated on developing his ideas at the highest level of application (as in *Capital*) rather than at the more concrete historical level (for example, there is no real analysis in Marx of the specific structures of the British nineteenth-century state, though there are many suggestive insights). Second, because the historical conditions for which Gramsci was writing were not the same as those in and for which Marx and Engels had written. (Gramsci had an acute sense of the historical conditions of theoretical production.) Third, because Gramsci felt the need for new conceptualizations at precisely the levels at which Marx's theoretical work was itself at its most sketchy and incomplete: that is, the levels of the analysis of specific historical conjunctures, or of the political and ideological aspects—the much-neglected dimensions of the analysis of social formations in classical Marxism.

These points help us, not simply to "place" Gramsci in relation to the Marxist tradition, but to make explicit the level at which Gramsci's work positively operates and the transformations this shift in the level of magnification required. It is to the generation of new concepts, ideas, and paradigms pertaining to the analysis of political and ideological aspects of social formations in the period after 1870, especially, that Gramsci's work most pertinently relates. Not that he *ever* forgot or neglected the critical element of the economic foundations of society and its relations. But he contributed relatively little by way of original formulations to *that* level of analysis. However, in the much-neglected areas of conjunctural analysis, politics, ideology and the state, the character of different types of political regimes, the importance of cultural and national-popular questions, and the role of civil society in the shifting balance of relations between different social forces in society—on *these* issues, Gramsci has an enormous amount to contribute. He is one of the first original "Marxist theorists" of the historical conditions which have come to dominate the second half of the twentieth century.

Nevertheless, in relation specifically to *racism*, his original contribution cannot be simply transferred wholesale from the existing context of his work. Gramsci did *not* write about race, ethnicity, or racism in their contemporary meanings or manifestations. Nor did he analyze in depth the colonial experience or imperialism, out of which so many of the characteristic "racist" experiences and relationships in the modern world have developed. His principal preoccupation was with his native Italy, and, behind that, the problems of socialist construction in western and eastern Europe, the failure of revolutions to occur in the developed capitalist societies of "the West," the threat posed by the rise of fascism in the interwar period, and the role of the party in the construction of hegemony. Superficially, all this might suggest that Gramsci belongs to that distinguished company of so-called "western Marxists" whom Perry Anderson identified, who, because of their preoccupations with more "advanced" societies, have little of relevance to say to the problems which have arisen largely in the non-European world, or in the relations of "uneven development" between the imperial nations of the capitalist "center" and the englobalized, colonized societies of the periphery.

To read Gramsci in *this* way would, in my opinion, be to commit the error of literalism (though, with qualifications, that is how Anderson reads him). Actually, though Gramsci does not write about racism and does not specifically address those problems, his *concepts* may still be useful to us in our attempt to think through the adequacy of existing social theory paradigms in these areas. Further, his own personal experience and formation, as well as his intellectual preoccupations, were not in fact quite so far removed from those questions as a first glance would superficially suggest.

Gramsci was born in Sardinia in 1891. Sardinia stood in a "colonial" relationship to the Italian mainland. His first contact with radical and socialist ideas was in the context of the growth of Sardinian nationalism, brutally repressed by troops from mainland Italy. Though, after his movement to Turin and his deep involvement with the Turin working-class movement, he abandoned his early "nationalism"; he never lost the concern, imparted to him in his early years, with peasant problems and the complex dialectic of class and regional factors. (For this and later, see Nowell Smith and Hoare's excellent "Introduction" to *Prison Notebooks* [1971].) Gramsci was acutely aware of the great line of division which separated the industrializing and modernizing "North" of Italy from the peasant, underdeveloped, and dependent "South." He contributed extensively to the debate on what came to be known as "the Southern question." At the time of his arrival in Turin in 1911, Gramsci almost certainly subscribed to what was known as a "Southernist" position. He retained an interest throughout his life in those relations of dependency and unevenness which linked "North" and "South": and the complex relations between city and countryside, peasantry and proletariat, clientism and modernism, feudalized and industrial social structures. He was thoroughly aware of the degree to which the lines of separation dictated by class relationships were compounded by the crosscutting relations of regional, cultural, and national difference; also, by differences in the tempos of regional or national historical development. When, in 1923, Gramsci, one of the founders of the Italian Communist Party, proposed *Unitá* as the title of the party's official newspaper, he gave as his reason "because . . . we must give special importance to the Southern question." In the years before and after the First World War, he immersed himself in every aspect of the political life of the Turin working class. This experience gave him an intimate, inside knowledge of one of the most advanced strata of the industrial "factory" proletarian class in Europe. He had an active and sustained career in relation to this advanced sector of the modern working class—first, as a political journalist on the staff of the Socialist Party weekly, *Il Grido del Popolo*; then during the wave of unrest in Turin (the so-called "Red Years"), the factory occupations and councils of labor; and finally, during his editorship of the journal *Ordine Nuovo* up to the founding of the Italian Communist Party. Nevertheless, he continued to reflect, throughout, on the strategies and forms of political action and organization which could *unite* concretely different kinds of struggle. He was preoccupied with the question of what basis could be found in the complex alliances of and relations between the different social strata for the foundation of a specifically *modern* Italian state. The preoccupation with the question of regional specificity, social alliances, and the social foundations of the state also directly links Gramsci's work with what we might think of today as "North/South," as well as "East/West," questions.

The early 1920s were taken up, for Gramsci, with the difficult problems of trying to conceptualize new forms of political "party" and with the question of distinguishing a path of development specific to Italian *national* conditions, in opposition to the hegemonizing thrust of the Soviet-based Comintern. All this led ultimately to the major contribution which the Italian Communist

Party has made to the theorization of the conditions of "national specific-ity" in relation to the very different concrete historical developments of the different societies, East and West. In the later 1920s, however, Gramsci's preoccupations were largely framed by the context of the growing threat of fascism, up to his arrest and internment by Mussolini's forces in 1929.

So, though Gramsci did not write directly about the problems of racism, the preoccupying themes of his work provide deeper intellectual and theo-retical lines of connection to many more of these contemporary issues than a quick glance at his writings would suggest.

II.

It is to these deeper connections, and to their fertilizing impact on the search for more adequate theorizations in the field, that we now turn. I will try to elucidate some of those core conceptions in Gramsci's work which point in that direction.

I begin with the issue which, in some ways, for the chronological student of Gramsci's work, comes more toward the end of his life: the question of his rigorous attack on all vestiges of "economism" and "reductionism" within classical Marxism. By "economism" I do not mean—as I hope I have already made clear—to neglect the powerful role which the economic foundations of a social order or the dominant economic relations of a society play in shap-ing and structuring the whole edifice of social life. I mean, rather, a spe-cific theoretical approach which tends to read the economic foundations of society as the *only* determining structure. This approach tends to see all other dimensions of the social formation as simply mirroring "the economic" on another level of articulation, and as having no other determining or structuring force in their own right. The approach, to put it simply, reduces everything in a social formation to the economic level and conceptual-izes all other types of social relations as directly and immediately "corre-sponding" to the economic. This collapses Marx's somewhat problematic formulation—the economic as "determining in the last instance"—to the re-ductionist principle that the economic determines, in an immediate way, in the first, middle, and last instances. In this sense, "economism" is a theoreti-cal reductionism. It simplifies the structure of social formations, reducing their complexity of articulation, vertical and horizontal, to a single line of determination. It simplifies the very concept of "determination" (which in Marx is actually a very complex idea) to that of a mechanical function. It flattens all the mediations between the different levels of a society. It presents social formations—in Althusser's words—as a "simple expressive totality," in which every level of articulation corresponds to every other, and which is, from end to end, structurally transparent. I have no hesitation in saying that this represents a gigantic crudification and simplification of Marx's work— the kind of simplification and reductionism which once led him, in despair, to say that "if that is Marxism, then I am not a Marxist." Yet there certainly are pointers in this direction in some of Marx's work. It corresponds closely to the orthodox version of Marxism, which did become canonized at the time of the Second International, and which is often even today advanced as the pure doctrine of "classical Marxism." Such a conception of the social formation and of the relationships between its different levels of articulation—it should be clear—has little or no theoretical room left in it for ways of conceptualizing the political and ideological dimensions, let alone ways of conceptualizing other types of social differentiation such as social divisions and contradictions arising around race, ethnicity, nationality, and gender.

Gramsci, from the outset, set his face against this type of economism; and in his later years, he developed a sustained theoretical polemic against precisely its canonization within the classical Marxist tradition. Two examples from different strands in his work must suffice to illustrate this point. In his essay titled "The Modern Prince" Gramsci is discussing how to set about analyzing a particular historical conjuncture. He substitutes, for the reductionist approach which would "read off" political and ideological developments from their economic determinations, a far more complex and differentiated type of analysis. This is based, not on a "one-way determination," but on the analysis of "the relations of force" and aims to differentiate (rather than to collapse as identical) the "various moments or levels" in the development of such a conjuncture (*Prison Notebooks* 180–181, hereafter *PN*). He pinpoints this analytic task in terms of what he calls "the decisive passage from the structure to the spheres of the complex superstructures." In this way he sets himself decisively against any tendency to reduce the sphere of the political and ideological superstructures to the economic structure or "base." He understands this as the most critical site in the struggle against reductionism. "It is the problem of the relations between structure and superstructure which must be accurately posed if the forces which are active in the history of a particular period are to be correctly analysed and the relations between them determined" (*PN*, 177). Economism, he adds, is an inadequate way, theoretically, of posing this critical set of relationships. It tends, among other things, to substitute an analysis based on "immediate class interests" (in the form of the question "Who profits directly from this?") for a fuller, more structured analysis of "economic class formations . . . with all their inherent relations" (PN, 163). It may be ruled out, he suggests, "that *immediate* economic crises of themselves produce fundamental historical events" (my italics). Does this mean that the economic plays no part in the development of historical crises? Not at all. But its role is, rather, to "create a terrain more favourable to the dissemination of certain modes of thought, and certain ways of posing and resolving questions involving the entire subsequent development of national life" (PN, 184). In short, until one has shown how "objective economic crises" actually develop, via the changing relations in the balance of social forces, into crises in the state and society, and germinate in the form of ethical-political struggles and formed political ideologies, influencing the conception of the world of the masses, one has not conducted a proper kind of analysis, rooted in the decisive and irreversible "passage" between structure and superstructure.

The sort of immediate infallibility which economic reductionism brings in its wake, Gramsci argues, "comes very cheap." It not only has no theoretical significance—it also has only minimal political implications or practical efficacy. "In general, it produces nothing but moralistic sermons and interminable questions of personality" (PN, 166). It is a conception based on "the iron conviction that there exist objective laws of historical development similar in kind to natural law, together with a belief in a predetermined teleology like that of a religion." There is no alternative to this collapse—which, Gramsci argues, has been incorrectly identified with historical materialism—except "the concrete posing of the problem of hegemony."

It can be seen from the general thrust of the argument in this passage that many of Gramsci's key concepts (hegemony, for example) and characteristic approaches (the approach via the analysis of "relations of social forces," for example) were consciously understood by him as a barrier against the tendency to economic reductionism in some versions of Marxism. He coupled with his critique of "economism" the related tendencies to positivism, empiricism, "scientism," and objectivism within Marxism.

This comes through even more clearly in "The Problems of Marxism," a text explicitly written as a critique of the "vulgar materialism" implicit in Bukharin's *Theory of Historical Materialism: A Manual of Popular Sociology*. The latter was published in Moscow in 1921, went through many editions, and was often quoted as an example of "orthodox" Marxism (even though

Lenin observed about it that Bukharin was unfortunately "ignorant of the dialectic"). In "Critical Notes on an Attempt at Popular Sociology," which forms the second part of his essay "The Problems of Marxism," Gramsci offers a sustained assault on the epistemologies of economism, positivism, and the spurious search for scientific guarantees. They were founded, he argues, on the falsely positivistic model that the laws of society and human historical development can be modeled directly on what social scientists conceived (falsely, as we now know) as the "objectivity" of the laws governing the natural scientific world. Terms like "regularity," "necessity," "law," and "determination," he argues, are not to be thought of "as a derivation from natural science but rather as an elaboration of concepts born on the terrain of political economy." Thus "determined market" must *really* mean a "determined relation of social forces in a determined structure of the productive apparatus," this relationship being guaranteed (that is, rendered permanent) by a "determined political, moral and juridical superstructure." The movement in Gramsci's formulation from an analytically reduced positivistic formula to a richer, more complex conceptualization framed with social science is lucidly clear from that substitution. It lends weight to Gramsci's summarizing argument, that

> the claim presented as an essential postulate of historical materialism, that every fluctuation of politics and ideology can be presented and expounded as an immediate expression of the structure (i.e., the economic base), must be contested in theory as primitive infantilism, and combated in practice with the authentic testimony of Marx, the author of concrete, political and historical works.

This shift of direction, which Gramsci set himself to bring about within the terrain of Marxism, was quite self-consciously accomplished—and decisive for the whole thrust of his subsequent thought. Without this point of theoretical departure, Gramsci's complicated relationship to the tradition of Marxist scholarship cannot be properly defined.

If Gramsci renounced the simplicities of reductionism, how then did he set about a more adequate analysis of a social formation? Here we may be helped by a brief detour, provided that we move with caution. Althusser (who was profoundly influenced by Gramsci) and his coauthors of *Reading Capital* (Althusser and Balibar [London: New Left Books, 1970]) make a critical distinction between "mode of production," which refers to the basic forms of economic relations which characterize a society, but which is an analytic abstraction, since no society can function by its economy alone, and, on the other hand, what they call the "social formation." By this latter term they meant to invoke the idea that societies are necessarily complexly structured totalities, with different levels of articulation (the economic, the political, the ideological instances) in different combinations, each combination giving rise to a different configuration of social forces and hence to a different type of social development. The authors of *Reading Capital* tended to give as the distinguishing feature of a "social formation" the fact that, in it, more than one mode of production could be combined. But, though this is true, and can have important consequences (especially for postcolonial societies, which we take up later), it is not, in my view, the most important point of distinction between the two terms. In "social formations" one is dealing with complexly structured societies composed of economic, political, and ideological relations, where the different levels of articulation do not by any means simply correspond or "mirror" one another but which are—in Althusser's felicitous metaphor—"overdetermining" on and for one another (Althusser, *For Marx* [Harmondsworth: Penguin, 1969]). It is this complex structuring of the different levels of articulation, not simply the existence of more than one mode of production, which constitutes the difference between the concept of "mode of production" and the necessarily more concrete and historically specific notion of a "social formation."

Now this latter concept *is* the conception to which Gramsci addressed himself. This is what he meant by saying that the relationship between "structure" and "superstructures," or the "passage" of any organic historical movement right through the whole social formation, from economic "base" to the sphere of ethico-political relations, was at the heart of any nonreductionist or economistic type of analysis. To pose and resolve *that* question was to conduct an analysis, properly founded on an understanding of the complex relationships of overdetermination between the different social practices in any social formation.

It is this protocol which Gramsci pursued when, in "The Modern Prince," he outlined his characteristic way of "analyzing situations." The details are complex and cannot be filled out in all their subtlety here, but the bare outlines are worth setting out, if only for purposes of comparison with a more "economistic" or reductionist approach. He considered this "an elementary exposition of the science and art of politics—understood as a body of practical rules for research and of detailed observations useful for awakening an interest in effective reality and for stimulating more rigorous and more vigorous political insights"—a discussion, he added, which must be *strategic* in character.

First of all, he argued, one must understand the fundamental structure—the objective relations—within society or "the degree of development of the productive forces," for these set the most fundamental limits and conditions for the whole shape of historical development. From here arise some of the major lines of tendency which *might* be favorable to this or that line of development. The error of reductionism is then to translate these tendencies and constraints *immediately* into their absolutely determined political and ideological effects, or, alternatively, to abstract them into some "iron law of necessity." In fact, they structure and determine only in the sense that they define the terrain on which historical forces move—they define the horizon of possibilities. But they can, in neither the first nor the last instance, fully determine the content of political and economic struggles, much less objectively fix or guarantee the outcomes of such struggles.

The next move in the analysis is to distinguish "organic" historical movements, which are destined to penetrate deep into society and be relatively long-lasting, from more "occasional, immediate, almost accidental movements." In this respect, Gramsci reminds us that a "crisis," if it is organic, can last for decades. It is not a static phenomenon but, rather, one marked by constant movement, polemics, contestations, etc., which represent the attempt by different sides to overcome or resolve the crisis and to do so in terms which favor their long-term hegemony. The theoretical danger, Gramsci argues, lies in "presenting causes as immediately operative which in fact only operate indirectly, or in asserting that the immediate causes are the only effective ones." The first leads to an excess of economism, the second to an excess of ideologism. (Gramsci was preoccupied, especially in moments of defeat, by the fatal oscillation between these two extremes, which in reality mirror one another in an inverted form.) Far from there being any "law-like" guarantee that some law of necessity will inevitably convert economic causes into immediate political effects, Gramsci insisted that the analysis only succeeds and is "true" *if* those underlying causes become a new reality. The substitution of the conditional tense for positivistic certainty is critical.

Next, Gramsci insisted on the fact that the length and complexity of crises cannot be mechanically predicted, but develop over longer historical periods; they move between periods of relative "stabilization" and periods of rapid and convulsive change. Consequently, *periodization* is a key aspect of the analysis. It parallels the earlier concern with historical specificity. "It is precisely the study of these 'intervals' of varying frequency which enables one to reconstruct the relations, on the one hand, between structure and superstructure, and on the other between the development of organic movement and conjunctural movement in the structure." There is nothing mechanical or prescriptive, for Gramsci, about this "study."

Having thus established the groundwork of a dynamic historical analytic framework, Gramsci turns to the analysis of the movements of historical forces—the "relations of force"—which constitute the actual terrain of political and social struggle and development. Here he introduces the critical notion that what we are looking for is *not* the absolute victory of this side over that, nor the total incorporation of one set of forces into another. Rather, the analysis is a relational matter—that is, a question to be resolved *relationally*, using the idea of "unstable balance" or "the continuous process of formation and superseding of unstable equilibria." The critical question is, are "relations of forces *favourable or unfavourable to this or that tendency*" (my italics)? This emphasis on "relations" and "unstable balance" reminds us that social forces which lose out in any particular historical period do not thereby disappear from the terrain of struggle, nor is struggle in such circumstances suspended. For example, the idea of the "absolute" and total victory of the bourgeoisie over the working class or the total incorporation of the working class into the bourgeois project is totally foreign to Gramsci's definition of hegemony—though the two are frequently confused in scholarly commentary. It is always the tendential balance in the relations of force which matters.

Gramsci then differentiates the "relations of force" into its different moments. He assumes no *necessary teleological evolution* between these moments. The first has to do with an assessment of the objective conditions which place and position the different social forces. The second relates to the political moment—the "degree of homogeneity, self-awareness and organization attained by the various social classes" (PN, 181). The important thing here is that so-called "class unity" is never *assumed*, a priori. It is understood that classes, while sharing certain common conditions of existence, are also crosscut by conflicting interests, historically segmented and fragmented in this actual course of historical formation. Thus the "unity" of classes is necessarily complex and has to be *produced*—constructed, created—as a result of specific economic, political, and ideological practices. It can never be taken as automatic or "given." Coupled with this radical historicization of the automatic conception of classes lodged at the heart of fundamentalist Marxism, Gramsci elaborates further on Marx's distinction between "class in itself" and "class for itself." He notes the different stages through which class consciousness, organization, and unity can—under the right conditions—develop. There is the "economic corporate" stage, where professional or occupational groups recognize their basic common interests but are conscious of no wider class solidarities. Then there is the "class corporate" moment, where class solidarity of interests develops, but only in the economic field. Finally, there is the moment of "hegemony," which transcends the corporate limits of purely economic solidarity, encompasses the interests of other subordinate groups, and begins to "propagate itself throughout society," bringing about intellectual and moral as well as economic and political unity, and "posing also the questions around which the struggle rages . . . thus creating the hegemony of a fundamental social group over a series of subordinate groups." It is this process of the coordination of the interests of a dominant group with the general interests of other groups and the life of the state as a whole that constitutes the "hegemony" of a particular historical bloc (*PN*, 182). It is only in such moments of "national popular" unity that the formation of what he calls a "collective will" becomes possible.

Gramsci reminds us, however, that even this extraordinary degree of organic unity does not *guarantee* the outcome of specific struggles, which can be won or lost on the outcome of the decisive tactical issue of the military and politico-military relations of force. He insists, however, that "politics must have priority over its military aspect, and only politics creates the possibility for manoeuvre and movement" (*PN*, 232).

Three points about this formulation should be particularly noted. First, "hegemony" is a very particular, historically specific, and temporary "moment" in the life of a society. It is rare for this degree of unity to be achieved, enabling a society to set itself a quite new historical agenda, under the leadership of a specific formation or constellation of social forces. Such periods of "settlement" are unlikely to persist forever. There is nothing automatic about them. They have to be actively constructed and positively maintained. Crises mark the beginning of their disintegration. Second, we must take note of the multidimensional, multiarena character of hegemony. It cannot be constructed or sustained on *one* front of struggle alone (for example, the economic). It represents a degree of mastery over a whole series of different "positions" at once. Mastery is not simply imposed or dominative in character. Effectively, it results from winning a substantial degree of popular consent. It thus represents the installation of a profound measure of social and moral authority, not simply over its immediate supporters but across society as a whole. It is this "authority," and the range and diversity of sites on which "leadership" is exercised, which makes possible the "propagation," for a time, of an intellectual, moral, political, and economic collective will throughout society. Third, what "leads" in a period of hegemony is no longer described as a "ruling class" in the traditional language, but as a historic bloc. This has its critical reference to "class" as a determining level of analysis, but it does *not* translate whole classes directly onto the political-ideological stage as unified historical actors. The "leading elements" in a historic bloc may be only one fraction of the dominant economic class—for example, finance rather than industrial capital, national rather than international capital. Associated with it, within the "bloc," will be strata of the subaltern and dominated classes, who have been won over by specific concessions and compromises and who form part of the social constellation but in a subordinate role. The "winning over" of these sections is the result of the forging of "expansive, universalizing alliances" which cement the historic bloc under a particular leadership. Each hegemonic formation will thus have its own, specific social composition and configuration. This is a very different way of conceptualizing what is often referred to, loosely and inaccurately, as the "ruling class."

Gramsci was not, of course, the originator of the term "hegemony." Lenin used it in an analytic sense to refer to the leadership which the proletariat in Russia was required to establish over the peasantry in the struggles to found a socialist state. This in itself is of interest. One of the key questions posed for us by the study of developing societies, which have not passed through the "classic" path of development to capitalism which Marx took as his paradigm case in *Capital* (that is, the English example), is the balance of and relations between different social classes in the struggle for national and economic development; the relative insignificance of the industrial proletariat, narrowly defined, in societies characterized by a relatively low level of industrial development; and above all, the degree to which the peasant class is a leading element in the struggles which found the national state and even, in some cases (China is the outstanding example, but Cuba and Vietnam are also significant examples), the *leading* revolutionary class. It was in this sort of context that Gramsci first employed the term "hegemony." In his unfinished 1926 "Notes on the Southern Question," he argued that the proletariat in Italy could only become the "leading" class insofar as it "succeeds in creating a system of alliances which allows it to mobilize the majority of the working population against capitalism and the bourgeois state . . . [which] means to the extent that it succeeds in gaining the consent of the broad peasant masses."

In fact, this is already a theoretically complex and rich formulation. It implies that the actual social or political force which becomes decisive in a moment of organic crisis will not be composed of a single homogeneous class but will have a complex social composition. Second, it is implicit that its basis of unity will have to be, not an automatic one, given by its position in the mode of economic production, but, rather, a "system of alliances." Third, though such a political and social force has its roots in the fundamental class division of society, the actual forms of the political struggle will have a *wider* social character—dividing society not simply along "class versus class" lines but, rather, polarizing it along the broadest front of antagonism ("the majority of the working population"): for example, between *all* the popular classes, on the one side, and those representing the interests of capital and the power bloc grouped around the state, on the other. In fact, in national and ethnic struggles in the modern world, the actual field of struggle is often actually polarized precisely in this more complex and differentiated way. The difficulty is that it often continues to be described, theoretically, in terms which *reduce* the complexity of its actual social composition to the more simple, descriptive terms of a struggle between two apparently simple and homogeneous class blocs. Further, Gramsci's reconceptualization puts firmly on the agenda such critical strategic questions as the terms on which a class like the peasantry can be won for a national struggle, not on the basis of compulsion but on the basis of "winning their consent."

In the course of his later writings, Gramsci went on to expand the conception of hegemony even further, moving forward from this essentially "class alliance" way of conceptualizing it. First, "hegemony" becomes a general term, which can be applied to the strategies of *all* classes, applied analytically to the formation of all leading historical blocs, not to the strategy of the proletariat alone. In this way, he converts the concept into a more general analytic term. Its applicability in this more general way is obvious. The way, for example, in which in South Africa the state is sustained by the forging of alliances between white ruling-class interests and the interests of white workers against blacks, or the importance in South African politics of the attempts to "win the consent" of certain subaltern classes and groups— for example, the colored strata or "tribal" blacks—in the strategy of forging alliances against the mass of rural and industrial blacks, or the "mixed" class character of all the decolonizing struggles for national independence in developing, postcolonial societies—these and a host of other concrete historical situations are significantly clarified by the development of this concept.

The second development is the difference Gramsci comes to articulate between a class which "dominates" and a class which "leads." Domination and coercion can maintain the ascendancy of a particular class over a society. But its "reach" is limited. It has to rely consistently on coercive means, rather than the winning of consent. For that reason it is not capable of enlisting the positive participation of different parts of society in a historic project to transform the state or renovate society. "Leadership," on the other hand, has its "coercive" aspects too. But it is "led" by the winning of consent, the taking into account of subordinate interests, the attempt to make itself popular. For Gramsci there is no pure case of coercion/consent—only different combinations of the two dimensions. Hegemony is not exercised in the economic and administrative fields alone, but encompasses the critical domains of cultural, moral, ethical, and intellectual leadership. It is only under those conditions that some long-term historic "project"—for example, to modernize society, to raise the whole level of performance of society or transform the basis of national politics—can be effectively put on the historical agenda. It can be seen from this that the concept of "hegemony" is *expanded* in Gramsci by making strategic use of a number of distinctions: for example, those between domination and leadership, coercion and consent, economic and corporate, and moral and intellectual.

Underpinning this expansion is another distinction based on one of Gramsci's fundamental historical theses. This is the distinction between state and civil society. In his essay titled "State and Civil Society," Gramsci elaborated this distinction in several ways. First, he drew a distinction between two types of struggle—the "war of manoeuvre," where everything is condensed into one front and one moment of struggle, and there is a single, strategic breach in the "enemy's defenses," which, once made, enables the new forces "to rush in and obtain a definitive (strategic) victory." Second, there is the "war of position," which has to be conducted in a protracted way, across many different and varying fronts of struggle, where there is rarely a single breakthrough which wins the war once and for all—"in a flash," as Gramsci puts it (PN, 233). What really counts in a war of position is not the enemy's "forward trenches" (to continue the military metaphor) but "the whole organizational and industrial system of the territory which lies to the rear of the army in the field"—that is, the whole structure of society, including the structures and institutions of civil society. Gramsci regarded "1917" as perhaps the last example of a successful "war of manoeuvre" strategy: it marked "a decisive turning-point in the history of the art and science of politics."

This was linked to a second distinction—between "East" and "West." These stand, for Gramsci, as metaphors for the distinction between eastern and western Europe, and between the model of the Russian Revolution and the forms of political struggle appropriate to the much more difficult terrain of the industrialized liberal democracies of "the West." Here, Gramsci addresses the critical issue, so long evaded by many Marxist scholars, of the failure of political conditions in "the West" to match or correspond with those which made 1917 in Russia possible—a central issue, since, despite these radical differences (and the consequent failure of proletarian revolutions of the classic type in "the West"), Marxists have continued to be obsessed by the "Winter Palace" model of revolution and politics. Gramsci is therefore drawing a critical analytic distinction between prerevolutionary Russia, with its long-delayed modernization, its swollen state apparatus and bureaucracy, and its relatively undeveloped civil society and low level of capitalist development, and, on the other hand, "the West," with its mass democratic forms, its complex civil society, the consolidation of the consent of the masses, through political democracy, into a more consensual basis for the state:

> In Russia the State was everything, civil society was primordial and gelatinous; in the West, there was a proper relation between State and civil society, and when the State trembled, a sturdy structure of civil society was at once revealed. The State was only an outer ditch, behind which there stood a powerful system of fortresses and earthworks: more or less numerous from one state to another. . . . This precisely necessitated an accurate reconnaissance of each individual country. (PN, 237–238)

Gramsci is not merely pinpointing a difference of historical specificity. He is describing a historical *transition*. It is evident, as "State and Civil Society" makes clear, that he sees the "war of position" *replacing* the "war of manoeuvre" more and more as the conditions of "the West" become progressively more characteristic of the modern political field in one country after another. (Here, "the West" ceases to be a purely *geographical* identification and comes to stand for a new terrain of politics, created by the emerging forms of state and civil society and new, more complex relations between them.) In these more "advanced" societies, "where civil society has become a very complex structure . . . resistant to the catastrophic 'incursions' of the immediate economic element, . . . the superstructures of civil society are like the trench-systems of modern warfare." A different type of political strategy is appropriate to this novel terrain. "The war of manoeuvre [is] reduced to more of a tactical than a strategic function," and one passes over from "frontal attack" to a "war of position" which requires "unprecedented concentration of hegemony" and is "concentrated, difficult and requires exceptional qualities of patience and inventiveness" because, once won, it is "decisive definitively" (PN, 238–239).

Gramsci bases this "transition from one form of politics to another" historically. It takes place in "the West" after 1870 and is identified with "the colonial expansion of Europe," the emergence of modern mass democracy, a complexification in the role and organization of the state, and an unprecedented elaboration in the structures and processes of "civil hegemony." What Gramsci is pointing to, here, is partly the diversification of social antagonisms, the "dispersal" of power, which occurs in societies where hegemony is not sustained exclusively through the enforced instrumentality of the state but, rather, is grounded in the relations and institutions of civil society. In such societies, the voluntary associations, relations, and institutions of civil society—schooling, the family, churches and religious life, cultural organizations, so-called private relations, gender, sexual and ethnic identities, etc.—become, in effect, "for the art of politics . . . the 'trenches' and the permanent fortifications of the front in the war of position: they render merely 'partial' the element of movement which before used to be 'the whole' of war" (PN, 243).

Underlying all this is therefore a deeper labor of theoretical redefinition. Gramsci in effect is progressively transforming the limited definition of the state, characteristic of some versions of Marxism, as essentially reducible to the coercive instrument of the ruling class, stamped with an exclusive class character which can only be transformed by being "smashed" with a single blow. He comes gradually to emphasize, not only the complexity of the formation of modern civil society, but also the parallel development in complexity of the formation of the modern state. The state is no longer conceived as simply an administrative and coercive apparatus—it is also "educative and formative." It is the point from which hegemony over society as a whole is ultimately exercised (though it is not the only place where hegemony is constructed). It is the point of condensation—not because all forms of coercive domination necessarily radiate outward from its apparatuses but because, in its contradictory structure, it *condenses* a variety of different relations and practices into a definite "system of rules." It is, for this reason, the site for conforming (that is, bringing into line) or "adapting the civilization and the morality of the broadest masses to the necessities of the continuous development of the economic apparatus of production."

Every state, he therefore argues, "is ethical in as much as one of its most important functions is to raise the great mass of the population to a particular cultural and moral level (or type) which corresponds to the needs of the productive forces for development, and hence to the interests of the ruling class" (PN, 258). Notice here how Gramsci foregrounds *new* dimensions of power and politics, new areas of antagonism and struggle—the ethical, the cultural, the moral. How, also, he ultimately returns to more "traditional" questions—"needs of the productive forces for development," "interests of the ruling class": but *not* immediately or reductively. They can only be approached *indirectly*, through a series of necessary displacements and "relays": that is, via the irreversible "passage from the structure to the sphere of the complex superstructures."

It is within this framework that Gramsci elaborates his new conception of the state. The modern state exercises moral and educative leadership—it "plans, urges, incites, solicits, punishes." It is where the bloc of social forces which dominates over it not only justifies and maintains its domination but wins by leadership and authority the active consent of those over whom it rules. Thus it plays a pivotal role in the construction of hegemony. In this reading, it becomes, not a *thing* to be seized, overthrown, or "smashed" with a single blow, but a complex *formation* in modern societies which must become the focus of a number of different strategies and struggles because it is an arena of different social contestations.

It should now be clearer how these distinctions and developments in Gramsci's thinking all feed back into and enrich the basic concept of "hegemony." Gramsci's actual formulations about the state and civil society vary from place to place in his work and have caused some confusion (Anderson, "The Antinomies of Antonio Gramsci," *New Left Review* 100 [1977]). But there is little question about the underlying thrust of his thought on this question. This points irrevocably to the increasing complexity of the interrelationships in modern societies *between* state and civil society. Taken together, they form a complex "system" which has to be the object of a many-sided type of political strategy, conducted on several different fronts at once. The use of such a concept of the state totally transforms, for example, much of the literature about the so-called "postcolonial state," which has often assumed a simple, dominative, or instrumental model of state power.

In this context, Gramsci's "East"/"West" distinction must not be taken too literally. Many so-called "developing" societies already have complex democratic political regimes (that is, in Gramsci's terms, they belong to the "West").

In others, the state has absorbed into itself some of the wider, educative, and "leadership" roles and functions which, in the industrialized Western liberal democracies, are located in civil society. The point is therefore not to apply Gramsci's distinction literally or mechanically but to use his insights to unravel the changing complexities in state/civil society relationships in the modern world and the decisive shift in the predominant character of strategic political struggles—essentially, the encompassing of civil society as well as the state as integral arenas of struggles—which this historic transformation has brought about. An enlarged conception of the state, he argues at one point (stretching the definitions somewhat), must encompass "political society and civil society" or "hegemony protected by the armour of coercion" (PN, 263). He pays particular attention to how these distinctions are differently articulated in different societies—for example, within the "separation of powers" characteristic of liberal parliamentary democratic states as contrasted with the collapsed spheres of fascist states. At another point, he insists on the ethical and cultural functions of the state—raising "the great mass of the population to a particular cultural and moral level," and to the "educative functions of such critical institutions as the school (a 'positive educative function') and the courts ('a repressive and negative educative function')." These emphases bring a range of new institutions and arenas of struggle into the traditional conceptualization of the state and politics. It constitutes them as specific and strategic centers of struggle. The effect is to multiply and proliferate the various fronts of politics and to differentiate the different kinds of social antagonisms. The different fronts of struggle are the various sites of political and social antagonism, and constitute the objects of modern politics when it is understood in the form of a "war of position." The traditional emphases, in which differentiated types of struggle, for example, around schooling, cultural or sexual politics, and institutions of civil society like the family, traditional social organizations, ethnic and cultural institutions, and the like, are *all* subordinated and reduced to an industrial struggle, condensed around the workplace, and a simple choice between trade-union and insurrectionary or parliamentary forms of politics, is here systematically challenged and decisively overthrown. The impact on the very conception of politics itself is little short of electrifying.

Of the many other interesting topics and themes from Gramsci's work which we could consider, I choose, finally, the seminal work on ideology, culture, the role of the intellectual, and the character of what he calls the "national-popular." Gramsci adopts what, at first, may seem a fairly traditional definition of ideology, a "conception of the world, any philosophy, which becomes a cultural movement, a 'religion,' a 'faith,' that has produced a form of practical activity or will in which a philosophy is contained as an implicit theoretical 'premise.'" "One might say," he adds, "ideology . . . on condition that the word is used in its best sense of a conception of the world that is implicitly manifest in art, in law, in economic activity and in all manifestations of individual and collective life." This is followed by an attempt clearly to formulate the problem ideology addresses in terms of its social function: "The problem is that of preserving the ideological unity of the entire social bloc which that ideology serves to cement and unify" (PN, 328). This definition is not as simple as it looks, for it assumes the essential link between the philosophical nucleus or premise at the center of any distinctive ideology or conception of the world and the necessary elaboration of that conception into practical and popular forms of consciousness, affecting the broad masses of society, in the shape of a cultural movement, political tendency, faith, or religion. Gramsci is *never* only concerned with the philosophical core of an ideology; he always addresses *organic* ideologies, which are organic because they touch practical, everyday common sense and they "organize human masses and create the terrain on which men move, acquire consciousness of their position, struggle, etc."

This is the basis of Gramsci's critical distinction between "philosophy" and "common sense." Ideology consists of two distinct "floors." The coherence of an ideology often depends on its specialized philosophical elaboration. But this formal coherence cannot guarantee its organic historical effectivity. That can only be found when and where philosophical currents enter into, modify, and transform the practical, everyday consciousness or popular thought of the masses. The latter is what he calls "common sense." "Common sense" is not coherent: it is usually "disjointed and episodic," fragmentary and contradictory. Into it the traces and "stratified deposits" of more coherent philosophical systems have sedimented over time without leaving any clear inventory. It represents itself as the "traditional wisdom or truth of the ages," but in fact, it is deeply a product of history, "part of the historical process." Why, then, is common sense so important? Because it is the terrain of conceptions and categories on which the practical consciousness of the masses of the people is actually formed. It is the already-formed and "taken-for-granted" terrain on which more coherent ideologies and philosophies must contend for mastery; the ground which new conceptions of the world must take into account, contest, and transform if they are to shape the conceptions of the world of the masses and in that way become historically effective:

> Every philosophical current leaves behind a sediment of "common sense"; this is the document of its historical effectiveness. Common sense is not rigid and immobile but is continually transforming itself, enriching itself with scientific ideas and with philosophical opinions which have entered ordinary life. Common sense creates the folklore of the future, that is as a relatively rigid phase of popular knowledge at a given place and time. (PN, 362, fn. 5)

It is this concern with the structures of *popular thought* which distinguishes Gramsci's treatment of ideology. Thus, he insists that everyone is a philosopher or an intellectual insofar as he or she thinks, since all thought, action, and language is reflexive, contains a conscious line of moral conduct, and thus sustains a particular conception of the world (though not everyone has the specialized function of "the intellectual").

In addition, a class will always have its spontaneous, vivid but not coherent or philosophically elaborated, instinctive understanding of its basic conditions of life and the nature of the constraints and forms of exploitation to which it is commonly subjected. Gramsci described the latter as its "good sense." But it always requires a further work of political education and cultural politics to renovate and clarify these constructions of popular thought—"common sense"—into a more coherent political theory or philosophical current. This "raising of popular thought" is part and parcel of the process by which a collective will is constructed, and requires extensive work of intellectual organization—an essential part of any hegemonic political strategy. Popular beliefs, the culture of a people, Gramsci argues, are not arenas of struggle which can be left to look after themselves. They "are themselves material forces" (PN, 165).

It thus requires an extensive cultural and ideological struggle to bring about or effect the intellectual and ethical unity which is essential to the forging of hegemony: a struggle which takes the form of "a struggle of political hegemonies and of opposing directions, first in the ethical field and then in that of politics proper" (PN, 333). This bears very directly on the type of social struggles we identify with national, anticolonial, and antiracist movements. In his application of these ideas, Gramsci is never simplistically "progressive" in his approach. For example, he recognizes, in the Italian case, the absence of a genuine popular national culture which could easily provide the groundwork for the formation of a popular collective will. Much of his work on culture, popular literature, and religion explores the potential terrain and tendencies in Italian life and society which might provide the basis of such a development. He documents, for example, in Italy, the extensive degree to which popular Catholicism can and has made itself a genuinely "popular force," giving it a unique importance in forming the traditional conceptions of the popular classes. He attributes this, in part, to Catholicism's scrupulous attention to the organization of ideas—especially to ensuring the relationship between philosophical thought or doctrine and popular life or common sense. Gramsci refuses all notions that ideas move and ideologies develop spontaneously and without direction. Like every other sphere of civil life, religion requires organization: it possesses its specific sites of development, specific processes of transformation, specific practices of struggle. "The relation between common sense and the upper level of philosophy," he asserts, "is assured by 'politics'" (PN, 331). Major agencies in this process are, of course, the cultural, educational, and religious institutions; the family and voluntary associations; but also political parties, which are also centers of ideological and cultural formation. The principal agents are intellectuals who have a specialized responsibility for the circulation and development of culture and ideology and who either align themselves with the existing dispositions of social and intellectual forces ("traditional" intellectuals) or align themselves with the emerging popular forces and seek to elaborate new currents of ideas ("organic" intellectuals). Gramsci is eloquent about the critical function, in the Italian case, of traditional intellectuals who have been aligned with classical, scholarly, or clerical enterprises and the relative weakness of the more emergent intellectual strata.

Gramsci's thinking on this question encompasses novel and radical ways of conceptualizing the *subjects* of ideology, which have become the object of considerable contemporary theorizing. He altogether refuses any idea of a pregiven unified ideological subject—for example, the proletarian with its "correct" revolutionary thoughts or blacks with their already-guaranteed current antiracist consciousness. He recognizes the "plurality" of selves or identities of which the so-called "subject" of thought and ideas is composed. He argues that this multifaceted nature of consciousness is not an individual but a collective phenomenon, a consequence of the relationship between "the self" and the ideological discourses which compose the cultural terrain of a society. "The personality is strangely composite," he observes. It contains "Stone Age elements and principles of a more advanced science, prejudices from all past phases of history . . . and intuitions of a future philosophy" (PN, 324). Gramsci draws attention to the contradiction in consciousness between the conception of the world which manifests itself, however fleetingly, in action and those conceptions which are affirmed verbally or in thought. This complex, fragmentary, and contradictory conception of consciousness is a considerable advance over the explanation by way of "false consciousness" more traditional to Marxist theorizing but which is an explanation that depends on self-deception and which he rightly treats as inadequate. The implicit attack which Gramsci advances on the traditional conception of the "given" and unified ideological class subject, which lies at the center of so much traditional Marxist theorizing in this area, matches in importance Gramsci's effective dismantling of the state, on which I commented earlier.

In recognizing that questions of ideology are always collective and social, not individual, Gramsci explicitly acknowledges the necessary complexity and interdiscursive character of the ideological field. There is never any one, single, unified, and coherent "dominant ideology" which pervades everything. Gramsci in this sense does not subscribe to what Nicholas Abercrombie et al. (*The Dominant Ideology Thesis* [Boston: Allen & Unwin, 1980]) call "the dominant ideology thesis." His is not a conception of the incorporation of one group totally into the ideology of another, and their inclusion of Gramsci in this category of thinkers seems to me deeply misleading. There coexist many systems and currents of philosophical thought. The object of analysis is therefore not the single stream of "dominant ideas" into which everything and everyone has been absorbed, but rather the analysis of ideology as a differentiated terrain, of the different discursive currents, their points of juncture and break, and the relations of power between them: in short, an ideological complex, ensemble, or discursive *formation*. The question is "how these ideological currents are diffused and why in the process of diffusion they fracture along certain lines and in certain directions."

I believe it is a clear deduction from this line of argument that, though the ideological field is always, for Gramsci, articulated to different social and political positions, its shape and structure do *not* precisely mirror, match, or "echo" the class structure of society. Nor can they be reduced to their economic content or function. Ideas, he argues, "have a centre of formation, of irradiation, of dissemination, of persuasion" (PN, 192). Nor are they "spontaneously born" in each individual brain. They are not psychologistic or moralistic in character "but structural and epistemological." They are sustained and transformed in their materiality within the institutions of civil society and the state. Consequently, ideologies are not transformed or changed by replacing one, whole, already-formed conception of the world with another, so much as by "renovating and making critical an already existing activity." The multiaccentual, interdiscursive character of the field of ideology is explicitly acknowledged by Gramsci when, for example, he describes how an old conception of the world is gradually displaced by another mode of thought and is internally reworked and transformed:

> What matters is the criticism to which such an ideological complex is subjected . . . This makes possible a process of differentiation and change in the relative weight that the elements of the old ideologies used to possess . . . what was previously secondary and subordinate . . . becomes the nucleus of a new ideological and theoretical complex. The old collective will dissolve into its contradictory elements since the subordinate ones develop socially.

This is an altogether more original and generative way of perceiving the actual process of ideological struggle. It also conceives of culture as the historically shaped terrain on which all "new" philosophical and theoretical currents work and with which they must come to terms. He draws attention to the given and determinate character of that terrain, and the complexity of the processes of deconstruction and reconstruction by which old alignments are dismantled and new alignments can be effected between elements in different discourses and between social forces and ideas. It conceives ideological change not in terms of substitution or imposition but rather in terms of the articulation and the disarticulation of ideas.

III.

It remains, now, to sketch some of the ways in which this Gramscian perspective could potentially be used to transform and rework some of the existing theories and paradigms in the analysis of racism and related social phenomena. Again, I emphasize that this is *not* a question of the immediate transfer of Gramsci's particular ideas to these questions. Rather, it is a matter of bringing a distinctive theoretical *perspective* to bear on the seminal theoretical and analytic problems which define the field.

First, I would underline the emphasis on historical specificity. No doubt there are certain general features to racism. But even more significant are the ways in which these general features are modified and transformed by the historical specificity of the contexts and environments in which they become active. In the analysis of particular historical forms of racism, we would do well to operate at a more concrete, historicized level of abstraction (that is, not racism in general but racisms). Even within the limited case that I know best (that is, Britain), I would say that the differences between British racism in its "high" imperial period and the racism which characterizes the British social formation now, in a period of relative economic decline, when the issue is confronted, not in the colonial setting but as part of the indigenous labor force and regime of accumulation within the domestic economy, are greater and more significant than the similarities. It is often little more than a gestural stance which persuades us to the misleading view that because racism is everywhere a deeply antihuman and antisocial practice, it is therefore everywhere *the same*—either in its forms, its relations to other structures and processes, or its effects. Gramsci does, I believe, help us to interrupt decisively this homogenization.

Second, and related, I would draw attention to the emphasis, stemming from the historical experience of Italy, which led Gramsci to give considerable weight to *national* characteristics, as an important level of determination, and to *regional* unevenness. There is no homogenous "law of development" which impacts evenly throughout every facet of a social formation. We need to understand better the tensions and contradictions generated by the uneven tempos and directions of historical development. Racism and racist practices and structures frequently occur in some but not all sectors of the social formation; their impact is penetrative but uneven, and their very unevenness of impact may help to deepen and exacerbate these contradictory sectoral antagonisms.

Third, I would underline the nonreductive approach to questions concerning the interrelationship between class and race. This has proved to be one of the most complex and difficult theoretical problems to address, and it has frequently led to the adoption of one or another extreme position. Either one "privileges" the underlying class relationships, emphasizing that all ethnically and racially differentiated labor forces are subject to the same exploitative relationships within capital, or one emphasizes the centrality of ethnic and racial categories and divisions at the expense of the fundamental class structuring of society. Though these two extremes appear to be the polar opposites of one another, in fact, they are inverse, mirror images of each other, in the sense that *both* feel required to produce a single and exclusive determining principle of articulation—class *or* race—even if they disagree as to which should be accorded the privileged sign. I believe the fact that Gramsci adopts a nonreductive approach to questions of class, coupled with his understanding of the profoundly historical shaping to any specific social formation, does help to point the way toward a nonreductionist approach to the race/class question.

This is enriched by Gramsci's attention to what we might call the culturally specific quality of class formations in any historically specific society. He never makes the mistake of believing that, because the general law of value has the tendency to homogenize labor power across the capitalist epoch, therefore, in any concrete society, this homogenization can be assumed to exist. Indeed, I believe Gramsci's whole approach leads us to question the validity of this general law in its traditional form, since, precisely, it has encouraged us to neglect the ways in which the law of value, operating on a global as opposed to a merely domestic scale, operates through and *because* of the culturally specific character of labor power rather than—as the classical theory would have us believe—by systematically eroding those distinctions as an inevitable part of a worldwide, epochal historical tendency. Certainly, whenever we depart from the "Eurocentric" model of capitalist development (and even within that model), what we actually find is the many ways in which capital can preserve, adapt to its fundamental trajectory, and harness and exploit these particularistic qualities of labor power, building them into its regimes. The ethnic and racial structuration of the labor force, like its gendered composition, may provide an inhibition to the rationalistically conceived "global" tendencies of capitalist development. And yet, these distinctions have been maintained, and indeed *developed and refined*, in the global expansion of the capitalist mode. They have provided the means for differentiated forms of exploitation of the different sectors of a fractured labor force. In that context, their economic, political, and social effects have been profound. We would get much further along the road to understanding how the regime of capital can function *through* differentiation and difference, rather than through similarity and identity, if we took more seriously this question of the cultural, social, national, ethnic, and gendered composition of historically different and specific forms of labor. Gramsci, though he is not a general theorist of the capitalist mode, does point us unalterably in that direction.

Moreover, his analysis does also point to the way different modes of production can be *combined* within the same social formation, leading not only to regional specificity and unevenness but to differential modes of incorporating so-called "backward" sectors within the social regime of capital (for example, southern Italy within the Italian formation; the "Mediterranean" South within the more advanced "northern" sectors of industrial Europe; the "peasant" economies of the hinterland in Asian and Latin American societies on the path to dependent capitalist development; "colonial" enclaves within the development of metropolitan capitalist regimes; historically, slave societies as an integral aspect of primitive capitalist development of the metropolitan powers; "migrant" labor forces within domestic labor markets; "Bantustans" within so-called sophisticated capitalist economies, etc.). Theoretically, what needs to be noticed is the persistent way in which *these* specific, differentiated forms of "incorporation" have consistently been associated with the appearance of racist, ethnically segmentary, and other similar social features.

Fourth, there is the question of the nonhomogeneous character of the "class subject." Approaches which privilege the class, as opposed to the racial, structuring of working classes or peasantries are often predicated on the assumption that because the mode of exploitation vis-à-vis capital is the same, the "class subject" of any such exploitative mode must be not only economically but politically and ideologically unified. As I have just argued, there is now good reason for qualifying the sense in which the operation of modes of exploitation toward different sectors of the labor force *are* "the same." In any case, Gramsci's approach, which differentiates the conditional process, the different "moments," and the contingent character of the passage from "class in itself" to "class for itself," or from the "economic-corporate" to the "hegemonic" moments of social development, does radically and decisively problematize such simple notions of unity. Even the "hegemonic" moment is no longer conceptualized as a moment of *simple* unity, but as a process of unification (never totally achieved), founded on strategic alliances between different sectors, not on their pre-given identity. Its character is given by the founding assumption that there is no automatic identity or correspondence between economic, political, and ideological practices. This begins to explain how ethnic and racial difference can be constructed as a set of economic, political, or ideological antagonisms *within* a class which is subject to roughly similar forms of exploitation with respect to ownership of and expropriation from the "means of production." The latter, which has come to provide something of a magical talisman, differentiating the Marxist definition of class from more pluralistic stratification models and definitions, has by now long outlived its theoretical utility when it comes to explaining the actual and concrete historical *dynamic* within and between different sectors and segments within classes.

Fifth, I have already referred to the lack of assumed correspondence in the Gramscian model between economic, political, and ideological dimensions. But here I would pull out for specific emphasis the *political* consequences of this noncorrespondence. This has the theoretical effect of forcing us to abandon schematic constructions of how classes *should*, ideally and abstractly, behave politically in place of the concrete study of how they actually *do* behave, in real historical conditions. It has frequently been a consequence of the old correspondence model that the analysis of classes and other related social forces *as* political forces, and the study of the terrain of politics itself, has become a rather automatic, schematic, and residual activity. If, of course, there is "correspondence," plus the "primacy" of the economic over other determining factors, then why spend time analyzing the terrain of politics when it only reflects, in a displaced and subordinate way, the determinations of the economic "in the last instance"? Gramsci certainly would not entertain that kind of reductionism for a moment. He knows he is analyzing structurally complex, not simple and transparent, formations. He knows that politics has its own "relatively autonomous" forms, tempos, and trajectories, which need to be studied in their own right, with their own distinctive concepts, and with attention to their real and retroactive effects. Moreover, Gramsci has put certain key concepts into play which help to differentiate this region, theoretically, of which such concepts as hegemony, historical bloc, "party" in its wider sense, passive revolution, transformism, traditional and organic intellectuals, and strategic alliance constitute only the beginnings of a distinctive and original range. It remains to be demonstrated how the study of politics in racially structured or dominated situations could be positively illuminated by the rigorous application of these newly formulated concepts.

Sixth, a similar argument could be mounted with respect to the state. In relation to racial and ethnic class struggles, the state has been consistently defined in an exclusively coercive, dominative, and conspiratorial manner. Again, Gramsci breaks irrevocably with all three. His domination/direction distinction coupled with the "educative" role of the state, its "ideological" character, its position in the construction of hegemonic strategies—however crude in their original formulation—could transform the study, both of the state in relation to racist practices and the related phenomenon of the "postcolonial state." Gramsci's subtle use of the state/civil society distinction—

even when it fluctuates in his own work—is an extremely flexible theoretical tool, and may lead analysts to pay much more serious attention to those institutions and processes in so-called "civil society" in racially structured social formations than they have been encouraged to do in the past. Schooling, cultural organizations, family and sexual life, the patterns and modes of civil association, churches and religions, communal or organizational forms, ethnically specific institutions, and many other such sites play an absolutely vital role in giving, sustaining, and reproducing different societies in a racially structured form. In any Gramscian-inflected analysis, they would cease to be relegated to a superficial place in the analysis.

Seventh, following the same line of thought, one might note the centrality which Gramsci's analysis always gives to the *cultural* factor in social development. By culture, here, I mean the actual, grounded terrain of practices, representations, languages, and customs of any specific historical society. I also mean the contradictory forms of "common sense" which have taken root in and helped to shape popular life. I would also include that whole distinctive range of questions which Gramsci lumped together under the title "the national-popular." Gramsci understands that these constitute a crucial site for the construction of a popular hegemony. They are a key stake as objects of political and ideological struggle and practice. They constitute a national resource for change as well as a potential barrier to the development of a new collective will. For example, Gramsci perfectly well understood how popular Catholicism had constituted, under specific Italian conditions, a formidable alternative to the development of a secular and progressive "national-popular" culture, how in Italy it would have to be engaged, not simply wished aside. He likewise understood, as many others did not, the role which fascism played in Italy in "hegemonizing" the backward character of the national-popular culture in Italy and refashioning it into a reactionary national formation, with a genuine popular basis and support. Transferred to other comparable situations, where race and ethnicity have always carried powerful cultural, national-popular connotations, Gramsci's emphasis should prove immensely enlightening.

Finally, I would cite Gramsci's work in the ideological field. It is clear that "racism," if not exclusively an ideological phenomenon, has critical ideological dimensions. Hence, the relative crudity and reductionism of materialist theories of ideology have proved a considerable stumbling block in the necessary work of analysis in this area. Especially, the analysis has been foreshortened by a homogeneous, noncontradictory conception of consciousness and of ideology, which has left most commentators virtually undefended when obliged to account, say, for the purchase of racist ideologies within the working class or within related institutions like trade unions, which, in the abstract, ought to be dedicated to antiracist positions. The phenomenon of "working-class racism," though by no means the *only* kind requiring explanation, has proved extraordinarily resistant to analysis.

Gramsci's whole approach to the question of the formation and transformation of the ideological field of popular consciousness, and its processes of formation, decisively undercuts this problem. He shows that subordinated ideologies are necessarily and inevitably contradictory: "Stone Age elements and principles of a more advanced science, prejudices from all past phases of history . . . and intuitions of a future philosophy." He shows how the so-called "self" which underpins these ideological formations is not a unified but a contradictory subject and a social construction. He thus helps us to understand one of the most common, least explained features of "racism": the "subjection" of the victims of racism to the mystifications of the very racist ideologies which imprison and define them. He shows how different, often contradictory elements can be woven into and integrated within different ideological discourses but, also, the nature and value of ideological struggle which seeks to transform popular ideas and the "common sense" of the masses. All this has the most profound importance for the analysis of racist ideologies and for the centrality, within that, of ideological struggle.

In all these different ways—and no doubt in other ways which I have not had time to develop here—Gramsci proves, on closer inspection, and *despite* his apparently "Eurocentric" position, to be one of the most theoretically fruitful, as well as one of the least known and least understood, sources of new ideas, paradigms, and perspectives in the contemporary studies of racially structured social phenomena.

NOTES

1   This essay was originally delivered to the colloquium titled "Theoretical Perspectives in the Analysis of Racism and Ethnicity" organized in 1985 by the Division of Human Rights and Peace, UNESCO, Paris. The original title was "Gramsci's Relevance to the Analysis of Racism and Ethnicity."

2   Some volumes of the planned eight-volume critical edition of the collected works have already been published, at the time of writing, as *Scriti* by Einaudi in Turin. A number of collections of his work, under various headings, exist in English, including the excellent edition of *Selections from the Prison Notebooks*

edited by Geoffrey Nowell Smith and Quintin Hoare (London: Lawrence and Wishart, 1971); *Selections from Political Writings, 1910–1920*, edited by Quintin Hoare (London: Lawrence and Wishart, 1977); and *Selections from Political Writings, 1921–1926*, edited by Quintin Hoare (London: Lawrence and Wishart, 1978); and the more recent *Selections from Cultural Writings*, edited by David Forgacs and Geoffrey Nowell Smith (London: Lawrence and Wishart, 1985). The references and quotations in this essay are all from the English translations cited above.

The Politics of Anti-Essentialism

The first chapter of part II is based on a talk given at a symposium on culture and globalization, held at the State University of New York in Binghamton, in the spring of 1989.[1] In it, Stuart synthesizes the key arguments contained in two talks given the previous year at the Institute for Contemporary Arts in London. Their context was a set of discussions of the dynamics of identity and race in British culture and politics, and of the representational issues raised by the emerging cinematic work of Isaac Julien, Sankofa, John Akomfrah, and the Black Audio Film Collective.[2] In the opening part of the chapter, Stuart situates the anti-essentialist sentiments of these arguments with reference to what he calls the "great decenterings" of modern thought. He traces the intellectual route through Marx's critique of political economy and the psychoanalytical "de-throning of the conscious mind" to the revelations in Saussurean linguistics concerning the unconscious foundations of language. On the basis of that groundwork, he then further updates his argument with reference to feminist critiques of masculinism and postcolonial perspectives on Eurocentric conceptions of modernity as a specifically western episteme and relates these issues to the insights (and dangers) of the Derridean reading of "différance."

It is within this theoretical framework that the analytical gains from the long process of deconstruction of the master concepts of identity (e.g., class) can then be transposed to the analysis of race and ethnicity. Nonetheless, the process of transposition also requires some very careful adaptations. Stuart's substantive argument on these questions involves a history in which he recounts the various stages of the politics of race in the UK. As he explains, this was a process in which, in the pursuit of "roots" as a symbolic counterweight to the processes of exclusion and marginalization, an antiracist politics was constructed through the deployment of the concept of blackness as an inclusive political category, articulating Afro-Asian identities such that new forms of antiracist politics and new conceptions of ethnicity could be facilitated.

However, as he explains, although at that stage ideas of ethnicity and multiculturalism were seen as unhelpfully divisive, there later came a point at which it had to be recognized that the construction of a singularly inclusive black identity also created many serious problems. Not least, it tended to silence all those who were subordinated within this category—notably, in the British case, people of various Asian ethnicities and, in all cases, those outside the normative category of heterosexual masculinity. To this extent, his argument is that, necessary as the moment of strategic essentialism had been in constructing a positive imagery of blackness around which to unite those marginalized and repressed by the racism of British culture, nonetheless, by the late 1980s, these silences could be maintained no longer. Thus, for him, as he explains here, in his discussion of the complex representation of matters of race, gender, sexuality, and ethnicity in films such as Stephen Frears and Hanif Kureishi's *My Beautiful Laundrette*, the time had come to take the necessary risk of abandoning the oversimplifications of the previous era. Correspondingly, he argued, only thus would it be possible to explore more fluid and dialogic conceptions of the various (and often contradictory) dimensions of identity. Race and ethnicity are always crucial factors in Stuart's analysis, but he insists that they are themselves unable to provide any kind of political guarantees.[3]

The following chapter, "What Is This 'Black' in Black Popular Culture?," first published in 1992, picks up and develops these same themes further.[4] As ever, Stuart begins from the premise that analysis must be attentive to the sociohistorical specificity of the contexts in which these issues are to be addressed. Hence he insists on trying to spell out some of the crucial differences between the Western European and North American forms of popular culture. As he notes, while Western European popular culture long failed to recognize that it was founded on any particular ethnicity at all, in America, the vernacular had always contained within it black traditions, even if they had been routinely marginalized and displaced. In a context where globalized, postmodern commercial cultures no longer simply repress that which is defined as primitive but rather serve to license the fascination with bodily and ethnic difference for their own commercial reasons, it is crucial that our analyses are subtle enough to register these distinctions.

Again, while Stuart is at pains to recognize the contribution made by the "necessary moment" of strategic essentialism, he is still concerned to spell out its weaknesses. One crucial problem is that it naturalizes and dehistoricizes difference, tearing the signifier "black" from its historical and cultural contexts and reducing it to a genetically transmitted and biologically constituted racial category, which is assumed to guarantee the value and progressive character of the politics at stake. For Stuart, that essentialist approach freezes differences into mutually exclusive binaries (e.g., that, in Britain, between the terms "black" and "British"), which it is imperative for us, ultimately, to transcend. Thus "identity politics #1" (as he terms it) privileges the problematic category of experience, as if black life is lived outside of representation—the very area in which so much new and exciting work was beginning to be done, by black filmmakers and photographers in the UK at this time.[5] Beyond this, he insists that we must attend to the diversity rather than the homogeneity of black experiences and to the way in which identities of gender, sexuality, class, and race refuse to coalesce around "a single axis of differentiation."

It is for these reasons that, as he ruefully notes here, he had been earlier driven to speak "in an unguarded moment" of the "end of the innocent notion of an essential black subject." He refers here to the intense debate generated by the initial publication of his "New Ethnicities" article, which had been heavily criticized by some activists in the UK for raising what some saw as unnecessarily complex theoretical problems that, it was argued, functioned as an unhelpful distraction from the fundamental struggle against racism.[6] However, rueful as he may have been about the controversies associated with what he calls here this "somewhat notorious" argument, Stuart would not be swayed from what he saw as its intellectual necessity, if we are to ever develop adequately dialogic—rather than simplistically oppositional—political perspectives and strategies.

This part concludes with Stuart's overview of these issues in his essay "The Multi-Cultural Question."[7] As ever, he begins by setting the question within a broad historical theoretical framework and insisting that, in the first place, one should speak of "multiculturalisms" in the plural, as it is, by definition, an unfinished and always-contested term, rather than the simple signifier of some preestablished Promised Land. It signifies neither a single doctrine or political strategy nor any already-achieved state of affairs. Moreover, he notes that it has a significant prehistory and far from being a new phenomenon was a constituent part of a variety of previous empires (Greek, Roman, and Ottoman). Today, he suggests, the crucial thing is to understand multicultur-alism within the context of the complex dynamics in which the homogenizing tendencies of globalization simultaneously meet the "subaltern prolifera-tion of differences." From this perspective, he insists, we can then better see how a variety of vernacular modernities might displace the binary division between a static concept of fixed "Tradition" and an abstracted vision of "Enlightenment Modernity." Thus, rather than accepting the conventional story in which particularistic backward traditions are replaced by a philo-sophically based set of universal principles, what we see is a process in which what had initially been a specifically Western form of particularism came to successfully hegemonize large parts of the globe while presenting itself as a form of global universalism. This is the context in which Stuart then situates what he calls the unraveling of the West, as the erstwhile margins of various empires reappear in the imperial centers. He describes this as the apotheosis of the West's global universalizing mission, which perhaps also signals the moment of its own "slow, uncertain . . . decentring."

Having established this analytical framework, Stuart then takes the changing situation of the UK as the case study to illustrate his arguments. He notes that the popular assumption that until recently the UK had always been a homogenous culture was always false, but nonetheless notes that in the postcolonial era, and specifically since the arrival of the early postwar Caribbean immigrants on the *Empire Windrush* in 1948, there has been a different scale and form of black and multicultural presence in the UK.[8] His concern here is with the shifting forms of debates (and assumptions) about any process of assimilation—and with all the complications arising from the fact that some categories of migrants have long been defined by race, while others have been defined by their ethnicity. He also highlights the signifi-cance of what he calls the processes of the ethnicization of race and the ra-cialization of ethnicity, as well as the "conflation of biological and culturally inferiorising discourses," and the more recent emergence of new forms of cultural racism. He insists on the need to move away from any absolutist vision of identity that is ultimately fixed and to prioritize the necessarily contradictory (and always incomplete) cultures of hybridity that have the great virtue of being "how newness enters the world."[9]

In the face of rising fundamentalisms on all sides, Stuart insists on the necessity of the double demand for both equality and the recognition of difference. Recognizing the dangers of ideas of ethnicity in any absolutist form, he further argues that we must pursue these demands without "reverting to new forms of ethnic closure." Thus, for him, if this whole process will (in Chantal Mouffe's terms) be inevitably "agonistic," and if there are no clear solutions at hand, there are nonetheless some compass points by which we can steer.[10] Thus, he avers, our aim must be to transcend the cul-de-sac created by a binary vision that insists that we either treat individuals as a free-floating entities, outside any particular culture, *or* communities as solidaristic, pregiven wholes in which the authority of a pregiven tradition must reign supreme. His argument is keenly alert to the extent to which, given the necessarily uncomfortable stresses and strains of multicultural societies, migrants (undermining, as they do, certainties previously thought to have been indelibly inscribed in the soil of the nation) so often come to function as scapegoats for the loss of that imaginary Golden Age of settled homogeneity.

Already, at the moment of the publication of the "What Is This 'Black' in Black Popular Culture?" in 1992, Stuart had been sensitive to the coming of a potential backlash to the decentering of the white, masculinized, Western narrative of history itself. He thus warns of the early signs—visible then and now, twenty-six years on, in full cry—of aggressive resistance to difference; of burgeoning attempts to restore the traditional artistic canon of Western civilization; of rising forms of ethnic absolutism, cultural racism, and xenophobia. Writing in 2009, in the context of an introduction to her collection of essays discussing Stuart's contribution to the analysis of race and ethnicity, Claire Alexander noted poignantly that the "relative optimism of the 'new ethnicities' moment (had) undoubtedly been superseded in the . . . climate of fear, religious and ethnic retrenchment and the resurgent assimilationist nationalism of 21st century Britain." She goes on to quote Stuart's own disillusionment at that moment, as he had come to feel that the points of reference around which he had organized his political perspective were crumbling, as the balance of social forces now came to be "stacked against hope," particularly in the wake of the hostile backlash against the Runnymede Trust's *Report on the Future of Multi-Ethnic Britain*.[11] In a newspaper article at the time, when Stuart was invited to respond to the critics of the Parekh report, he nonetheless stuck firmly to his guns, insisting that the report was quite right to argue that historically the idea of Britishness had carried "largely unspoken racial connotations" insofar as—in the common understanding—Britain was then, and is still, usually imagined as white.[12]

For him and his fellow commissioners, he robustly argued, the central point was that if people from ethnic minorities were ever to become not only citizens but an integral part of the national culture, the term "British" would have to be hyphenated in a variety of ways, so as to accommodate their differences and become more inclusive of their experiences. In the end, his analysis was sensitive to both the positive and negative factors in play, noting the coincidence of the well-publicized and widely supported fiftieth anniversary celebrations, in 1998, of the arrival of the *Windrush* and the damning report chaired by Sir William Macpherson into the 1993 murder of the black teenager Stephen Lawrence by white racists. Their crimes had met with the collusion of what Macpherson, in his report, described as an "institutionally racist" police force, demonstrating that it was still "perfectly possible for multiculturalism and racism to coexist."[13] In the wake of the burgeoning Islamophobia of recent decades and of the key role that the issue of immigration played in the British public's decision to vote itself out of Europe in the Brexit referendum of 2016, it would certainly seem that even stormier clouds are now gathering, and the toxic appeal of racism, right across Europe, is all too evident. In the North American context, the tragic deaths dramatically protested by the Black Lives Matter movement have shown just how very much the question of racist policing remains of vital importance.[14]

NOTES

1 The talk published here in a reedited version was originally published in Anthony King, ed., *Culture, Globalisation and the World System* (London: Macmillan, 1991).

2 Stuart Hall, "Minimal Selves," in *Identity: The Real Me*, ICA Documents no. 6, ed. Lisa Appignanesi (London: Institute of Contemporary Arts, 1987); and Hall, "New Ethnicities," in *Black Film, British Cinema*, ICA Documents no. 7, ed. Kobena Mercer (London: Institute of Contemporary Arts, 1988).

3 Here we return to that signature rhetorical trope.

4 Stuart Hall, "What Is This 'Black' in Black Popular Culture?," first published in Gina Dent, ed., *Black Popular Culture: A Project by Michele Wallace* (Seattle: Bay Press, 1992).

5 See the general introduction for my earlier brief commentary on this work. For a more detailed survey of these issues, see John Akomfrah, "The Partisan's Prophecy: Handsworth Songs and Its Silent Partners," and Mark Sealy, "The

Historical Conditions of Existence: On Stuart Hall and the Photographic Moment," both in *Stuart Hall: Conversations, Projects and Legacies*, ed. Julian Henriques and David Morley, with Vana Goblot (London: Goldsmiths Press, 2018).

6   Principal among his critics was the influential activist and commentator Ambalavaner Sivanandan, formerly director of the Institute of Race Relations and editor of the journal *Race and Class*. See "All That Melts Into Air Is Solid" in his *Communities of Resistance: Writings on Black Struggles for Socialism* (London: Verso, 1990).

7   This essay was originally given as the Pavis lecture at the Open University in 1998 and published by the Open University Faculty of Science as no. 4 in the Pavis Papers series, and was subsequently republished in Barnor Hesse, ed., *Un/settled Multiculturalisms: Diasporas, Entanglements, Transruptions* (London: Zed, 2000).

8   For another version of Hall's arguments on these issues, see his "Whose Heritage? Unsettling the Heritage, Reimagining the Post-Nation," *Third Text*, no. 49 (2000): 3–13.

9   See also Stuart's later commentaries on these themes in the interviews in part 7.

10 Chantal Mouffe, "Deliberative Democracy or Agonistic Pluralism?" *Social Research* 66, no. 3 (1999): 745–758.

11 Claire Alexander, introduction to "Stuart Hall and Race," special issue of *Cultural Studies* 23, no. 4 (2009): 457–482. See also Bhikhu C. Parekh, ed., *The Future of Multi-Ethnic Britain* (London: Runnymede Commission, 2000).

12 Stuart Hall, "A Question of Identity (II)," *Observer*, October 15, 2000.

13 Mike Phillips and Trevor Phillips, *Windrush: The Irresistible Rise of Multi-racial Britain* (London: HarperCollins, 1998); William Macpherson, *The Stephen Lawrence Inquiry: Report of an Inquiry by Sir William Macpherson*, UK Government Command Papers, Cm 4262-I, London, February 1999.

14 Alexander, "Introduction." For a recent commentary on the situation in the US, see Angela Davis, "*Policing the Crisis* Today," in *Stuart Hall: Conversations, Projects and Legacies*, ed. Julian Henriques and David Morley, with Vana Goblot. And for discussion of Stuart's work in relation to Black Lives Matter, see the papers of the conference held in Stuart's honor in New York in the fall of 2015: "*Policing the Crisis* Today," Barnard College/Stony Brook University/Columbia University, New York, September 24–26, 2015.

CHAPTER 2

Old and New Identities, Old and New Ethnicities

Previously, I've tried to open out the questions about the local and the global from their somewhat closed, somewhat overintegrated, and somewhat over-systematized formulations. My argument was that we need to think about the processes which are now revealing themselves in terms of the local and the global, in those two spaces, but we also need to think of these as more contradictory formulations than we usually do. Unless we do, I was concerned that we are likely to be disabled in trying to think those ideas politically.

I was therefore attempting—certainly not to close out the questions of power and appropriation which I think are lodged at the very center of any notion of a shift between the dispositions of the local and the global in the emergence of a cultural politics on a world scale—but rather to conceptualize that within a more open-ended and contingent cultural politics.

In the course of these reflections, however, I was obliged to ask if there is a politics, indeed, a counterpolitics of the local. If there are new globals and new locals at work, who are the new subjects of this politics of position? What conceivable identities could they appear in? Can identity itself be re-thought and relived, in and through difference?

It is this question which I want to address here. I have called it "Old and New Identities, Old and New Ethnicities," and what I am going to do first is to return to the question of identity and try to look at some of the ways in which we are beginning to reconceptualize that within contemporary theoretical discourses. I shall then go back from that theoretical consideration to the ground of a cultural politics. Theory is always a detour on the way to something more important.

I return to the question of identity because the question of identity has returned to us; at any rate, it has returned to us in British politics and British cultural politics today. It has not returned in the same old place; it is not the traditional conception of identity. It is not going back to the old identity politics of the 1960s social movements. But it is, nevertheless, a kind of return to some of the ground which we used to think in that way. I will make a comment at the very end about what is the nature of this theoretical-political work which seems to lose things on the one side and then recover them in a different way from another side, and then have to think them out all over again just as soon as they get rid of them. What is this never-ending theoretical work which is constantly losing and regaining concepts? I talk about identity here as a point at which, on the one hand, a whole set of new theoretical discourses intersect and where, on the other, a whole new set of cultural practices emerge. I want to begin by trying, very briefly, to map some of those points of intersection theoretically, and then to look at some of their political consequences.

The old logics of identity are ones with which we are extremely familiar, either philosophically or psychologically. Philosophically, the old logic of identity which many people have critiqued in the form of the old Cartesian subject was often thought in terms of the origin of being itself, the ground of action. Identity is the ground of action. And we have in more recent times a psychological discourse of the self which is very similar: a notion of the continuous, self-sufficient, developmental, unfolding, inner dialectic of self-hood. We are never quite there, but always on our way to it, and when we get there, we will at last know exactly who it is we are.

Now this logic of identity is very important in a whole range of political, theoretical, and conceptual discourses. I am interested in it also as a kind of existential reality because I think the logic of the language of identity is extremely important to our own self-conceptions. It contains the notion of the true self, some real self inside there, hiding inside the husks of all the false selves that we present to the rest of the world. It is a kind of guarantee of authenticity. Not until we get really inside and hear what the true self has to say do we know what we are "really saying."

There is something guaranteed about that logic or discourse of identity. It gives us a sense of depth, out there and in here. It is spatially organized. Much of our discourse of the inside and the outside, of the self and other, of the individual and society, of the subject and the object, are grounded in that particular logic of identity. And it helps us, I would say, to sleep well at night.

Increasingly, I think one of the main functions of concepts is that they give us a good night's rest. Because what they tell us is that there is a kind of stable, only very slowly changing ground inside the hectic upsets, discontinuities, and ruptures of history. Around us history is constantly breaking in unpredictable ways but we, somehow, go on being the same.

That logic of identity is, for good or ill, finished. It is at an end for a whole range of reasons. It is at an end in the first instance because of some of the great decenterings of modern thought. One could discuss this very elaborately—I could spend the rest of the time talking about it, but I just want to slot the ideas into place very quickly by using some names as reference points.

It is not possible to hold to that logic of identity after Marx because although Marx does talk about man (he does not talk about women making history, but perhaps they were slotted in, as the nineteenth century so often slotted women in under some other masculine title), about men and women making history but under conditions which are not of their own choosing. And having lodged either the individual or collective subject always within historical practices, we as individuals or as groups cannot be, and can never have been, the sole origin or authors of those practices. That is a profound historical decentering in terms of social practice.

If that was not strong enough, knocking us sideways as it were, Freud came knocking from underneath, like Hamlet's ghost, and said, "While you're being decentered from left to right like that, let me decenter you from below a bit, and remind you that this stable language of identity is also set from the psychic life about which you don't know very much, and can't know very much. And which you can't know very much about simply by taking it at face value: the great continent of the unconscious speaks most clearly when it's slipping rather than when it's saying what it means." This makes the self begin to seem a pretty fragile thing.

Now, buffeted on one side by Marx and upset from below by Freud, just as it opens its mouth to say, "Well, at least I speak so therefore I must be something," Saussure and linguistics come along and say, "That's not true either, you know. Language was there before you. You can only say something by positioning yourself in the discourse. The tale tells the teller, the myth tells the myth-maker. The enunciation is always from some subject who is positioned by and in discourse." That upsets that. Philosophically, one comes to the end of any kind of notion of a perfect transparent continuity between our language and something out there which can be called the real, or the truth, without any quotation marks.

These various upsets, these disturbances in the continuity of the notion of the subject and the stability of identity, are indeed what modernity is like. It is not, incidentally, modernity itself. That has an older, and longer, history. But this is the beginning of modernity as trouble. Not modernity as enlightenment and progress, but modernity as a problem.

It is also upset by other enormous historical transformations which do not have, and cannot be given, a single name, but without which the story could not be told. In addition to the three or four that I have quoted, we could mention the relativization of the Western narrative itself, the Western episteme, by the rise of other cultures to prominence, and fifthly, the displacement of the masculine gaze.

Now, the question of trying to come to terms with the notion of identity in the wake of those theoretical decenterings is an extremely problematic enterprise. But that is not all that has been disturbing the settled logic of identity. Because, as I was saying earlier when I was talking about the relative decline, erosion, or instability of the nation-state, of the self-sufficiency of national economies, and consequently, of national identities as points of reference, there has simultaneously been a fragmentation and erosion of collective social identity.

I mean here the great collective social identities which we thought of as large-scale, all-encompassing, homogenous, unified collective identities, which could be spoken about almost as if they were singular actors in their own right but which, indeed, placed, positioned, stabilized, and allowed us to understand and read, almost as a code, the imperatives of the individual self: the great collective social identities of class, race, nation, gender, and the West.

These collective social identities were formed in, and stabilized by, the huge, long-range historical processes which have produced the modern world, just as the theories and conceptualizations that I just referred to very briefly are what constituted modernity as a form of self-reflection. They were staged and stabilized by industrialization, by capitalism, urbanization, the formation of the world market, the social and the sexual division of labor, the great punctuation of civil and social life into the public and the private, the dominance of the nation-state, and the identification between Westernization and the notion of modernity itself.

I spoke in my previous talk about the importance, to any sense of where we are placed in the world, of the national economy, the nation-state, and national cultural identities. Let me say a word here about the great class identities which have stabilized so much of our understanding of the immediate and not-so-immediate past.

Class was the main locator of social position, that which organized our understanding of the main grid and group relations between social groups. They linked us to material life through the economy itself. They provided the code through which we read one another. They provided the codes through which we understood each others' languages. They provided, of course, the notions of collective action itself, that which would unlock politics. Now as I tried to say previously, the great collective social identities rise and fall, and it is almost as difficult to know whether they are more dangerous when they are falling than when they are rising.

These great collective social identities have not disappeared. Their purchase and efficacy in the real world that we all occupy is ever present. But the fact is that none of them is, any longer, in either the social, historical, or epistemological place where they were in our conceptualizations of the world in the recent past. They cannot any longer be thought in the same homogenous form. We are as attentive to their inner differences, their inner contradictions, their segmentations, and their fragmentations as we are to their already-completed homogeneity, their unity, and so on.

They are not already-produced stabilities and totalities in the world. They do not operate like totalities. If they have a relationship to our identities, cultural and individual, they do not any longer have that suturing, structuring, or stabilizing force, so that we can know what we are simply by adding up the sum of our positions in relation to them. They do not give us the code of identity as I think they did in the past.

It is a moot point by anybody who takes this argument directly on the pulses, as to whether they ever functioned in that way. Perhaps they never functioned in that way. This may be, indeed, what the narrative of the West is like: the notion that we told of the story we told ourselves, about their functioning in that way. We know that the great homogenous function of the collective social class is extremely difficult for any good historian to actually lay his or her finger on. It keeps disappearing just over the horizon, like the organic community.

You know the story about the organic community? The organic community was just always in the childhood you have left behind. Raymond Williams has a wonderful essay on these people, a range of social critics who say you can measure the present in relation to the past, and you know the past because back then it was much more organic and integrated. When was "back then"? Well, when I was a child, there was always some adult saying, "When I was a child, it was much more integrated." And so, eventually, some of these great collectivities are rather like those people who have an activity of historical nostalgia going on in their retrospective reconstructions. We always reconstructed them more essentially, more homogenously, more unified, less contradictorily than they ever were, once you actually know anything about them.

That is one argument. Whatever the past was like, they may have all marched forth, unified and dictating history forward, for many decades in the past. They sure aren't doing it now.

Now, as I have said, the question of how to begin to think questions of identity, either social or individual, not in the wake of their disappearance but in the wake of their erosion, of their fading, of their not having the kind of purchase and comprehensive explanatory power they had before, that is what it seems to me has gone. They used to be thought of—and it is a wonderfully gendered definition—as "master concepts," the "master concepts" of class.

It is not tolerable any longer to have a "master concept" like that. Once it loses its "master" status, its explanatory reach weakens, becomes more problematic. We can think of some things in relation to questions of class, though always recognizing its real historical complexity. Yet there are certain other things it simply will not, or cannot, decipher or explain. And this brings us face to face with the increasing social diversity and plurality, the technologies of the self which characterize the modern world in which we live.

Well, we might say, where does this leave any discourse on social identity at all? Haven't I now abolished it from about as many sides as I could think of? As has been true in theoretical work over the past twenty years, the moment a concept disappears through the left-hand door, it returns through the right-hand window, but not in quite the same place. There is a wonderful moment in an Althusser text where he says, "I can now abolish the notion of ideas." And he actually writes the word "ideas" and draws a line through it to convince himself that we need never use the word again.

In exactly the same way, the old discourse of the subject was abolished, put in a deep container, concrete poured over it, with a half-life of a million years. We will never look at it again, when, bloody hell, in about five minutes, we are talking about subjectivity, and the subject in discourse, and it has come roaring back in. So it is not, I think, surprising that, having lost one sense of identity, we find we need it. Where are we to find it?

One of the places that we have to go to is certainly in the contemporary languages which have rediscovered but repositioned the notion of the subject, of subjectivity. That is, principally, and preeminently, the languages of feminism and of psychoanalysis.

I do not want to go through that argument, but I want to say something about how one might begin to think questions of identity from this new set of theoretical spaces. And I have to do this programmatically. I have to state what I think, from this position, identity is and is not as a sort of protocol, although each one could take me a very long time.

It makes us aware that identities are never completed, never finished, that they are always, as subjectivity itself is, in process. That itself is a pretty difficult task. Though we have always known it a little bit, we have always thought about ourselves as getting more like ourselves every day. But that is a sort of Hegelian notion, of going forward to meet that which we always were. I want to open that process up considerably. Identity is always in the process of formation.

Secondly, identity means, or connotes, the process of identification, of saying that this here is the same as that, or we are the same together, in this respect. But something we have learned from the whole discussion of identification, in feminism and psychoanalysis, is the degree to which that structure of identification is always constructed through ambivalence. Always constructed through splitting.

Splitting between that which one is and that which is the other. The attempt to expel the other to the other side of the universe is always compounded by the relationships of love and desire. This is a different language from the language of, as it were, the Others who are completely different from oneself.

This is the Other that belongs inside one. This is the Other that one can only know from the place from which one stands. This is the self as it is inscribed in the gaze of the Other. And this notion which breaks down the boundaries between outside and inside, between those who belong and those who do not, between those whose histories have been written and those whose histories they have depended on but whose histories cannot be spoken. That the unspoken silence in between that which can be spoken is the only way to reach for the whole history. There is no other history except to take the absences and the silences along with what can be spoken. Everything that can be spoken is on the ground of the enormous voices that have not yet been, or cannot yet be, heard.

This doubleness of discourse, this necessity of the Other to the self, this inscription of identity in the look of the other finds its articulation profoundly in the ranges of a given text. And I want to cite one which I am sure you know but will not remember necessarily, though it is a wonderful, majestic moment in Fanon's *Black Skin, White Masks*, when he describes himself as a young Antillean, face to face with the white French child and her mother. And the child pulls the hand of the mother and says, "Look, Mama, a black man." And he said, "For the first time, I knew who I was. For the first time, I felt as if I had been simultaneously exploded in the gaze, in the violent gaze of the other, and at the same time, recomposed as another." The notion that identity in that sense could be told as two histories, one over here, one over there, never having spoken to one another, never having anything to do with one another, when translated from the psychoanalytic to the historical terrain, is simply not tenable any longer in an increasingly globalized world. It is just not tenable any longer.

People like me who came to England in the 1950s have been there for centuries; symbolically, we have been there for centuries. I was coming home. I am the sugar at the bottom of the English cup of tea. I am the sweet tooth, the sugar plantations that rotted generations of English children's teeth. There are thousands of others beside me that are, you know, the cup of tea itself. Because they don't grow it in Lancashire, you know. Not a single tea plantation exists within the United Kingdom. This is the symbolization of English identity—I mean, what does anybody in the world know about an English person except that they cannot get through the day without a cup of tea?

Where does it come from? Ceylon/Sri Lanka, India. That is the outside history that is inside the history of the English. There is no English history without that other history. The notion that identity has to do with people who look the same, feel the same, call themselves the same, is nonsense. As a process, as a narrative, as a discourse, it is always told from the position of the Other.

What is more is that identity is always in part a narrative, always in part a kind of representation. It is always within representation. Identity is not something which is formed outside and then we tell stories about it. It is that which is narrated in one's own self. I will say something about that in terms of my own narration of identity in a moment—you know, that wonderful moment where Richard II says, "Come let us sit down and tell stories about the death of kings." Well, I am going to tell you a story and ask you to tell one about yourself.

We have the notion of identity as contradictory, as composed of more than one discourse, as composed always across the silences of the other, as written in and through ambivalence and desire. These are extremely important ways of trying to think an identity which is not a sealed or closed totality.

Now we have within theory some interesting ways of trying to think difference in this way. We have learned a lot about sexual difference in feminist writers. And we have learned a lot about questions of difference from people like Derrida. I do think that there are some important ways in which Derrida's use of the notion of the difference between "difference" and "différance," spelt with an "a," is significant. The "a," the anomalous "a" in Derrida's spelling of différance, which he uses as a kind of marker that sets up a disturbance in our settled understanding of translation of our concept of difference is very important, because that little "a," disturbing as it is, which you can hardly hear when spoken, sets the word in motion to new meanings, yet without obscuring the trace of its other meanings in its past.

His sense of différance, as one writer has put it, remains suspended between the two French verbs "to differ" and "to defer," both of which contribute to its textual force, neither of which can fully capture its meaning. Language depends on difference, as Saussure has shown: the structure of distinctive propositions which make up its economy. But where Derrida breaks new ground is in the extent to which "differ" shades into "defer."

Now this notion of a différance is not simply a set of binary, reversible oppositions, thinking sexual difference not simply in terms of the fixed opposition of male and female, but of all those anomalous sliding positions ever in process, between which opens up the continent of sexuality to increasing points of disturbance. That is what the odyssey of difference now means in the sense in which I am trying to use it.

That is about difference, and you might ask the question, Where does identity come in to this infinite postponement of meaning that is lodged in Derrida's notion of the trace of something which still retains its roots in one meaning while it is, as it were, moving to another, encapsulating another, with endless shiftings, slidings, of that signifier?

The truth is that Derrida does not help us as much as he might here in thinking about the relationship between identity and difference. And the appropriators of Derrida in America, especially in American philosophical and literary thought, help us even less. By taking Derrida's notion of différance precisely out of the tension between the two textual connotations, "defer" and "differ," and lodging it only in the endless play of difference, Derrida's politics is in that very moment uncoupled.

From that moment unrolls that enormous proliferation of extremely sophisticated, playful deconstruction which is a kind of endless academic game. Anybody can do it, and on and on it rolls. No signifier ever stops; no one is ever responsible for any meaning; all traces are effaced. The moment anything is lodged, it is immediately erased. Everybody has a great time; they go to conferences and do it, as it were. The very notion of the politics which requires the holding of the tension between that which is both placed and not stitched in place, by the word which is always in motion between positions, which requires us to think both positionality and movement (both together, not one and the other), not playing with difference, or "finding nights to rest under" identity, but living in the tension of identity and difference, is uncoupled.

We have then to go on thinking beyond that mere playfulness into the really hard game which the play of difference actually means to us historically. For if signification depends upon the endless repositioning of its differential terms, meaning in any specific instance depends on the contingent and arbitrary stop, the necessary break. It is a very simple point.

Language is part of an infinite semiosis of meaning. To say anything, I have got to shut up. I have to construct a single sentence. I know that the next sentence will open the infinite semiosis of meaning again, so I will take it back. So each stop is not a natural break. It does not say, "I'm about to end a sentence and that will be the truth." It understands that it is contingent. It is a positioning. It is the cut of ideology which, across the semiosis of language, constitutes meaning. But you have to get into that game or you will never say anything at all.

You think I am joking. I know graduate students of mine who got into this theoretical fix in the 1970s, one enormous French theoretician after another, throwing them aside, until they could not commit a single word to paper at all because to say anything was to open oneself to the endless sliding of the signifier. So if they said, what I think Derrida really, in—really—ooh—start again, yes, start again.

Meaning is in that sense a wager. You take a bet. Not a bet on truth, but a bet on saying something. You have to be positioned somewhere in order to speak. Even if you are positioned in order to unposition yourself, even if you want to take it back, you have to come into language to get out of it. There is no other way. That is the paradox of meaning.

To think it only in terms of difference and not in terms of the relational position between the suturing, the arbitrary, overdetermined cut of language which says something which is instantly opened again to the play of meaning; not to think of meaning always, in supplement, that there is always something left over, always something which goes on escaping the precision; the attempt of language to code, to make precise, to fix, to halt, etc.; not to think it in that way is to lose hold of the two necessary ends of the chain to which the new notion of identity has to be conceptualized.

Now I can turn to questions of politics. In this conception of an identity which has to be thought through difference, is there a general politics of the local to bring to bear against the great, overriding, powerful, technologically based, massively invested unrolling of global processes which I was trying to describe in my previous talk, which tend to mop up all differences, and occlude those differences? Which means, as it were, they are different—but it does not make any difference that they are different, they are just different.

No, there is no general politics. I have nothing in the kitbag. There is nothing I can pull out. But I have a little local politics to tell you about. It may be that all we have, in bringing the politics of the local to bear against the global, is a lot of little local politics. I do not know if that is true or not. But I would like to spend some time later talking about the cultural politics of the local, and of this new notion of identity. For it is in this new frame that identity has come back into cultural politics in Britain. The formation of the black diasporas in the period of postwar migration in the 1950s and '60s has transformed English social, economic, and political life.

In the first generations, the majority of people had the same illusion that I did: that I was about to go back home. That may have been because everybody always asked me when I was going back home. We did think that we were just going to get back on the boat; we were here for a temporary sojourn. By the '70s, it was perfectly clear that we were not there for a temporary sojourn. Some people were going to stay, and then the politics of racism really emerged.

Now one of the main reactions against the politics of racism in Britain was what I would call "Identity Politics One," the first form of identity politics. It had to do with the constitution of some defensive collective identity against the practices of racist society. It had to do with the fact that people were being blocked out of and refused an identity and identification within the majority nation, having to find some other roots on which to stand. Because people have to find some ground, some place, some position on which to stand. Blocked out of any access to an English or British identity, people had to try to discover who they were. This is the moment I defined in my previous talk. It is the crucial moment of the rediscovery or the search for roots.

In the course of the search for roots, one discovered not only where one came from; one began to speak the language of that which is home in the genuine sense, that other crucial moment which is the recovery of lost histories. The histories that have never been told about ourselves that we could not learn in schools, that were not in any books, and that we had to recover.

This is an enormous act of what I want to call imaginary political reidentification, reterritorialization and reidentification, without which a counterpolitics could not have been constructed. I do not know an example of any group or category of the people of the margins, of the locals, who have been able to mobilize themselves socially, culturally, economically, and politically in the past twenty or twenty-five years who have not gone through some such series of moments in order to resist their exclusion, their marginalization. That is how and where the margins begin to speak. The margins begin to contest, and the locals begin to come to representation.

The identity which that whole, enormous political space produced in Britain, as it did elsewhere, was the category black. I want to say something about this category which we all now so take for granted. I will tell you some stories about it.

I was brought up in a lower-middle-class family in Jamaica. I left there in the early 1950s to go and study in England. Until I left, though I suppose 98 percent of the Jamaican population is either black or colored in one way or another, I had never ever heard anybody either call themselves, or refer to anybody else as, "black." Never. I heard a thousand other words. My grandmother could differentiate about fifteen different shades between light brown and dark brown. When I left Jamaica, there was a beauty contest in which the different shades of women were graded according to different trees, so that there was Miss Mahogany, Miss Walnut, etc.

People think of Jamaica as a simple society. In fact, it had the most complicated color stratification system in the world. Talk about practical semioticians; anybody in my family could compute and calculate anybody's social status by grading the particular quality of their hair versus the particular quality of the family they came from and which street they lived on, including their physiognomy, shading, etc. You could trade off one characteristic against another. Compared with that, the normal class stratification system is absolute child's play.

But the word "black" was never uttered. Why? No black people around? Lots of them, thousands and thousands of them. Black is not a question of pigmentation. The black I am talking about is a historical category, a political category, a cultural category. In our language, at certain historical moments, we have to use the signifier. We have to create an equivalence between how people look and what their histories are. Their histories are in the past, inscribed on their skin. But it is not because of their skin that they are black in their heads.

I heard "black" for the first time in the wake of the civil rights movement, in the wake of the decolonization and nationalistic struggles. "Black" was created as a political category in a certain historical moment. It was created as a consequence of certain symbolic and ideological struggles. We said, "You have spent five, six, seven hundred years elaborating the symbolism through which black is a negative factor. Now I don't want another term. I want that term, that negative one, that's the one I want. I want a piece of that action. I want to take it out of the way in which it has been articulated in religious discourse, in ethnographic discourse, in literary discourse, in visual discourse. I want to pluck it out of its articulation and rearticulate it in a new way."

In that very struggle is a change of consciousness, a change of self-recognition, a new process of identification, the emergence into visibility of a new subject. A subject that was always there, but emerging, historically.

You know that story, but I do not know if you know the degree to which that story is true of other parts of the Americas. It happened in Jamaica in the 1970s. In the 1970s, for the first time, black people recognized themselves as black. It was the most profound cultural revolution in the Caribbean, much greater than any political revolution they have ever had. That cultural revolution in Jamaica has never been matched by anything as far-reaching as the politics. The politics has never caught up with it.

You probably know the moment when the leaders of both major political parties in Jamaica tried to grab hold of Bob Marley's hand. They were trying to put their hands on black; Marley stood for black, and they were trying to get a piece of the action. If only he would look in their direction he would have legitimated them. It was not politics legitimating culture, it was culture legitimating politics.

Indeed, the truth is I call myself all kinds of other things. When I went to England, I would not have called myself an immigrant either, which is what we were all known as. It was not until I went back home in the early 1960s that my mother, who, as a good middle-class colored Jamaican woman, hated all black people (you know, that is the truth), said to me: "I hope they don't think you're an immigrant over there."

And I said, "Well, I just migrated. I've just emigrated." At that very moment, I thought, that is exactly what I am. I have just left home—for good.

I went back to England, and I became what I had been named. I had been hailed as an immigrant. I had discovered who I was. I started to tell myself the story of my migration.

Then black erupted and people said, "Well, you're from the Caribbean, in the midst of this, identifying with what's going on, the black population in England. You're black."

At that very moment, my son, who was two and a half, was learning the colors. I said to him, transmitting the message at last, "You're black." And he said, "No. I'm brown." And I said, "Wrong referent. Mistaken concreteness, philosophical mistake. I'm not talking about your paintbox, I'm talking about your head." That is something different. The question of learning, learning to be black. Learning to come into an identification.

What that moment allows to happen are things which were not there before. It is not that what one then does was hiding away inside as my true self. There was not any bit of that true self in there before that identity was learned. Is that, then, the stable one, is that where we are? Is that where people are?

I will tell you something now about what has happened to that black identity as a matter of cultural politics in Britain. That notion was extremely important in the antiracist struggles of the 1970s: the notion that people of diverse societies and cultures would all come to Britain in the 1950s and '60s as part of that huge wave of migration from the Caribbean, East Africa, and the Asian subcontinent, and all identified themselves politically as black.

What they said was, "We may be different actual color skins but vis-à-vis the social system, vis-à-vis the political system of racism, there is more that unites us than what divides us." People begin to ask, "Are you from Jamaica? Are you from Trinidad? Are you from Barbados?" You can just see the process of divide and rule. "No. Just address me as I am. I know you can't tell the difference so just call me black. Try using that. We all look the same, you know. Certainly can't tell the difference. Just call me black. Black identity." Antiracism in the 1970s was only fought and only resisted in the community, in the localities, behind the slogan of a black politics and the black experience.

In that moment, the enemy was ethnicity. The enemy had to be what we called "multiculturalism." Because multiculturalism was precisely what I called previously "the exotic." The exotica of difference. Nobody would talk about racism, but they were perfectly prepared to have "International Evenings," when we would all come and cook our native dishes, sing our own native songs, and appear in our own native costume. It is true that some people, some ethnic minorities in Britain, do have indigenous, very beautiful indigenous forms of dress. I didn't. I had to rummage in the dressing-up box to find mine. I have been deracinated for four hundred years. The last thing I am going to do is dress up in some native Jamaican costume and appear in the spectacle of multiculturalism.

Has the moment of the struggle organized around this constructed black identity gone away? It certainly has not. So long as that society remains in its economic, political, cultural, and social relations in a racist way to the variety of black and Third World peoples in its midst, and it continues to do so, that struggle remains.

Why, then, don't I just talk about a collective black identity replacing the other identities? I can't do that either, and I'll tell you why.

The truth is that in relation to certain things, the question of black, in Britain, also has its silences. It had a certain way of silencing the very specific experiences of Asian people. Because though Asian people could identify, politically, in the struggle against racism, when they came to using their own culture as the resources of resistance, when they wanted to write out of their own experience and reflect on their own position, when they wanted to create, they naturally created within the histories of the languages, the cultural tradition, the positions of people who came from a variety of different historical backgrounds. And just as black was the cutting edge of a politics vis-a-vis one kind of enemy, it could also, if not understood properly, provide a kind of silencing in relation to another. These are the costs, as well as the strengths, of trying to think of the notion of black as an essentialism.

What is more, there were not only Asian people of color, but also black people who did not identify with that collective identity. So that one was aware of the fact that always, as one advanced to meet the enemy, with a solid front, the differences were raging behind. Just shut the doors and conduct a raging argument to get the troops together, to actually hit the other side.

A third way in which black was silencing was to silence some of the other dimensions that were positioning individuals and groups in exactly the same way. To operate exclusively through an unreconstructed conception of black was to reconstitute the authority of black masculinity over black women, about which, as I am sure you know, there was also, for a long time, an unbreakable silence about which the most militant black men would not speak.

To organize across the discourses of blackness and masculinity, of race and gender, and forget the way in which, at the same moment, blacks in the underclass were being positioned in class terms, in similar work situations, exposed to the same deprivations of poor jobs and lack of promotion that certain members of the white working class suffered, was to leave out the critical dimension of positioning.

What, then, does one do with the powerful, mobilizing identity of the black experience and of the black community? Blackness as a political identity in light of the understanding of any identity is always complexly composed, always historically constructed. It is never in the same place but always positional. One always has to think about the negative consequences of the positionality. You cannot, as it were, reverse the discourses of any identity simply by turning them upside down. What is it like to live, by attempting to valorize and defeat the marginalization of the variety of black subjects and to really begin to recover the lost histories of a variety of black experiences, while at the same time recognizing the end of any essential black subject?

That is the politics of living identity through difference. It is the politics of recognizing that all of us are composed of multiple social identities, not of one. That we are all complexly constructed through different categories, of different antagonisms, and these may have the effect of locating us socially in multiple positions of marginality and subordination, but positions which do not yet operate on us in exactly the same way. It is also to recognize that any counterpolitics of the local which attempts to organize people through their diversity of identifications has to be a struggle which is conducted positionally. It is the beginning of antiracism, antisexism, and anticlassism as a war of positions, as the Gramscian notion of the war of position.

The notion of the struggles of the local as a war of positions is a very difficult kind of politics to get one's head around; none of us knows how to conduct it. None of us even knows whether it can be conducted. Some of us have had to say there is no other political game, so we must find a way of playing this one.

Why is it difficult? It has no guarantees. Because identifications change and shift, they can be worked on by political and economic forces outside of us, and they can be articulated in different ways. There is absolutely no political guarantee already inscribed in an identity. There is no reason on God's earth why the film is good because a black person made it. There is absolutely no guarantee that all the politics will be right because a woman does it.

There are no political guarantees of that kind. It is not a free-floating open space because history has lodged on it the powerful, tendential organization of a past. We bear the traces of a past, the connections of the past. We cannot conduct this kind of cultural politics without returning to the past, but it is never a return of a direct and literal kind. The past is not waiting for us back there to recoup our identities against. It is always retold, rediscovered, reinvented. It has to be narrativized. We go to our own pasts through history, through memory, through desire, not as a literal fact.

It is a very important example. Some work has been done, in feminist history, in black history, and in working-class history recently which recovers the oral testimonies of people who, for a very long time, from the viewpoint of the canon and the authority of the historian, have not been considered to be historymakers at all. That is a very important moment. But it is not possible to use oral histories and testimonies, as if they are just, literally, the truth. They also have to be read. They are also stories, positionings, narratives. You are bringing new narratives into play, but you cannot mistake them for some "real," back there, by which history can be measured.

There is no guarantee of authenticity like that in history. One is ever afterward in the narrativization of the self and of one's histories. Just as in trying to conduct cultural politics as a war of positions, one is always in the strategy of hegemony. Hegemony is not the same thing as incorporating everybody, of making everybody the same, though nine-tenths of the people who have marginally read Gramsci think that that is what he means. Gramsci uses the notion of hegemony precisely to counteract the notion of incorporation.

Hegemony is not the disappearance or destruction of difference. It is the construction of a collective will through difference. It is the articulation of differences which do not disappear. The subaltern class does not mistake itself for people who were born with silver spoons in their mouths. They know they are still second on the ladder, somewhere near the bottom. People are not cultural dopes. They are not waiting for the moment when, like an overnight conversion, false consciousness will fall from their eyes, the scales will fall away, and they will suddenly discover who they are.

They know something about who they are. If they engage in another project, it is because it has interpellated them, hailed them, and established some point of identification with them. It has brought them into the historical project. And that notion of a politics which, as it were, increasingly is able to address people through the multiple identities which they have—understanding that those identities do not remain the same, that they are frequently contradictory, that they crosscut one another, that they tend to locate us differently at different moments, conducting politics in light of the contingent, in the face of the contingent—is the only political game that the locals have left at their disposal, in my view.

If they are waiting for a politics of maneuver, when all the locals, in every part of the world, will all stand up at the same moment and go in the same direction, and roll back the tide of the global in one great historical activity, it is not going to happen. I do not believe it anymore; I think it is a dream. In order to conduct the politics really, we have to live outside of the dream, to wake up, to grow up, to come into the world of contradiction. We have to come into the world of politics. There is no other space to stand in.

Out of that notion some of the most exciting cultural work is now being done in England. Third-generation young black men and women know they come from the Caribbean, know they are black, know they are British. They want to speak from all three identities. They are not prepared to give up any one of them. They will contest the Thatcherite notion of Englishness, because they say this Englishness is black. They will contest the notion of blackness because they want to make a differentiation between people who are black from one kind of society and people who are black from another. Because they need to know that difference, that difference that makes a difference in how they write their poetry, how they make their films, how they paint. It makes a difference. It is inscribed in their creative work. They need it as a resource. They are all those identities together. They are making astonishing cultural work, the most important work in the visual arts. Some of the most important work in film and photography and nearly all the most important work in popular music is coming from this new recognition of identity that I am speaking about.

Very little of that work is visible elsewhere, but some of you have seen, though you may not have recognized, the outer edge of it. Some of you, for example, may have seen a film made by Stephen Frears and Hanif Kureishi called *My Beautiful Laundrette*. This was originally made as a television film for local distribution only and was shown once at the Edinburgh Festival, where it received an enormous reception. If you have seen *My Beautiful Laundrette*, you will know that it is the most transgressive text there is. Anybody who is black, who tries to identify it, runs across the fact that the central characters of this narrative are two gay men. What is more, anyone who wants to separate the identities into their two clearly separate points will discover that one of these gay men is white and one of these gay men is brown. Both of them are struggling in Thatcher's Britain. One of them has an uncle who is a Pakistani landlord who is throwing black people out of the window.

This is a text that nobody likes. Everybody hates it. You go to it looking for what are called "positive images," and there are none. There aren't any positive images like that with which one can, in a simple way, identify. Because as well as the politics—and there is certainly a politics in that and in Kureishi's other work, but it is not a politics which invites easy identification—it has a politics which is grounded in the complexity of identifications which are at work.

I will read you something which Hanif Kureishi said about the question of responding to his critics who said: "Why don't you tell us good stories about ourselves, as well as good/bad stories? Why are your stories mixed about ourselves?" He spoke about the difficult moral position of the writer from an oppressed or persecuted community and the relation of that writing to the rest of the society. He said it is a relatively new one in England, but it will arise more and more as British writers with a colonial heritage and from a colonial or marginal past start to declare themselves.

"There is sometimes," he said, "too simple a demand for positive images. Positive images sometimes require cheering fictions—the writer as Public Relations Officer. And I'm glad to say that the more I looked at *My Beautiful Laundrette*, the less positive images I could see. If there is to be a serious attempt to understand present-day Britain with its mix of races and colors, its hysteria and despair, then writing about it has to be complex. It can't apologize, or idealize. It can't sentimentalize. It can't attempt to represent any one group as having the total, exclusive, essential monopoly on virtue.

"A jejune protest or parochial literature, be it black, gay or feminist, is in the long run no more politically effective than works which are merely public relations. What we need now, in this position, at this time, is imaginative writing that gives us a sense of the shifts and the difficulties within our society as a whole.

"If contemporary writing which emerges from oppressed groups ignores the central concerns and major conflicts of the larger society, and if these are willing simply to accept themselves as marginal or enclave literatures, they will automatically designate themselves as permanently minor, as a sub-genre. They must not allow themselves now to be rendered invisible and marginalized in this way by stepping outside of the maelstrom of contemporary history."

CHAPTER 3

What Is This "Black" in Black Popular Culture?

I begin with a question: What sort of moment is this in which to pose the question of black popular culture? These moments are always conjunctural. They have their historical specificity, and although they always exhibit similarities and continuities with the other moments in which we pose a question like this, they are never the same moment. And the combination of what is similar and what is different defines not only the specificity of the moment, but the specificity of the question, and therefore the strategies of cultural politics with which we attempt to intervene in popular culture, and the form and style of cultural theory and criticizing that has to go along with such an intermatch. In his important essay "The New Cultural Politics of Difference," Cornel West offers a genealogy of what this moment is, a genealogy of the present that I find brilliantly concise and insightful.[1] His genealogy follows, to some extent, positions I tried to outline in an article that has become somewhat notorious, but it also usefully maps the moment into an American context and in relation to the cognitive and intellectual philosophical traditions with which it engages.[2]

According to West, the moment, this moment, has three general coordinates. The first is the displacement of European models of high culture, of Europe as the universal subject of culture, and of culture itself in its old Arnoldian reading as the last refuge . . . I nearly said of scoundrels, but I won't say who it is of. At least we know who it was against—culture against the barbarians, against the people rattling the gates as the deathless prose of anarchy flowed away from Arnold's pen. The second coordinate is the emergence of the United States as a world power and, consequently, as the center of global cultural production and circulation. This emergence is both a displacement and a hegemonic shift in the *definition* of culture—a movement from high culture to American mainstream popular culture and its mass-cultural, image-mediated, technological forms. The third coordinate is the decolonization of the Third World, culturally marked by the emergence of the decolonized sensibilities. And I read the decolonization of the Third World in Frantz Fanon's sense: I include in it the impact of civil rights and black struggles on the decolonization of the minds of the peoples of the black diaspora.

Let me add some qualifications to that general picture, qualifications that, in my view, make this present moment a very distinctive one in which to ask the question about black popular culture. First, I remind you of the ambiguities of that shift from Europe to America, since it includes America's ambivalent relationship to European high culture and the ambiguity of America's relationship to its own internal ethnic hierarchies. Western Europe did not have, until recently, any ethnicity at all. Or did not recognize it had any. America has always had a series of ethnicities, and consequently, the construction of ethnic hierarchies has always defined its cultural politics. And, of course, silenced and unacknowledged, the fact of American popular culture itself, which has always contained within it, whether silenced or not, black American popular vernacular traditions. It may be hard to remember that, when viewed from outside of the United States, American mainstream popular culture has always involved certain traditions that could only be attributed to black cultural vernacular traditions.

The second qualification concerns the nature of the period of cultural globalization in progress now. I hate the term "the global postmodern," so empty and sliding a signifier that it can be taken to mean virtually anything you like. And, certainly, blacks are as ambiguously placed in relation to postmodernism as they were in relation to high modernism: even when denuded of its wide European, disenchanted Marxist, French intellectual provenance and scaled down to a more modest descriptive status, postmodernism remains extremely unevenly developed as a phenomenon in which the old center peripheries of high modernity consistently reappear. The only places where one can genuinely experience the postmodern ethnic cuisine are Manhattan and London, not Calcutta. And yet it is impossible to refuse "the global postmodern" entirely, insofar as it registers certain stylistic shifts in what I want to call the cultural dominant. Even if postmodernism is not a new cultural epoch, but only modernism in the streets, that, in itself, represents an important shifting of the terrain of culture toward the popular—toward popular practices, toward everyday practices, toward local narratives, toward the decentering of old hierarchies and the grand narratives. This decentering or displacement opens up new spaces of contestation and affects a momentous shift in the high culture of popular culture relations, thus presenting us with a strategic and important opportunity for intervention in the popular cultural field.

Third, we must bear in mind postmodernism's deep and ambivalent fascination with difference—sexual difference, cultural difference, racial difference, and above all, ethnic difference. Quite in opposition to the blindness and hostility that European high culture evidenced on the whole toward ethnic difference—its inability even to speak ethnicity when it was so manifestly registering its effects—there is nothing that global postmodernism loves better than a certain kind of difference: a touch of ethnicity, a taste of the exotic, and, as we say in England, "a bit of the other" (which in the United Kingdom has a sexual as well as an ethnic connotation). Michele Wallace was quite right, in her seminal essay "Modernism, Postmodernism and the Problem of the Visual in Afro-American Culture," to ask whether this reappearance of a proliferation of difference, of a certain kind of ascent of the global postmodern, isn't a repeat of that "now you see it, now you don't" game that modernism once played with primitivism, to ask whether it is not once again achieved at the expense of the vast silencing about the West's fascination with the bodies of black men and women of other ethnicities.[3] And we must ask about that continuing silence within postmodernism's shifting terrain, about whether the forms of licensing of the gaze that this proliferation of difference invites and allows, at the same time as it disavows, is not really, along with Benetton and the mixed male models of *The Face*, a kind of difference that doesn't make a difference of any kind.

Hal Foster writes (Wallace quotes him in her essay): "The primitive is a modern problem, a crisis in cultural identity"—hence, the modernist construction of primitivism, the fetishistic recognition and disavowal of the primitive difference.[4] But this resolution is only a repression; delayed into our political unconscious, the primitive returns uncannily at the moment of its apparent political eclipse. This rupture of primitivism, managed by modernism, becomes another postmodern event. That managing is certainly evident in the difference that may not make a difference, which marks the ambiguous appearance of ethnicity at the heart of global postmodernism. But it cannot be only that. For we cannot forget how cultural life, above all in the West, but elsewhere as well, has been transformed in our lifetimes by the voicing of the margins.

Within culture, marginality, though it remains peripheral to the broader mainstream, has never been such a productive space as it is now. And that is not simply the opening within the dominant of spaces that those outside it can occupy. It is also the result of the cultural politics of difference, of the struggles around difference, of the production of new identities, of the appearance of new subjects on the political and cultural stage. This is true not only in regard to race but also for other marginalized ethnicities, as well as around feminism and around sexual politics in the gay and lesbian movement, as a result of a new kind of cultural politics. Of course, I don't want to suggest that we can counterpose some easy sense of victories won to the eternal story of our own marginalization—I'm tired of those two continuous, grand counternarratives. To remain within them is to become trapped in that endless either/or, either total victory or total incorporation, which almost never happens in cultural politics, but with which cultural critics always put themselves to bed.

What we are talking about is the struggle over cultural hegemony, which is these days waged as much in popular culture as anywhere else. That high/popular distinction is precisely what the global postmodern is displacing. Cultural hegemony is never about pure victory or pure domination (that's not what the term means); it is never a zero-sum cultural game; it is always about shifting the balance of power in the relations of culture; it is always about changing the dispositions and the configurations of cultural power, not getting out of it. There is a kind of "nothing ever changes, the system always wins" attitude, which I read as the cynical protective shell that, I'm sorry to say, American cultural critics frequently wear, a shell that sometimes prevents them from developing cultural strategies that can make a difference. It is as if, in order to protect themselves against the occasional defeat, they have to pretend they can see right through everything—and it's just the same as it always was.

Now cultural strategies that can make a difference—that's what I'm interested in: those that can make a difference and can shift the dispositions of power. I acknowledge that the spaces "won" for difference are few and far between, that they are very carefully policed and regulated. I believe they are limited. I know, to my cost, that they are grossly underfunded, that there is always a price of incorporation to be paid when the cutting edge of differ-ence and transgression is blunted into spectacularization. I know that what replaces invisibility is a kind of carefully regulated, segregated visibility. But it does not help simply to name-call it "the same." That name-calling merely reflects the particular model of cultural politics to which we remain attached, precisely, the zero-sum game—our model replacing their model, our identities in place of their identities—what Antonio Gramsci called cul-ture as a once-and-for-all "war of manoeuvre," when, in fact, the only game in town worth playing is the game of cultural "wars of position."

Lest you think, to paraphrase Gramsci, my optimism of the will has now completely outstripped my pessimism of the intellect, let me add a fourth element that comments on the moment. For, if the global postmodern rep-resents an ambiguous opening to difference and to the margins and makes a certain kind of decentering of the Western narrative a likely possibility, it is matched, from the very heartland of cultural politics, by the backlash: the aggressive resistance to difference; the attempt to restore the canon of West-ern civilization; the assault, direct and indirect, on multiculturalism; the re-turn to grand narratives of history, language, and literature (the three great supporting pillars of national identity and national culture); the defense of ethnic absolutism, of a cultural racism that has marked the Thatcher and the Reagan eras; and the new xenophobias that are about to overwhelm Fortress Europe. The last thing to do is read me as saying the cultural dialectic is finished. Part of the problem is that we have forgotten what sort of space the space of popular culture is. And black popular culture is not exempt from that dialectic, which is historical, not a matter of bad faith. It is therefore necessary to deconstruct the popular once and for all. There is no going back to an innocent view of what it consists of.

Popular culture carries that affirmative ring because of the prominence of the word "popular." And, in one sense, popular culture always has its base in the experiences, the pleasures, the memories, the traditions of the people. It has connections with local hopes and local aspirations, local tragedies and local scenarios that are the everyday practices and everyday experiences of ordinary folks. Hence, it links with Mikhail Bakhtin's conception of "the vulgar"—the popular, the informal, the underside, the grotesque. That is why it has always been counterposed to elite or high culture and is thus a site of alternative traditions. And that is why the dominant tradition has always been deeply suspicious of it, quite rightly. They suspect that they are about to be overtaken by what Bakhtin calls "the carnivalesque." This fundamental mapping of culture between the high and the low has been charted into four symbolic domains by Peter Stallybrass and Allon White in their important book *The Politics and Poetics of Transgression.* They talk about the mapping of high and low in psychic forms, in the human body, in space, and in the social order.[5] And they discuss the high/low distinction as a fundamental basis to the mechanism of ordering and of sense-making in European and other cultures despite the fact that the contents of what is high and what is low change from one historical moment to another.

The important point is the ordering of different aesthetic morals, social aesthetics, the orderings of culture that open up culture to the play of power, not an inventory of what is high versus what is low at any particular moment. That is why Gramsci gave the question of what he called "the national-popular" such strategic importance. The role of the "popular" in popular culture is to fix the authenticity of popular forms, rooting them in the experiences of popular communities from which they draw their strength, allowing us to see them as expressive of a particular subordinate social life that resists its being constantly made over as low and outside.

However, as popular culture has historically become the dominant form of global culture, so it is at the same time the scene, par excellence, of commodification, of the industries where culture enters directly into the circuits of a dominant technology—the circuits of power and capital. It is the space of homogenization where stereotyping and the formulaic mercilessly process the material and experiences it draws into its web, where control over narratives and representations passes into the hands of the established cultural bureaucracies, sometimes without a murmur. It is rooted in popular experience and available for expropriation at one and the same time. I want to argue that this is necessarily and inevitably so. And this goes for black popular culture as well. Black popular culture, like all popular cultures in the modern world, is bound to be contradictory, and this is not because we haven't fought the cultural battle well enough.

By definition, black popular culture is a contradictory space. It is a sight of strategic contestation. But it can never be simplified or explained in terms of the simple binary oppositions that are still habitually used to map it out: high and low, resistance versus incorporation, authentic versus inauthentic, experiential versus formal, opposition versus homogenization. There are always positions to be won in popular culture, but no struggle can capture popular culture itself for our side or theirs. Why is that so? What consequences does this have for strategies of intervention in cultural politics? How does it shift the basis for black cultural criticism?

However deformed, incorporated, and inauthentic are the forms in which black people and black communities and traditions appear and are represented in popular culture, we continue to see, in the figures and the repertoires on which popular culture draws, the experiences that stand behind them. In its expressivity, its musicality, its orality, in its rich, deep, and varied attention to speech, in its inflections toward the vernacular and the local, in its rich production of counternarratives, and above all, in its metaphorical use of the musical vocabulary, black popular culture has enabled the surfacing, inside the mixed and contradictory modes even of some mainstream popular culture, of elements of a discourse that is different—other forms of life, other traditions of representation.

I do not propose to repeat the work of those who have devoted their scholarly, critical, and creative lives to identifying the distinctiveness of these diasporic traditions, to exploring their modes and the historical experiences and memories they encode. I say only three inadequate things about these traditions, since they are germane to the point I want to develop. First, I ask you to note how, within the black repertoire, *style*—which mainstream cultural critics often believe to be the mere husk, the wrapping, the sugar-coating on the pill—has become *itself* the subject of what is going on. Second, mark how, displaced from a logocentric world—where the direct mastery of cultural modes meant the mastery of writing and, hence, both of the criticism of writing (logocentric criticism) and the deconstruction of writing—the people of the black diaspora have, in opposition to all of that, found the deep form, the deep structure of their cultural life in music. Third, think of how these cultures have used the body—as if it was, and it often was, the only cultural capital we had. We have worked on ourselves as the canvases of representation.

There are deep questions here of cultural transmission and inheritance, and of the complex relations between African origins and the irreversible scatterings of the diaspora, questions I cannot go into. But I do believe that these repertoires of black popular culture—which, since we were excluded from the cultural mainstream, were often the only performative spaces we had left—were overdetermined from at least two directions: they were partly determined from their inheritances, but they were also critically determined by the diasporic conditions in which the connections were forged.

Selective appropriation, incorporation, and rearticulation of European ideologies, cultures, and institutions, alongside an African heritage—this is Cornel West again—led to linguistic innovations in rhetorical stylization of the body, forms of occupying an alien social space, heightened expressions, hairstyles, ways of walking, standing, and talking, and a means of constituting and sustaining camaraderie and community.

The point of underlying overdetermination—black cultural repertoires constituted from two directions at once—is perhaps more subversive than you think. It is to insist that in black popular culture, strictly speaking, ethnographically speaking, there are no pure forms at all. Always these forms are the product of partial synchronization, of engagement across cultural boundaries, of the confluence of more than one cultural tradition, of the negotiations of dominant and subordinate positions, of the subterranean strategies of receding and transcoding, of critical signification, of signifying. Always these forms are impure, to some degree hybridized from a vernacular base. Thus, they must always be heard, not simply as the recovery of a lost dialogue bearing clues for the production of new musics (because there is never any going back to the old in a simple way), but as what they are—adaptations, molded to the mixed, contradictory, hybrid spaces of popular culture. They are not the recovery of something pure that we can, at last, live by. In what Kobena Mercer calls the necessity for a diaspora aesthetic, we are obliged to acknowledge they are what the modern is.

It is this mark of difference *inside* forms of popular culture—which are by definition contradictory and which therefore appear as impure, threatened by incorporation or exclusion—that is carried by the signifier "black" in the term "black popular culture." It has come to signify the black community, where these traditions were kept, and whose struggles survive in the persistence of the black experience (the historical experience of black people in the diaspora), of the black aesthetic (the distinctive cultural repertoires out of which popular representations were made), and of the black counternarratives we have struggled to voice. Here, black popular culture returns to the ground I defined earlier. "Good" black popular culture can pass the test of authenticity—the reference to black experience and to black expressivity. These serve as the guarantees in the determination of which black popular culture is right on, which is ours and which is not.

I have the feeling that, historically, nothing could have been done to intervene in the dominated field of mainstream popular culture, to try to win some space there, without the strategies through which those dimensions were condensed into the signifier "black." Where would we be, as bell hooks once remarked, without a touch of essentialism? Or, what Gayatri Spivak calls strategic essentialism, as a necessary moment? The question is whether we are any longer in that moment, whether that is still a sufficient basis for the strategies of new interventions. Let me try to set forth what seem to me to be the weaknesses of this essentializing moment and the strategies, creative and critical, that flow from it.

This moment essentializes differences in several senses. It sees difference as "their traditions versus ours," not in a positional way, but in a mutually exclusive, autonomous, and self-sufficient one. And it is therefore unable to grasp the dialogic strategies and hybrid forms essential to the diaspora aesthetic. A movement beyond this essentialism is not an aesthetic or critical strategy without a cultural politics, without a marking of difference. It is not simply rearticulation and reappropriation for the sake of it. What it evades is the essentializing of difference into two mutually opposed either/ ors. What it does is to move us into a new kind of cultural positionality, a different logic of difference. To encapsulate what Paul Gilroy has so vividly put on the political and cultural agenda of black politics in the United Kingdom: blacks in the British diaspora must, at this historical moment, refuse the binary black or British. They must refuse it because the "or" remains the site of *constant contestation* when the aim of the struggle must be, instead, to replace the "or" with the potentiality or the possibility of an "and." That is, the logic of coupling rather than the logic of a binary opposition. You can be black *and* British, not only because that is a necessary position to take in the 1990s, but also because even those two terms, joined now by the coupler "and" instead of opposed to one another, do not exhaust all of our identities. Only some of our identities are sometimes caught in that particular struggle.

The essentializing moment is weak because it naturalizes and dehistoricizes difference, mistaking what is historical and cultural for what is natural, biological, and genetic. The moment the signifier "black" is torn from its historical, cultural, and political embedding and lodged in a biologically constituted racial category, we valorize, by inversion, the very ground of the racism we are trying to deconstruct. In addition, as always happens when we naturalize historical categories (think about gender and sexuality), we fix that signifier outside of history, outside of change, outside of political intervention. And once it is fixed, we are tempted to use "black" as sufficient in itself to guarantee the progressive character of the politics we fight under the banner—as if we don't have any other politics to argue about except whether something's black or not. We are tempted to display that signifier as a device which can purify the impure, bring the straying brothers and sisters who don't know what they ought to be doing into line, and police the boundaries—which are of course political, symbolic, and positional boundaries—as if they were genetic. For which, I'm sorry to say, read "jungle fever"—as if we can translate from nature to politics using a racial category to warrant the politics of a cultural text and as a line against which to measure deviation.

Moreover, we tend to privilege experience itself, as if black life is lived experience outside of representation. We have only, as it were, to express what we already know we are. Instead, it is only through the way in which we represent and imagine ourselves that we come to know how we are constituted and who we are. There is no escape from the politics of representation, and we cannot wield "how life really is out there" as a kind of test against which the political rightness or wrongness of a particular cultural strategy or text can be measured. It will not be a mystery to you that I think that "black" is none of these things in reality. It is not a category of essence, and, hence, this way of understanding the floating signifier in black popular culture now will not do.

There is, of course, a very profound set of distinctive, historically defined black experiences that contribute to those alternative repertoires I spoke about earlier. But it is to the diversity, not the homogeneity, of black experience that we must now give our undivided creative attention. This is not simply to appreciate the historical and experiential differences within and between communities, regions, countries and cities, across national cultures, between diasporas, but also to recognize the other kinds of difference that place, position, and locate black people. The point is not simply that, since our racial differences do not constitute all of us, we are always different, negotiating different kinds of differences—of gender, of sexuality, of class. It is also that these antagonisms refuse to be neatly aligned; they are simply not reducible to one another; they refuse to coalesce around a single axis of differentiation. We are always in negotiation, not with a single set of oppositions that place us always in the same relation to others, but with a series of different positionalities. Each has for us its point of profound subjective identification. And that is the most difficult thing about this proliferation of the field of identities and antagonisms: they are often dislocating in relation to one another.

Thus, to put it crudely, certain ways in which black men continue to live out their counteridentities as black masculinities and replay those fantasies of black masculinities in the theaters of popular culture are, when viewed from along other axes of difference, the very masculine identities that are oppressive to women, that claim visibility for their hardness only at the expense of the vulnerability of black women and the feminization of gay black men. The way in which a transgressive politics in one domain is constantly sutured and stabilized by reactionary or unexamined politics in another is only to be explained by this continuous cross-dislocation of one identity by another, one structure by another. Dominant ethnicities are always underpinned by a particular sexual economy, a particular figured masculinity, a particular class identity. There is no guarantee, in reaching for an essentialized racial identity of which we think we can be certain, that it will always turn out to be mutually liberating and progressive on all the other dimensions. It *can* be won. There *is* a politics there to be struggled for. But the invocation of a guaranteed black experience behind it will not produce that politics. Indeed, the plurality of antagonisms and differences that now seek to destroy the unity of black politics, given the complexities of the structures of subordination that have been formed by the way in which we were inserted into the black diaspora, is not at all surprising.

These are the thoughts that drove me to speak, in an unguarded moment, of the end of the innocence of the black subject or the end of the innocent notion of an essential black subject. And I want to end simply by reminding you that this end is also a beginning. As Isaac Julien said in an interview with bell hooks in which they discussed his new film *Young Soul Rebels*, his attempt in his own work to portray a number of different racial bodies, to constitute a range of different black subjectivities, and to engage with the positionalities of a number of different kinds of black masculinities: "blackness as a sign is never enough. What does that black subject do, how does it act, how does it think politically . . . being black isn't really good enough for me: I want to know what your cultural politics are."[6]

I want to end with two thoughts that take that point back to the subject of popular culture. The first is to remind you that popular culture, commodified and stereotyped as it often is, is not at all, as we sometimes think of it, the arena where we find who we really are, the truth of our experience. It is an arena that is *profoundly* mythic. It is a theater of popular desires, a theater of popular fantasies. It is where we discover and play with the identifications of ourselves, where we are imagined, where we are represented, not only to the audiences out there who do not get the message, but to ourselves for the first time. As Freud said, sex (and representation) mainly takes place in the head. Second, though the terrain of the popular looks as if it is constructed with single binaries, it is not. I reminded you about the importance of the structuring of cultural space in terms of high and low, and the threat of the Bakhtinian carnivalesque. I think Bakhtin has been profoundly misread. The carnivalesque is not simply an upturning of two things which remain locked within their oppositional frameworks; it is also crosscut by what Bakhtin calls the dialogic.

I simply want to end with an account of what is involved in understanding popular culture, in a dialogic rather than in a strictly oppositional way, from *The Politics and Poetics of Transgression* by Stallybrass and White:

> A recurrent pattern emerges: the "top" attempts to reject and eliminate the "bottom" for reasons of prestige and status, only to discover, not only that it is in some way frequently dependent upon the low-Other . . . but also that the top *includes* that low symbolically, as a primary eroticized constituent of its own fantasy life. The result is a mobile, conflictual fusion of power, fear, and desire in the construction of subjectivity: a psychological dependence upon precisely those others which are being rigorously opposed and excluded at the social level. It is for this reason that what is socially peripheral is so frequently *symbolically* central.[7]

NOTES

1 Cornel West, "The New Cultural Politics of Difference," in *Out There: Marginalization and Contemporary Cultures*, ed. Russell Ferguson et al. (Cambridge, MA: MIT Press in association with the New Museum of Contemporary Art, 1990), 19–36.

2 Stuart Hall, "New Ethnicities," in *Black Film/British Cinema*, ICA Document 7, ed. Kobena Mercer (London: Institute of Contemporary Arts, 1988), 27–31.

3 Michele Wallace, "Modernism, Postmodernism and the Problem of the Visual in Afro-American Culture," in *Out There: Marginalization and Contemporary Cultures*, ed. Russell Ferguson et al., 39–50.

4 Hal Foster, *Recodings: Art, Spectacle, and Cultural Politics* (Port Townsend, WA: Bay Press, 1985), 204.

5 Peter Stallybrass and Allon White, *The Politics and Poetics of Transgression* (Ithaca, NY: Cornell University Press, 1986), 3.

6 bell hooks, "States of Desire: Interview with Isaac Julien," *Transition* 1, no. 3 (1990): 175.

7 Stallybrass and White, *The Politics and Poetics of Transgression*, 5.

CHAPTER 4

The Multicultural Question

My starting point is Homi Bhabha's observation that "multiculturalism" is a heterogeneously expanded portmanteau term and that "multicultural" has become a floating signifier. The first part of the chapter undertakes a deconstructive critique of these key terms. It considers their conditions of emergence and disseminated existence in contemporary British society and political discourse. The second half picks up from Barnor Hesse's idea of the "transruptive effects" of the multicultural question and traces these through in a number of domains. The chapter ends by trying in a tentative way to rescue a new multicultural political "logic" from the debris of existing political vocabularies which the eruption of the multicultural question has left in its wake.

The term "multiculturalism" is now universally deployed. However, this proliferation has neither stabilized nor clarified its meaning. Like other related terms—for example, "race," ethnicity, identity, diaspora—multiculturalism is now so discursively entangled that it can only be used "under erasure" (Hall 1996a). Nevertheless, since we have no less implicated concepts to think this problem with, we have no alternative but to go on using and interrogating it.

The Multicultural/Multiculturalism Distinction

It might be useful to draw a distinction here between "multicultural" and "multiculturalism."[1] Here multicultural is used adjectivally. It describes the social characteristics and problems of governance posed by any society in which different cultural communities are obliged by historical circumstances to live together and attempt to build a common life while retaining something of their "original" identity. By contrast, "multiculturalism" is substantive. It references the strategies and policies adopted to govern or manage the problems of diversity and multiplicity which multicultural societies throw up. It is usually used in the singular, signifying the distinctive philosophy or doctrine which underpins multicultural strategies. "Multicultural," however, is, by definition, plural. There are many kinds of multicultural society. The US, Canada, Britain, France, Holland, Bosnia, Malaysia, Sri Lanka, New Zealand, Indonesia, South Africa, and Nigeria all qualify. They are "multicultural" in significantly different ways. However, they all share one characteristic. They are, by definition, culturally heterogeneous. They differ in this respect from liberal-constitutional, "modern," Western nation-states which are predicated on the (usually unspoken) assumption of cultural homogeneity organized around "universal" liberal-individualist secular values (Goldberg 1994).

The two terms are now so interdependent that it is virtually impossible to disentangle them. However, "multiculturalism" presents specific difficulties. It stands for "a wide range of social articulations, ideals and practices." The problem is that the "-ism" tends to convert "multiculturalism" into a political doctrine and "reduces [it] to a formal singularity, fixing it into a cemented condition. . . . Thus converted, . . . the heterogeneity characteristic of multicultural conditions is reduced to a pat and pedestrian doctrine" (Caws 1994). In fact, "multiculturalism" is not a single doctrine, does not characterize one political strategy, and does not represent an already-achieved state of affairs. It is not a covert way of endorsing some ideal, utopian state. It describes a variety of political strategies and processes which are everywhere incomplete. Just as there are different multicultural societies, so there are very different "multiculturalisms." Conservative multiculturalism follows Hume (Goldberg 1994) in insisting on the assimilation of difference into the traditions and customs of the majority. Liberal multiculturalism seeks to integrate the different cultural groups as fast as possible into the "mainstream" provided by a universal individual citizenship, tolerating only in private particularistic cultural practices. Pluralist multiculturalism formally enfranchises the differences between groups along cultural lines and accords different group rights to different communities within a more communal or communitarian political order. Commercial multiculturalism assumes that if the diversity of individuals from different communities is best recognized in the marketplace, then the problems of cultural difference will be (dis)solved through private consumption, without any need for a redistribution of power and resources. Corporate multiculturalism (public or private) seeks to "manage" minority cultural differences in the interests of the center. Critical or "revolutionary" multiculturalism foregrounds power, privilege, the hierarchy of oppressions, and the movements of resistance (McLaren 1997). It seeks to be "insurgent, polyvocal, heteroglossial and anti-foundational" (Goldberg 1994). And so on.

Far from being a settled doctrine, "multiculturalism" is a deeply contested idea (May 1999). It is contested by the conservative Right, in defense of the purity and cultural integrity of the nation. It is contested by liberals, who claim that the "cult of ethnicity" and the pursuit of difference threaten the universalism and neutrality of the liberal state, undermining personal autonomy, individual liberty, and formal equality. Multiculturalism, some liberals also say, legitimates the idea of "group rights," which threatens individualism. But this subverts the dream that one nation and one citizenship can be constructed out of the diverse cultures of different peoples—e pluribus unum.[2] Multiculturalism is also contested by modernizers of different political persuasions. For them, the triumph of the universalism of Western civilization over the particularism of ethnic and racial belonging established in the Enlightenment marked a fateful and irreversible transition from Traditionalism to Modernity. This shift must never be reversed. Some postmodern versions of "cosmopolitanism," which treat "the subject" as wholly contingent and unencumbered, are sharply opposed to multiculturalism, where subjects are more located. It is also challenged from several positions on the Left. Antiracists argue that it—wrongly—privileges culture and identity over economic and material questions. Radicals believe it divides the united front of race and class against injustice and exploitation along ethnically and racially particularistic lines. Others point to various versions of commercialized, consumerist, or "boutique" multiculturalism (Fish 1998), which celebrate difference without making a difference.[3] There is also what Sarat Maharaj (in an unpublished paper) felicitously calls "multi-cultural managerialism," which is often indistinguishable from "a spook-lookalike of Apartheid logic."

Can a concept which means so many different things and so effectively draws the fire of such diverse and contradictory enemies really have anything to say to us? Alternatively, is its contested status not precisely its value? After all, "a sign which has been withdrawn from the pressures of the social struggle inevitably loses force, degenerating into allegory and becoming the object . . . of [mere] philological comprehension" (Volosinov and Bakhtin

1973). For good or ill, we are inevitably implicated in its practices, which characterize and define "late-modern societies." In Michele Wallace's terms,

> Everybody knows . . . that multiculturalism is not the promised land. . . . [However,] even at its most cynical and pragmatic, there is something about multiculturalism which continues to be worth pursuing. . . . We do need to find ways of publicly manifesting the significance of cultural diversity, [and] of integrating the contributions of people of colour into the fabric of society. (Wallace 1994)

Conditions of Emergence

Multicultural societies are not new. Long before the age of European expansion (from the fifteenth century onward)—and with increasing intensity since—the migration and movement of peoples has been the rule rather than the exception of global history, producing societies which are ethnically or culturally "mixed." "Movement and migration . . . are the defining sociohistorical conditions of humanity" (Goldberg 1994). People have moved for many reasons—natural disasters, climate and ecological change, war, conquest, famine, poverty, labor exploitation, colonization, slavery, indenture, political repression, civil war, economic underdevelopment. Empires, the product of conquest and domination, are often multicultural. The Greek, Roman, Islamic, Ottoman, and European Empires were all, in different ways, both multiethnic and multicultural. Colonialism—always a double inscription—attempted to convene the colonized within the "empty, homogeneous time" of global modernity, without effacing deep differences or disjunctures of time, place, and tradition (Bhabha 1994; Hall 1996a). The plantation systems of the Western world, the indentured systems of Southeast Asia, colonial India, as well as the many nation-states consciously carved out of a more fluid ethnic canvas—in Africa, by the colonizing powers, in the Middle East, the Balkans, and Central Europe, by the Great Powers—all loosely fit the multicultural description.

These historical examples are not irrelevant to how multiculturalism has surfaced in the postwar world. They provide some of the latter's conditions of emergence. But there is no linear connection between the colonial and the postcolonial. Since World War II, the multicultural question has not only changed its forms but become intensified. It has also become more salient, taking center stage in the field of political contestation. This is the result of a series of decisive shifts—a strategic reconfiguration of social forces and relations across the globe.

First, the winding up of the old European imperial system and the completion of the decolonizing and national independence struggles. In the wake of the dismantling of the old empires, many *new* multiethnic and multicultural nation-states were created. However, they continue to reflect their prior conditions of existence under colonialism.[4] These new states are relatively weak, economically and militarily. Many lack a developed civil society. They remain dominated by the imperatives of the early independence nationalist movements. They govern populations with a variety of different ethnic, cultural, or religious traditions. The indigenous cultures, dislocated if not destroyed by colonialism, are not inclusive enough to provide the basis for a new national or civic culture. These difficulties are compounded by extensive poverty and underdevelopment, in the context of deepening global inequality and an unregulated neoliberal economic world order. Increasingly, crises in these societies assume a multicultural or ethnicized form.

There is a close relationship between the reemergence of "the multicultural question" and the phenomenon of the "postcolonial." The latter concept could take us on a detour through a conceptual labyrinth from which few travelers return. It must suffice at this point simply to assert that the "postcolonial" does *not* signal a simple before/after chronological succession. The movement from colonization to postcolonial times does *not* imply that the problems of colonialism have been resolved or replaced by some conflict-free era. Rather, the "postcolonial" marks the passage from one historical power configuration or conjuncture to another (Hall 1996a).[5] Problems of dependency, underdevelopment, and marginalization, typical of the "high" colonial period, persist into the postcolonial. However, these relations are *resumed* in a new configuration. Once they were articulated as unequal relations of power and exploitation between colonized and colonizing societies. Now they are restaged and displaced as struggles between indigenous social forces, as internal contradictions and sources of destabilization *within* the decolonized society, or between them and the wider global system. Think of the ways in which the instability of democratic rule in, say, Pakistan, Iraq, Iran, Indonesia, Nigeria, or Algeria, or the continuing problems of political legitimacy and stability in Afghanistan, Namibia, Mozambique, or Angola have clear roots in their recent imperial history. This postcolonial "double inscription" is taking place in a global context where direct rule, governance, or protectorship by an imperial power has been replaced by an asymmetric globalized system of power which is postnational, transnational, and neo-imperial in character. Its main features are structural inequality, within a deregulated free-trade and free-capital-flow system dominated by the First World, and programs of structural readjustment, in which Western interests and models of governance are paramount.

The second factor is the ending of the Cold War. Its main features are the post-1989 breakup of the Soviet Union as a transethnic, transnational forma-tion, the decline of state communism as an alternative model of industrial development, and the waning of the Soviet sphere of influence, especially in Eastern Europe and Central Asia. This has had regional effects similar in certain ways to the dismantling of the old imperial systems. The year 1989 has been followed by the attempt, under US leadership, to construct "a new world order." One aspect of this drive has been the relentless pressure by the West, designed to drag these very different, relatively underdeveloped East European societies kicking and screaming, overnight, into what is called "*the* market." This mysterious entity is propelled into old, complex cultures and authoritarian polities as an abstract and denuded principle, without any attention to the cultural, political, social, and institutional embeddedness which markets *always* require. One result is that the unsolved problems of social development have combined with the resurgent traces of older, still unrequited ethnic and religious nationalisms, allowing the tensions in these societies to resurface in a multicultural form.

It should be emphasized that this is no simple revival of archaic ethnicities, though such elements persist. Older traces are combined with new, emergent forms of "ethnicity," which are often a product of uneven globalization and failed modernization. This explosive mix selectively revalorizes older dis-courses, condensing in a lethal combination what Hobsbawm and Ranger (1993) called "the invention of tradition" with what Michael Ignatieff (1994) has called (after Freud) "the narcissism of minor differences." (Serbian na-tionalism and ethnic cleansing in Bosnia and Kosovo are obvious examples.) Their reinvention of the past in the present is reminiscent of the Janus-faced character of nationalist discourse (Nairn 1997). These revivalist movements remain deeply attached to the idea of "the nation."[6] They see the nation as an engine of modernization and a guarantor of a place in the new world system, at precisely the moment when globalization is bringing the nation-state-driven phase of capitalist modernity to a hesitant close.

The third factor is our old friend "globalization." Again, globalization is not new. European exploration, conquest, and colonization were early forms of the same secular, historical process. (Marx once called it "the formation of the world market.") But since the 1970s, the process has assumed new forms while also being intensified (Held et al. 1999). Contemporary globalization is associated with the rise of new, deregulated financial markets, with global capital and currency flows large enough to destabilize medium-sized economies, transnational forms of production and consumption, the exponential growth of the new cultural industries and new information technologies, and the rise of "the knowledge economy." Characteristic of this phase is time-space compression (Harvey 1989), which struggles—however incompletely—to cohere particular times, places, histories, and markets within a homogeneous, "global" space-time chronotope. It is also marked by the uneven disembedding of social relations and processes of detraditionalization (Giddens 1999) which are not restricted to developing societies. Western societies can no more defend themselves against these effects than societies of the periphery.

This system is global in the sense that its sphere of operations is planetary. Few places are beyond the reach of its destabilizing interdependencies. It has significantly weakened national sovereignty and eroded the "reach" of the older Western nation-states (the engines of earlier phases of globalization) without entirely displacing them. The system, however, is *not* global, if by that we understand that the process is uniform in character, impacts everywhere in the same way, operates without contradictory effects, or produces equal outcomes across the globe. It remains a system of deep, indeed deepening, global inequalities and instabilities, of which no power—not even the US, which is the most economically and militarily powerful nation on earth—is any longer completely in control.

Like the postcolonial, contemporary globalization is both novel and contradictory. Its economic, financial, and cultural circuits are Western-driven and US-dominated. Ideologically, it is governed by a global neoliberalism which is fast becoming the common sense of the age (Fukuyama 1992). Its dominant cultural tendency is homogenization. However, this is not the only trend. It has also had extensive *differentiating* effects within and between different societies. From this perspective, globalization is *not* a natural and inevitable process whose imperatives, like Fate, cannot be resisted or inflected, only obeyed.[7] Rather, it is a hegemonizing process, in the proper Gramscian sense. It is "structured in dominance," but it cannot control or saturate everything within its orbit. Indeed, it produces as one of its unintended effects subaltern formations and emergent tendencies which it cannot control but must try to "hegemonize" or harness to its wider purposes. It is a system for *conforming difference* rather than a convenient synonym for the obliteration of difference. This argument is critical if we are to take account of how and where resistances and counterstrategies are likely to successfully develop. This perspective entails a more discursive model of power in the new global environment than is common among the "hyper-globalizers" (Held et al. 1999).

The Subaltern Proliferation of Difference

Alongside globalization's homogenizing tendencies, there is "the subaltern proliferation of difference." It is a paradox of contemporary globalization that, culturally, things appear to look more alike (a sort of Americanization of global culture, for example); however, at the same time, there is a proliferation of "differences." The "vertical" of American cultural, economic, technological power seems to be constantly crosscut and offset by lateral connections, producing the sense of a world composed of many "local" differences, with which the "global-vertical" is obliged to reckon (Hall 1991). In this model, the classic Enlightenment binary between Traditionalism and Modernity is displaced by a disseminated set of "vernacular modernities." Consider, for example, the way News International's effort to saturate India and China with the staple diet of Western television was forced into a tactical retreat. It could advance only through an "indigenization" of the local television industries, which greatly complicates the range of images offered locally and sets in motion the development of an indigenous industry rooted in different cultural traditions. Some see this as just a slower version of the westernization of Indian and Chinese culture when exposed to the global market. Others see it as the way in which the peoples in these areas try to enter "modernity," acquire the fruits of its technologies, and yet do so to some extent on their terms. In the global context, the struggle here between "local" and "global" interests is not yet finally resolved.

This is what, in another context, Derrida calls différance: "the playing movement that 'produces' . . . these differences, these effects of difference" (Derrida 1981, 1982).[8] This is *not* the binary form of difference, between what is absolutely the same and what is absolutely "Other." It is a "weave" of similarities and differences, which refuses to separate into fixed binary oppositions. Différance characterizes a system where "every concept [or meaning] is inscribed in a chain or in a system within which it refers to the other, to other concepts [meanings], by means of the systematic play of differences" (Derrida 1972).

Meaning here has no origin or final destination, cannot be finally fixed, is always *in process*, "positional" along a spectrum. Its political value cannot be essentialized but only relationally determined.

Strategies of différance are not able to inaugurate totally different forms of life (they do not work with the notion of a totalizing dialectical "overcoming"). They cannot conserve older, traditional ways of life intact. They operate best in what Homi Bhabha calls "the borderline time" of minorities (Bhabha 1997). However, différance does prevent any system from stabilizing itself as a fully sutured totality. It arises in the gaps and aporias, which constitute potential sites of resistance, intervention, and translation. Within these interstices lie the possibility of a disseminated set of vernacular modernities. Culturally, these cannot frontally stem the tide of Westernizing techno-modernity. However, they continue to inflect, deflect, and "translate" its imperatives from below.[9] They constitute the basis for a new kind of "localism" that is not self-sufficiently particular, but arises *within*, without being simply a simulacrum of, the global (Hall 1991). This "localism" is no mere residue of the past. It is something new—globalization's accompanying shadow: what is left aside in globalization's panoramic sweep but returns to trouble and disturb globalization's cultural settlements. It is globalization's "constitutive outside" (Laclau and Mouffe 1985; Butler 1993). Here we find the "return" of the particular and specific—of the specifically different—at the center of globalization's universalist, panoptic aspiration to closure. "The local" has no stable, transhistorical character. It resists universalism's homogenizing sweep with different, conjunctural times. It has no fixed political inscription. It can be either progressive or regressive and fundamentalist—open or closed—in different contexts (Hall 1993). Its political thrust is determined not by its essential content (usually caricatured as "Tradition's resistance to Modernity"), but by its articulation with other forces. It emerges at many sites, one of the most significant being that planned and unplanned, compelled and so-called "free," migration, which has brought the margins to the center, the multicultural disseminated "particular" to the heart of the metropolitan Western city. Only in such a context can we understand why what threatens to become the moment of the West's global closure—the apotheosis of its global universalizing mission—is *at the same time* the moment of the West's slow, uncertain, protracted decentering.

The Margins in the Center: The British Case

How has this untimely appearance of the margins in the center—the heart of "the multicultural question"—become what Barnor Hesse has called "a transruptive force" within the political and social institution of Western states and societies?

The British case can be briefly put in place in relation to the wider argument. The national story assumes that Britain was a unified and homogeneous culture until the postwar migrations from the Caribbean and Asian subcontinent. This is a highly simplistic version of a complex history (Hall 1999a, 1999b, 1999c, 1999d). Britain is not a sceptered isle which arose, fully formed and separate, as an integral nation-state, from the North Sea. Though "assumed to be fixed and eternal," it was in fact constituted out of a series of conquests, invasions, and settlements (Davies 1999). It was part of the European landmass until the sixth century BC, dominated for centuries by the French, and integrally related to Europe until the Reformation. Britain has really only existed as a nation-state since the eighteenth century, by virtue of the civil pact (rooted, in fact, in an Anglo-Saxon, Protestant ascendancy), which associated significantly different cultures—Scotland and Wales—with England. The Act of Union with Ireland (1801), which ended in Partition, never succeeded in integrating the Irish people or the Celtic-Catholic element into the British imaginary. Indeed, Ireland has been Britain's earliest "colony" and the Irish the first group to be systematically "racialized." The so-called homogeneity of "Britishness" as a national culture has been considerably exaggerated. It was always contested by the Scots, Welsh, and Irish; challenged by rival local and regional allegiances; and crosscut by class, gender, and generation. There have always been many different ways of being "British." Most national achievements—from free speech and a universal franchise to the welfare state and NHS [National Health Service]— were won only as the result of bitter struggles between one kind of "British" person and another. Only retrospectively were these radical differences smoothly reintegrated into the seamless web of a discourse of transcendent "Britishness." Britain was also the center of the largest imperium of modern times, governing a variety of different cultures. This imperial experience profoundly shaped British national identity and British ideas of greatness as well as its place in the world (C. Hall 1992). This more or less continuous intercourse with "difference," which was at the heart of colonization, has framed the "other" as a constitutive element of British identity.

There has been a "black" presence in Britain since the sixteenth century and an Asian presence since the eighteenth. But the type and scale of migration into Britain from the nonwhite global periphery which has seriously challenged the settled notion of British identity and posed "the multicultural question" is a post–Second World War, postcolonial phenomenon. Historically, it began with the arrival of the *Empire Windrush* in 1948, bringing returning Caribbean volunteer servicemen and the first civilian Caribbean migrants leaving the depressed economies of the region in search of a better life. The flow was quickly reinforced from the Caribbean, then from the Asian subcontinent and the Asians expelled from East Africa, together with Africans and others from the Third World, until the late 1970s, when immigration legislation effectively closed the door.

The old relations of colonization, slavery, and colonial rule, linking Britain with the Empire for over four hundred years, marked out the pathways which these migrants followed. But these historic relations of dependency and subordination were *reconfigured*—in the now-classic postcolonial way—when reconvened on domestic British soil. In the wake of decolonization, and masked by a collective amnesia about, and systematic disavowal of, empire (which descended like a Cloud of Unknowing in the 1960s), this encounter was interpreted as "a new beginning." Most British people looked at these "children of empire" as if they could not imagine where "they" had come from, why, or what possible connection they could have with Britain.

By and large, migrants found poor housing and unskilled, poorly paid jobs in the cities and industrial regions, themselves recovering from the war and affected by the steep decline in Britain's economic fortunes. Today, they and their offspring constitute about 7 percent of the British population.[10] However, they already constitute 25 percent of the population of London and some other cities, reflecting the selective density of settlement. They have been subjected to all the effects of social exclusion, racialized disadvantage, and informal and institutionalized racism, which is typical across western Europe today in the face of similar processes affecting France, Spain, Portugal, Germany, Italy, and Greece. Their postwar history has been marked by the struggles against racialized disadvantage, confrontations with racist groups and the police, and institutional racism in those institutions and public authorities which differentially manage and distribute the support systems on which migrant communities are heavily dependent. In broad terms, the majority are clustered at the lower end of the social deprivation spectrum, characterized by high relative levels of poverty, unemployment, and educational underachievement. In 1991, less than two-thirds of the men and less than half of the women of working age were actually working.

However, their social and economic positioning has become markedly more differentiated over time (Modood et al. 1997). Some Indians, East African Asians, and Chinese, despite being highly qualified, are experiencing the "glass ceiling" of blocked promotion at the upper levels of the professional ladder. The Pakistani communities are considerably active, entrepreneurially, in the small business sector. Nevertheless, a few Asian millionaires cannot disguise the fact that countless Indian and Pakistani families still live in serious household poverty. Bangladeshis are on average four times more "deprived" than any other identifiable group. Gender differences play a critical role. Young Afro-Caribbean men are seriously vulnerable to unemployment and educational underachievement, and are overrepresented in school exclusions, stop-and-search arrests, and the prison population. Afro-Caribbean women, however, now have higher job mobility, earnings, and educational participation rates than their white counterparts. The picture is no longer one of uniform deprivation, though socioeconomic disadvantage continues to be extensive.

What kinds of "community" have they formed? How unified and homogeneous are their cultures? What is their relationship to so-called "mainstream" society? What strategies are appropriate to their fuller integration within society?

The term "community" (as in "ethnic minority communities") accurately reflects the strong sense of group identity found among them. However, it can be dangerously misleading. The model is an idealization of the face-to-face relationships of the one-class village, connoting homogeneous groups with strong, binding, internal ties and very clear boundaries separating them from the outside world. So-called "ethnic minorities" have indeed formed strongly marked, cultural communities and maintain in everyday life, especially in familial and domestic contexts, distinctive social customs and practices. There are continuing links with their places of origin. This is especially the case in the densely settled areas, such as Afro-Caribbean communities in Brixton, Peckham, and Tottenham; in Manchester Moss Side, Liverpool, and Handsworth; or Asian communities in places like Southall, Tower Hamlets, Birmingham's Balsall Heath, Bradford, and Leeds. But there are also differences which refuse to be consolidated. Caribbeans from the different islands come from quite distinctive racial and ethnic mixes, though they all tend (wrongly) to be seen as "Jamaican." "Asians" are also lumped together as a single group. However, "despite sharing some cultural traits in common . . . [Asians] belong to different ethnic, religious and linguistic groups and bring with them different fears and historical memories" (Parekh 1999). All these communities are ethnically and racially mixed, with substantial white populations. None is a racially or ethnically segregated ghetto. They are significantly less segregated than, say, nonwhite minorities are in many US cities. As with the white population, class and gender are highly significant in determining differential positioning across the British society (Brah 1996; Yuval-Davis 1997; Phoenix 1998). A more accurate picture would have to begin with the lived complexity emerging in these diaspora communities, where so-called "traditional" ways of life derived from the cultures of origin remain important to community self-definitions, but consistently operate alongside extensive daily interaction at every level, with British mainstream social life.

Maintaining racialized, ethno-cultural, and religious identities is clearly important to self-understanding in these communities. "Blackness" is as critical to third-generation Afro-Caribbeans' identity[11] as the Hindu or Muslim faiths are to some second-generation Asians. But these are certainly not communities immured in an unchanging "Tradition." As in most diasporas, traditions are variable from person to person, and even within persons, and are constantly being revised and transformed in response to the migration experience. There is very considerable variation, both of commitment and of practice, between and within different communities—between different nationalities and linguistic groups, within religious faiths, between men and women, and across the generations. Young people from all the communities express some continuing allegiance to their "traditions," alongside a visible decline in actual practice. Identities declare, not some primordial identity, but rather a positional choice of the group with which they wish to be associated. Identity choices are more political than anthropological, more "associational," and less ascribed (Modood et al. 1997).

Generalizations are therefore extremely difficult to make in the face of this multicultural complexity. Bhikhu Parekh, an acute observer, adopts a *strong* definition of "ethnic communities": "The Asian and Afro-Caribbean communities are ethnic in nature, that is, physically distinguishable, bonded by social ties arising out of shared customs, language and practice of inter-marriage, and having their distinct history, collective memories, geographical origins, views of life and modes of social organization." Nevertheless, he recognizes that contrary to popular impression, great changes are afoot within ethnic communities and every family has become a terrain of subdued or explosive struggles. In every family, husband and wife, parents and children, brothers and sisters are having to re-negotiate and re-define their patterns of relationship in a manner that takes account both of their traditional values and those characteristic of their adopted country. Different families reach their own inherently tentative conclusions. (Parekh 1991)

It is therefore a fundamental error to mistake their diasporic ways of life as simply in slow transition to full assimilation (an idea quietly and decisively laid to rest, in Britain at least, in the 1970s). They represent a novel cultural configuration—to borrow an oxymoron, "cosmopolitan communities"—marked by extensive transculturation (Pratt 1992). In turn, they have had a massive, pluralizing impact on public and private social life in Britain, literally transforming many British cities into multicultural metropolises. They were the "cool" in that transient New Labour phenomenon, "Cool Britannia." One sign that they have outrun the commonsense categories is that they are simultaneously invoked as representing that "sense of community" that liberal society is supposed to have lost, and as the most advanced signifiers of the urban postmodern metropolitan experience!

Readers may want to quarrel with the detail of the process as described (which is, of necessity, generalized and abstract). However, unless the fundamental picture is substantively challenged, it is worth reflecting on the enormous dis- or (as Barnor Hesse puts it) "trans-ruptive" consequences for a political strategy or approach to the multicultural question which this development poses. The rest of this essay is concerned with tracing through some of these transruptive effects.

Disrupting the Language of "Race" and Ethnicity

The first of these is the disruptive impact on the traditional categories of "race" and ethnicity. The emergence of the multicultural question has produced a differentiated "racialization" of central areas of British life and culture.[12] Increasingly, the British have been obliged to think of themselves and their relations with others within the UK in racialized terms. Ethnicity, too, has entered the British domestic vocabulary. Whereas in the American self-understanding the US is a society composed of ethnicities, Britain (though in origins quite diverse) has always applied the term to everyone else—Britishness being the empty signifier, the norm against which "difference" (ethnicity) is measured. The rising visibility of ethnic communities, together with the movement toward devolved government, has posed questions about the "homogeneity" of British culture and "Englishness" as an ethnicity, precipitating the multicultural question at the center of a crisis of national identity.

Of course, Britishness as a category has always been racialized through and through—when has it connoted anything but "whiteness"? But this fact has been carefully segregated from the national discourse, popular and scholarly. "Race" has struggled to be seriously acknowledged in mainstream political theory, in journalistic or scholarly thinking.[13] This silencing is breaking down as these terms force their way into public consciousness. Their growing visibility is, inevitably, a fraught and difficult process. What's more, this is now "race" in quotation marks, "race" under erasure, "race" in a new configuration with ethnicity. This epistemic shift is one of the multicultural's most transruptive effects.

Of the two largest nonwhite post-migration communities in Britain, "race" is usually applied to Afro-Caribbeans, "ethnicity" to Asians. In fact, these terms map only very roughly onto these actual communities. "Race" is thought to make sense of Afro-Caribbean experience because of the significance of skin color, a biologically derived idea. In fact, the color spectrum among Afro-Caribbeans is extremely wide—the result of the extensive miscegenation of Caribbean plantation society and centuries of "transculturation" (Ortiz 1940; Brathwaite 1971; Glissant 1981; Pratt 1992). Asians are not a "race" at all, nor indeed a single "ethnicity." Nationality is often as important as ethnicity. Indians, Pakistanis, Bangladeshis, Sri Lankans, Ugandans, Kenyans, and the Chinese are all crosscut by regional, urban/rural, cultural, ethnic, and religious differences.

Conceptually, "race" is not a scientific category. The differences attributable to "race" within a population are as great as that between racially defined populations. "Race" is a political and social construct. It is the organizing discursive category around which a system of socioeconomic power, exploitation, and exclusion—i.e., racism—has been constructed. However, as a discursive practice, racism has its own "logic" (Hall 1990). It claims to ground the social and cultural differences which legitimate racialized exclusion in genetic and biological differences: i.e., in Nature. This "naturalizing effect" appears to make racial difference a fixed, scientific "fact," unresponsive to change or reformist social engineering. This discursive reference to Nature is something which antiblack racism shares with antisemitism and sexism (where, too, "biology is destiny"), though less with class. The problem is that the genetic level is not immediately visible. Hence, in this type of discourse, genetic differences (supposed to be hidden in the gene structure) are "materialized" and can be "read off" in easily recognizable, visible signifiers of the body (which is only too visible) such as skin color, physical characteristics of hair, features, (e.g., the Jewish hooked nose), body type, etc., enabling them to function as discursive closure mechanisms in everyday situations.[14]

"Ethnicity," by contrast, generates a discourse where difference is grounded in *cultural and religious* features. It is often, on these grounds, counterposed to "race." But this binary opposition can be too simplistically drawn. Biological racism privileges markers like skin color. But those signifiers have always *also* been used, by discursive extension, to connote social and cultural differences. "Blackness" has functioned as a sign that people of African descent are closer to nature, and *therefore* more likely to be lazy, indolent, and lack the higher intellectual faculties; driven by emotion and feeling rather than reason; oversexualized; with low self-control and prone to violence, etc. Correspondingly, those who are stigmatized on ethnic grounds, because they are "culturally different" and therefore inferior, are often *also* characterized as physically different in significant ways (though not perhaps as visibly as blacks), underpinned by sexual stereotypes which are correlated with the body (blacks being overmasculinized, Orientals feminized, etc.). The biological referent is therefore never wholly absent from discourses of ethnicity, though it is more indirect. The more "ethnicity" matters, the more its characteristics are represented as relatively fixed; inherent within a group; transmitted from generation to generation, not just by culture and education but by biological inheritance; inscribed on the body; and stabilized above all by kinship and endogamous marriage rules, which ensure that the ethnic group remains genetically, and therefore culturally, "pure." Ethnicity is underpinned by characteristics which are "physically distinguishable . . . arising out of . . . [the] practice of inter-marriage" (Parekh 1991). In short, the articulation of difference with nature (biology and the genetic) is present in the discourse of ethnicity but *displaced through kinship and intermarriage*.

Both the discourses of "race" and "ethnicity," then, work by establishing a discursive articulation or "chain of equivalences" (Laclau and Mouffe 1985) between the social/cultural and the biological registers, which allows differences in one signifying system to be "read off" against equivalents in the other chain (Hall 1990). Biological racism and cultural differentialism therefore constitute, not two different systems, but racism's two registers. In most situations, the discourses of biological and cultural difference are simultaneously in play. In antisemitism Jews were multiply racialized on biological, cultural, and religious grounds. As Wieviorka argues, racism exists "where there is an association of these two main strategies, whose unique combination depends on the specificities of experience, the historical moment and individual preference" (Wieviorka 1995). It seems therefore more appropriate to speak, not of "racism" *versus* "cultural difference," but of racism's "two logics."[15]

There seem to be three reasons for the current conceptual confusion. The first is empirical. Afro-Caribbean migrants—viewed largely in racialized terms—arrived in Britain earlier. Asians, characterized by religious and cultural difference, arrived and became visible as a so-called "problem" later. In the 1970s, antiracist struggles by both groups tended to cluster under the affirmative identity of "black," defined by their shared racialized difference from white society. However, one unintended effect was to privilege the Afro-Caribbean experience over that experienced by Asians. As the salience of what Taylor (1994) has called "the politics of recognition" has grown, stressing the right to cultural difference, so the two trajectories have become more separate. "Black" has become descriptively normalized for people of African descent, and Asians have tended to revert to ethnically specific terms of identification. Hence the anomalous current description—"black and Asian"—which combines "race" and "ethnicity." Secondly, there are many more situations in the world where ethnicity rather than "race" has provided the focus of violent exclusionary conflict (e.g., Indonesia, Sri Lanka, Rwanda, Bosnia, and Kosovo). Thirdly, there has been a significant rise in discrimination and exclusion either based on religion or with a strong religious component (Richardson 1999), in particular against Muslim communities, related to the worldwide politicization of Islam. Some writers feel that a multiculturalism focused on biological racism rather than cultural differentialism ignores this religious dimension (e.g., Modood et al. 1997).

In the 1980s some commentators observed a decline in biologically based racism and a rise in "the new cultural racism" (Barker 1981). Modood indeed speaks of an "effacing of colour racism" and a "reinforcing [of] cultural racism at a micro-level" in Britain. It is not clear that current developments bear out this zero-sum account empirically (racist attacks on Asian families and violent assaults in the street on black youths continue apace) or that it is particularly helpful to trade one against the other in this either/or way. What seems more appropriate is an expanded conception of racism, which acknowledges the way in which, in its discursive structure, biological racism and cultural differentialism are articulated and combine. These two "logics" are always present, though in different combinations and differently foregrounded in different contexts and in relation to different subject populations. Of course, the actual histories of racialized and ethnicized closure are very different in different places (e.g., the US and the UK), emerge at different moments and in different forms, and have very different political and social effects. They should not be homogenized. However, the conflation of biological and culturally inferiorizing discourses seems to be a defining characteristic of "the multi-cultural moment."[16]

Given the way "black"—originally a negative epithet—has become a term of positive cultural identification (Bonnett 1999), we may speak here of the "ethnicization" of "race."[17] At the same time, cultural difference has taken on a more violent, politicized, and oppositional meaning—which we might think of as the "racialization" of ethnicity (e.g., "ethnic cleansing"). The consequence is to place on the agenda of a British multiculturalism two related but different political demands which have hitherto been considered mutually exclusive: the demand (against a differentiated racism) for social equality and racial justice, and the demand (against a universalizing ethnocentrism) for the recognition of cultural difference. We return to the political significance of this double demand below.

Unsettling "Culture"

The second transruptive effect is that which "the multicultural question" has on our understanding of culture. The binary opposition derived from the Enlightenment—Particularism versus Universalism or Tradition versus Modernity—produces a certain way of understanding culture. There are the distinctive, homogeneous, self-contained, strongly bounded cultures of so-called traditional societies. In this anthropological definition, cultural tradition saturates whole communities, subordinating individuals to a communally sanctioned form of life. This is counterposed to the "culture of modernity"—open, rational, universalist, and individualistic. In the latter, particular cultural attachments must be set aside in public life—always trumped by the neutrality of the civic state—so that the individual is formally free to write his or her own script. These characteristics are held to be fixed by the essentialized content of each. The idea that liberal society could act in a "fundamentalist" way or that the "traditionalism" of, say, Islam could combine with modern ways of life appears a contradiction in terms. Tradition is represented as set in stone.[18]

However, since the inception of the global "project" of the West at the end of the fifteenth century, this Tradition/Modernity binary has been progressively undermined. Colonized traditional cultures remained distinctive, but they inevitably became "conscripts of modernity."[19] They may be more strongly bounded than so-called modern societies. But they are no longer (if ever they were) organic, fixed, self-sustaining, self-sufficient entities. As a result of globalization in its longer, historical sense, many have become more "hybrid" formations, though some, in reaction against globalization, have become more "traditional." Tradition functions, in general, less as doctrine than as significant *repertoires of meaning*. Increasingly, individuals draw upon these frameworks, and the attachments they inscribe to help them to make sense of the world, without being rigorously bound by and into them in every detail of existence.[20] They have become part of a larger dialogical relation to "the other." Precolonial cultures were—to very different degrees— progressively *convened*, globally under the rubric of Western capitalist modernity and the imperial system without their distinctiveness being wholly erased. This left them (as C. L. R. James once remarked of the Caribbean) "in but not of Europe." As Aijaz Ahmad (no natural ally of the hybridizing intelligentsia) has observed, "The cross fertilization of cultures has been endemic to all movements of people . . . and all such movements in history have involved travel, contact, transmutation, hybridization of ideas, values and behavioural norms" (Ahmad 1995).

One term which has been used to characterize the increasingly mixed and diasporic cultures of such communities is "hybridity." Its meaning, however, has been widely misunderstood.[21] Hybridity is not a reference to the mixed racial composition of population. It is really another term for the cultural logic of *translation*. This logic is increasingly evident in the multicultural diasporas and other mixed and minority communities of the postcolonial world. New and old diasporas governed by this ambivalent, inside/outside position are to be found everywhere. It defines the combined and uneven cultural logic of the way so-called Western "modernity" has impacted on the rest of the world ever since the onset of Europe's globalizing project (Hall 1996a).

Hybridity does *not* refer to hybrid individuals, who can be contrasted as fully formed subjects with "traditionals" and "moderns." It is a process of cultural translation, which is agonistic because it is never completed, but rests with its indecidability. It is not simply appropriation or adaptation; it is a process through which cultures are required to revise their own systems of reference, norms and values by departing from their habitual or "inbred" rules of transformation. Ambivalence and antagonism accompany any act of cultural translation because negotiating with the "difference of the other" reveals the radical insufficiency of our own systems of meaning and signification. (Bhabha 1997)

In its many variants, "tradition" and "translation" are variously combined (Robbins 1991). It is not simply celebratory, because it has deep and disabling "costs" deriving from its multiple forms of dislocation and habitation (Clifford 1998). As Homi Bhabha has suggested, it signifies an

ambiguous, anxious moment of . . . transition, that nervously accompanies any mode of social transformation [which is] without the promise of celebratory closure or transcendence of the complex, even conflictual conditions that attend the process. . . . [It] insists on displaying . . . the dissonances that have to be crossed despite the proximate relations; the disjunctions of power or position that have to be contested; the values, ethical and aesthetic, that have to be "translated" but will not seamlessly transcend the process of transfer. (Bhabha 1997)

However, it is also often "how newness enters the world" (Rushdie 1991).

The idea of culture embedded in "ethnic minority communities" does not reference a fixed relation between Tradition and Modernity. It neither remains within one boundary nor transcends boundaries. In practice it refuses those binaries.[22] *Necessarily*, its notion of "community" covers a wide variety of actual practices. Some individuals remain deeply committed to "traditional" practices and values, though rarely without a diasporic inflection. For others, so-called traditional identifications have been intensified (e.g., by hostility from the "host" community, racism, or by changing world conditions, such as the rising salience of Islam). For others, still, hybridization is far advanced, but rarely in any assimilationist sense. This is a radically dislocated, and more complex, picture of culture and community than are inscribed in the conventional sociological or anthropological literature. "Hybridity" marks the place of this incommensurability.

In diasporic conditions people are often obliged to adopt shifting, multiple, or hyphenated positions of identification. About two-thirds of those from minority communities asked in the *Fourth National Survey of Ethnic*

Minorities whether they thought of themselves as "British" agreed, though they also felt that, for example, being British and Pakistani did not compete strongly in their minds (Modood et al. 1997). Black-and-British or British-Asian are increasingly identities the young are willing to answer to. Some women, who believe that their communities have a right to have their differences respected, do not wish their lives as women, their rights to education, or their marital choices to be governed by norms which are wholly communally regulated and policed. Even where the more traditionally oriented sections are concerned, the principle of *heterogeneity* continues to be strongly operative. In our terms, then, the besuited Asian chartered accountant vividly invoked by Modood (1998), who lives in suburbia, sends his children to private school and reads *Readers Digest* and the *Bhagavad-Gita*, or the black teenager who is a dancehall DJ and plays jungle music but supports Manchester United, or the Muslim student who wears baggy, hip-hop, street-style jeans but is never absent from Friday prayers are *all*, in their different ways, "hybridized." Were they to return to their villages of origin, the most traditional would be regarded as "Westernized"—if not hopelessly diaspora-ized. They are all negotiating culturally somewhere along the spectrum of différance, in which disjunctures of time, generation, spatialization, and dissemination refuse to be neatly aligned.

Unsettling the Foundations of the Liberal-Constitutional State

A third disruptive effect of "the multicultural question" is its challenge to the dominant discourses of Western political theory and the foundations of the liberal state. In the face of the dissemination of unstable differences, the settled argument between liberals and communitarians, which now dominates the Western political tradition, has been seriously disturbed.

The post-Enlightenment, liberal, rational, humanist universalism of Western culture looks not less historically significant but less *universal* by the minute. Many great ideas—liberty, equality, autonomy, democracy—have been honed within the liberal tradition. However, it is now clear that liberalism is not the "culture that is beyond cultures" but the culture that won: that particularism which successfully universalized and hegemonized itself across the globe. Its triumph in virtually setting the limits to the domain of "the political" was not, in retrospect, the result of a disinterested mass conversion to the Rule of Universal Reason but something closer to a more earthy, Foucauldian, power-knowledge sort of "game." There have been theoretical critiques of the "dark" sides of the Enlightenment project before. But it is "the multicultural question" which has most effectively blown its contemporary cover.

Universal citizenship and the cultural neutrality of the state are two cornerstones of Western liberal universalism. Of course, citizenship rights have never been universally applicable—either to African Americans at the hands of the founding fathers or to colonial subjects at the dispensation of imperial rule. This gap between ideal and practice, between formal and substantive equality, between negative and positive freedom, has haunted liberalism's conception of citizenship from its inception. As to the cultural neutrality of the liberal state, its achievements are not to be lightly discarded. Religious toleration, free speech, the rule of law, formal equality, and procedural legality, a universal franchise—though seriously contested—are positive achievements. However, the neutrality of the state only works when a broad cultural homogeneity among the governed can be assumed. This assumption has indeed underpinned Western liberal democracies until recently. Under the new multicultural conditions, however, this premise seems less and less valid.

The claim is that the liberal state has sloughed off its ethnic-particularistic skin and emerged in its culturally cleansed, universalistic, civic form. Britain, however, like all civic nationalisms, is not only a sovereign political and territorial entity but also "an imagined community." It is the latter which is the focus of identification and belongingness. The discourses of the nation do not, as we are led to suppose, reflect an already-achieved unified state. Their purpose is, rather, to forge or construct a unified form of identification out of the many differences of class, gender, region, religion, and locality which actually crosscut the nation (Hall 1992; Bhabha 1990). To achieve this, these discourses must deeply embed and enmesh the so-called culture-free "civic" state in a dense entanglement of cultural meanings, traditions, and values which come to stand for or represent the nation. It is only *within* culture and representation that identification with this "imagined community" can be constructed at all.

All so-called modern, liberal nation-states thus combine the so-called rational, reflective, civic form of allegiance to the state with a so-called intuitive, instinctual, ethnic allegiance to the nation. That heterogeneous formation, "Britishness," grounds the United Kingdom, the political entity, as an "imagined community." As that great patriot, Enoch Powell, observed: "The life of nations, no less than of men [*sic*], is lived largely in the mind." Britain's rational and constitutional foundations are given lived meaning and texture through a system of cultural representation. They are grounded in the customs, habits, and rituals of everyday life, the social codes and conventions, the dominant versions of masculinity and femininity, the socially constructed memory of national triumphs and disasters, the imagery, imagined landscapes and distinctive national characteristics which produce the idea of "Britain." These aspects are no less important because many of them are "invented" (Hobsbawm and Ranger 1993). Though the nation constantly reinvents itself as an ongoing process, however, it is represented as something which has existed from the origins of time (Davis 1999). Of course, it does not follow that because the "universal" state is grounded in very distinct cultural particularities, the state is nothing but a playground for rival definitions of the good. What however cannot any longer be sustained, in the face of the "multicultural question," is the binary contrast between the particularism of "their" demands for the recognition of difference versus the universalism of "our" civic rationality.[23]

In fact, the so-called homogeneity of British culture has been massively overstated. There have always been very different ways of "being British." Britain was always crosscut by deep cleavages around gender, class, and region. Serious differences in material and cultural power between the different "kingdoms" of the UK were masked by the hegemony of the English over the rest and "Englishness" over "Britishness." The Irish never properly belonged. The poor have always been excluded. The mass of the people were not enfranchised until the beginning of the twentieth century. To this we must add the growing cultural diversity of British social life itself. The effects of globalization, the decline of Britain's economic fortunes and world position, the end of empire, the rising pressures to devolve government and power, the growth of internal nationalisms, local and regional sentiment, and the challenge of Europe have all unsettled the so-called homogeneity of Britishness, producing a major internal crisis of national identity. There is also the astonishing pace of social pluralism and economic and technological change, which have undermined the older class and gender settlements, made British society a less predictable place, and are the sources of a massive internal diversification of social life.[24] Today, it would be difficult to find a significant national consensus around any of the critical social issues, about which there are in fact deep differences of opinion and lived experience. People belong to many different, overlapping "communities" which sometimes exert contrary pulls. Britain is "a multiculturally diverse" society, long before one begins to consider the impact of postmigration multiethnic communities. Indeed, it sometimes appears as if the latter are the symbolic bearers of a complex pattern of change, diversification, and "loss" for which they are only the most convenient scapegoats.

The multicultural question has also helped to deconstruct some of the other incoherences of the liberal constitutional state. The "neutrality" of the liberal state (i.e., the fact that it is represented as pursuing in the *public* realm no particular notion of "the good") is said to secure the personal autonomy and liberty of the individual to pursue his or her own conception of "the good," provided it is done *in private*. The ethically neutral legal order of the liberal state thus depends on the strict separation between the public and private spheres. But this is harder and harder to deliver in a stable form. The law and politics increasingly intervene in the so-called private realm. Private conduct and judgments intrude into the public realm. In the wake of the new feminism, we understand better how the sexual contract underpins the social contract. Domains like the family, sexuality, health, food, and dress, which used to belong quintessentially to the private domain have become part of an expanded public and political realm of contestation. The easy distinctions between the republic and the domestic spheres is no longer tenable, especially since the massive entry of women and the "privatized" activities which used to be associated with that sphere. Everywhere, "the personal" has become "the political."

What Michael Walzer famously called "Liberalism 1" constitutes one of the great discursive systems of the modern world, making in recent years virtually a clean sweep of political theory. Only a thin definition of culture and a highly attenuated notion of collective rights is compatible with the individualist emphasis at the center of this market-liberal conception.[25] It does not recognize the degree to which the individual is what Taylor (1994) calls "dialogic"—not in the binary sense of dialogue between two already-constituted subjects, but in the sense of its relation to the other being fundamentally constitutive of the subject, which can position itself as an "identity" only in relation to what it lacks—its other, its "constitutive outside" (Lacan 1977; Laclau and Mouffe 1985; Butler 1993). The meaningful individual life is always embedded in cultural contexts within which alone its "free choices" make sense.

> From a normative point of view, the integrity of the individual legal person cannot be guaranteed without protecting the inter-subjectively shared experiences and life-contexts in which the person has been socialized and formed his or her identity. The identity of the individual is in-

terwoven with collective identities and can be stabilized only in a cultural network that cannot be appropriated as private property, any more than the mother tongue itself can. Hence the individual remains the bearer of "rights to cultural membership." (Habermas 1994)

In practice, under the pressure of multicultural difference, some Western constitutional states like Britain have been obliged to move to what Walzer calls "Liberalism 2," or what in a less constricted vocabulary in Europe would be called a "social-democratic" reformist program.[26] The state has formally recognized and reflects publicly the differentiated social needs and growing cultural diversity of its citizens, acknowledging some group—as well as individually defined rights. It has had to develop redistributive public support strategies (e.g., affirmative action programs, equal opportunities legislation, publicly funded compensatory grants, and a welfare state for deprived groups), even to ensure the "level playing field" so beloved by formal liberalism. It has adopted into law some alternative definitions of "the good life" and legalized certain "exceptions" on essentially cultural grounds. For example, in recognizing the right of Sikhs to wear turbans without suspending the obligations of employers under health-and-safety regulations or by accepting consensual arranged marriages as legal, but declaring the imposition of an arranged marriage on a nonconsenting woman to be coercive and thus illegal, British law has gone in practice some way to striking a balance between *cultural pluralism* defined in relation to communities and *liberal conceptions* of the liberty of the individual subject.[27] In Britain, however, this move has so far been piecemeal and, since the New Labour erosion of the commitment to the welfare state, uncertain: a haphazard response to the growing visibility and presence of the ethnic communities at the heart of British life. It has constituted a species of "multi-cultural drift" (Hall 1999a).

Beyond the Existing Political Vocabularies

What would be required for this "drift" to become a sustained movement, a concerted effort of political will? To put this another way, what are the premises behind a radically distinctive form of British multiculturalism? It would need to be grounded, not in some abstract notion of nation and community, but in the analysis of what "community" actually means and how the different communities which now compose the nation actually interact on the ground. In addressing the sources of disadvantage, it would have to reflect what we have called "racism's two registers"—the interdependence of biological racism and cultural differentialism. The commitment to expose and confront racism in any of its forms would have to become a positive objective of, and a statutory obligation on, government, on which its very claim to representative legitimacy would be seen to depend. It would have to address the double political demand, which arises from this interplay between the gross inequalities and injustices arising from the absence of substantive equality and justice, and exclusion and inferiorization arising from the lack of recognition and insensitivity to difference. Finally, rather than a strategy for improving the lot of the so-called "ethnic" or racialized minorities alone, it would have to be a strategy which broke with that majoritarian logic and attempted to reconfigure or reimagine the nation as a whole—in a radical postnational form (Hall 1999d).

The double demand for equality and difference appears to outrun our existing political vocabularies. Liberalism has consistently failed to come to terms with cultural difference or to deliver equality and justice for minority citizens. By contrast, communitarians argue that, since the self cannot be independent of its ends, the conceptions of "the good life" embedded in communities should take precedence over the individual. Cultural pluralists ground this idea in a very strong definition of community: "distinct cultures which embody concepts charged with historical memories and associations . . . which shape their understandings and approach to the world and constitute cultures of distinct and cohesive communities" (Parekh).

As we have tried to show, ethnic minority communities are not integrated collective actors, such as would allow them to become the legal subjects of all-encompassing community rights. The temptation to essentialize "community" has to be resisted—it is a fantasy of plenitude in circumstances of imagined loss. Migrant communities bear the imprint of diaspora, "hybridization," and différance in their very constitution. Their vertical integration into their traditions of origin exist side by side with their lateral linkages to other "communities" of interest, practice and aspiration, real and symbolic. Individual members, especially the younger generations, experience the contradictory pulls which these different forces exert. Many are making their own negotiated "settlements" within and outside their communities. Women who respect the traditions of their communities feel free to challenge their patriarchal character and the sexism with which their authority is sometimes exercised. Some are happy to conform. Others, while unwilling to trade identities, insist on their individual "right to exit," where there is no consent, and rightly claim the support of the law and other social agencies to make the exercise of that right practically effective.[28] The same is true of political and religious dissent.

In making the move toward greater cultural diversity at the heart of modernity, therefore, we must take care lest we simply reverse into new forms of ethnic closure. We should remember that "ethnicity," and its naturalized relationship to "community," is another term operating "under erasure." We all locate ourselves in cultural vocabularies, and without them we are incapable of enunciation as cultural subjects. We all come from and speak from "somewhere": we are located—and in that sense even the most "modern" bear the traces of an "ethnicity." As Laclau paraphrases Derrida, we can only think "within a tradition." However, he reminds us, this is only possible "if one conceives one's relation to that past as a critical reception" (Laclau 1996). Cosmopolitan critics are right to remind us that, in late modernity, we tend to draw on the fragmented traces and broken repertoires of several cultural and ethical languages. It is not a denial of culture to insist that "the social world [does not] divide up neatly into distinct particular cultures, one to every community, [nor] that what everyone needs is just *one* of those entities—a single, coherent culture—to give shape and meaning to . . . life" (Waldron 1992, emphasis in original). We often operate with too simplistic a conception of "belonging." Sometimes we are most "spoken" by our attachments when we struggle to be free of them, quarrel with, criticize, or dissent radically from them. Like parental relationships, cultural traditions shape us *both* when they nurture and sustain us *and* when we have to break irrevocably with them in order to survive. And beyond—though we don't always recognize it—there are always the "attachments" we have to those who share our world with us but who are different from us. The pure assertion of difference is only viable in a rigidly segregated society. Its ultimate logic is that of *apartheid*.

MUST PERSONAL LIBERTY and individual choice, then, in the end, trump every particularity in modern societies, as liberalism always claimed? Not necessarily. The right to live one's life "from within," which is at the heart of a modern conception of individuality, was indeed honed and developed within the Western liberal tradition. But it is no longer a value restricted to the West—in part because the forms of life in which it developed are no longer exclusively "Western." It has become a cosmopolitan value and, in the form of the discourse of human rights, is as pertinent to Third World workers struggling at the periphery of the global system, women in the developing world up against patriarchal conceptions of a women's role, or political dissenters subject to the threat of torture as it is to Western consumers in the weightless economy. In that sense, paradoxically, cultural belongingness (ethnicity) is something, in its very specificity, of which everyone partakes. It is a universal particular, a "concrete universal."

Another way of putting the point would be to note that, by definition, a multicultural society always involved more than one group. There has to be some framework in which serious conflicts of outlook, belief, and interest can be negotiated, and this cannot be simply the framework of one group writ large, which was the problem with Eurocentric assimilationism. The specific and particular "difference" of a group or community cannot be asserted absolutely, without regard to the wider context provided by all those "others" in relation to whom "particularity" acquires a relative value. Philosophically, the logic of différance means that the meaning/identity of every concept is constituted in relation to all the other concepts in the system in terms of which alone it signifies. A particular cultural identity cannot be defined only by its positive presence and content. All identity terms depend on marking their limits—defining what they are in relation to what they are not. As Laclau argues, "I cannot assert a differential identity without distinguishing it from a context, and in the process of making the distinction, I am asserting the context at the same time" (Laclau 1996). Identities, then, are constructed within power relations (Foucault 1986). Every identity is founded on an exclusion and in that sense is an "effect of power." There must be something which is external to an identity (Laclau and Mouffe 1985; Butler 1993). That "outside" is constituted by all the other terms of the system, whose "absence" or lack is constitutive of its "presence" (Hall 1996). "I am a subject precisely because I cannot be an absolute consciousness, because something constitutively alien confronts me." Each particular identity, then, is *radically insufficient* in terms of its "others." "This means that the universal is part of my identity as far as I am penetrated by a constitutive lack" (Laclau 1996).[29]

The problem is that this argument seems to provide an alibi for the surreptitious return by the back door of the old liberal universalism. However, as Laclau notes, "European imperialist expansion had to be presented in terms of a universalizing civilizing function, modernization and so forth. The resistances of other cultures were . . . presented not as struggles between particular identities and cultures, but as part of an all-embracing and epochal struggle between universality and particularisms" (Laclau 1996). In short Western particularism was rewritten as a global universalism.

In this paradigm, then, universalism is opposed at every point to particularity and difference. However, if the "other" in fact is part of the difference we are asserting (the absence that allows a presence to signify), then any generalized claim which includes the "other" does not come from outer space but arises from *within the particular*. "The universal emerges out of the particular, not as some principle underlying and explaining the particular but as an incomplete horizon suturing a dislocated particular identity" (Laclau 1996). Why incomplete? Because it cannot—as it is in the liberal conception—be filled by a specific and unchanging content. It will be redefined whenever a particular identity, in taking account of its others and its own radical insufficiency, expands the horizon within which the demands of all can and must be negotiated. Laclau is right to insist that its content cannot be known in advance—in this sense the universal is an empty sign, an "always receding signifier." It is that horizon to which every particular difference must orient itself if it is not to fall back into absolute difference (which, of course, is the antithesis of a multicultural society). What we said about the generalizing across cultures of the individual's wish to live his or her life "from within" is an example of this process. A demand, arising from within a particular culture, is expanded and its link with the originating culture transformed as it is obliged to negotiate its meaning with other traditions within a wider "horizon" which now includes them both.

How, then, can the particular and the universal, the claims of both difference and equality, be recognized? This is the dilemma, the conundrum—the multicultural question—at the heart of the multicultural's transruptive and reconfigurative impact. It requires us to think beyond the traditional boundaries of the existing political discourses and their ever-ready "solutions." It suggests that we have to put our minds seriously, not to reiterating the sterile arguments between liberals and communitarians, but to some new and novel ways of *combining* difference and identity, drawing together on the same terrain those formal incommensurables of political vocabularies—liberty and equality *with* difference, "the good" *and* "the right."

Formally, this antagonism may not be amenable to resolution in the abstract. But it can be negotiated in practice. A process of final political adjudication between rival definitions of "the good" would be inimical to the whole multicultural project, since its effect would be to constitute every political space as a "war of manoeuvre" between entrenched and absolutized particular differences. The only circumstances in which this is not a simple zero-sum game is within the framework of an agonistic form of democratic negotiation (Mouffe 1993). However, the emphasis needs to be on the "agonistic"—democracy as an ongoing struggle without final resolution. We cannot simply reaffirm "democracy." But the multicultural question also suggests that the moment of "difference" is essential to defining democracy *as a genuinely heterogeneous space*. In our anxiety to identify the points of possible articulation, we must be careful not emphasize the ineradicable necessity of this moment of différance.[30] However, what is clear is that the process cannot be allowed to remain with this political assertion of a radical particularity. It must attempt to construct a diversity of new public spheres in which all the particulars will be transformed by being obliged to negotiate within a broader horizon. But it is essential for this space to remain heterogeneous and pluralistic, and for the elements negotiating within it to retain their différance. They must resist the drive to be integrated by a process of formal equivalence, such as is inscribed in a liberal conception of citizenship, which is to recoup an Enlightenment assimilationist strategy via a long detour. As Laclau recognizes, "This universalization and its open character certainly condemns all identity to an unavoidable hybridization, but hybridization does not necessarily mean decline through the loss of identity. It can also mean empowering existing identities through the opening of new possibilities. Only a conservative identity, closed on itself, could experience hybridization as loss" (Laclau 1996).

Toward a New Political Logic

In the latter part of the essay we have been struggling to identify and disinter the bare outlines of a new multicultural political logic. Such a strategy would seek to do, conjuncturally, what is said in the liberal-constitutional model to be incommensurable in principle: to effect a radical reconfiguration of the particular and the universal, of liberty and equality with difference. The aim has been to begin to reframe the inheritances from the liberal, pluralist, cosmopolitan, and democratic discourses in light of the multicultural character of late-modern societies. No easy final resolution seems possible. Instead, we have tried to sketch an approach in which, in pushing for vigorous and uncompromising strategies to be adopted which confront and try to eradicate racism, exclusion, and inferiorization (the old antiracist or race equality agenda, which is as relevant today as it ever was), certain limits have nevertheless to be respected (in the new multicultural circumstances of difference in which those strategies now operate).

Thus, we cannot simply reaffirm individual liberty and formal equality (what New Labour disarmingly calls "equality of worth"), because we can see both their inadequacy to the complexities of attachment, belongingness, and identity which multicultural society introduces, and the deep injustices of inequality, social exclusion, and injustice which continue to be perpetrated in their name. Individual choice, however tarted up with a thin veneer of communitarianism, cannot supply the bonds of recognition, reciprocity, and connection which give meaning to our lives as social beings. *This is the cultural or communitarian limit on liberal (including "market-liberal") forms of multiculturalism.* Conversely, we cannot enfranchise the claims of community cultures and norms over individuals without at the same time expanding—not only ideally but in practice—the right of individuals as bearers of rights to dissent from, exit from, and oppose if necessary their communities of origin. There are palpable dangers in slipping into a more formally separate, plural form of political representation. There is a danger in simply valorizing the distinctive values of "community" as if they are not always in a moving relationship to all the other competing values around them. The return to ethnicity in its "ethnically absolutist" form (Gilroy 1993a, 1993b) is only too capable of producing its own kinds of violence. It overessentializes cultural difference, fixes racial binaries, freezes them in time and history, gives power to established authority over others, privileges "the fathers and the Law," and leads to the policing of difference. This seems to be the critical frontier where cultural pluralism or ethnic communitarianism *encounters its liberal limit.*

However, the fact is that neither individuals as free-floating entities nor communities as solidaristic wholes occupy the social space on their own. Each is constituted in and through its relation to that which is other and different from itself. If this is not to result in either "the war of all against all" or a segregated communalism, then we must look for how both the greater recognition of difference and greater equality and justice for all can become part of a common "horizon." It seems to be the case, as Laclau suggests, *both* that "the universal is incommensurable with the particular" *and* that the former "cannot exist without the latter." Far from undermining democracy, this so-called "failure" is "the precondition for democracy" (Laclau 1996). Accordingly, this multicultural political logic requires at least two further conditions of existence: a deepening expansion and radicalization of democratic practices in our social life, and the unrelenting contestation of every form of racialized and ethnicized exclusionary closure (whether practiced by others on minority communities, or within communities). For racialized disadvantage and exclusion block the access of everyone, including "minorities" of *all* kinds, to the process of defining a more inclusive "Britishness" with which, *only then*, might everyone be legitimately invited to identify. This constitutes *the democratic or cosmopolitan limit on both liberal and communitarian alternatives.*

The difficulties in the way of practically and politically expanding this multicultural political logic are legion, and it has not been possible within the scope of this essay, to address them. However, one could not leave the argument without at least indicating the difficulties. On the one hand, in Britain, this is a propitious moment to raise the multicultural question—because Britishness as a national identity is in a transitional state, beset by problems and up for extensive renovation and renegotiation. However, such opportunities are also always moments of profound danger. For, just as the multicultural question opens up from below issues which were considered closed—settled—in the Western political institutions, so it is seen by many as the straw that broke the camel's back. It points toward the redefinition of what it means to be British, where the unthinkable might come to pass—it might be possible to be black-and-British, or Asian-and-British (or even British-and-gay)! However, the idea that *everyone* should have access to the processes by which such new forms of "Britishness" are redefined, coupled with the loss of empire and decline as a world power, is literally driving some of its citizens crazy. The "pollution" of Little England—as some see it—is calculated to produce not just a resurgence of the old biological stereotypes but a proliferating lexicon of new exclusionary binaries, grounded in a racialized "cultural difference": a British version of the new racisms which are abroad everywhere and gaining ground.

Both processes are alive and well in Britain at the turn of the millennium. Both thrive hand in hand in a fateful symbiosis. The celebration of the anniversary of the arrival of the *Empire Windrush*—described by some as "the irresistible rise of multi-racial Britain" (Phillips and Phillips 1998)—occurred within a year of the long-delayed Macpherson Inquiry into the murder of the black teenager Stephen Lawrence by five white youths, with its finding of "institutional racism" (Macpherson 1999). Both these events are deeply paradigmatic of the contradictory state of British multiculturalism, and their appearance together, in the same conjuncture, is essential to an understanding of Britain's confused and problematic response to "the multicultural question."

1 This essay first appeared in Barnor Hesse's collection *Un/settled Multicultural-isms*. To some extent, the distinction I make here overlaps with that offered in Hesse's introduction but also departs from it in certain important respects.

2 In fact, as Kymlicka (1989) has argued, the problems posed by multiculturalism are not adequately represented as necessitating a strong conception of collective rights since, in his perspective, individuals must remain the bearers of rights. Conversely, Parekh (1991) argues that many rights already acknowledged by liberal societies (for example, trade-union legislation, the Race Relations and Equal Opportunities Acts, Sikh exemption from health and safety requirements) are, in fact, group based or collectivity defined.

3 Hazel Carby (1998) has remarked on the "stark reversal of visibility of the black male body," where images of black men have made a remarkable transition straight from the drug-soaked ghetto to the front covers of the fashion magazines, while their actual bodies have remained largely where they were, an inordinate number of them in jail.

4 "In 1983 there were 144 recognized nations in the world. By the late 1990s this number had grown to just under 200. More will certainly come into being over the next few years as local ethnic groups and 'nations without a state' press for greater autonomy" (Giddens 2000, 153).

5 No conjuncture is ever wholly new. It is always a transformed combination of existing and emergent elements—in Gramsci's terms, the rearticulation of a disarticulation. See Gramsci (1971) and Hall (1998).

6 "Globalization in a post-imperial age only permits a post-nationalist consciousness for cosmopolitans who are lucky enough to live in the wealthy west" (Ignatieff 1994).

7 Globalization as fate seems to be a key feature of the Blair/New Labour/Third Way position. Giddens, who also advanced similar arguments, now makes a stronger argument for the regulation of global corporate power (Giddens 2000).

8 I am, of course, translating from philosophy to culture and expanding Derrida's (1972) concept without warrant—though not, I hope, against the spirit of his meaning.

9 For Derrida (1972), "différance" is both "to differ" and "to defer." It is grounded in strategies of delay, reprieve, referral, elision, detour, postponement, and reserving.

10 One needs to compare this figure with the size of the African American, Latino, Caribbean, Korean, and Vietnamese populations in the US to get a sense of comparative scale.

11 There is some evidence to suggest that "blackness" was not strongly marked among the earliest Caribbean migrants and developed in Britain in the 1960s as a response to racism.

12 The impact of the official inquiry into the death of Stephen Lawrence and the *Macpherson Report* (1999) is the most striking recent example of this.

13 Paul Gilroy speaks correctly of "the inability to take race seriously and an iron-jawed disinclination to recognize the equal human worth and dignity of people who are not white" (Gilroy 1999).

14 In discursive terms, racism has a metonymic structure—the genetic differences which are hidden being displaced along the chain of signification through their inscription onto the surface of the body (which, of course, is visible). This is what Frantz Fanon meant by *epidermalization*, or the "corporeal schema" (see Hall 1990, 1996b).

15 This is the position adopted by Balibar (1991) in his discussion of "differentialist racism" and by Wieviorka (1995). The term is borrowed from Pierre-André Taguieff. Modood (1997), however, in my opinion goes too far in attempting to distinguish "cultural racism" from any connection with fixity or the biological and draws, too, a sharp opposition between "biological racism" and "cultural differentialism." I think this misreading comes from not taking the discursive character of racism sufficiently into account. Modood is therefore misled into taking the biological referent in "biological racism" too literally.

16 Here I differ from the way the race/ethnicity distinction is drawn by, for example, Pnina Werbner (1997) in an important contribution.

17 This was the result of an extensive struggle of resignification. Judith Butler (1993) makes the argument that what is important about terms such as "black" or "queer," which have moved from a negative to a positive connotation, is that they retain the traces of the struggle to change within them. This may constitute an alternative strategy to "political correctness" which attempts to cleanse the language of all traces of negativity.

18 Whereas it needs to be understood as "the changing same" (Gilroy 1993a) or as "a discursive concept . . . [which] seeks to connect, authoritatively, within the structure of its narrative, a relation among past, community and identity" (Scott 1999). Fixture is something which *happens* to tradition under certain conditions—how it ceases to be creative and becomes immured in "authority."

19 See Scott (1999).

20 This is the important distinction between the conception of culture as a "way of life" and the conception of culture as "signifying practice" (Hall 1998).

21 Thus, I do not take seriously Robert Young's argument (that the use of the term "hybridity" simply restores the old racialized discourse of difference which one was attempting to supersede). This is semantic quibbling. Surely, terms can be disarticulated and rearticulated from their originary meanings: what is this pre-post-structuralist conception of language in which meaning is fixed eternally to its racialized referent? Clearly, my concern throughout has been with *cultural* hybridity, which I relate to the novel combination of heterogeneous cultural elements in a new synthesis—e.g., "creolization" and "transculturation"—and which cannot be fixed by, or dependent on, the so-called racial character of the people whose culture I am discussing.

22 Tradition does not mean something fixed. It is, rather, a recognition of the embodied character of all discourse. "It is a special sort of discursive concept in the sense that it performs a distinctive kind of labour; it seeks to connect authoritatively, within the structure of its narrative, a relation among past, community and identity. It depends upon a play of conflict and contention. It is a space of dispute as much as of consensus, of discourse as much as of accord" (Scott 1999).

23 Rawls made an important concession to his communitarian critics in recognizing that his theory of justice was particularly appropriate for a liberal-pluralist society, where the desire for political cooperation is already widespread (i.e., depended on certain particularistic culture assumptions). See Thompson, in Archibugi, Held, and Kohler (1998).

24 This includes uneven patterns of economic and technological change, the revolution in the position of women and the feminization of the workforce, the decline in manual male working-class culture and the older occupational communities; new patterns of consumption and the religion of the free market, new family forms and styles of parenting, generational differences in an aging population, the decline of organized religion, profound shifts in sexual behavior and moral culture, the decline of deference, the rise of managerialism, the heroization of the entrepreneur, the new individualism and the new hedonism.

25 Walzer talks, confusingly (and in view of recent developments, optimistically), about the US "choosing Liberalism 1 from within Liberalism 2." In fact, recent American public policy with its assault against affirmative action programs in the name of individual liberty looks more like a concerted effort to drag the US back to Liberalism 1 from its brief flirtation with Liberalism 2! Kymlicka, from a Canadian perspective, argues that certain individually defined group rights are compatible with the liberal conception and stretches the liberal conception to its limits in order to make them so. Taylor (1994) suggests that they are not; first, because of the individualistic foundational assumptions of liberalism, and second, because the protection of collective identities conflicts with the right to individual liberties. Liberalism therefore requires to be reformed in order to accommodate the multicultural demand for "recognition." Habermas (1998), however, argues that, of course, individuality is constituted intersubjectively, but that, correctly understood, a theory of rights not only accommodates but requires a politics of recognition that protects the integrity of the individual as a bearer of rights; this is compatible with liberalism, provided there is "the consistent actualization of the system of rights."

26 John Rex, who supports the general proposition of the cultural neutrality of the state, correctly argues that this approach differs from that of liberal individualism. It has been underpinned, at least until the advent of New Labour, by a social-democratic welfare program including substantial redistributive measures, which it would be misleading to subsume under an all-inclusive liberal rubric just because it respects the rights of the individual.

27 For a persuasive argument on the complexities of evaluating differences between cultural practices in a nonabsolutist way, see Parekh (1999).

28 See the extended debates on this question by Women against Fundamentalism.

29 In what follows, I am particularly indebted to the way the argument about universalism/particularism is conducted in Ernesto Laclau's recent work, especially his *Emancipations* (1996).

30 This may be a matter of emphasis rather than fundamental disagreement. Laclau, for example, writes as if the proliferation of identities is something which has simply happened to late-modern societies: his focus is on how such a disseminated field could nevertheless be hegemonized through a certain type of "universalization." When advanced by some proponents, this often becomes a recuperation of difference and a reassertion of the old Enlightenment universalist argument. However, from the multicultural perspective, the heterogenization of the social field—the pluralization of positionalities—is itself a necessary and positive, though not sufficient, moment and must be retained (in its hybridized forms), alongside the efforts (always incomplete) to define from within their particularities of a more universal horizon.

REFERENCES

Ahmad, A. 1995. "The Politics of Literary Post-Coloniality." *Race and Class* 36, no. 3.

Balibar, E. 1991. "Is There a 'Neo-Racism?'" In E. Balibar and I. Wallenstein, *Race, Nation and Class*. London: Verso.

Barker, M. 1981. *The New Racism*. London: Junction Books.

Bhabha, H. 1990. *Nation and Narration*. London: Routledge.

Bhabha, H. 1994. *The Location of Culture*. London: Routledge.

Bhabha, H. 1997. "The Voice of the Dom." *Times Literary Supplement*, no. 4923.

Bonnett, A. 1999. "Anti-Racist Dilemmas." *Race and Class* 36, no. 3.

Brah, A. 1996. *Cartographies of Diaspora*. London: Routledge.

Brathwaite, E. K. 1971. *The Development of Creole Society in Jamaica, 1770–1820*. Oxford: Oxford University Press.

Butler, J. 1993. *Bodies That Matter*. London: Routledge.

Carby, H. V. 1998. *Race Men: The W. E. B. Du Bois Lectures*. Cambridge, MA: Harvard University Press.

Caws, P. 1994. "Identity, Trans-cultural and Multi-cultural." In D. Goldberg, ed., *Multiculturalism*. London: Blackwell.

Clifford, J. 1998. "Introduction: The Pure Products Go Crazy." In J. Clifford, ed., *The Predicament of Culture*. Cambridge, MA: Harvard University Press.

Davies, N. 1999. *The Isles*. Basingstoke: Macmillan.

Derrida, J. 1972. *Positions*. Chicago: University of Chicago Press.

Derrida, J. 1981. *Dissemination*. London: Althorne.

Derrida, J. 1982. *Margins of Philosophy*. Brighton: Harvester.

Fish, S. 1998. "Boutique Multiculturalism." In A. Meltzer et al., eds., *Multiculturalism and American Democracy*. Lawrence: University of Kansas Press.

Fukayama, F. 1992. *The End of History*. New York: Free Press.

Giddens, A. 2000. *The Third Way and Its Critics*. London: Polity.

Gilroy, P. 1993a. *The Black Atlantic: Modernity and Double Consciousness*. London: Verso.

Gilroy, P. 1993b. *Small Acts*. London: Serpent's Tail.

Gilroy, P. 1999. "Joined-up Politics and Post-colonial Melancholia." The 1999 Diversity Lecture. London: Institute of Contemporary Arts.

Glissant, É. 1981. *Le discours antillais*. Paris: Seuil.

Goldberg, D. 1994. "Introduction." In D. Goldberg, ed., *Multiculturalism*. London: Blackwell.

Gramsci, A. 1971. *Selections from the Prison Notebooks*. Edited and translated by Q. Hoare and G. Nowell Smith. New York: International.

Habermas, J. 1994. "Struggles for Recognition in the Democratic Constitutional State." In A. Gutman, ed., *Multiculturalism*. Princeton, NJ: Princeton University Press.

Hall, C. 1992. *White, Male and Middle Class*. Cambridge: Polity.

Hall, S. 1990. "Cultural Identity and Diaspora." In J. Rutherford, ed., *Identity, Community, Culture, Difference*. London: Lawrence and Wishart.

Hall, S. 1991. "The Local and the Global: Globalization and Ethnicity." In A. D. King, ed., *Culture, Globalization and the World System*. Binghamton: State University of New York Press.

Hall, S. 1992. "New Ethnicities." In J. Donald and A. Rattansi, eds., *"Race," Culture and Difference*. London: Sage.

Hall, S. 1993. "Culture, Community, Nation." *Cultural Studies* 7, no. 3.

Hall, S. 1996a. "When Was the 'Post-colonial?' Thinking at the Limit." In I. Chambers and L. Curti, eds., *The Post-colonial Question*. London: Routledge.

Hall, S. 1996b. "Who Needs Identity?" In S. Hall and P. du Gay, eds., *Questions of Cultural Identity*. London: Sage.

Hall, S. 1998. "Aspiration and Attitude . . . Reflections on Black Britain in the Nineties." *New Formations*, no. 3.

Hall, S. 1999a. "From Scarman to Stephen Lawrence." *History Workshop Journal*, no. 48.

Hall, S. 1999b. "National and Cultural Identity." Paper for the Runnymede Commission on the Future of Multi-Ethnic Britain, London.

Hall, S. 1999c. "Thinking the Diaspora." *Small Axe*, no. 6.

Hall, S. 1999d. "Whose Heritage? Unsettling the Heritage, Re-imagining the Post-Nation." *Third Text*, no. 49 (winter).

Held, D., A. McGrew, D. Goldblatt, and J. Perraton, eds. 1999. *Global Transformations*. Cambridge: Polity.

Hesse, B. 2000. *UnSettled Multiculturalisms*. London: Zed.

Hobsbawm, E., and T. Ranger, eds. 1993. *The Invention of Tradition*. Cambridge: Cambridge University Press.

Ignatieff, M. 1994. *Blood and Belonging*. London: Vintage.

Kymlicka, W. 1989. *Liberalism, Community and Culture*. Oxford: Clarendon.

Lacan, J. 1977. *Écrits*. London: Tavistock.

Laclau, E. 1996. *Emancipations*. London: Verso.

Laclau, E., and C. Mouffe. 1985. *Hegemony and Socialist Strategy*. London: Verso.

Macpherson, W. 1999. *The Stephen Lawrence Inquiry—Report of an Inquiry by Sir William Macpherson of Cluny*. London: Stationery Office.

May, S., ed. 1999. *Critical Multiculturalism: Re-thinking Multicultural and Anti-racist Education*. Brighton: Falmer.

McLaren, P. 1997. *Revolutionary Multiculturalism—Pedagogies of Dissent for the New Millennium*. Boulder, CO: Westview.

Modood, T., R. Berthould, et al., eds. 1997. *Ethnic Minorities in Britain: Diversity and Disadvantage*. London: Policy Studies Institute.

Mouffe, C. 1993. *The Return of the Political*. London: Verso.

Nairn, T. 1997. *The Break-up of Britain*. London: Verso.

Ortiz, F. 1940. *Cuban Counterpoint: Tobacco and Sugar*. Durham, NC: Duke University Press.

Parekh, B. 1991. "British Citizenship and Cultural Difference." In Geoff Andrews, ed., *Citizenship*. London: Lawrence and Wishart.

Parekh, B. 1999. "The Logic of Inter-cultural Evaluation." In J. Horton and S. Mendes, eds., *Toleration, Identity and Difference*. Basingstoke: Macmillan.

Phillips, M., and T. Phillips. 1998. *Windrush—the Irresistable Rise of Multi-Racial Britain*. London: HarperCollins.

Phoenix, A. 1998. "'Multiculture,' 'Multiracisms' and Young People: Contradictory Legacies of *Windrush*." *Soundings*, 10.

Pratt, M. L. 1992. *Imperial Eyes: Travel Writing and Transculturation*. London: Routledge.

Richardson, R. 1999. *Islamophobia*. London: Runnymede Trust.

Robbins, K. 1991. "Tradition and Translation." In J. Corner and S. Harvey, eds., *Enterprise and Heritage*. London: Routledge.

Rushdie, S. 1991. *Imaginary Homelands*. London: Granta.

Scott, D. 1999. *Refashioning Futures: Criticism after Post-Coloniality*. Princeton, NJ: University of Princeton Press.

Taylor, C. 1994. "The Politics of Recognition." In A. Gutman, ed., *Multiculturalism*. Princeton, NJ: Princeton University Press.

Thompson, J. 1998. "Community, Identity and World Citizenship." In A. Archibugi, D. Held, and M. Kohler, eds., *Re-imagining Political Community*. Cambridge: Polity.

Voloshinov, V. N., and M. Bakhtin. 1973. *Marxism and the Philosophy of Language*. London and New York: Seminar Press.

Waldron, J. 1992. "Minority Cultures and the Cosmopolitan Alternative." In W. Kymlicka, ed., *The Rights of Minority Cultures*. Oxford: Oxford University Press.

Wallace, M. 1994. "The Search for the Good-Enough Mammy." In D. Goldberg, ed., *Multiculturalism*. London: Blackwell.

Werbner, P. 1997. "The Dialectics of Cultural Hybridity." In P. Werbner and T. Modood, eds., *Debating Cultural Hybridity*. London: Zed.

Wieviorka, M. 1995. "Is It So Difficult to Be an Anti-racist?" In P. Werbner and T. Modood, eds., *Debating Cultural Hybridity*. London: Zed.

Yuval-Davis, N. 1997. *Gender and Nation*. London: Saga.

PART III

THE POSTCOLONIAL AND
THE DIASPORIC

The panoramic essay titled "The West and the Rest: Discourse and Power" frames this whole part. It was originally published in 1992 as part of a textbook accompanying an Open University course called "Understanding Modern Society," and it is included here for both substantive and formal reasons.[1] Substantively, its intellectual originality is noteworthy in offering what Stuart calls an "externalist" account of the rise of modernity in the West, which sees it as implicated, from its very beginnings, in its exploitative relations to "the Rest" of the world.[2]

At a formal level, the essay has also been chosen as an example of Stuart's writing in an explicitly pedagogic mode: here, writing as a member of a course team and, as in the introduction to the second edition of *Policing the Crisis* (volume 1, chapter 12), participating in the collective work that was his preferred mode of intellectual endeavor. As noted earlier, he had a very significant investment in his identity as a teacher, and his move from the Centre for Contemporary Cultural Studies (CCCS) to the Open University (OU) in 1979 was largely driven by his desire to try to reach a much broader, popular audience than the graduate students at CCCS. He said he wanted to take the "high paradigm" of Cultural Studies and attempt to transform it into a popular pedagogy, for people without an academic background: "I thought . . . in that more open, interdisciplinary, unconventional setting, some of the aspirations of my generation—of talking to ordinary people, to women and black students in non-academic settings—might just be possible. . . . It served some of my political aspirations. . . . I wanted Cultural Studies to be open to that sort of challenge."[3] On arrival at the OU, he enthusiastically embraced the whole apparatus of radio, television, and video modes of presentation, which could be used to convey complex ideas to the broadest possible audience. Indeed, among the insomniacs and the merely curious who, alongside the OU's students, made up the (large) nocturnal audiences for these educational broadcasts, Stuart was so ubiquitous that, at one point, he acquired the nickname of "the dawn telly Don." These audiovisually mediated encounters could in some cases be dramatically consequential. Thus the black British filmmaker John Akomfrah credits the youthful experience of seeing one of Stuart's OU broadcasts with inspiring him to want to go on to make films himself, having seen in Stuart a potential role model for a "man of colour who wasn't crooning, dancing or running."[4]

In fact, as anyone familiar with the OU's educational texts will realize, the essay as presented here is much simplified from its original version. In its original OU format, the essay contained a whole variety of supplementary readings, exercises, illustrations, questions, and commentaries to guide the students through the argument—all of which have had to be omitted here, for technical reasons. However, the pedagogic tone and purpose of the text is still clear. The essay presents an important and original perspective on the history of globalization and modernity as represented by the imperial powers of the northwest of the globe. Its main purpose is to offer an overview, enabling the student reader to self-reflexively place the perspective offered here in relation to a broad range of earlier work in anthropology, history, and sociology. Most importantly, perhaps, in this connection, the essay not only discusses Edward Said's perspectives on Orientalism but also deals at some length with Foucault's contribution to the analysis of discourses of power and regimes of truth. Elsewhere, Stuart is critical of what he sees as the limitations of Foucauldian perspectives (not least in terms of what he sees as the inadequacy of their overgeneralized and insufficiently specified accounts of the limits of power, and of the particular sources of potential resistance in a given conjuncture). However, this essay as well as the section on modes of discourse analysis in his "The Work of Representation" are perhaps the two places where Stuart most clearly indicates his admiration for Foucault and his influence on his own later work.[5]

As indicated earlier, the main thrust of the argument is to critique previous accounts of the development of Western modernity as entirely the result of forces internal to that geographical region. He argues that the very idea of the West's special place in world history and its relations (post-Enlightenment) of superiority to the rest of the world were central to its own development from the very beginning. This was always so, he argues, both in terms of the material relations of exploitation and extraction of the treasures of the exotic realms discovered by the Western explorers, and in terms of the discursive and ideological relations of superiority constructed between them. Thus the supposed enlightenments of the West were defined precisely in relation to the presumed inferiority of the Others—who were not even necessarily admitted to the realm of humanity. The essay explores the history of how the very definition of Europe itself was constructed in relation to its enemies, inferiors, and opponents, and goes on to offer an exposition of Said's account of the role of the West in the discursive construction of the Orient as exotic, backward, and primitive. Rather than staying within the limited terms of the classical Marxist critique of imperialism, the essay also examines the gendering of relations of power between the colonialists and the objects of their conquests. It also introduces psychoanalytic perspectives on the rituals of degradation involved in the splitting of the noble West from the realm of the cannibals and ignoble savages—to whom it sees itself bringing the precious gift of civilization.[6] In doing all this, the essay, in conclusion, offers a damning critique of the models of development offered by conventional sociology. It insists on the recognition of the extent to which the discourses of civilization, refinement, and modernity were always constructed on the basis of the repression of the dark side of Enlightenment, represented by the Others relegated to the invisibility of its margins.

Shifting from these macroperspectives to the level of microhistory, in the interview with Kuan-Hsing Chen, "The Formation of a Diasporic Intellectual" (chapter 6), Stuart speaks autobiographically of his family upbringing in Jamaica. He reflects on being the one who did not fit in, and who found that experience of marginality both replicated and amplified upon coming to England to study, and of knowing both places intimately but belonging to neither. The account is offered as a way of elucidating not simply his own autobiography but the more general phenomenon of diasporic experience. The story quoted earlier of how "as they hauled down the flag, we got on the banana boat and sailed right into London" also functions as a kind of emotional history of how it *felt* to be part of that post-imperial phenomenon.[7] When, in "Old and New Identities," Stuart figures himself as the "sugar at the bottom of the English cup of tea . . . the sweet tooth, the sugar plantation that rotted generations of English children's teeth" (see chapter 2, this volume), there is a sense of wicked delight (or perhaps even of sweet revenge) in this destabilization of any secure category of (white) Englishness.

Stuart was always clear that the major problem with traditional Marxist theory's account of the development of capitalism was its relative neglect of the question of imperialism and colonialism. As he puts it in "Cultural Identity and Diaspora," the missing (third) term is quite particularly his own: "the Caribbean as the Third New World . . . the empty land . . . where strangers from every other part of the globe collided . . . the primal scene where the fateful/fatal encounter was staged between Africa and the West."[8] The account that Stuart gives here of the traumas of his own familial life in the "pigmentocracy" of Jamaican skin tones, where the body is painfully inserted into crisscrossing hierarchies of class, race, and color, movingly demonstrates how structural conditions of colonization and exploitation come to be lived as personal dramas.[9]

Here Stuart returns to the theme of how his Jamaican education had already inserted him into the structures of feeling and knowledge characteristic of the England whence they had originally been exported. Thus his position as the doubly displaced "familiar stranger"—both in relation to the context of colonial Jamaica, from which he felt he must escape, and in relation to the Imperial center, to which he then traveled. What is also at stake here, as demonstrated in his comments later in the interview, is that, just as an understanding of the development of capitalist modernity cannot be generated adequately by dealing only with its internal dynamics, nor can any history of resistances to those structures. His account of his time as a student at Oxford demonstrates the key role played in the formation of the New Left of the 1950s and 1960s by colonial intellectuals from a variety of "elsewheres." What is also striking here is the account Stuart gives of how his own later reconnection with Jamaica, as it became a self-consciously black society in the 1970s, was enabled and mediated through his work with the black diasporic populations of the UK.[10]

Through the 1990s, Stuart's work on the Caribbean flourished, and he made a BBC television series, *Redemption Song*, which focused on many of the issues discussed in the third piece in this section, "Thinking the Diaspora"— itself originally presented in 1998 in a lecture marking the fiftieth anniversary of the founding of the University of the West Indies.[11] Having earlier spoken of his own psychic difficulties with the idea of "going home" (chapter 6), here Stuart deconstructs in more theoretical terms the foundational myth of the possibility of the exiled diaspora's return to the authentic original culture of its mythological homeland. He notes the continuing affiliations of diasporic populations with their cultures of origin, as articulated through multisite households (these days, of course, often taking significantly virtual forms) and across generations, but he is concerned to escape any easy teleologies in which cultures are represented as having essential cores that can be maintained (or rescued). He starts with the fact that the Caribbean has long been populated by people who themselves had come—or, in many cases, forcibly been brought—from Africa, the East Indies, and China, having been conscripted into slavery or indenture, bringing with them a rich variety of cultures: hence their descendants must themselves be understood as the "diaspora of the diaspora," as he puts it.[12]

His central concern is with the syncretic and creolizing, transcultural logic that he argues is characteristic of the region, giving rise to different versions of Africa, India, and China, and mixing together Christianity, Hinduism, and voodoo alongside the variously English, French, and Spanish cultures of the original colonists. All this has produced the particular cultural syntheses that constitute contemporary Haiti or Martinique, as opposed to Barbados, Trinidad, or Jamaica. The ambition of his analysis is to transcend any merely national imaginary and to recognize the Caribbean as constituted through a diasporic aesthetic of creative intermingling and hybridity. Rather than seeking any continuity of transmission of cultural roots, he argues for the need to trace the complex routes through which given cultural elements have been transformed and reworked in different contexts. It is this vernacular system of cosmopolitan exchange that lies at the heart of his concerns—and most particularly the syncretic processes through which its dominant cultural forms are deconstructed into local modes of life. To return to the concerns of "The West and the Rest"—for him, this marks the end of modernity defined exclusively in Western terms and its reemergence in new vernacular forms in different parts of the globe.[13]

NOTES

1 Stuart Hall and Bram Gieben, eds., *Formations of Modernity* (Cambridge: Polity Press/Open University, 1992).

2 For an earlier and specifically Caribbean perspective, see Walter Rodney, *How Europe Underdeveloped Africa* (London: Bogle L'Ouverture, 1972).

3 Stuart Hall, "The Formation of a Diasporic Intellectual," in this volume. The version of the interview reprinted here omits some sections of the 1996 text (494–496 and

498–500 in the original) in order to maintain a clearer focus on the question of diaspora.

4   Akomfrah, quoted in Ashley Clark, "'The Stuart Hall Project' Reviewed," in *The Stuart Hall Project: Revolution, Politics, Culture and the New Left Experience* (London: British Film Institute, 2013), 13.

5   See the section titled "Discourse, Power and the Subject" in Hall's "The Work of Representation," in *Representation: Cultural Representations and Signifying Practices*, ed. Stuart Hall (London: Sage/Open University Press, 1997), and Stuart Hall, "Foucault: Power, Knowledge and Discourse," in *Discourse—Theory and Practice: A Reader*, ed. Margaret Wetherall, Stephanie Taylor, and Simeon J. Yates (London: Sage/Open University Press, 2011).

6   Beyond this, the analysis also points to the further splitting of the "good native" (as noble savage) from the realm of the "bad native" (the violent warrior) in a complex process of psychic disavowal.

7   Stuart Hall, "The Local and the Global," in *Culture Globalisation and the World System*, ed. Anthony King (London: Macmillan, 1991).

8   Stuart Hall, "Cultural Identity and Diaspora," in *Identity: Community, Culture, Difference*, ed. Jonathan Rutherford (London: Lawrence and Wishart, 1990), 234.

9   This account is vividly reprised in some of the archival footage in John Akomfrah's *The Stuart Hall Project*, 2013.

10 It was this work that also laid the foundations for his later involvements with the third generation of black British filmmakers and photographers around questions of race, ethnicity, and cultural identity. See also Stuart Hall, "Black Diaspora Artists in Britain," *History Workshop Journal*, no. 61 (2006): 1–24.

11 BBC2 (prod. Barraclough Carey), June–August 1991, in seven episodes. See also Stuart Hall, "Negotiating Caribbean Identities," *New Left Review*, no. 1/209 (1995): 3–14.

12 See also Stuart Hall, "Cosmopolitanism, Globalisation and Diaspora," in *Anthropology and the New Cosmopolitanism*, ed. Pnina Werbner (Oxford: Berg, 2009).

13 On this, see Stuart Hall, "When Was the Post-Colonial?," in *The Post-Colonial Question: Common Skies, Divided Horizons*, ed. Lidia Curti and Iain Chambers (London: Routledge, 1996), and Stuart Hall, "Diaspora and Hybridity in the Context of Globalisation," in *Documenta 11: Platform 3—Creolité and Creolisation*, ed. Okwui Enwezor et al. (Ostfildern-Ruit: Hatje Cantz, 2003).

CHAPTER 5

The West and the Rest: Discourse and Power

Introduction

This essay explores the role which societies *outside* Europe played in the process of their becoming (or unevenly becoming) "modern." It examines how an idea of "the West and the Rest" was constituted, how relations between Western and non-Western societies came to be represented. We refer to this as the formation of the "discourse" of "the West and the Rest."

Where and What Is "the West"?

This question puzzled Christopher Columbus and remains puzzling today. Nowadays, many societies aspire to become "Western"—at least in terms of achieving Western standards of living. But in Columbus's day (the end of the fifteenth century) going West was important mainly because it was believed to be the quickest route to the fabulous wealth of the East. Indeed, even though it should have become clear to Columbus that the New World he had found was not the East, he never ceased to believe that it was, and even spiced his reports with outlandish claims: on his fourth voyage, he still insisted that he was close to Quinsay (the Chinese city now called Hangchow, or Hangzhou), where the Great Khan lived, and probably approaching the source of the Four Rivers of Paradise! Our ideas of "East" and "West" have never been free of myth and fantasy, and even to this day they are not primarily ideas about place and geography.

We have to use shorthand generalizations like "West" and "Western," but we need to remember that they represent very complex ideas and have no simple or single meaning. At first sight, these words may seem to be about matters of geography and location. But even this, on inspection, is not straightforward since we also use the same words to refer to a type of society, a level of development, and so on. It's true that what we call "the West," in this second sense, *did* first emerge in western Europe. But "the West" is no longer only in Europe, and not all of Europe is in "the West." The historian John Roberts has remarked that "Europeans have long been unsure about where Europe 'ends' in the east. In the west and to the south, the sea provides a splendid marker . . . but to the east the plains roll on and on and the horizon is awfully remote" (Roberts 1985, 149). Eastern Europe doesn't (doesn't yet? never did?) belong properly to "the West," whereas the United States, which is not in Europe, definitely does. These days, technologically speaking, Japan is "Western," though on our mental map it is about as far "East" as you can get. By comparison, much of Latin America, which is in the Western Hemisphere, belongs economically to the Third World, which is struggling—not very successfully—to catch up with "the West." What are these different societies "east" and "west" of, exactly? Clearly, "the West" is as much an idea as a fact of geography.

The underlying premise of this chapter is that "the West" is a *historical*, not a geographical, construct. By "Western" we mean the type of society that is developed, industrialized, urbanized, capitalist, secular, and modern. Such societies arose at a particular historical period—roughly, during the sixteenth century, after the Middle Ages and the breakup of feudalism. They were the result of a specific set of historical processes—economic, political, social, and cultural. Nowadays, any society, wherever it exists on a geographical map, which shares these characteristics can be said to belong to "the West." The meaning of this term is therefore virtually identical to that of the word "modern."

"The West" is therefore also an idea, a concept—and this is what interests us most in this chapter. How did the idea, the language, of "the West" arise, and what have been its effects? What do we mean by calling it a *concept*?

The concept or idea of "the West" can be seen to function in the following ways:

First, it allows us to characterize and classify societies into different categories—i.e., "Western," "non-Western." It is a tool to think with. It sets a certain structure of thought and knowledge in motion.

Second, it is an image, or set of images. It condenses a number of different characteristics into one picture. It calls up in our mind's eye—it *represents* in verbal and visual language—a composite picture of what different societies, cultures, peoples, and places are like. It functions as part of a language, a "system of representation." (I say "system" because it doesn't stand on its own but works in conjunction with other images and ideas with which it forms a set: for example, "Western" = urban = developed, or "non-Western" = nonindustrial = rural = agricultural = underdeveloped.)

Third, it provides a standard or model of comparison. It allows us to compare to what extent different societies resemble, or differ from, one another. Non-Western societies can accordingly be said to be "close to" or "far away from" or "catching up with" the West. It helps to explain *difference*.

Fourth, it provides criteria of evaluation against which other societies are ranked and around which powerful positive and negative feelings cluster. (For example, "the West" = developed = *good* = desirable, or the "non-West" = underdeveloped = *bad* = undesirable.) It produces a certain kind of *knowledge* about a subject and certain attitudes toward it. In short, it functions as an *ideology*.

This chapter discusses all these aspects of the idea of "the West."

We know that the West itself was produced by certain historical processes operating in a particular place in unique (and perhaps unrepeatable) historical circumstances. Clearly, we must also think of the *idea* of "the West" as having been produced in a similar way. These two aspects are, in fact, deeply connected, though exactly how is one of the big puzzles in sociology. We cannot attempt to resolve here the age-old sociological debate as to which came first: the idea of "the West," or Western societies. What we can say is that as these societies emerged, so a concept and language of "the West" crystallized. And yet, we can be certain that the idea of "the West" did not simply reflect an already-established Western society: rather, it was essential to the very formation of that society.

What is more, the idea of "the West," once produced, became productive in its turn. It had real effects: it enabled people to know or speak of certain things in certain ways. It produced knowledge. It became *both* the organizing factor in a system of global power relations *and* the organizing concept or term in a whole way of thinking and speaking.

The central concern of this chapter is to analyze the formation of a particular pattern of thought and language, a "system of representation," which has the concepts of "the West" and "the Rest" at its center.

The emergence of an idea of "the West" was central to the Enlightenment. The Enlightenment was a very European affair. European society, it assumed, was the most advanced type of society on earth, European man the pinnacle of human achievement. It treated the West as the result of forces largely *internal* to Europe's history and formation.

However, in this chapter we argue that the rise of the West is also a *global* story. As Roberts observes, "'Modern' history can be defined as the approach march to the age dominated by the West" (Roberts 1985, 41). The West and the Rest became two sides of a single coin. What each now is and what the terms we use to describe them mean depend on the relations which were established between them long ago. The so-called uniqueness of the West was, in part, produced by Europe's contact and self-comparison with other, non-Western societies (the Rest), very different in their histories, ecologies, patterns of development, and cultures from the European model. The difference of these other societies and cultures from the West was the standard against which the West's achievement was measured. It is within the context of these relationships that the idea of "the West" took on shape and meaning.

The importance of such perceived difference needs itself to be understood. Some modern theorists of language have argued that *meaning* always depends on the relations that exist between the different terms or words within a meaning system. Accordingly, we know what "night" means because it is different from—in fact, opposite to—"day." The Swiss linguist who most influenced this approach to meaning, Ferdinand de Saussure (1857–1912), argued that the words "night" and "day" on their own can't mean anything; it is the *difference* between "night" and "day" which enables these words to carry meaning (to signify).

Likewise, many psychologists and psychoanalysts argue that an infant first learns to think of itself as a separate and unique "self" by recognizing its separation—its difference—from others (principally, of course, its mother). By analogy, national cultures acquire their strong sense of identity by contrasting themselves with other cultures. Thus, we argue, the West's sense of itself—its identity—was formed not only by the internal processes that gradually molded western European countries into a distinct type of society but also through Europe's sense of difference from other worlds—how it came to represent itself in relation to these "others." In reality, differences often shade imperceptibly into each other. (When, exactly, does "night" become "day"? Where, exactly, does "being English" end and "being Scottish" begin?) But, in order to function at all, we seem to need distinct, positive concepts, many of which are sharply polarized toward each other. Such "binary oppositions" seem to be fundamental to all linguistic and symbolic systems and to the production of meaning itself.

This chapter, then, is about the role which "the Rest" played in the formation of the idea of "the West" and a "Western" sense of identity. At a certain moment, the fates of what had been for many centuries separate and distinct worlds became—some would say, fatally—harnessed together in the same historical time frame. They became related elements in the same *discourse*, or way of speaking. They became different parts of one global social, economic, and cultural system, one interdependent world, one language.

A word of warning must be entered here. In order to bring out the distinctiveness of this "West and the Rest" discourse, I have been obliged to be selective and to simplify my representation of the West, and you should bear this in mind as you read. Terms like "the West" and "the Rest" are historical and linguistic constructs whose meanings change over time. More importantly, there are many different discourses, or ways in which the West came to speak of and represent other cultures. Some, like "the West and the Rest," were very Western-centered, or Eurocentric. Others, however, which I do not have space to discuss here, were much more culturally relativistic. I have elected to focus on what I call the discourse of "the West and the Rest" because it became a very common and influential discourse, helping to shape public perceptions and attitudes down to the present.

Another qualification concerns the very term "the West," which makes the West appear unified and homogeneous—essentially one place, with one view about other cultures and one way of speaking about them. Of course, this is not the case. The West has always contained many internal differences— between different nations, between Eastern and western Europe, between the Germanic northern and the Latin southern cultures, between the Nordic, Iberian, and Mediterranean peoples, and so on. Attitudes toward other cultures within the West varied widely, as they still do between, for example, the British, the Spanish, the French, and the German.

It is also important to remember that, as well as treating non-European cultures as different and inferior, the West had its own *internal* "others." Jews, in particular, though close to Western religious traditions, were frequently excluded and ostracized. West Europeans often regarded Eastern Europeans as "barbaric," and, throughout the West, Western women were represented as inferior to Western men.

The same necessary simplification is true of my references to "the Rest." This term also covers enormous historical, cultural, and economic distinctions—for example, between the Middle East, the Far East, Africa, Latin America, indigenous North America, and Australasia. It can equally encompass the simple societies of some North American Indians and the developed civilizations of China, Egypt, or Islam.

These extensive differences must be borne in mind as you study the analysis of the discourse of "the West and the Rest" in this chapter. However, we can actually use this simplification to make a point about discourse. For simplification is precisely what this discourse itself does. It represents what are, in fact, very differentiated (the different European cultures) as homogeneous (the West). And it asserts that these different cultures are united by one thing: the fact that *they are all different from the Rest*. Similarly, the Rest, though different among themselves, are represented as the same in the sense that *they are all different from the West*. In short, the discourse, as a "system of representation," *represents* the world as divided according to a simple dichotomy: the West/the Rest. That is what makes the discourse of "the West and the Rest" so destructive. It draws crude and simplistic distinctions and constructs an oversimplified conception of "difference."

Europe Breaks Out

"The voyages of discovery were the beginning of a new era, one of worldwide expansion by Europeans, leading in due course to an outright, if temporary, European . . . domination of the globe" (Roberts 1985, 175). In this section, we offer a broad sketch of the early stages of this process of expansion. When did it begin? What were its main phases? What did it "break out" from? Why did it occur?

When and How Did Expansion Begin?

Long historical processes have no exact beginning or end and are difficult to date precisely. A particular historical pattern is the result of the interplay between a number of different causal processes. In order to describe them, we are forced to work within very rough-and-ready chronologies and to use *historical generalizations* which cover long periods and pick out the broad patterns, but leave much of the detail aside. There is nothing wrong with this—historical sociology would be impossible without it—provided we know at what level of generality our argument is working. For example, if we are answering the question, "When did western Europe first industrialize?," it may be sufficient to say, "During the second half of the eighteenth century." However, a close study of the origins of industrialization in, say, Lancashire, would require a more refined timescale.

We can date the onset of the expansion process roughly in relation to two key events:

1. The early Portuguese explorations of the African coast (1430–1498); and
2. Columbus's voyages to the New World (1492–1502).

Broadly speaking, European expansion coincides with the end of what we call "the Middle Ages" and the beginning of the "modern age." Feudalism was already in decline in western Europe, while trade, commerce, and the market were expanding. The centralized monarchies of France, England, and Spain were emerging. Europe was on the threshold of a long, secular boom in productivity, improving standards of living, rapid population growth, and that explosion in art, learning, science, scholarship, and knowledge known as the Renaissance. (Leonardo had designed flying machines and submarines prior to 1519; Michelangelo started work on the Sistine Chapel in 1508; Thomas More's *Utopia* appeared in 1516.) For much of the Middle Ages, the arts of civilization had been more developed in China and the Islamic world than in Europe. Many historians would agree with Michael Mann that "the point at which Europe 'overtook' Asia must have been about 1450, the period of European naval expansion and the Galilean revolution in science"; though, as Mann also argues, many of the processes which made this possible had earlier origins (Mann 1988, 7). We return to this question at the end of the section.

Five Main Phases

The process of expansion can be divided, broadly, into five main phases:

1. The period of exploration, when Europe "discovered" many of the "new worlds" for itself for the first time (they all, of course, already existed).
2. The period of early contact, conquest, settlement, and colonization, when large parts of these "new worlds" were first annexed to Europe as possessions, or harnessed through trade.

3. The time during which the shape of permanent European settlement, colonization, or exploitation was established (e.g., plantation societies in North America and the Caribbean; mining and ranching in Latin America; the rubber and tea plantations of India, Ceylon, and the East Indies). Capitalism now emerged as a global market.
4. The phase when the scramble for colonies, markets, and raw materials reached its climax. This was the "high noon of Imperialism" and led into the First World War and the twentieth century.
5. The present, when much of the world is economically dependent on the West, even when formally independent and decolonized.

There are no neat divisions between these phases, which often overlapped. For example, although the main explorations of Australia occurred in our first phase, the continent's shape was not finally known until after Cook's voyages in the eighteenth century. Similarly, the Portuguese first circumnavigated Africa in the fifteenth century, yet the exploration of the African interior below the Sahara and the scramble for African colonies is really a nineteenth-century story.

This chapter concentrates on the first two phases—those involving early exploration, encounter, contact, and conquest—in order to trace how "the West and the Rest" as a "system of representation" was formed.

The Age of Exploration

This began with Portugal, after the Moors (the Islamic peoples who had conquered Spain) had finally been expelled from the Iberian Peninsula. Prince Henry "The Navigator," the pioneer of Portuguese exploration, was himself a Crusader who fought the Moors at the battle of Ceuta (North Africa; 1415) and helped to disperse the Moorish pirates who lurked at the entrance to the Mediterranean. As Eric Newby explains:

> With the pirates under control there was a real possibility that the Portuguese might be able to take over the caravan trade—an important part of which was in gold dust—that Ceuta enjoyed with the African interior. In the event, the attempt to capture this trade failed. . . . And so there emerged another purpose. This was to discover from which parts of Africa the merchandise, particularly the gold dust, emanated and, having done so, to contrive to have it re-routed . . . to stations on the Atlantic coast in

which the inhabitants would already have been converted to Christianity and of which the King of Portugal would be the ruler. (1975, 62)

This comment pinpoints the complex factors—economic, political, and spiritual—which motivated Portuguese expansion. Why, then, hadn't they simply sailed southward before? One answer is that they thought their ships were not sufficiently robust to endure the fierce currents and contrary winds to be encountered around the curve of the North African coastline. Another equally powerful factor was what is called the "Great Barrier of Fear"— evident, for example, in the belief that beyond Cape Bojador lay the mouth of Hell, where the seas boiled and people turned black because of the intense heat. The late-medieval European conception of the world constituted as much of a barrier to expansion as technological and navigational factors.

In 1430, the Portuguese sailed down the west coast of Africa, hoping to find not only the sources of the African gold, ivory, spice, and slave trades but also the legendary black Christian ruler "Prester John." In stages (each consolidated by papal decree giving Portugal a monopoly "in the Ocean Sea . . . lying southward and eastward"), the Portuguese pushed down the African coast and past the "Great Barrier of Fear." In 1441, the first cargo of African slaves captured by Europeans arrived in Portugal—thereby beginning a new era of slave-trading.

In 1487–1488, Bartolomeu Dias rounded the Cape of Good Hope, and Pedro da Covilhão, taking the caravan route overland, reached the Sudan from where he sailed to India (1488). Later, Vasco da Gama sailed around Africa and then, with the aid of a Muslim pilot, across the Indian Ocean to the city of Calicut (1497–1498). Within ten years, Portugal had established the foundations of a naval and commercial empire. Displacing the Arab traders who had long plied the Red Sea and Indian Ocean, they established a chain of ports to Goa, the East Indies, the Moluccas, and Timor. In 1514, a Portuguese mission reached Canton in China, and in 1542 the first contact was made with Japan.

By comparison, the exploration of the New World (America) was at first largely a Spanish affair. After long pleading, Columbus, the Genoese navigator, finally persuaded King Ferdinand and Queen Isabella of Spain to support his "western Enterprise" to find a westerly route to the treasures of the East. Deliberately underestimating the distance of Asia from Europe (he chose the shortest of a number of guesses on offer from medieval and classical sources), he sailed into the "Green Sea of Darkness" in 1492. In four remarkable voyages, he became the first European to land on most of the islands of the Caribbean and on the Central American mainland. He never relinquished his belief that "I am before Zaiton (Japan) and Quinsay (China), a hundred leagues, a little more or less" (Columbus 1969, 26). The misnamed "West Indies" are a permanent reminder that the Old World "discovered" the New by accident. But Columbus opened up a whole continent to Spanish expansion, founded on the drive for gold and the Catholic dream of converting the world to the Christian faith. Shortly afterward, Amerigo Vespucci (to whom the American continents owe their name) sailed north to Carolina, and south along the coast of Brazil to Rio, Patagonia, and the Falkland Islands.

In 1500, a Portuguese called Pedro Cabral, sailing to India, was blown out into the Atlantic and landed fortuitously on the coast of Brazil, giving Portugal her first foothold in what was to become Latin America. The threatened Spanish–Portuguese rivalry was aggravated by papal decrees favoring the Spanish but was finally settled by the Treaty of Tordesillas (1494), which divided the "unknown world" between the Spanish and the Portuguese along a line of longitude running about 1,500 miles west of the Azores. This line was subsequently revised many times, and other nations, like Spain's archenemy and Protestant rival, England, greedy to partake of the riches of the New World, soon made nonsense of it with their buccaneering exploits and raids along the Spanish Main. "Nevertheless," as John Roberts observes of the treaty,

> it is a landmark of great psychological and political importance: Europeans, who by then had not even gone round the globe, had decided to divide between themselves all its undiscovered and unappropriated lands and peoples. The potential implications were vast. . . . The conquest of the high seas was the first and greatest of all the triumphs over natural forces which were to lead to domination by western civilisation of the whole globe. Knowledge is power, and the knowledge won by the first systematic explorers . . . had opened the way to the age of western world hegemony. (Roberts 1985, 194)

In 1519–1522, a Portuguese expedition led by Magellan circumnavigated the globe, and Sir Francis Drake repeated this feat in 1577–1580.

The early Spanish explorers of the New World opened the way to that ruthless band of soldier-adventurers, the conquistadors, who completed the conquest of Central and South America, effecting the transition from exploration to conquest and colonization.

In 1513 Balboa, having explored the northern coast of South America, crossed the Isthmus of Darien to the Pacific. And in 1519 Cortés landed in Mexico and carried through the destruction of the Aztec empire. Pizarro pushed south through Ecuador to the Andes and Peru and destroyed the Inca empire (1531–1534), after which Orellana crossed the continent by way of the Amazon (1541–1542). The conquistadors were driven by the prospect of vast, unlimited fortunes. "We Spaniards," Cortés confessed, "suffer from a disease that only gold can cure" (quoted in Hale 1966, 105).

The Spanish proceeded to push up into what is now New Mexico, Arizona, Florida, and Arkansas (1528–1542). Meanwhile, farther north, other nations were also busy exploring. John Cabot, a Venetian sailing under English patronage, landed at Nova Scotia, Newfoundland, and New England (1497–1498). In 1500–1501, the Portuguese Corte Real, and in 1524, the Italian Verrazano, explored the Atlantic seaboard of North America. They were followed in 1585–1587 by Sir Walter Raleigh, and a number of British colonies were soon established: Newfoundland (1583), Roanoke (1585), and Jamestown (1607).

Yet farther north, British explorers such as Gilbert, Frobisher, Davis, Hudson, and Baffin (1576–1616) tried in vain to find an alternative route to the East via a northwest passage through the arctic seas. This quest was partly responsible for the opening up of North America, and Dutch, French, and English colonies sprang up along the Atlantic seaboard. Nevertheless, the serious exploration of Canada and North America was led largely by the French: Cartier, Champlain, and their followers exploring the St. Lawrence River, the Great Lakes, and the Mississippi River down to the Gulf of Mexico (1534–1682).

The Spanish and Portuguese established an early presence in the Far East, and soon the Spanish were exploring the Pacific, colonizing islands, and even commuting out of Manila in the Philippines to the west coast of America (1565–1605). But the Dutch and the English set out to flout the Spanish and Portuguese commercial monopolies. The British East India Company was founded in 1599, the Dutch East India Company in 1602. After their independence from Spain in 1584, the Dutch became one of the most powerful commercial nations, their East Indies trade laying the basis for the flourishing of Dutch *bourgeois* culture (Schama 1977). From a base in the old spice empire, the Dutch reached Fiji, the East Indies, Polynesia, Tasmania, and New Zealand, and in 1606 were the first Europeans to catch sight of Australia. Over the next thirty years, they gradually pieced together the Australian jigsaw puzzle, though the Australian coast was not completely mapped until after Cook's famous voyages (1768–1779) to Tahiti, the South Pacific, and the Antarctic.

By the eighteenth century, then, the main European world players—Portugal, Spain, England, France, and Holland—were all in place. The serious business of bringing the far-flung civilizations they had discovered into the orbit of Western trade and commerce, and exploiting their wealth, land, labor, and natural resources for European development, had become a major enterprise. (China and India remained closed for longer, except for trading along their coasts and the efforts of Jesuit missionaries.) Europe began to imprint its culture and customs on the new worlds. European rivalries were constantly fought out and settled in the colonial theaters. The colonies became the "jewels in the crown" of the new European empires. Through trade monopolies and the mercantilist commercial system, each of these empires tried to secure exclusive control of the flow of trade for its own enrichment. The wealth began to flow in: in 1554, America yielded 11 percent of the Spanish Crown's income; in 1590, 50 percent.

Breaking the Frame

Toward the end of the fifteenth century, then, Europe broke out of its long confinement. What had bottled it up for so long? This is a difficult question to answer, but we can identify two sets of factors: the first, material and the second, cultural.

Physical Barriers to the East

The Middle Ages represented an actual *loss* of contact with and knowledge of the outside world. Alexander the Great's conquests (336–323 BC) had taken the Macedonian-Greek armies as far east as the Himalayas. Only his troops' reluctance prevented him from reaching what he believed to be the limits of the inhabited world. The Roman Empire stretched from Britain to the Arabian deserts. But in the Middle Ages, Europe closed in on itself. It retained some knowledge of India (especially among Venetian traders), but beyond that lay unknown territory. Though every port and trade route on the Mediterranean was mapped, the basic contours of other seas and continents were shrouded in mystery. For example, though Europe bought great quantities of Chinese silk, transported by caravan across Central Asia, it took little interest in the great civilization from which the silk came.

A key factor in this was that after the seventh century AD, "sea-routes and land-routes alike were barred by the meteoric rise of Islam, which interposed its iron curtain between West and East" (Latham 1958, 8). It was Arab middlemen who brought eastern goods to the European seaports of the Mediterranean and Black Sea to sell. The Crusades (1095–1291) were the long, and for a time unsuccessful, struggle of Christian Europe to roll back this "infidel threat." But just when, at last, Europe seemed to be winning, a thunderbolt struck from a quarter unexpected by both Islam and Christendom: the invasions of the Mongol and Tartar nomads from the Central Asian steppes (1206–1260), which left a trail of devastation in their wake. However, Islam suffered even more than Christendom from the Tartar invasions, and in the thirteenth century, the eastern curtain lifted briefly.

During this interval, the Venetian Marco Polo and other members of his family undertook their famous travels to the court of the Great Khan, China, and Japan (1255–1295).

Marco Polo's *Travels* with its tales of the fabulous wealth of the East played a decisive role in stimulating the European imagination to search for a westerly route to the East, a search that became increasingly important. For soon the eastern opening became blocked again by the rise of a new Islamic power, the Ottoman Empire, and China, under the Ming dynasty, once more turned inward.

This had profound effects. It stimulated expansion westward, favoring the European powers of the Atlantic seaboard (Spain, Portugal, Britain, Holland, and France). It also tended to isolate Western from Eastern Europe—a process reinforced by the growing split between Western (Catholic) and Eastern (Orthodox) churches. From this point onward, the patterns of development within Western and Eastern Europe sharply diverged.

The Barriers in the Mind

A second major obstacle to the East lay in the mind—consisting not only of the sketchy knowledge that Europeans had of the outside world but of the way they conceptualized and imagined it. To the north, they believed, there was "nothing—or worse . . . barbarian peoples who, until civilized by the church, were only a menace" (Roberts 1985, 117). To the east, across the plains, there were barbarians on horseback: Huns, Mongols, and Tartars. To the south lay the shifting empires of Islam, which, despite their early tolerance of Christianity and of the Jews, had advanced deep into Europe—to Poitiers and Constantinople, across North Africa and into Spain, Portugal, and Southern Italy. The cradle of European civilization and trade was the Mediterranean. In the eastern Mediterranean, there was Byzantium—a civilization which was part of Christendom. But the Catholic and Orthodox churches were drawing farther apart as the centuries passed.

For what lay beyond, Europe relied on other sources of knowledge—classical, biblical, legendary, and mythological. Asia remained largely a world of elephants and other wonders almost as remote as sub-Saharan Africa. There were four continents—Europe, Africa, Asia, and "Terra Australis Incognita" ("The Unknown Southern Land")—the way to the latter being judged impassable. On medieval maps, the landmass crowded out the oceans: there was no Pacific, and the Atlantic was a narrow, and extremely dangerous, waterway. The world was often represented as a wheel, superimposed on the body of Christ, with Jerusalem at its hub. This conception of the world did not encourage free and wide-ranging travel.

The Consequences of Expansion for the Idea of "the West"

Gradually, despite their many internal differences, the countries of western Europe began to conceive of themselves as part of a single family or civilization—"the West." The challenge from Islam was an important factor in hammering western Europe and the idea of "the West" into shape. Roberts notes that "the word 'Europeans' seems to appear for the first time in an eighth-century reference to Charles Martel's victory [over Islamic forces] at Tours. All collectivities become more self-aware in the presence of an external challenge, and self-awareness promotes cohesiveness" (1985, 122). And Peter Hulme speaks of "the consolidation of an ideological identity through the testing of [Europe's] Eastern frontiers prior to the adventure of Atlantic exploration. . . . A symbolic end to that process could be considered Pius III's 1458 identification of Europe with Christendom" (1986, 84).

But in the Age of Exploration and Conquest, Europe began to define itself in relation to a new idea—the existence of many new "worlds," profoundly different from itself. The two processes—growing internal cohesion and the conflicts and contrasts with external worlds—reinforced each other, helping to forge that new sense of identity that we call "the West."

Discourse and Power

We have looked at the historical process by which an idea of "the West" emerged from Europe's growing internal cohesion and its changing relations to non-Western societies. We turn, next, to the formation of the languages or "discourses" in which Europe began to describe and represent the *difference* between itself and these "others" it encountered during the course of its expansion. We are now beginning to sketch the formation of the "discourse" of "the West and the Rest." However, we first need to understand what we mean by the term "discourse."

What Is a "Discourse"?

In commonsense language, a *discourse* is simply "a coherent or rational body of speech or writing; a speech, or a sermon." But here the term is being used in a more specialized way. By "discourse," we mean a particular way of *representing* "the West," "the Rest," and the relations between them. A discourse is a group of statements which provide a language for talking about—i.e., a way of representing—a particular kind of knowledge about a topic. When statements about a topic are made within a particular discourse, the discourse makes it possible to construct the topic in a certain way. It also limits the other ways in which the topic can be constructed.

A discourse does not consist of one statement but of several statements working together to form what the French social theorist Michel Foucault (1926–1984) calls a "discursive formation." The statements fit together because any one statement implies a relation to all the others: "They refer to the same object, share the same style and support 'a strategy . . . a common institutional . . . or political drift or pattern'" (Cousins and Hussain 1984, 84–85).

One important point about this notion of discourse is that it is not based on the conventional distinction between thought and action, language and practice. Discourse is about the production of knowledge through language. But it is itself produced by a practice: "discursive practice"—the practice of producing meaning. Since all social practices entail *meaning*, all practices have a discursive aspect. So discourse enters into and influences all social practices. Foucault would argue that the discourse of the West about the Rest was deeply implicated in practice—i.e., in how the West behaved toward the Rest.

To get a fuller sense of Foucault's theory of discourse, we must bear the following points in mind.

1. A discourse can be produced by many individuals in different institutional settings (e.g., families, prisons, hospitals, and asylums). Its integrity or "coherence" does not depend on whether it issues from one place or from a single speaker or "subject." Nevertheless, every discourse constructs positions from which alone it makes sense. Anyone deploying a discourse must position themselves *as if* they were the subject of the discourse. For example, we may not ourselves believe in the natural superiority of the West. But if we use the discourse of "the West and the Rest," we will necessarily find ourselves speaking from a position that holds that the West is a superior civilization. As Foucault puts it, "To describe a . . . statement does not consist in analysing the relations between the author and what he [*sic*] says . . . but in determining what position can and must be occupied by any individual if he is to be the subject of it [the statement]" (1972, 95–96).

2. Discourses are not closed systems. A discourse draws on elements in other discourses, binding them into its own network of meanings. Thus, as we saw in the preceding section, the discourse of "Europe" drew on the earlier discourse of "Christendom," altering or translating its meaning. Traces of past discourses remain embedded in more recent discourses of "the West."

3. The statements within a discursive formation need not all be the same. But the relationships and differences between them must be regular and systematic, not random. Foucault calls this a "system of dispersion": "Whenever one can describe, between a number of statements, such a system of dispersion, whenever . . . one can define a regularity . . . [then] we will say . . . that we are dealing with a *discursive formation*" (1972, 38; emphasis in original).

These points will become clearer when we apply them to particular examples, as we do later in this chapter.

Discourse and Ideology

A discourse is similar to what sociologists call an "ideology": a set of statements or beliefs which produce knowledge that serves the interests of a particular group or class. Why, then, use "discourse" rather than "ideology"?

One reason which Foucault gives is that ideology is based on a distinction between *true* statements about the world (science) and *false* statements (ideology), and the belief that the facts about the world help us to decide between true and false statements. But Foucault argues that statements about the social, political, or moral world are rarely ever simply true or false, and "the facts" do not enable us to decide definitively about their truth or falsehood, partly because "facts" can be construed in different ways. The very language we use to describe the so-called facts interferes in this process of finally deciding what is true, and what false.

For example, Palestinians fighting to regain land on the West Bank from Israel may be described either as "freedom fighters" or as "terrorists." It is a fact that they are fighting, but what does the fighting *mean*? The facts alone cannot decide. And the very language we use—"freedom fighters/terrorists"— is part of the difficulty. Moreover, certain descriptions, even if they appear false to us, can be *made* "true" because people act on them believing that they are true, and so their actions have real consequences. Whether the Palestinians are terrorists or not, if we think they are, and act on that "knowledge," they in effect become terrorists because we treat them as such. The language (discourse) has real effects in practice: the description becomes "true."

Foucault's use of "discourse," then, is an attempt to side-step what seems an unresolvable dilemma—deciding which social discourses are true or scientific, and which false or ideological. Most social scientists now accept that our values enter into all our descriptions of the social world, and therefore most of our statements, however factual, have an ideological dimension. What Foucault would say is that knowledge of the Palestinian problem is produced by competing discourses—those of "freedom fighter" and "terrorist"—and that each is linked to a contestation over power. It is the outcome of *this* struggle which will decide the "truth" of the situation.

You can see, then, that although the concept of "discourse" sidesteps the problem of truth/falsehood in ideology, it does *not* evade the issue of power. Indeed, it gives considerable weight to questions of power since it is power, rather than the facts about reality, which make things "true": "We should admit that power produces knowledge. . . . That power and knowledge directly imply one another; that there is no power relation without the correlative constitution of a field of knowledge, nor any knowledge that does not presuppose and constitute . . . power relations" (Foucault 1980, 27).

Can a Discourse Be "Innocent"?

Could the discourse which developed in the West for talking about the Rest operate outside power? Could it be, in that sense, purely scientific—i.e., ideologically innocent? Or was it influenced by particular class interests?

Foucault is very reluctant to *reduce* discourse to statements that simply mirror the interests of a particular class. The same discourse can be used by groups with different, even contradictory, class interests. But this does not mean that discourse is ideologically neutral or "innocent." Take for example, the encounter between the West and the New World. There are several reasons why this encounter could not be innocent, and therefore why the discourse which emerged in the Old World about the Rest could not be innocent either.

First, Europe brought its own cultural categories, languages, images, and ideas to the New World in order to describe and represent it. It tried to fit the New World into existing conceptual frameworks, classifying it according to its own norms and absorbing it into Western traditions of representation. This is hardly surprising: we often draw on what we already know about the world in order to explain and describe something novel. It was never a simple matter of the West just looking, seeing and describing the New World/the Rest without preconceptions.

Second, Europe had certain definite purposes, aims, objectives, motives, interests, and strategies in setting out to discover what lay across the "Green Sea of Darkness." These motives and interests were mixed. The Spanish, for example, wanted to

1 get their hands on gold and silver,
2 claim the land for their Catholic majesties, and
3 convert the heathen to Christianity.

These interests often contradicted one another. But we must not suppose that what Europeans said about the New World was simply a cynical mask for their own self-interest. When King Manuel of Portugal wrote to Ferdinand and Isabella of Spain that "the principal motive of this enterprise [da Gama's voyage to India] has been . . . the service of God our Lord, and our own advantage" (quoted in Hale 1966, 38)—thereby neatly and conveniently bringing God and Mammon together into the same sentence—he probably saw no obvious contradiction between them. These fervently religious Catholic rulers fully believed what they were saying. To them, serving God and pursuing "our advantage" were not necessarily at odds. They lived and fully believed their own ideology.

So, while it would be wrong to attempt to reduce their statements to naked self-interest, it is clear that their discourse was molded and influenced by the play of motives and interests across their language. Of course, motives and interests are almost never wholly conscious or rational. The desires which drove the Europeans were powerful, but their power was not always subject to rational calculation. Marco Polo's "treasures of the East" were tangible enough. But the seductive power which they exerted over generations of Europeans transformed them more and more into a myth. Similarly, the gold that Columbus kept asking the natives for very soon acquired a mystical, quasi-religious significance.

Finally, the discourse of "the West and the Rest" could not be innocent because it did not represent an encounter between equals. The Europeans had outsailed, outshot, and outwitted peoples who had no wish to be "explored," no need to be "discovered," and no desire to be "exploited." The Europeans stood, vis-à-vis the Others, in positions of dominant power. This influenced what they saw and how they saw it, as well as what they did not see.

Foucault sums up these arguments as follows. Not only is discourse always implicated in *power*, but discourse is one of the "systems" through which power circulates. The knowledge which a discourse produces constitutes a kind of power exercised over those who are "known." When that knowledge is exercised in practice, those who are "known" in a particular way will be subject (i.e., subjected) to it. This is always a power relation (see Foucault 1980, 201.) Those who produce the discourse also have the power to *make it true*—i.e., to enforce its validity, its scientific status.

This leaves Foucault in a highly relativistic position with respect to questions of truth because his notion of discourse undermines the distinction between true and false statements—between science and ideology—to which many sociologists have subscribed. These epistemological issues (about the status of knowledge, truth, and relativism) are too complex to take further here (some of them are addressed further in Hall et al. 1992). However, the important idea to grasp now is the deep and intimate relationship which Foucault establishes between discourse, knowledge, and power. According to Foucault, when power operates so as to enforce the "truth" of any set of statements, then such a discursive formation produces a "regime of truth":

> Truth isn't outside power. . . . Truth is a thing of this world; it is produced only by virtue of multiple forms of constraint . . . and it induces regular effects of power. Each society has its regime of truth, its "general polities" of truth; that is, the types of discourse which it accepts and makes function as true; the mechanisms and instances which enable one to distinguish "true" and "false" statements; the means by which each is sanctioned; and the techniques and procedures accorded value in the acquisition of truth; the status of those who are charged with saying what counts as true. (Foucault 1980, 131)

Summary

Let us summarize the main points of this argument. Discourses are ways of talking, thinking, or representing a particular subject or topic. They produce meaningful knowledge about that subject. This knowledge influences social practices, and so has real consequences and effects. Discourses are not reducible to class interests but always operate in relation to power—they are part of the way power circulates and is contested. The question of whether a discourse is true or false is less important than whether it is effective in practice. When it is effective—organizing and regulating relations of power (say, between the West and the Rest)—it is called a "regime of truth."

Representing the Other

So far, the discussion of discourse has been rather abstract and conceptual. The concept may be easier to understand in relation to example. One of the best examples of what Foucault means by a "regime of truth" is provided by Edward Said's study of Orientalism. In this section, I want to look briefly at this example and then see how far we can use the theory of discourse and the example of Orientalism to analyze the discourse of "the West and the Rest."

Orientalism

In his book *Orientalism*, Edward Said analyzes the various discourses and institutions which constructed and produced, as an object of knowledge, that entity called "the Orient." Said calls this discourse "Orientalism." Note that, though we tend to include the Far East (including China) in our use of the word "Orient," Said refers mainly to the Middle East, the territory occupied principally by Islamic peoples. Also, his main focus is French writing about the Middle East. Here is Said's own summary of the project of his book:

> My contention is that without examining Orientalism as a discourse one cannot possibly understand the enormously systematic discipline by which European culture was able to manage—and even produce—the Orient politically, sociologically, militarily, ideologically, scientifically, and imaginatively during the post-Enlightenment period. Moreover, so authoritative a position did Orientalism have that I believe no one writing, thinking, or acting on the Orient could do so without taking account of the limita-

tions on thought and action imposed by Orientalism. In brief, because of Orientalism, the Orient was not (and is not) a free subject of thought and action. This is not to say that Orientalism unilaterally determines what can be said about the Orient, but that it is the whole network of interests inevitably brought to bear on (and therefore always involved in) any occasion when that peculiar entity "the Orient" is in question. . . . This book . . . tries to show that European culture gained in strength and identity by setting itself off against the Orient as a sort of surrogate and even underground self. (1985, 3)

We now analyze the discourse of "the West and the Rest" as it emerged between the end of the fifteenth and eighteenth centuries using Foucault's ideas about "discourse" and Said's example of "Orientalism." How was this discourse formed? What were its main themes—its "strategies" of representation?

The "Archive"

Said argues that "in a sense Orientalism was a library or archive of information commonly . . . held. What bound the archive together was a family of ideas and a unifying set of values proven in various ways to be effective. These ideas explained the behaviour of Orientals; they supplied Orientals with a mentality, a genealogy, an atmosphere; most important, they allowed Europeans to deal with and even to see Orientals as a phenomenon possessing regular characteristics" (1985, 41–42). What sources of common knowledge, what "archive" of other discourses, did the discourse of "the West and the Rest" draw on? We can identify four main sources:

Classical Knowledge

This was a major source of information and images about "other worlds." Plato (c. 427–347 BC) described a string of legendary islands, among them Atlantis, which many early explorers set out to find. Aristotle (384–322 BC) and Eratosthenes (c. 276–194 BC) both made remarkably accurate estimates of the circumference of the globe, which were consulted by Columbus. Ptolemy's *Geographia* (second century AD) provided a model for mapmakers more than a thousand years after it had been produced. Sixteenth-century explorers believed that in the outer world lay, not only Paradise, but that "Golden Age," a place of perfect happiness and "springtime of the human race," of which the classical poets, including Horace (65–8 BC) and Ovid (43 BC–AD 17), had written.

The eighteenth century was still debating whether what they had discovered in the South Pacific was Paradise. In 1768, the French Pacific explorer Bougainville renamed Tahiti "The New Cythera" after the island where, according to classical myth, Venus first appeared from the sea. At the opposite extreme, the descriptions by Herodotus (484–425 BC) and Pliny (AD 23–79) of the barbarous peoples who bordered Greece left many grotesque images of "other" races which served as self-fulfilling prophecies for later explorers who found what legend said they would find. Paradoxically, much of this classical knowledge was lost in the Dark Ages and only later became available to the West via Islamic scholars, themselves part of that "other" world.

Religious and Biblical Sources

These were another source of knowledge. The Middle Ages reinterpreted geography in terms of the Bible. Jerusalem was the center of the earth because it was the Holy City. Asia was the home of the Three Wise Kings; Africa that of King Solomon. Columbus believed the Orinoco (in Venezuela) to be a sacred river flowing out of the Garden of Eden.

Mythology

It was difficult to tell where religious and classical discourses ended and those of myth and legend began. Mythology transformed the outer world into an enchanted garden, alive with misshapen peoples and monstrous oddities. In the sixteenth century Sir Walter Raleigh still believed he would find, in the Amazon rain forests, the king "El Dorado" ("The Gilded One"), whose people were alleged to roll him in gold, which they would then wash off in a sacred lake.

Travelers' Tales

Perhaps the most fertile source of information was travelers' tales—a discourse where description faded imperceptibly into legend. The following fifteenth-century German text summarizes more than a thousand years of travelers' tales, which themselves often drew on religious and classical authority:

> In the land of Indian there are men with dogs' heads who talk by barking [and] . . . feed by catching birds. . . . Others again have only one eye in the forehead. . . . In Libya many are born without heads and have a mouth and eyes. Many are of both sexes. . . . Close to Paradise on the River Ganges live

men who eat nothing. For . . . they absorb liquid nourishment through a straw [and] . . . live on the juice of flowers. . . . Many have such large under-lips that they can cover their whole faces with them. . . . In the land of Ethiopia many people walk bent down like cattle, and many live four hundred years. Many have horns, long noses and goats' feet. . . . In Ethiopia towards the west many have four eyes . . . [and] in Eripia there live beautiful people with the necks and bills of cranes. (Quoted in Newby 1975, 17)

A particularly rich repository was Sir John Mandeville's *Travels*—in fact, a compendium of fanciful stories by different hands. Marco Polo's *Travels* was generally more sober and factual but nevertheless achieved mythological status. His text (embellished by Rusticello, a romance writer) was the most widely read of the travelers' accounts and was instrumental in creating the myth of "Cathay" ("China" or the East generally), a dream that inspired Columbus and many others. The point of recounting this astonishing mixture of fact and fantasy which constituted late medieval "knowledge" of other worlds is not to poke fun at the ignorance of the Middle Ages. The point is: (a) to bring home how these very different discourses, with variable statuses as "evidence," provided the cultural framework through which the peoples, places, and things of the New World were seen, described, and represented; and (b) to underline the conflation of fact and fantasy that constituted "knowledge." This can be seen especially in the use of analogy to describe first encounters with strange animals. Penguins and seals were described as being like geese and wolves, respectively; the tapir as a bull with a trunk like an elephant, the opossum as half fox, half monkey.

A "Regime of Truth"

Gradually, observation and description vastly improved in accuracy. The medieval habit of thinking in terms of analogies gave way to a more sober type of description of the fauna and flora, ways of life, customs, physical characteristics, and social organization of native peoples. We can here begin to see the outlines of an early ethnography or anthropology.

But the shift into a more descriptive, factual discourse, with its claims to truth and scientific objectivity, provided no guarantees. A telling example of this is the case of the "Patagonians." Many myths and legends told of a race of giant people. And in the 1520s, Magellan's crew brought back stories of having encountered, in South America, such a race of giants whom they dubbed *patagones* (literally, "big feet"). The area of the supposed encounter became known as "Patagonia," and the notion became fixed in the popular imagination, even though two Englishmen who visited Patagonia in 1741 described its people as being of average size.

When Commodore John Byron landed in Patagonia in 1764, he encountered a formidable group of natives—broad-shouldered, stocky, and inches taller than the average European. They proved quite docile and friendly. However, the newspaper reports of his encounter wildly exaggerated the story, and Patagonians took on an even greater stature and more ferocious aspect. One engraving showed a sailor reaching only as high as the waist of a Patagonian giant, and the Royal Society elevated the topic to serious scientific status. "The engravings took the explorers' raw material and shaped them into images familiar to Europeans" (Withey 1987, 1175–1176). Legend had taken a late revenge on science.

Idealization

"Orientalism," Said remarks, "is the discipline by which the Orient was (and is) approached systematically, as a topic of learning, discovery and practice." "In addition," he adds, Orientalism "designate[s] that collection of dreams, images and vocabularies available to anyone who has tried to talk about what lies east of the dividing line" (1985, 73). Like the Orient, the Rest quickly became the subject of the languages of dream and Utopia, the object of a powerful fantasy.

Between 1590 and 1634, the Flemish engraver Theodor de Bry published his *Historia Americae* in ten illustrated volumes. These were leading examples of a new popular literature about the New World and the discoveries there. De Bry's books contained elaborate engravings of life and customs of the New World. Here we see the New World reworked—re-presented—within European aesthetic conventions, Western "ways of seeing." Different images of America are superimposed on one another. De Bry, for example, transformed the simple, unpretentious sketches which John White had produced in 1587 of the Algonquian Indians he had observed in Virginia. Facial features were retouched, gestures adjusted, and postures reworked according to more classical European styles. The effect overall, Hugh Honour observes, was "to tame and civilize the people White had observed so freshly" (1976, 75). The same transformation can be seen in the three representations of the inhabitants of Tierra del Fuego.

A major object of this process of idealization was Nature itself. The fertility of the Tropics was astonishing even to Mediterranean eyes. Few had ever seen landscapes like those of the Caribbean and Central America. However, the line between description and idealization is almost impossible to draw. In describing Cuba, for example, Columbus refers to "trees of a thousand kinds . . . so tall they seem to touch the sky," sierras and high mountains "most beautiful and of a thousand shapes," nightingales and other birds, marvelous pine groves, fertile plains, and varieties of fruit (quoted in Honour 1976, 5). Columbus's friend, Peter Martyr, later used his descriptions to express a set of rich themes which resound across the centuries: "The inhabitants live in that Golden World of which old writers speak so much, wherein men lived simply and innocently, without enforcement of laws, without quarrelling, judges and libels, content only to satisfy Nature. . . . [There are] naked girls so beautiful that one might think he [sic] beheld those splendid naiads and nymphs of the fountains so much celebrated by the ancients" (quoted in Honour 1978, 6).

The key themes in this passage are worth identifying since they reappear in later variants of "the West and the Rest":

1 The Golden World, an Earthly Paradise;
2 the simple, innocent life;
3 the lack of developed social organization and civil society;
4 people living in a pure state of Nature;
5 the frank and open sexuality, the nakedness, the beauty of the women.

In these images and metaphors of the New World as an Earthly Paradise, a Golden Age, or Utopia, we can see a powerful European fantasy being constructed.

Sexual Fantasy

Sexuality was a powerful element in the fantasy which the West constructed, and the ideas of sexual innocence and experience, sexual domination and submissiveness, play out a complex dance in the discourse of "the West and the Rest."

When Captain Cook arrived in Tahiti in 1769, the same idyll of a sexual paradise was repeated all over again. The women were extremely beautiful, the vegetation lush and tropical, the life simple, innocent, and free; Nature nourished the people without the apparent necessity to work or cultivate; the sexuality was open and unashamed—untroubled by the burden of European guilt. The naturalist on Bougainville's voyage to the Pacific said that the Tahitians were "without vice, prejudice, needs or dissention and knew no other god but Love" (Moorhead 1968, 51). "In short," Joseph Banks, the gentleman-scientist who accompanied Cook, observed, "the scene that we saw was the truest picture of an Arcadia, of which we were going to be kings, that the imagination can form" (quoted in Moorhead 1987, 38). As Cook's biographer, J. C. Beaglehole, remarks: "They were standing on the beach of the dream-world already, they walked straight into the Golden Age and embraced their nymphs" (quoted in Moorhead 1968, 66). The West's contemporary image of tropical paradise and exotic holidays still owes much to this fantasy.

Popular accounts by other explorers, such as Amerigo Vespucci (1451–1512), were explicit—where Columbus had been more reticent—about the sexual dimension. New World people, Vespucci said, "lived according to Nature" and went naked and unashamed; "the women . . . remained attractive after childbirth, were libidinous, and enlarged the penises of their lovers with magic potions" (quoted in Honour 1976, 56).

The very language of exploration, conquest, and domination was strongly marked by gender distinctions and drew much of its subconscious force from sexual imagery. In "Europe," the colonizer stands bold and upright, a commanding male figure, his feet firmly planted on terra firma. Around him are the insignia of power: the standard of Their Catholic Majesties of Spain, surmounted by a cross; in his left hand, the astrolabe that guided him, the fruit of Western knowledge; behind him, the galleons, sails billowing. Vespucci presents an image of supreme mastery. Hulme comments that, "in line with existing European conventions, the 'new' continent was often allegorized as a woman"—here, naked, in a hammock, surrounded by the emblems of an exotic landscape: strange plants and animals and, above all, a cannibal feast (see Hulme 1986, xii).

Misrecognizing Difference

Said says that "the essence of Orientalism is the ineradicable distinction between Western superiority and Oriental inferiority" (Said 1985, 42). How was this strong marking of difference constructed?

Europeans were immediately struck by what they interpreted as the absence of government and civil society—the basis of all "civilization"—

among peoples of the New World. In fact, these peoples did have several, very different, highly elaborated social structures. The New World the Europeans discovered was already home to millions of people who had lived there for centuries, whose ancestors had migrated to America from Asia across the neck of land which once connected the two continents. It is estimated that sixteen million people were living in the Western Hemisphere when the Spanish "discovered" it. The highest concentration was in Mexico, while only about a million lived in North America. They had very different standards and styles of life. The Pueblo of Central America were village people. Others were hunter-gatherers on the plains and in the forests. The Arawaks of the Caribbean islands had a relatively simple type of society based on subsistence farming and fishing. Farther north, the Iroquois of the Carolinas were fierce, nomadic hunters.

The high civilization of the Maya, with its dazzling white cities, was based on a developed agriculture; it was stable, literate, and composed of a federation of nations, with a complex hierarchy of government. The civilizations of the Aztecs (Mexico) and the Inca (Peru) were both large, complex affairs, based on maize cultivation and with a richly developed art, culture, and religion. Both had a complex social structure and a centralized administrative system, and both were capable of extraordinary engineering feats. Their temples outstripped in size anything in Europe, and the Royal Road of the Incas ran for nearly two thousand miles through mountainous terrain— farther than the extent of the Roman Empire from York to Jerusalem (see Newby 1975, 95–97).

These were functioning societies. What they were not was "European." What disturbed Western expectations, what had to be negotiated and explained, was their *difference*. As the centuries passed, Europeans came to know more about the specific characteristics of different "native American" peoples. Yet, in everyday terms, they persisted in describing them *all* as "Indians," lumping all distinctions together and suppressing differences in one, inaccurate stereotype (see Berkhofer 1978).

Another illustration of the inability to deal with difference is provided by Captain Cook's early experience of Tahiti (1769). The Englishmen knew that the Tahitians held property communally and that they were therefore unlikely to possess a European concept of "theft." In order to win over the natives, the crew showered them with gifts. Soon, however, the Tahitians began to help themselves. At first, the pilfering amused the visitors. But when the natives snatched Banks's spyglass and snuffbox, he threatened them with his musket until they were returned. Cook's crew continued to be plagued by incidents like this. A similar misunderstanding was to lead to Cook's death at the hands of the Hawaiians, in 1779.

The first actual contact with local inhabitants was often through an exchange of gifts, quickly followed by a more regular system of trade. Eventually, of course, this trade was integrated into a whole commercial system organized by Europe. Many early illustrations represent the inauguration of these unequal exchanges.

In Theodor de Bry's famous engraving of Columbus being greeted by the Indians, Columbus adopts a familiar heroic pose. On the left, the Cross is being planted. The natives (looking rather European) come bearing gifts and offering them in a gesture of welcome. As Columbus noted in his logbook, the natives were "marvellously friendly towards us." "In fact," he says, disarmingly, "they very willingly traded everything they had" (Columbus 1969, 55). Subsequent illustrations showed the Indians laboring to produce gold and sugar (described by the caption as a "gift") *for* the Spaniards.

The behavior of the Europeans was governed by the complex understandings and norms which regulated their own systems of monetary exchange, trade, and commerce. Europeans assumed that, since the natives did not have such an economic system, they therefore had no system at all and offered gifts as a friendly and suppliant gesture to visitors whose natural superiority they instantly recognized. The Europeans therefore felt free to organize the continuous supply of such "gifts" for their own benefit. What the Europeans found difficult to comprehend was that the exchange of gifts was part of a highly complex, but different, set of social practices—the practices of reciprocity—which only had meaning within a certain cultural context. Caribbean practices were different from, though as intricate in their social meaning and effects as, the norms and practices of European exchange and commerce.

Rituals of Degradation

The image of the cannibal feast in these early representations points to a set of themes, evident from the first contact, which were, in fact, the reverse side—the exact opposites—of the themes of innocence, idyllic simplicity, and proximity to Nature discussed earlier. It was as if everything which Europeans represented as attractive and enticing about the natives could also be used to represent the exact opposite: their barbarous and depraved character. One account of Vespucci's voyages brought these two sides together in the same passage: "The people are thus naked . . . well-formed in body, their heads, necks, arms, privy part, feet of women and men slightly covered with feathers. No one owns anything but all things are in common. . . . The men have as wives those that please them, be they mothers, sisters or friends. . . . They also fight with each other. They also eat each other" (quoted in Honour 1976, 8).

There were disturbing reversals being executed in the discourse here. The innocent, friendly people in their hammocks could also be exceedingly unfriendly, and hostile. Living close to Nature meant that they had no developed culture—and were therefore "uncivilized." Welcoming to visitors, they could also fiercely resist, and had warlike rivalries with other tribes. (The New World was no freer of rivalry, competition, conflict, war and violence than the Old.) Beautiful nymphs and naiads could also be "warlike and savage." At a moment's notice, Paradise could turn into "barbarism." Both versions of the discourse operated simultaneously. They may seem to negate each other, but it is more accurate to think of them as *mirror images*. Both were exaggerations, founded on stereotypes, feeding off each other. Each required the other. They were in opposition but systematically related: part of what Foucault calls a "system of dispersion."

From the beginning, *some* people described the natives of the New World as "lacking both the power of reason and the knowledge of God," as "beasts in human form." It is hard, they said, to believe God had created a race so obstinate in its viciousness and bestiality. The sexuality which fed the fantasies of some outraged many others. The natives were more addicted, it was said, to incest, sodomy, and licentiousness than any other race. They had no sense of justice, were bestial in their customs and inimical to religion. The characteristic which condensed all this into a single image was their (alleged) consumption of human flesh.

The question of cannibalism represents a puzzle which has never been resolved. Human sacrifice—which may have included cannibalism—was associated with some religious rituals. There may have been ritual sacrifice, involving some cannibalism, of captured enemies. But careful reviews of the relevant literature now suggest that the hard evidence is much sketchier and more ambiguous than has been assumed. The extent of any cannibalism was considerably exaggerated: it was frequently attributed by one tribe to "other people"—who were rivals or enemies. Much of what is offered as having been witnessed firsthand turns out to be second- or thirdhand reports; the practice had usually just ended months before the European visitors arrived. The evidence that, as a normal matter, of course, outside ritual occasions, New World Indians regularly sat down to an evening meal composed of juicy limbs of their fellow humans is extremely thin. (See, for example, the extensive analysis of the anthropological literature in Arens 1978.)

Peter Hulme (1986) offers a convincing account of how cannibalism became the prime symbol or signifier of "barbarism," thus helping to fix certain stereotypes. Columbus reported (January 13, 1493) that in Hispaniola he met a warlike group, whom he judged "must be one of the Caribs who eat men" (Columbus 1969, 40). The Spanish divided the natives into two distinct groupings: the "peaceful" Arawaks and the "warlike" Caribs. The latter were said to invade Arawak territory, steal their wives, resist conquest, and be "cannibals." What started as a way of describing a social group turned out to be a way of "establishing which Amerindians were prepared to accept the Spaniards on the latter's terms, and which were hostile, that is to say prepared to defend their territory and way of life" (Hulme 1986, 72).

In fact, so entrenched did the idea become that the "fierce" Caribs were eaters of human flesh that their ethnic name (Carib) came to be used to refer to anyone thought guilty of this behavior. As a result, we today have the word "cannibal," which is actually derived from the name "Carib."

Summary: Stereotypes, Dualism, and "Splitting"

We can now try to draw together our sketch of the formation and modes of operation of this discourse or "system of representation" we have called "the West and the Rest."

Hugh Honour, who studied European images of America from the period of discovery onward, has remarked that "Europeans increasingly tended to see in America an idealized or distorted image of their own countries, onto which they could project their own aspirations and fears, their self-confidence and . . . guilty despair" (1976, 3). We have identified some of these *discursive strategies* in this section. They are:

1 idealization;
2 the projection of fantasies of desire and degradation;
3 the failure to recognize and respect difference; and
4 the tendency to impose European categories and norms, to see difference through the modes of perception and representation of the West.

These strategies were all underpinned by the process known as *stereotyping*. A stereotype is a one-sided description which results from the collapsing of complex differences into a simple "cardboard cut-out." Different characteristics are run together or condensed into one. This exaggerated simplification is then attached to a subject or place. Its characteristics become the signs, the "evidence" by which the subject is known. They define its being, its *essence*. Hulme noted that,

> as always, the stereotype operates principally through a judicious combination of adjectives, which establish [certain] characteristics as [if they were] eternal verities ["truths"], immune from the irrelevancies of the historical moment: [e.g.,] "ferocious," "warlike," "hostile," "truculent and vindictive"—these are present as innate characteristics, irrespective of circumstances. . . . [Consequently, the Caribs] were locked as "cannibals" into a realm of "beingness" that lies beyond question. This stereotypical dualism has proved stubbornly immune to all kinds of contradictory evidence. (1986, 49–50)

By "*stereotypical dualism*," Hulme means that the stereotype is split into two opposing elements. These are two key features of the discourse of "the Other":

1 First, several characteristics are collapsed into one simplified figure which stands for or represents the essence of the people; this is stereotyping.
2 Second, the stereotype is split into two halves—its "good" and "bad" sides; this is "splitting," or *dualism*.

Far from the discourse of "the West and the Rest" being unified and monolithic, "splitting" is a regular feature of it. The world is first divided, symbolically, into good/bad, us/them, attractive/disgusting, civilized/uncivilized, the West/the Rest. All the other, many differences between and within these two halves are collapsed, simplified—i.e., stereotyped. By this strategy, the Rest becomes defined as everything that the West is not—its mirror image. It is represented as absolutely, essentially different, *other*: the Other. This Other is then itself split into two "camps": friendly/hostile, Arawak/Carib, innocent/depraved, noble/ignoble.

"In the Beginning, All the World Was America"

Writing about the use of stereotypes in the discourse of "the Other," Sander Gilman argues that "these systems are inherently bi-polar [i.e., polarized into two parts], generating pairs of antithetical signifiers [i.e., words with apparently opposing meanings]. This is how the deep structure of the stereotype reflects the social and political ideologies of the time" (1985, 27). He goes on to say:

> With the split of both the self and the world into "good" and "bad" objects, the "bad" self is distanced and identified with the mental representation of the "bad" object. This act of projection saves the self from any confrontation with the contradictions present in the necessary integration of "bad" and "good" aspects of the self. The deep structure of our own sense of self and the world is built upon the illusionary [sic] image of the world divided into two camps, "us" and "them." "They" are either "good" or "bad." (17)

The example Gilman gives is that of the "noble" versus the "ignoble savage." In this section, we examine the "career" of this stereotype. How did it function in the discourse of "the West and the Rest"? What was its influence on the birth of modern social science?

Are They "True Men"?

The question of how the natives and nations of the New World should be treated in the evolving colonial system was directly linked to the question of what sort of people and societies they were—which in turn depended on the West's knowledge of them, on how they were represented. Where did the Indians stand in the order of Creation? Where were their nations placed in the order of civilized societies? Were they "true men [sic]"? Were they made in God's image? The point was vital because if they were "true men," they could not be enslaved. The Greek philosophers argued that man (women rarely figured in these debates) was a special creation, endowed with the divine gift of reason; the Church taught that man was receptive to divine grace. Did the Indians' way of life, their lack of "civilization," mean that they were so low on the scale of humanity as to be incapable of reason and faith?

The debate raged for most of the fifteenth century. Ferdinand and Isabella issued decrees saying that "a certain people called Cannibals" and "any, whether called cannibals or not, who were not docile" could be enslaved.

One view was that "they probably descended from another Adam . . . born after the deluge and . . . perhaps have no souls" (see Honour 1978, 58). However, Bartolomé de Las Casas (1474–1566), the priest who made himself the champion of the Indians, protested vigorously at the brutality of the Spaniards in putting Indians to work as forced labor. Indians, he insisted, *did* have their own laws, customs, civilization, and religion, and were "true men" whose cannibalism was much exaggerated. "All men," Las Casas claimed, "however barbarous and bestial, . . . necessarily possess the faculty of Reason" (quoted in Honour 1978, 59). The issue was formally debated before Emperor Charles X at Valladolid in 1550.

One paradoxical outcome of Las Casas's campaign was that he got Indian slavery outlawed, but was persuaded to accept the alternative of replacing Indians with African slaves, and so the door opened to the horrendous era of New World African slavery. A debate similar to that about the Indians was held about African slavery prior to Emancipation (1834). The charter of the Royal Africa Company, which organized the English slave trade, defined slaves as "commodities." As slavery expanded, a series of codes was constructed for the Spanish, French, and English colonies governing the status and conduct of slaves. These codes defined the slave as a chattel— literally, "a thing," not a person. This was a problem for some churches. But in the British colonies, the Church of England, which was identified with the planters, accommodated itself to this definition without too much difficulty and made little effort to convert slaves until the eighteenth century. Later, however, the dissenters in the antislavery movement advocated abolition precisely because every slave *was* "a man and brother" (C. Hall 1991).

"Noble" versus "Ignoble Savages"

Another variant of the same argument can be found in the debate about the "noble" versus the "ignoble savage." The English poet John Dryden provides one of the famous images of the "noble savage":

> I am as free as Nature first made man,
> E're the base Laws of Servitude began,
> When wild in woods the noble Savage ran.
> > (*The Conquest of Granada*, Vol. 1, I.i.207–209)

Earlier, the French philosopher Montaigne, in his essay "Des Cannibales" (1580), had placed his noble savage in America. The idea quickly took hold on the European imagination. The famous painting of "The Different Nations of America" by Le Brun in Louis XIV's (1638–1715) Versailles Palace was dominated by a "heroic" representation of an American Indian—grave, tall, proud, independent, statuesque, and naked (see Honour 1978, 118). Paintings and engravings of American Indians dressed like ancient Greeks or Romans became popular. Many paintings of Cook's death portrayed both Cook and the natives who killed him in "heroic" mold. As Beaglehole explains, the Pacific voyages gave new life and impetus to the idealization of the "noble savage," who "entered the study and drawing room of Europe in naked majesty, to shake the preconceptions of morals and polities" (quoted in Moorhead 1987, 62). Idealized "savages" spoke on stage in ringing tones and exalted verse. The eponymous hero in Aphra Behn's novel *Oroonoko* (1688) was one of the few "noble" Africans (as opposed to American Indians) in seventeenth-century literature and was fortunate enough to have "long hair, a Roman nose and shapely mouth."

"Heroic savages" have peopled adventure stories, westerns, and other Hollywood and television films ever since, generating an unending series of images of "the Noble Other."

The "noble savage" also acquired sociological status. In 1749, the French philosopher Rousseau produced an account of his ideal form of society: simple, unsophisticated man living in a state of Nature, unfettered by laws, government, property, or social divisions. "The savages of North America," he later said in *The Social Contract*, "still retain today this method of government, and they are very well governed" (Rousseau 1968, 114). Tahiti was the perfect fulfilment of this preconceived idea, "one of those unseen stars which eventually came to light after the astronomers have proved that it must exist" (Moorhead 1987, 62).

The French Pacific explorer Bougainville (1729–1811) had been captivated by the way of life on Tahiti. Diderot, the philosopher and editor of the *Encyclopédie*, wrote a famous *Supplement* about Bougainville's voyage, warning Tahitians against the West's intrusion into their innocent happiness. "One day," he prophesied correctly, "they [Europeans] will come, with crucifix in one hand and the dagger in the other to cut your throats or to force you to accept their customs and opinions" (quoted in Moorhead 1987). Thus the "noble savage" became the vehicle for a wide-ranging critique of the overrefinement, religious hypocrisy and divisions by social rank that existed in the West.

This was only one side of the story. For, at the same time, the opposite image—that of the "ignoble savage"—was becoming the vehicle for a profound reflection in European intellectual circles on the nature of social development. There were eighteenth-century figures, such as Horace Walpole, Edmund Burke, and Dr. Johnson, who poured scorn on the idea of the noble savage. Ronald Meek has remarked that contemporary notions of savagery influenced eighteenth-century social science by generating a critique of society through the idea of the *noble* savage: "It is not quite so well known . . . that they also stimulated the emergence of a new theory of the development of society through the idea of the *ignoble* savage" (Meek 1976, 2).

The questions which concerned the social philosophers were: What had led the West to its high point of refinement and civilization? Did the West evolve from the same simple beginnings as "savage society," or were there different paths to "civilization"?

Many of the precursors and leading figures of the Enlightenment participated in this debate. Thomas Hobbes, the political philosopher, argued in *Leviathan* (1651) that it was because of their lack of "industry . . . and consequently no culture of the earth, no navigation, nor use of commodities" that "the savage people in many places of America . . . live at this day in [their] brutish manner" (Hobbes 1946, 82–83). The English satirist Bernard Mandeville, in his *Fable of the Bees* (1723), identified a series of "steps" or stages in which economic factors like the division of labor, money, and the invention of tools played the major part in the progress from "savagery" to "civilization." The philosopher John Locke claimed that the New World provided a prism through which one could see "a pattern of the first ages in Asia and Europe"—the origins from which Europe had developed. "In the beginning," Locke said, "all the World was America" (1976, 26). He meant by this that the world (i.e., the West) had evolved from a stage very much like that discovered in America—unfilled, undeveloped, and uncivilized. America was the "childhood of mankind," Locke claimed, and Indians should be classed with "children, idiots and illiterates because of their inability to reason in abstract, speculative . . . terms" (quoted in Marshall and Williams 1982, 192).

The History of "Rude" and "Refined" Nations

The "noble-ignoble" and the "rude-refined" oppositions belonged to the same discursive formation. This "West and the Rest" discourse greatly influenced Enlightenment thinking. It provided the framework of images in which Enlightenment social philosophy matured. Enlightenment thinkers believed that there was *one* path to civilization and social development, and that all societies could be ranked or placed early or late, lower or higher, on the same scale. The emerging "science of society" was the study of the forces which had propelled all societies, by stages, along this single path of development, leaving some, regrettably, at its "lowest" stage—represented by the American savage—while others advanced to the summit of civilized development, represented by the West.

This idea of a universal criterion of progress modeled on the West became a feature of the new "social science" to which the Enlightenment gave birth. For example, when Edmund Burke wrote to the Scottish Enlightenment historian William Robertson on the publication of his *History of America* (1777), he said that "the great map of Mankind is unrolled at once, and there is no state or gradation of barbarism, and no mode of refinement which we have not at the same moment under our view; the very different civility of Europe and China; the barbarism of Persia and of Abyssinia; the erratic manners of Tartary and of Arabia; the savage state of North America and of New Zealand" (quoted by Meek 1976, 173). Enlightenment social science reproduced within its own conceptual framework many of the preconceptions and stereotypes of the discourse of "the West and the Rest."

The examples are too voluminous to refer to in detail. Meek argues that "no one who reads the work of the French and Scottish pioneers [of social science] of the 1750s can fail to notice that all of them, without exception, were very familiar with the contemporary studies of the Americans; that most of them had evidently pondered deeply about their significance and that some were almost obsessed by them. . . . The studies of Americans provided the new social scientists with a plausible working hypothesis about the basic characteristics of the 'first' or 'earliest' stage of socio-economic development" (1976, 128). Many of the leading names of the French Enlightenment— Diderot, Montesquieu, Voltaire, Turgot, Rousseau—used the studies of early American Indians in this way.

This is also the case with the Scottish Enlightenment. In Adam Smith's *Theory of the Moral Sentiments* (1759), American Indians are used as the pivot for elaborate contrasts between "civilized nations" and "savages and barbarians." They are also pivotal in Henry Kames's *Sketches of the History of Man* (1774), John Millar's *Origin of the Distinction of Ranks* (1771), and Adam Ferguson's *Essay on the History of Civil Society* (1767).

The contribution which this debate about "rude-refined nations" made to social science was not simply descriptive. It formed part of a larger theoretical framework, about which the following should be noted:

1 It represented a decisive movement away from mythological, religious, and other "causes" of social evolution to what are clearly recognizable as material causes—sociological, economic, environmental, etc.

2 It produced the idea that the history of "mankind" [*sic*] occurred along a single continuum, divided into a series of stages.

3 Writers differed over precisely which material or sociological factors they believed played the key role in propelling societies through these stages. But one factor assumed increasing importance—the "mode of subsistence":

> In its most specific form, the theory was that society had "naturally" or "normally" progressed over time through four more or less distinct and consecutive stages, each corresponding to a different mode of subsistence, these stages being defined as hunting, pasturage, agriculture and commerce. To each of these modes of subsistence . . . there corresponded different sets of ideas and institutions relating to law, property, and government and also different sets of customs, manners and morals. (Meek 1976, 2)

Here, then, is a surprising twist. The Enlightenment aspired to be a "science of man." It was the matrix of modern social science. It provided the language in which "modernity" first came to be defined. In Enlightenment discourse, the West was the model, the prototype, and the measure of social progress. It was *Western* progress, civilization, rationality, and development that were celebrated. And yet, all this depended on the discursive figures of the "noble versus ignoble savage," and of "rude and refined nations" which had been formulated in the discourse of "the West and the Rest." So the Rest was critical for the formation of Western Enlightenment—and therefore for modern social science. Without the Rest (or its own internal "others"), the West would not have been able to recognize and represent itself as the summit of human history. The figure of "the Other," banished to the edge of the conceptual world and constructed as the absolute opposite, the negation, of everything which the West stood for, reappeared at the very center of the discourse of civilization, refinement, modernity, and development in the West. "The Other" was the "dark" side—forgotten, repressed, and denied, and the reverse image of enlightenment and modernity.

From "the West and the Rest" to Modern Sociology

In response to this argument, you may find yourself saying, "Yes, perhaps the early stages of the 'science of man' *were* influenced by the discourse of 'the West and the Rest.' But all that was a long time ago. Since then, social science has become more empirical, more 'scientific.' Sociology today is, surely, free of such 'loaded images'?" But this is not necessarily the case. Discourses don't stop abruptly. They go on unfolding, changing shape, as they make sense of new circumstances. They often carry many of the same unconscious premises and unexamined assumptions in their bloodstream.

For example, readers may have recognized in the Enlightenment concept of "modes of subsistence" the outline of an idea which Karl Marx (1818–1883), a "founding father" of modern sociology, was subsequently to develop into one of the most powerful sociological tools: his theory that society is propelled forward by the class struggle, that it progresses through a series of stages marked by different modes of production, the critical one for capitalism being the transition from feudalism to capitalism. Of course, there is considerable divergence between the Enlightenment's "four stages of subsistence" and Marx's "modes of production." But there are also some surprising similarities. In his *Grundrisse*, Marx speaks in broad outlines of the Asiatic, ancient, feudal, and capitalist or bourgeois modes of production. He argues that each is dominated by a particular social class which expropriates the economic surplus through a specific set of social relations. The Asiatic mode (which is only sketchily developed) is that to which, in Marx's view, countries such as China, India, and those of Islam belong. It is characterized by: (a) stagnation, (b) an absence of dynamic class struggle, and (c) the dominance of a swollen state acting as a sort of universal landlord. The conditions for capitalist development are here absent. Marx hated the capitalist system; nevertheless, he saw it, in contrast with the Asiatic mode, as progressive and dynamic, sweeping old structures aside, driving social development forward.

There are some interesting parallels here with Max Weber (1864–1920), another of sociology's founding fathers. Weber used a very dualistic model which contrasted Islam with western Europe in terms of modern social development. For Weber, the essential conditions for the transition to capitalism and modernity were: (a) ascetic forms of religion, (b) rational forms of law, (c) free labor, and (d) the growth of cities. All these, in his view, were missing from Islam, which he represented as a "mosaic" of tribes and groups, never cohering into a proper social system but existing under a despotic rule which absorbed social conflicts in an endlessly repeating cycle of factional struggles, with Islam as its monolithic religion. Power and privilege, Weber believed, had been kept within, and rotated between, the ruling Islamic families, who merely syphoned off the wealth through taxation. He called this a "patrimonial" or "prebendary" form of authority. Unlike feudalism, it did not provide the preconditions for capitalist accumulation and growth.

These are, of course, some of the most complex and sophisticated models in sociology. The question of the causes and preconditions for the development of capitalism in the West have preoccupied historians and social scientists for centuries.

However, it has been argued by some social scientists that *both* Marx's notion of the "Asiatic" mode of production and Weber's "patrimonial" form of domination contain traces of, or have been deeply penetrated by, "Orientalist" assumptions. Or, to put it in our terms, both models provide evidence that the discourse of "the West and the Rest" is still at work in some of the conceptual categories, the stark oppositions and the theoretical dualisms of modern sociology.

In his studies of *Weber and Islam* (1974) and *Marx and the End of Orientalism* (1978), Bryan Turner has argued that both sociology and Marxism have been unduly influenced by "Orientalist" categories, or, if you lift the argument out of its Middle Eastern and Asian context, by the discourse of "the West and the Rest":

> This can be seen . . . in Weber's arguments about the decline of Islam, its despotic political structure and the absence of autonomous cities. . . . Weber employs a basic dichotomy between the feudal economies of the West and the prebendal/patrimonial political economies of the East. . . . [He] overlays this discussion . . . with two additional components which have become the staples of the *internalist* version of development—the "Islamic ethic" and the absence of an entrepreneurial urban bourgeoisie. (Turner 1978, 7, 45–46; emphasis in original)

Marx's explanation of the lack of capitalist development in the East is very different from Weber's. But his notion that this was due to the "Asiatic mode of production" takes a similar path. Turner summarizes Marx's argument thus:

> Societies dominated by the "Asiatic" mode of production have no internal class conflicts and are consequently trapped within a static social context.

The social system lacks a basic ingredient of social change, namely class struggle between landlords and an exploited peasantry. . . . [For example,] "Indian society has no history at all." (1978, 26–27)

Despite their differences, both Weber and Marx organize their arguments in terms of broad, simple, contrasting oppositions which mirror quite closely the West-Rest, civilized-rude, developed-backward oppositions of "the West and the Rest" discourse. Weber's is an "internalist" type of explanation because "he treats the main problems of 'backward societies' as a question of certain characteristics *internal* to societies, considered in isolation from any international societal context" (Turner 1978, 10; emphasis in original). Marx's explanation also looks like an "internalist" one. But he adds certain "externalist" features. By "externalist," we mean "relating to a theory of development which identifies the main problems facing 'developing' societies as external to the society itself, which is treated as a unit located within a structured international context" (Turner 1978, 11). In this chapter, we have adopted an "externalist" or "global" rather than a purely "internalist" account of the rise of the idea of the West.

However, these additional features of Marx's argument lead his explanation in a very surprising direction. "Asiatic"-type societies, he argues, cannot develop into modern ones because they lack certain preconditions. Therefore, "only the introduction of dynamic elements of Western capitalism" can trigger development. This makes "capitalist colonialism" a (regrettable) historical necessity for these societies, since it alone can "destroy the pre-capitalist modes which prevent them from entering a progressive historical path." Capitalism, Marx argues, must expand to survive, drawing the whole world progressively into its net, and it is this expansion which "revolutionizes and undermines pre-capitalist modes of production at the periphery of the capitalist world" (Turner 1978, 11). Many classical Marxists have indeed argued that, however stunting and destructive it may have been, the expansion of Western capitalism through conquest and colonization was historically inevitable and would have long-term progressive outcomes for "the Rest."

Earlier, we discussed some of the forces which pushed a developing western Europe to expand outward into "new worlds." But whether this was inevitable, whether its effects have been socially progressive, and whether this was the only possible path to "modernity" are subjects increasingly debated in the social sciences today (Hall et al. 1992). In many parts of the world, the expansion of Western colonization has *not* destroyed the precapitalist barriers to development. It has conserved and reinforced them. Colonization and imperialism have not promoted economic and social development in these societies, most of which remain profoundly underdeveloped. Where development has taken place, it has often been of the "dependent" variety.

The destruction of alternative ways of life has *not* ushered in a new social order in these societies. Many remain in the grip of feudal ruling families, religious elites, military cliques, and dictators who govern societies beset by endemic poverty. The destruction of indigenous cultural life by Western culture is, for most of them, a very mixed blessing. And as the human, cultural, and ecological consequences of this form of "Western development" become more obvious, the question of whether there is only one path to modernity is being debated with increasing urgency. The historically inevitable and necessarily progressive character of the West's expansion into the Rest is no longer as obvious as perhaps it once seemed to Western scholars.

We must leave these issues as open questions at this stage. However, this is a useful point to summarize the main thrust of the argument of this chapter.

Conclusion

Conventional perspectives on these issues focus on the distinctive form of society which we call "modern" emerged, and on the major processes which led to its formation. They also look at the emergence of the distinctive form of knowledge which accompanied that society's formation—at what the Enlightenment called the "sciences of man," which provided the framework within which modern social science and the idea of "modernity" were formulated. On the whole, their emphasis is "internalist." The story is largely framed from within western Europe (the West), where these processes of formation first emerged.

This chapter reminds us that this formation was also a "global" process. It had crucial "externalist" features—aspects which could not be explained without taking into account the rest of the world, where these processes were not at work and where these kinds of society did not emerge. This is a huge topic in its own right, and I could tell only a small part of the story here. I could have focused on the economic, political, and social consequences of the global expansion of the West; instead, I briefly sketched the outline history of that expansion, up to roughly the eighteenth century. I also wanted to show the *cultural* and *ideological* dimensions of the West's expansion. For if the Rest was necessary for the political, economic, and social formation of the West, it was also essential to the West's formation both of its own sense of itself—a "Western identity"—and of Western forms of knowledge.

This is where the notion of "discourse" came in. A discourse is a way of talking about or representing something. It produces knowledge that shapes perceptions and practice. It is part of the way in which power operates. Therefore, it has consequences for both those who employ it and those who are "subjected" to it. The West produced many different ways of talking about itself and "the Others." But what we have called the discourse of "the West and the Rest" became one of the most powerful and formative of these discourses. It became the dominant way in which, for many decades, the West represented itself and its relation to "the Other." In this chapter, I have traced how this discourse was formed and how it worked. We analyzed it as a "system of representation"—a "regime of truth."

In transformed and reworked forms, this discourse continues to inflect the language of the West, its image of itself and "others," its sense of "us" and "them," its practices and relations of power toward the Rest. It is especially important for the languages of racial inferiority and ethnic superiority which still operate so powerfully across the globe today. So, far from being a "formation" of the past, and of only historical interest, the discourse of "the West and the Rest" is alive and well in the modern world. And one of the surprising places where its effects can still be seen is in the language, theoretical models, and hidden assumptions of modern sociology itself.

REFERENCES

Abercrombie, N., S. Hill, and B. S. Turner, eds. 1988. *The Penguin Dictionary of Sociology.* 2nd ed. Harmondsworth: Penguin.

Arens, W. 1977. *The Man-Eating Myth: Anthropology and Anthropophagy.* New York: Oxford University Press.

Asad, T. 1973. *Anthropology and the Colonial Encounter.* London: Ithaca Press.

Barker, A. J. 1978. *The African Link: British Attitudes to the Negro in the Era of the Atlantic Slave Trade, 1550–1807.* London: Frank Cass.

Baudet, H. 1963. *Paradise on Earth: European Images of Non-European Man.* New Haven, CT: Yale University Press.

Beaglehole, J. C., ed. 1961. *The Journals of Captain Cook on His Voyages of Discovery.* Vol. 2. Cambridge: Cambridge University Press.

Berkhofer, R. 1978. *The White Man's Indian: Images of the American Indian from Columbus to the Present.* New York: Knopf.

Chiappelli, F., ed. 1978. *First Images of America: The Impact of the New World.* 2 vols. Berkeley: University of California Press.

Columbus, C. 1969. *The Four Voyages of Christopher Columbus.* Edited by J. M. Cohen. Harmondsworth: Penguin.

Cousins, M., and A. Hussain. 1984. *Michel Foucault.* London: Macmillan.

Dryden, J. 1978. *The Works of John Dryden.* Vol. 11. Berkeley: University of California Press.

Fairchild, H. 1961. *The Noble Savage: A Study in Romantic Naturalism.* New York: Russell and Russell.

Foucault, M. 1972. *The Archaeology of Knowledge.* London: Tavistock.

Foucault, M. 1980. *Power/Knowledge.* Brighton: Harvester.

Gilman, S. 1985. *Difference and Pathology: Stereotypes of Sexuality, Race, and Madness.* Ithaca, NY: Cornell University Press.

Hakluyt, R. 1972. *Voyages and Discoveries.* Harmondsworth: Penguin.

Hale, J. R., et al. 1966. *Age of Exploration.* New York: Time-Life International.

Hall, C. 1991. "Missionary Positions." In *Cultural Studies Now and in the Future,* ed. L. Grossberg and C. Nelson. London: Routledge.

Hall, S., D. Held, and A. McGrew, eds. 1992. *Modernity and Its Futures.* Cambridge: Polity Press.

Harris, M. 1977. *Cannibals and Kings: The Origins of Cultures.* New York: Random House.

Hobbes, T. 1946. *Leviathan.* Oxford: Blackwell.

Honour, H. 1976. *The New Golden Land: European Images of America.* London: Allen Lane.

Hulme, P. 1986. *Colonial Encounters: Europe and the Native Caribbean, 1492–1797.* London: Methuen.

Jennings, F. 1976. *The Invasion of America: Indians, Colonialism, and the Cant of Conquest.* New York: W. W. Norton.

Joppien, R., and B. Smith. 1985. *The Art of Captain Cook's Voyages.* 2 vols. New Haven, CT: Yale University Press.

Latham, R., ed. 1958. *Marco Polo: The Travels.* Harmondsworth: Penguin.

Léon-Portilla, M. 1962. *The Broken Spears: The Aztec Account of the Conquest of Mexico.* London: Constable.

Locke, J. 1976. *The Second Treatise on Government.* Oxford: Basil Blackwell.

Mandeville, B. 1924. *The Fable of the Bees.* Oxford: Clarendon Press.

Mandeville, Sir J. 1964. *The Travels.* New York: Dover.

Mann, M. 1988. "European Development: Approaching a Historical Explanation." In *Europe and the Rise of Capitalism,* ed. J. Baechler et al. Oxford: Blackwell.

Marshall, P., and G. Williams. 1982. *The Great Map of Mankind: British Perceptions of the World in the Age of the Enlightenment.* London: Dent.

Marx, K. 1964. *Precapitalist Economic Formations.* Edited by E. J. Hobsbawm. London: Lawrence and Wishart.

Marx, K. 1973. *Grundrisse.* Harmondsworth: Pelican.

Meek, R. 1976. *Social Science and the Ignoble Savage*. Cambridge: Cambridge University Press.

Montaigne, M. 1964. *Selected Essays*. Boston: Houghton Mifflin.

Moorhead, A. 1987. *The Fatal Impact: An Account of the Invasion of the South Pacific, 1767–1840*. Harmondsworth: Penguin.

Newby, E. 1975. *The Mitchell Beazley World Atlas of Exploration*. London: Mitchell Beazley.

Parry, J. H., ed. 1968. *The European Reconnaissance: Selected Documents*. New York: Harper and Row.

Parry, J. H. 1971. *Trade and Dominion: The European Oversea Empires in the Eighteenth Century*. London: Weidenfeld and Nicolson.

Roberts, J. M. 1985. *The Triumph of The West*. London: British Broadcasting Corporation.

Rousseau, J.-J. 1968. *The Social Contract*. Harmondsworth: Penguin.

Said, E. W. 1985. *Orientalism: Western Concepts of the Orient*. Harmondsworth: Penguin.

Sale, K. 1991. *The Conquest of Paradise: Christopher Columbus and the Columbian Legacy*. London: Hodder and Stoughton.

Schama, S. 1987. *The Embarrassment of Riches: An Interpretation of Dutch Culture*. New York: Knopf.

Smith, B. 1988. *European Vision and the South Pacific*. New Haven, CT: Yale University Press.

Turner, B. S. 1974. *Weber and Islam*. London: Routledge.

Turner, B. S. 1978. *Marx and the End of Orientalism*: London, Allen and Unwin.

Wallace, W. M. 1959. *Sir Walter Raleigh*. Princeton, NJ: Princeton University Press.

Williams, E. E. 1970. *From Columbus to Castro: The History of the Caribbean, 1492–1969*. London: André Deutsch.

Withey, L. 1987. *Voyages of Discovery: Captain Cook and the Exploration of the Pacific*. London: Hutchinson.

CHAPTER 6

The Formation of a Diasporic Intellectual:
An Interview with Stuart Hall by Kuan-Hsing Chen

KUAN-HSING CHEN: In your later work on race and ethnicity, diaspora seems to have become central, one of the critical sites in which the question of cultural identity is articulated; bits and pieces of your own diasporic experiences have been narrated powerfully in order to address both theoretical and political problematics.[1] What I am interested in is how the specificities of the various historical trajectories came to shape your diasporic experiences, your own intellectual and political position?

STUART HALL: I was born in Jamaica and grew up in a middle-class family. My father spent most of his working life in the United Fruit Company. He was the first Jamaican to be promoted in every job he had; before him, those jobs were occupied by people sent in from the head office in America. What's important to understand is both the class fractions and the color fractions from which my parents came. My father's and my mother's families were both middle class but from very different class formations. My father belonged to the colored lower-middle class. His father kept a drugstore in a poor village in the country outside Kingston. The family was ethnically very mixed—African, East Indian, Portuguese, Jewish. My mother's family was much fairer in color; indeed, if you had seen her uncle, you would have thought he was an English expatriate, nearly white, or what we would call "local white." She was adopted by an aunt, whose sons—one a lawyer, one a doctor—trained in England. She was brought up in a beautiful house on the hill, above a small estate where the family lived. Culturally present in my own family was therefore this lower-middle class, Jamaican country legacy, manifestly dark skinned, and then this lighter-skinned, English-oriented, plantation-oriented fraction.

So what was played out in my family, culturally, from the very beginning, was the conflict between the local and the imperial in the colonized context. Both these class fractions were opposed to the majority culture of poor Jamaican black people: highly race and color conscious, and identifying with the colonizers.

I was the blackest member of my family. The story in my family, which was always told as a joke, was that when I was born, my sister, who was much fairer than I, looked into the crib and she said, "Where did you get this coolie baby from?" Now, "coolie" is the abusive word in Jamaica for a poor East Indian, who was considered the lowest of the low. So she wouldn't say, "Where did you get this black baby from?," since it was unthinkable that she could have a black brother. But she *did* notice that I was a different color from her. This is very common in colored middle-class Jamaican families, because they are the product of mixed liaisons between African slaves and European slave-masters, and the children then come out in varying shades.

So I always had the identity in my family of being the one from the outside, the one who didn't fit, the one who was blacker than the others, "the little coolie." And I performed that role throughout. My friends at school, many of whom were from good middle-class homes but blacker in color than me, were not accepted at my home. My parents didn't think I was making the right kind of friends. They always encouraged me to mix with more middle-class, more higher-color friends, and I didn't. Instead, I withdrew emotionally from my family and met my friends elsewhere. My adolescence was spent continuously negotiating these cultural spaces.

My father wanted me to play sport. He wanted me to join the clubs that he joined. But I always thought that he himself did not quite fit in this world. He was negotiating his way into this world. He was accepted on sufferance by the English; I could see the way they patronized him. I hated that more than anything else. It wasn't just that he belonged to a world which I rejected. I couldn't understand how *he* didn't see how much they despised him. I said to myself, "Don't you understand when you go into that club they think you are an interloper?" And, "But you want to put me into that space, to be humiliated in the same way?"

Because my mother was brought up in this Jamaican plantation context, she thought she was practically "English." She thought England was the mother country; she identified with the colonial power. She had aspirations for us, her family, which materially we couldn't keep up with, but which she aspired to, culturally.

I'm trying to say that those classic colonial tensions were lived as part of my personal history. My own formation and identity was very much constructed out of a kind of refusal of the dominant and cultural models which were held up for me. I didn't want to beg my way like my father into acceptance by the American or English expatriate business community, and I couldn't identify with that old plantation world, with its roots in slavery, but which my mother spoke of as a "golden age." I felt much more like an independent Jamaican boy. But there was no room for that as a subjective position in the culture of my family.

Now, this is the period of the growth of the Jamaican independence movement. As a young student, I was very much in favor of that. I became anti-imperialist and identified with Jamaican independence. But my family was not. They were not even identified with the ambitions for independence of the national bourgeoisie. In that sense, they were different from even their own friends, who thought, once the transition to national independence began, "Well, at least we'll be in power." My parents, my mother especially, regretted the passing of that old colonial world more than anything else. This was a huge gap between their aspirations for me and how I identified myself.

KHC: So you are saying that your impulse to "revolt" partly came from the Jamaican situation. Can you elaborate?

SH: Going to school as a bright, promising scholar and becoming politically involved, I was therefore interested in what was going on politically, namely, the formation of Jamaican political parties, the emergence of the trade unions and the labor movement after 1938, the beginnings of a nationalist independence movement at the end of the war; all of these were part of the postcolonial or decolonizing revolution. Jamaica began to move toward independence once the war was over. So bright kids like me and my friends, of varying colors and social positions, were nevertheless caught up in that movement, and that's what we identified with. We were looking forward to the end of imperialism, Jamaica governing itself, self-autonomy for Jamaica.

KHC: What was your intellectual development during this early period?

SH: I went to a small primary school, then I went to one of the big colleges. Jamaica had a series of big girls' schools and boys' schools, strongly modeled after the English public school system. We took English high school exams, the normal Cambridge School Certificate, and A-level examinations. There were no local universities, so if you were going to university you would have to go abroad, off to Canada, the United States, or England to study. The curriculum was not yet indigenized. Only in my last two years did I learn anything about Caribbean history and geography. It was a very "classical" education: very good, but in very formal academic terms. I learned Latin, English history, English colonial history, European history, English literature, etc. But because of my political interest, I also became interested in other questions. In order to get a scholarship, you have to be older than eighteen, and I was rather younger, so I took the final A-level exam twice; I had three years in the sixth form. In the last year, I started to read T. S. Eliot, James Joyce, Freud, Marx, Lenin, and some of the surrounding literature and modern poetry. I got a wider reading than the usual, narrowly academic British-oriented education. But I was very much formed like a member of a colonial intelligentsia.

KHC: Can you recall any figure who influenced your intellectual development at that point in time?

SH: There was no single one. There was a whole series of them, and they did two things for me. First of all, they gave me a strong sense of self-confidence, of academic achievement. Second, they themselves being teachers were identified with these emerging nationalist tendencies. Although they were strongly academic and English oriented, they were also attentive to the rising Caribbean nationalist movement. So I learned a good deal about that from them. For instance, a Barbadian who studied at Codrington College taught me Latin and ancient history. A Scottish, ex-Corinthian footballer made me do the modern current affairs paper in my final history exam. The current affairs paper was about postwar history, about the war and afterwards, which wasn't taught formally. I learned for the first time about the Cold War, I learned about the Russian Revolution, about American politics. I became interested in international affairs and about Africa. He introduced me to certain political texts—though mainly to "inoculate" me against dangerous "Marxist" ideas. I devoured them. I belonged to a local library, called the Institute of Jamaica. We would go down there on Saturday mornings, and we would read books about slavery. It introduced me to Caribbean literature. I started to read Caribbean writers. Much of that time, I read on my own, trying to make sense of them, and dreaming of one day becoming a creative writer.

The war was very important to me. I was a child during the war; the war was a dominating experience. It's not that we were attacked or anything like that, but it was a real presence. I was very aware of that. I used to play games about the war and learned a lot about where these places were, about them. I learned about Asia following the American war in the Philippines. I learned about Germany. I just followed current historical events throughout the war. When I think back, I learned a lot just by looking at the maps about the war, about the invasion of the Far East, and playing "war games" with my friends (I was often a German general, and wore a monocle!).

KHC: How important was Marx, or the tradition of Marxist literature?

SH: Well, I read Marx's essays (*The Communist Manifesto*, *Wage Labour and Capital*), and I read Lenin on imperialism. It was important for me more in the context of colonialism than about Western capitalism. The questions of class were clearly present in the political conversation about colonialism going on in Jamaica, the question of poverty, the problem of economic development, etc. A lot of my young friends who went to university at the same time I did studied economics. Economics was supposed to be the answer to the poverty which countries like Jamaica experienced, as a consequence of imperialism and colonialism. So I was interested in the economic question from a colonial standpoint. If I had an ambition at that point, the ambition was not to go into business like my father, but to become a lawyer; becoming a lawyer was already, in Jamaica, a major route into politics. Or, I could become an economist. But actually, I was more interested in literature and history than in economics. When I was seventeen, my sister had a major nervous breakdown. She began a relationship with a young student doctor who had come to Jamaica from Barbados. He was middle class, but black, and my parents wouldn't allow it. There was a tremendous family row, and she, in effect, retreated from the situation into a breakdown. I was suddenly aware of the contradiction of a colonial culture, of how one lives out the color-class-colonial dependency experience and of how it could destroy you, subjectively.

I am telling this story because it was very important for my personal development. It broke down forever, for me, the distinction between the public and the private self. I learned about culture, first, as something which is deeply subjective and personal, and at the same moment as a structure you live. I could see that all these strange aspirations and identifications which my parents had projected onto us, their children, destroyed my sister. She was the victim, the bearer of the contradictory ambitions of my parents in this colonial situation. From then on, I could never understand why people thought these structural questions were not connected with the psychic—with emotions and identifications and feelings because, for me, those structures are things you live. I don't just mean they are personal, they are, but they are also institutional; they have real structural properties; they break you, destroy you.

It was a very traumatic experience, because there was little or no psychiatric help available in Jamaica at that time. My sister went through a series of ECT [electroconvulsive therapy] treatments given by a GP [general practitioner], from which she's never properly recovered. She never left home after that. She looked after my father until he died. Then she looked after my mother until she died. She took care of my brother, who became blind, until he died. That's a complete tragedy, which I lived through with her, and I decided I couldn't take it; I couldn't help her, I couldn't reach her, although I understood what was wrong. I was seventeen, eighteen.

But it crystallized my feelings about the space I was called into by my family. I was not going to stay there. I was not going to be destroyed by it. I had to get out. I felt that I must never put myself back into it, because I would be destroyed. When I look at the snapshots of myself in childhood and early adolescence, I see a picture of a depressed person. I don't want to be who they want me to be, but I don't know how to be somebody else. And I am depressed by that. All of that is the background to explain why I eventually migrated.

KHC: From then on, you maintained a very close relationship with your sister. Psychoanalytically speaking, you identified with her?

SH: No, not really. Though the whole system had messed up her life, she never revolted. So I revolted, in her place, as it were. I'm also guilty, because I left her behind to cope with it. My decision to emigrate was to save myself. She stayed.

I left in 1951, and I didn't know until 1957 that I wasn't going back; I never really intended to go back, though I didn't know it at the time. In a way, I am able to write about it now because I'm at the end of a long journey. Gradually, I came to recognize I was a black West Indian, just like everybody else; I could relate to that; I could write from and out of that position. It has taken a very long time, really, to be able to write in that way, personally. Previously, I was only able to write about it analytically. In that sense, it has taken me fifty years to come home. It wasn't so much that I had anything to conceal. It was the space I couldn't occupy, a space I had to learn to occupy.

You can see that this formation—learning the whole destructive, colonized experience—prepared me for England. I will never forget landing there. My mother brought me, in my felt hat, in my overcoat, with my steamer trunk. She brought me, as she thought, "home," on the banana boat, and delivered me to Oxford. She gave me to the astonished college scout and said, "There is my son, his trunks, his belongings. Look after him." She delivered me, signed and sealed, to where she thought a son of hers had always belonged—Oxford.

My mother was an overwhelmingly dominant person. My relationship with her was close and antagonistic. I hated what she stood for, what she tried to represent to me. But we all had a close bond with her, because she dominated our lives. She dominated my sister's life. It was compounded by the fact that my brother, who was the eldest, had very bad sight, and eventually went blind. From a very early age, he was very dependent on my parents. When I came along, this pattern of mother-son dependency was clearly established. They tried to repeat it with me. And when I began to have my own interests and my own positions, the antagonism started. At the same time, the relationship was intense, because my mother always said I was the only person who fought her. She wanted to dominate me, but she also despised those whom she dominated. So she despised my father because he would give in to her. She despised my sister, because she was a girl, and, as my mother said, women were not interesting. In adolescence, my sister fought her all along, but once my mother broke her, she despised her. So we had that relationship of antagonism. I was the youngest. She thought I was destined to oppose her, but she respected me for that. Eventually, when she knew what I had become in England—fulfilling all her most paranoid fantasies of the rebellious son—she didn't want me to come back to Jamaica, because by then I would have represented my own thing, rather than her image of me. She found out about my politics and said, "Stay over there. Don't come back here and make trouble for us with those funny ideas."

I felt easier in relation to Jamaica, once they were dead, because before that, when I went back, I had to negotiate Jamaica through them. Once my parents were dead, it was easier to make a relationship to the new Jamaica that emerged in the 1970s. This Jamaica was not where I had grown up. For one thing, it had become, culturally, a black society, a postslave, postcolonial society, whereas I had lived there at the end of the colonial era. So I could negotiate it as a "familiar stranger."

Paradoxically, I had exactly the same relationship to England. Having been prepared by the colonial education, I knew England from the inside. But I'm not and never will be "English." I know both places intimately, but I am not wholly of either place. And that's exactly the diasporic experience, far away enough to experience the sense of exile and loss, close enough to understand the enigma of an always-postponed "arrival."

It's interesting, in relation to Jamaica, because my close friends whom I left behind then went through experiences which I didn't. They lived 1968 there, the birth of black consciousness and the rise of Rastafarianism, with its memories of Africa. They lived those years in a different way from me, so I'm not of their generation either. I was at school with them, and I've kept in touch with them, but they have an entirely different experience from mine. Now that gap cannot be filled. You can't "go home" again.

So you have what Simmel talked about: the experience of being inside and outside, the "familiar stranger." We used to call that "alienation," or deracination. But nowadays it's come to be the archetypal late-modern condition. Increasingly, it's what everybody's life is like. So that's how I think about the articulation of the postmodern and the postcolonial. Postcoloniality, in a curious way, prepared one to live in a "postmodern" or diasporic relationship to identity. Paradigmatically, it's a diasporic experience. Since migration has turned out to be *the* world-historical event of late modernity, the classic postmodern experience turns out to be the diasporic experience.

KHC: But when was the diasporic experience registered, in a conscious way?

SH: In modern times, since 1492, with the onset of the "Euro-imperial" adventure—in the Caribbean, since European colonization and the slave trade—since that time, in the "contact zones" of the world, culture has developed in a "diasporic" way. When I wrote about Rastafarianism, about reggae, in the 1960s, when I thought about the role of religion in Caribbean life, I've always been interested in this relationship of the "translation" between Christianity and the African religions, or the mixtures in Caribbean music. I've been interested in what turns out to be the thematic of the diaspora for a long time, without necessarily calling it that. For a long time, I wouldn't use the term "diaspora" because it was mainly used in relation to Israel. That was the dominant political usage, and it's a usage I have problems about, in relation to the Palestinian people. That is the originary meaning of the term "diaspora," lodged in the sacred text, fixed in the original landscape, which requires you to expel everybody else and reclaim a land already settled by more than one people. That diasporic project, of "ethnic cleansing," was not tenable for me. Although, I also have to say, there are certain very close relations between the black diaspora and the Jewish diaspora—for example, in the experience of suffering and exile, and the culture of deliverance and redemption, which flow out of it. That is why Rastafarianism uses the Bible, why reggae uses the Bible, because it is a story of a people in exile dominated by a foreign power, far from "home" and the symbolic power of the redemptive myth. So the whole narrative of coloniality, slavery, and colonization is reinscribed in the Jewish one. And in the post-Emancipation period, there were a lot of African American writers who used the Jewish experience, very powerfully, as a metaphor. For the black churches in the States, escape from slavery and deliverance from "Egypt" were parallel metaphors.

Moses is more important for the black slave religions than Jesus, because he led his people out of Babylon, out of captivity. So I've always been interested in this double text, this double textuality. Paul Gilroy's book *The Black Atlantic* is a wonderful study of "the black diaspora" and of the role of that concept in African American thought.[2] Another landmark text for me, in this respect, is Bakhtin's *The Dialogic Imagination*, which develops a range of related concepts about language and meaning—heteroglossia, carnival, or multiaccentuality, from Bakhtin-Volosinov—which we developed in Cultural Studies theoretically, really in the context of the question of language and ideology, but which turned out to be discursive tropes classically typical of diaspora.[3]

KHC: Then you went to England in 1951. What happened then?

SH: Arriving on a steamer in Bristol with my mother, getting on the train to come to Paddington, I'm driving through this West Country landscape; I've never seen it, but I know it. I read Shakespeare, Hardy, the Romantic poets. Though I didn't occupy the space, it was like finding again, in one's dreams, an already-familiar idealized landscape. In spite of my anticolonial politics, it had always been my aspiration to study in England. I always wanted to study there. It took quite a while to come to terms with Britain, especially with Oxford, because Oxford is the pinnacle of Englishness, it's the hub, the motor, that creates Englishness.

There were two phases. Up until 1954, I was saturated in West Indian expatriate politics. Most of my friends were expatriates and went back to play a role in Jamaica, Trinidad, Barbados, Guyana. We were passionate about the colonial question. We followed the expulsion of the French from Indochina with a massive celebration dinner. We discovered, for the first time, that we were "West Indians." We met African students for the first time. With the emerging postcolonial independence, we dreamt of a Caribbean federation, merging these countries into a larger entity. If that had happened, I would have gone back to the Caribbean.

Several West Indian students actually lived together, for a while, in this house in Oxford, which also spawned the New Left. They were the first-generation, black, anticolonial, or postcolonial intelligentsia, who studied in England, did graduate work, trained to be economists. A lot of them were sent by their governments and went back to become the leading cadre of the postindependence period. I was very much formed, politically and personally, in conversation with that, in the early Oxford days.

At that time, I was still thinking of going back to Jamaica, having a political career, being involved in West Indian federation politics, or teaching at the University of the West Indies. Then I got a second scholarship and decided to stay on in Oxford to do graduate work. At that point, most of my immediate Caribbean circle went home. During that time, I also got to know people on the Left, mainly from the Communist Party and the Labour Club. I had a very close friend, Alan Hall, to whom I dedicated an essay on the New Left in *Out of Apathy*.[4] He was a Scotsman, a classical archaeologist, who was interested in cultural and political questions. We met Raymond Williams together. We were very close to some people in the Communist Party then, but never members of it—people like Raphael Samuel, Peter Sedgwick. Another close friend was the philosopher Charles Taylor. Charles was another person, like Alan Hall and me, who was of the "independent Left." We were interested in Marxism, but not dogmatic Marxists, anti-Stalinist, not defenders of the Soviet Union, and therefore we never became members of the Communist Party, though we were in dialogue with them, refusing to be cut off by the Cold War, as the rulers of the Labour Club of that time required. We formed this thing called the Socialist Society, which was a place for meetings of the independent minds of the Left. It brought together postcolonial intellectuals and British Marxists, people in the Labour Party and other Left intellectuals. Perry Anderson, for example, was a member of that group. This was before 1956. Many of us were foreigners or internal immigrants: a lot of the British people were provincial, working class, or Scottish, or Irish, or Jewish.

When I decided to stay on to do graduate work, I opened a discussion with some of the people in this broad Left formation. I remember going to a meeting and opening a discussion with members of the Communist Party, arguing against the reductionist version of the Marxist theory of class. That must have been in 1954, and I seem to have been arguing the same thing ever since. In 1956, Alan Hall, myself, and two other friends, both of them painters, went away for a long summer vacation. Alan and I were going to write this book on British culture. We took away three chapters of *Culture and Society*,[5] *The Uses of Literacy*,[6] Crosland's book *The Future of Socialism*, Strachey's book *After Imperialism*; we took away Leavis, with whose work we'd had a long engagement. The same issues were also breaking culturally. We took away the novelist Kingsley Amis's *Lucky Jim*, new things that were happening in cinema in the British documentary movement—like Lindsay Anderson's essay in *Sight and Sound*. This was the time when the Soviet Union marched on Hungary and the British invaded Suez. That was the end of that. The world turned. That was the formation, the moment of the New Left. We were into something else.

Most of the people who had been in our circles, in the Communist Party, left it, and the Oxford branch collapsed. For a moment in Oxford, this funny grouping, the Socialist Society, became the conscience of the Left, because we had opposed Stalinism *and* opposed imperialism. We had the moral capital to criticize both the Hungarian invasion and the British invasion. That is the political space—of the birth of the first British New Left. Raphael Samuel persuaded us to start this journal, the *Universities and Left Review*, and I got caught up in that. I became more and more involved in the journal. There were four editors: Charles Taylor, Raphael Samuel, Gabriel Pearson, and myself. Once I decided to leave Oxford, in 1957, I came to London and taught in secondary school as a supply teacher, mainly in Brixton and the Oval in south London. I used to leave the school at four o'clock and go to the center of London, to Soho, to edit the journal. So I didn't leave England, at first, because I became involved, in a new kind of way, in British politics.

It's important to say what my feelings are now about that second moment. I never felt defensive about the New Left, but in a broader political sense I remain identified with the project of the *first* New Left. I always had problems in that period about the pronoun "we." I didn't know quite who I meant when I said, "We should do X." I have a funny relationship to the British working-class movement and the British institutions of the labor movement: the Labour Party, and the code unions, identified with it. I'm in it but not culturally of it. I was one of the people, as editor of *Universities and Left Review*, mainly negotiating that space, but I didn't feel the continuity that people who were born in it did, or like people for whom it was an essential part of their "Englishness," like Edward Thompson; I was still learning about it, in a way, as well as negotiating with it. I did have a diasporic "take" on my position in the New Left. Even if I was not then writing about the diaspora, or writing about black politics (there weren't yet many black settlers in Britain), I looked at the British political scene very much as somebody who had a different formation. I was always aware of that difference. I was aware that I'd come from the periphery of this process, that I was looking at it from a different vantage point. I was learning to appropriate it, rather than feeling that the culture was already mine. I was always reluctant to go canvassing for the Labour Party. I don't find it easy to say, straight, face to face with an English working-class family, "Are you going to vote for us?" I just don't know how to utter that sentence.

KHC: Was the New Left essentially an intellectual formation, or did it have an organized mass basis?

SH: It had no organized mass base. In the high period of the New Left, during the years between 1956 and 1962, it had much stronger links with political forces and social movements on the ground. The New Left Club in London was not just composed of intellectuals. The New Left's work on race, during the 1958 racial upheaval in Notting Hill, was organizing on the ground, organizing tenants' associations, organizing defense grouping for black people. We set up the clubs, *Universities and Left Review* and *New Left Review* clubs, and at one stage there were twenty-six clubs. They had people from the Labour Party, the trade unions, students, and so on. So they were not only intellectuals; though since the journal, *Universities and Left Review*, played the leading role, it was the intellectuals who took the lead. Then we made a very strong link with the CND [Campaign for Nuclear Disarmament], antinuclear movement. The link with the CND, with the peace movement, was again not only class movement, but it did represent a deep involvement with what was one of the earliest "new social movements," what was to become, post-1968, the "new politics."

I am not trying to present the New Left as wider, in its social composition, than it actually was. But it is not true that at its high point it was composed exclusively of students and intellectuals, in an American sense. Remember, in Britain, universities were never large enough to form the autonomous space of politics. So, for a long time, the New Left had a wider formation. It emerged in that very moment of the 1960s, when there was a major shift in class formation going on. There were a lot of people in transition between the traditional classes. There were people with working-class backgrounds, who were scholarship boys going to colleges and art schools for the first time, beginning to get professional jobs, training to be teachers, and so on. The New Left was in touch with people who were themselves moving between classes. A lot of our clubs were in new towns where people had parents who might have been manual workers, but they themselves got a better education, had gone to university, and come back as teachers. Hoggart and Williams, who both were from working-class backgrounds and became intellectuals through the adult education movement, are the classic members of the New Left, representatives of the audiences for the New Left Clubs of readers of the New Left journals. We were more a "new social movement" than a proto-political party.

KHC: Why wasn't there an attempt to get these "audiences" organized into something?

SH: What a very much pre–"new social movements" question! That's what we kept asking ourselves—not knowing that the "tyranny of structureless-ness" was a problem for all "new social movements." But there were two reasons. One was the presence of the Labour Party. The overwhelming fact of the Labour Party, as a mass social democratic party, suggested that if *only* one could build a new alliance within the Labour Party, there already was a mass movement of the Left, which could be penetrated by New Left ideas. The Labour Party was like a prize waiting to be won. If only that transformation, from an Old Left to a New Left Party, could be brought about. Is all this beginning to have a familiar ring? It is the dilemma of the Left in Britain, writ large.

Second, because the New Left was, from its origins, anti-Stalinist, and because it was opposed to the bureaucracy of the Cold War, to the bureaucratic apparatuses of the party during the early 1950s, and so on, it anticipated the new social movements, in being very antiorganizational. So we didn't want any structure, we didn't want any leadership, we didn't want any permanent party apparatuses. You belonged to the New Left by affiliating with it. We didn't want anybody to pay any dues. We may have been quite wrong about that, in many ways, but we were very antiorganizational. In very much the same way in which early feminism was antistructure. It was the spirit of 1968, avant la lettre.

KHC: So there was this possibility of forming, or articulating, an alliance without any organizational hierarchy?

SH: Yes, that was the ambition, but I don't think we knew how to do it. One couldn't just set up the New Left because, after all, the working class already had its own institutions, the Labour Party, the trade unions. And there were people sympathetic to New Left ideas in the Labour and trade union movements. We were, in the light of the Stalinist experience, deeply suspicious of the bureaucratic apparatus of the political party. So we decided to sidestep that question. What matters, we argued, was what new ideas the Left subscribed to, not which party label it adopted. It was a struggle for the renewal of socialist ideas, not for the renovation of the party. "One foot in, one out," we said. What is interesting is "What are you doing on the ground? Do you have a local CND? Are you going into the local market?" It was like occupying a space without organizing it, without imposing on people a choice of institutional loyalty.

Remember, there was no such thing as a "new social movement" then. We hadn't identified this as a new phase (or form) of politics. We thought we were still in the old political game but conducting it in a rather new way. It's only retrospectively that we came to understand that New Left as an early anticipation of the era of the "new social movements." Exactly what I'm describing later happened in CND: the antinuclear movement as an autonomous, independent movement.

KHC: Now about the *New Left Review*, what was the situation which put you on the spot, with all the more established or earlier generation people, such as Thompson and Williams, around?

SH: The situation was this: there were originally two groups, the *New Reasoner* and *Universities and Left Review*. People on the *New Reasoner*'s editorial board—Edward and Dorothy Thompson, John Saville, Alasdair MacIntyre—were from a slightly older generation, one basically formed in the old Communist tradition, the dissident Communist tradition that grew up, especially amongst Marxist historians of the 1930s and 1940s, the same generation as Raymond Williams, although Raymond was only briefly, as a student at Cambridge, a member of the party. Raymond then broke off and had an independent formation, and, as a consequence, became one of the mediating figures, belonging to the *Reasoner* generation in age, but closer to us in his pre-occupations. We were the next generation, who started the *Universities and Left Review*. We were related to Marxism, but much more critical of it, more willing to think new things, especially to open new spaces in relation to questions of popular culture, television, etc.—which the older generation did not regard as politically significant. Nevertheless, these two formations were so close together, shared so much in common, and found it so difficult, in financial terms, to keep two different journals going, that gradually the two editorial boards began to meet together. Then the idea emerged to form one journal. The obvious editor was Edward Thompson, the leading figure on the *New Reasoner*. But Edward, by then, had been locked into the struggle since 1956; first of all, fighting inside the Communist Party after the horrors of Stalinism were exhumed in Khrushchev's twentieth Congress speech, then being expelled, then trying to keep the *New Reasoner* going with very little funds. He had two kids, and I think he and Dorothy simply couldn't go on any longer living like that. So the editorship passed to me, though the ambiguity of Edward's position, in relation to me, continued to be a source of tension on the editorial board.

KHC: What about Raymond Williams? Was he the mediator?

SH: Yes, Raymond played a different role. Raymond never took on a detailed editorial role. He was a major figure; his writing influenced all of us. He wrote for both journals, especially the *Universities and Left Review*, and his writing helped to give the project of the New Left a distinctive and original identity. I was very much influenced by his work. Then there was the younger generation: Charles Taylor, myself, Raphael Samuel. Raphael was the dynamo and inspiration, absolutely indispensable, full of energy and ideas, though he wasn't the person to put in charge of getting the journal out regularly. By 1958, in effect I had become the full-time editor of the *Universities and Left Review*. Charles Taylor had already gone to Paris to study with Merleau-Ponty. Charles was very important to me, personally. I remember the first discussions of Marx's 1844 *Economic and Philosophical Manuscripts*, which he brought back from Paris, and the discussions about alienation, humanism, and class.

KHC: You mentioned, in *Out of Apathy*, Doris Lessing. What role did she play?

SH: Doris was not involved in the editorial work of the journal. She contributed to it. She was very close to the Edward Thompson generation, and was one of those independent intellectuals in the Communist Party in the 1940s. She joined the *New Left Review* editorial board, but she was already taking her distance from active politics.

KHC: Then, after two years' editorship, in 1961, you were completely burned out. What did you do after that?

SH: I left the *Review* to teach media, film, and popular culture at Chelsea College, University of London. I went to teach what was then called complementary studies, and what we would now call Cultural Studies. I was brought in by a group of people teaching there, who were sympathetic towards the New Left, interested in the work of Hoggart and Williams, but also in the work which Paddy Whannel and I were doing in film studies for the British Film Institute, the BFI. I was appointed at Chelsea to teach film and mass media studies. I don't think there was a lectureship in film and mass media studies anywhere at that time. I had done work on film and TV with Paddy Whannel, through the Education Department of the BFI. And there was also the connection with "Free Cinema," the British documentary movement associated with Lindsay Anderson et al., then *Screen* and the Society for Education in Film and Television. Between 1962 and 1964, Paddy and I did the work which finally resulted in *The Popular Arts*.[7]

KHC: Before that, you were going to write your dissertation on Henry James. Did you give it up because of the *New Left Review*?

SH: I gave it up literally because of 1956. I gave it up in a deeper sense because I was increasingly using my research time to read about culture and to follow that line of interest. I spent a great deal of time in Rhodes House library, reading the anthropological literature and absorbing the debate about African "survivals" in Caribbean and New World culture. Actually, my thesis on Henry James was not as distant from these preoccupations as all that. It was on the theme of "America" versus "Europe" in James's novels. It dealt with the cultural-moral contrasts between America and Europe, one of the great cross-cultural themes in James. I was also interested in James in terms of the destablization of the narrative "I," the last such moment in the modernist western novel, before Joyce. Joyce represented the dissolution of the narrative "I"; James is poised perilously on the edge of that. His language is almost overrunning the capacity of the narrative "I." So I was interested in these two questions, which have major Cultural Studies implications. On the other hand, I didn't feel it was right for me to go on thinking cultural questions in "pure" literary terms.

While teaching at Chelsea, I kept in touch with Williams and Hoggart. I organized the first occasion at which Richard Hoggart and Raymond Williams met. It was for a conversation republished in the *Universities and Left Review*. They discussed *Culture and Society* and *The Uses of Literacy*. Hoggart had then decided to leave Leicester and go to Birmingham as a professor of English. He wanted to continue graduate work in the area covered by *The Uses of Literacy*, rather than straight literary studies. And Birmingham University said to him, "You can do that but we don't have any money to support you." But he had testified in the *Lady Chatterley's Lover* trial, for Penguin Books, and he went to the head of Penguin Books, Sir Allen Lane, and persuaded him to give us some money to start a research center. So Allen Lane gave Hoggart a few thousand pounds a year, which Penguin could write off against tax, because it was an education covenant. With this money, Hoggart decided to hire somebody who would look after this end of the work while he remained professor of English, and he invited me to Birmingham to take it on. Hoggart had read *Universities and Left Review* and *New Left Review*, and *The Popular Arts*, and he thought that, with my combination of interests in television, film, and popular literature; my knowledge of the Leavis debate; and my interest in cultural politics, I would be a good person. I went to Birmingham in 1964 and got married to Catherine—who transferred to Birmingham from Sussex—the same year.

KHC: Getting back to the question of the diaspora. Some of the diasporic intellectuals I know of have exercised their power, for better or worse, back home, but you have not. And some of them are trying to move back, in whatever way. So, in that sense, you are very peculiar.

SH: Yes. But remember, the diaspora came to me. I turned out to be in the first wave of a diaspora over here. When I came to Britain, the only blacks here were students—and all the black students wanted to go back after college. Gradually, during my postgraduate and early New Left days, a working black population settled here, and this became the diaspora of a diaspora. The Caribbean is already the diaspora of Africa, Europe, China, Asia, and India, and this diaspora rediasporized itself here. So that's why more of my recent work is not only just about the postcolonial, but has to be with black photographers, black filmmakers, with black people in the theater; it's with the third-generation black British.

KHC: But you never tried to exercise your intellectual power back home.

SH: There have been moments when I have intervened in my home parts. At a certain point, before 1968, I was engaged in dialogue with the people I knew in that generation, principally to try to resolve the difference between a black Marxist grouping and a black nationalist tendency. I said, you ought to be talking to one another. The black Marxists were looking for the Jamaican proletariat, but there were no heavy industries in Jamaica; they were not listening to the cultural revolutionary thrust of the black nationalists and Rastafarians, who were developing a more persuasive cultural, or subjective, language. But essentially I never tried to play a major political role there. It's partly because the break in the politics there—the cultural revolution that made Jamaica a "black" society for the first time in the 1970s—coincided with a break in my own life. I would have gone back, had the Caribbean Federation lasted, and tried to play a role there. That dream was over at the moment in the 1950s when I decided to stay, and to open a "conversation" with what became the New Left—the possibility of the scenario in which I might have been politically active in the Caribbean closed at the very moment when personally I found a new kind of political space here. After that, once I decided I was going to live here rather than there, once Catherine and I got married, the possibility of return became more difficult. Catherine was an English social historian, a feminist; her politics were here. Of course, paradoxically, she is now working on Jamaica, and the imperial relationship, and she now knows more Jamaican history than I do, and she loves being there. But in the 1960s, it was very difficult for a white British feminist to feel anything but an outsider in relation to Jamaican politics. My "reconnection" with the Caribbean happened because of the formation of a black diasporic population here. I began to write about it again in the context of the studies of ethnicity and racism for UNESCO, then I wrote about it in *Policing the Crisis*,[8] focusing on race and racism, and their internal relation to the crisis of British society, and now I write very much in terms of cultural identities.

KHC: So diaspora is defined by the historical conjunctures both personally and structurally, and the creative energies and power of the diaspora come, in part, from these unresolvable tensions?

SH: Yes, but it is very specific, and it never loses its specificities. That is the reason why the way in which I'm trying to think questions of identity is slightly different from a postmodernist "nomadic." I think cultural identity is not fixed—it's always hybrid. But this is precisely because it comes out of very specific historical formations, out of very specific histories and cultural repertoires of enunciation, that it can constitute a "positionality," which we call, provisionally, identity. It's not just anything. So each of those identity-stories is inscribed in the positions we take up and identify with, and we have to live this ensemble of identity-positions in all its specificities.

[August 8, 1992]

NOTES

1 For Stuart Hall's work on race and ethnicity, see "Gramsci's Relevance for the Study of Race and Ethnicity," in this volume; "Minimal Selves," *ICA Document* 6 (1987); "New Ethnicities," *ICA Document* 7 (1988); "Ethnicity: Identity and Difference," *Radical America* 23, no. 4 (1989); "Cultural Identity and Diaspora," in *Identity: Community, Culture, Difference*, ed. Jonathan Rutherford (London: Lawrence and Wishart, 1990); "The Local and Global: Globalization and Ethnicity," and "Old and New Identities, Old and New Ethnicities," in *Culture, Globalization and the World-System*, ed. Anthony D. King (London: Macmillan, 1991); David A. Bailey and Stuart Hall, eds., "Critical Decade: Black British Photography in the 80s," *Ten.8*, 2, no. 3 (1992); "What Is This 'Black' in Black Popular Culture?," in *Black Popular Culture*, ed. Gina Dent (Seattle: Bay Press, 1992); "The Question of Cultural Identities," in *Modernity and Its Futures*, ed. Stuart Hall, David Held, and Tony McGrew (Cambridge: Polity Press and the Open University, 1992).

2 Paul Gilroy, *The Black Atlantic* (London: Verso, 1993).

3 Mikhail Bakhtin, *The Dialogic Imagination* (Austin: University of Texas Press, 1981).

4 Stuart Hall, "The 'First' New Left: Life and Times," in *Out of Apathy: Voices of the New Left 30 Years On*, ed. Oxford University Socialist Discussion Group (London: Verso, 1989).

5 Raymond Williams, *Culture and Society: 1780–1950* (Harmondsworth: Penguin 1958.

6 Richard Hoggart, *The Uses of Literacy* (Harmondsworth: Penguin, 1958).

7 Paddy Whannel and Stuart Hall, *The Popular Arts* (London: Hutchinson, 1964).

8 Stuart Hall, Chas Critcher, Tony Jefferson, John Clarke, and Brian Roberts, *Policing the Crisis: Mugging, the State, and Law and Order* (London: Macmillan, 1978).

CHAPTER 7

Thinking the Diaspora: Home-Thoughts from Abroad

The occasion for this lecture was the fiftieth anniversary of the founding of the University of the West Indies (UWI). The year 1948 was also, as it happens, the year of the arrival at Tilbury Docks in the UK of the *Empire Windrush*, the troopship, with its cargo of West Indian migrants. This event signified the start of postwar Caribbean migration to Britain and stands symbolically as the birth date of the Afro-Caribbean postwar black diaspora. Its anniversary in 1998 was celebrated as symbolizing "the irresistible rise of multi-racial Britain."[1]

Migration has been a constant motif of the Caribbean story. But the *Windrush* initiated a new phase of diaspora formation whose legacy is the black Caribbean settlements in the UK. The purpose here is not to offer a historical account of the evolution of this diaspora—though its troubled history deserves to be better known in the Caribbean, even, one (dare one suggest) more systematically studied. The fate of Caribbean people living in the UK, the US, or Canada is no more "external" to Caribbean history than the empire was "external" to the so-called domestic history of Britain, though that is indeed how contemporary historiography constructs them. At all events, the question of diaspora is posed here primarily because of the light that it throws on the complexities not simply of building, but of imagining, Caribbean nationhood and identity in an era of intensifying globalization.

Nations, Benedict Anderson suggests, are not only sovereign political entities but "imagined communities."[2] Thirty years after independence, how are Caribbean nations imagined? This question is central, not only to their peoples but to the arts and culture they produce, where some "imagined subject" is always in play. Where do their boundaries begin and end, when regionally each is culturally and historically so closely related to its neighbors, and so many live thousands of miles from "home"? How do we imagine their relation to "home," the nature of their "belongingness"? And how are we to think of national identity and "belongingness" in the Caribbean in light of this diaspora experience?

The black settlements in Britain are not totally separated from their roots in the Caribbean. Mary Chamberlain's *Narratives of Exile and Return*, with its life histories of Barbadian migrants to the UK, emphasizes how strong the links remain.[3] As is common to most transnational communities, the extended family—as network and site of memory—is the critical conduit between the two locations. Barbadians, she suggests, have kept alive in exile a strong sense of what "home" is like and tried to maintain a Barbadian "cultural identity." This picture is confirmed by research among Caribbean migrants in general in the UK that suggests that, among the so-called ethnic minorities in Britain, what we might call "associational identification" with the cultures of origin remains strong, even into the second and third generation, though the places of origin are no longer the only source of identification.[4] The strength of the umbilical tie is also reflected in the growing numbers of retired Caribbean returnees. Chamberlain's judgment is that "a determination to construct autonomous Barbadian identities in Britain, . . . if current trends continue, is likely to be enhanced rather than diminished by time."[5]

However, it would be wrong to see these trends as singular or unambiguous. In the diaspora situation, identities become multiple. Alongside an associative connection with a particular island "home" there are other centripetal forces: there is the West-Indianness that they share with other West Indian migrants. (George Lamming once remarked that his—and, incidentally, my—generation became "West Indian" not in the Caribbean but in London!) There are the similarities with other so-called ethnic minority populations, emergent "black British" identities, the identification with the localities of settlement, also the symbolic reidentifications with "African" and more recently with "African American" cultures—all jostling for place alongside, say, their "Barbadianness."

Mary Chamberlain's interviewees also speak eloquently of how difficult many returnees find reconnecting with the societies of their birth. Many miss the cosmopolitan rhythms of life to which they have become acclimatized.

Many feel that "home" has changed beyond all recognition. In turn, they are seen as having had the natural and spontaneous chains of connection disturbed by their diasporic experiences. They are happy to be home. But history has somehow irrevocably intervened.

This is the familiar, deeply modern, sense of dislocation which—it increasingly appears—we do not have to travel far to experience. Perhaps we are all, in modern times—after the Fall, so to speak—what the philosopher Heidegger called "Unheimlichkeit": literally, "not-at-home." As Iain Chambers eloquently expresses it:

> We can never go Home, return to the primal scene, to the forgotten moment of our beginnings and "authenticity," for there is always something else between. We cannot return to a bygone unity, for we can only know the past, memory, the unconscious through its effects, that is when it is brought into language and from there embark on an (interminable) analysis. In front of the "forest of signs" (Baudelaire) we find ourselves always at the crossroads, holding our stories and memories ("secularized reliques," as Benjamin, the collector, describes them) while scanning the constellation full of tension that lies before us, seeking the language, the style, that will dominate movement and give it form. Perhaps it is now a question of seeking to be at home here, in the only time and context we have.[6]

What light, then, does the diaspora experience throw on issues of cultural identity in the Caribbean? Since this is a conceptual and epistemological, as well as an empirical, question, what does the diaspora experience do to our models of cultural identity? How are we to conceptualize or imagine identity, difference, and belongingness, after diaspora? Since "cultural identity" carries so many overtones of essential unity, primordial oneness, indivisibility, and sameness, how are we to "think" identities inscribed within relations of power and constructed across difference and disjuncture?

Essentially, it is assumed that cultural identity *is* fixed by birth, part of nature, imprinted through kinship and lineage in the genes, constitutive of our innermost selves. It is impermeable to something as "worldly," secular, and superficial as temporarily moving one's place of residence. Poverty, underdevelopment, the lack of opportunities—the legacies of empire everywhere—may force people to migrate, bringing about the scattering: the dispersal. But each dissemination carries with it the promise of the redemptive return.

This powerful interpretation of the concept of "diaspora" is the one most familiar to Caribbean people. It has become part of our newly constructed collective sense of self and deeply written in the subtext of nationalist histories. It is modeled on the modern history of the Jewish people (from whom the term "diaspora" was first derived), whose fate in the Holocaust—one of the few world-historical events comparable in barbarity to that of modern slavery—is well known. More significant, however, for the Caribbean is the Old Testament version of the story. There we find the analogue, critical to our history, of "the chosen people," taken away by violence into slavery in "Egypt"; their "suffering" at the hands of "Babylon"; the leadership of Moses, followed by the Great Exodus—"movement of Jah People"—out of bondage and the return to the Promised Land. This is the ur-source of that great New World narrative of freedom, hope, and redemption which is repeated again and again throughout slavery: the Exodus and the "Freedom Ride." It has provided every black New World liberatory discourse with its governing metaphor. Many believe this Old Testament narrative to be much more powerful for the popular imaginary of New World black people than the so-called Christmas story. Indeed, in the very week in which this lecture was first delivered at the UWI Cave Hill campus, the *Barbados Advocate*—looking forward to independence celebrations—attached the honorific titles of "Moses" and "Aaron" to the "founding fathers" of Barbadian independence, Errol Barrow and Cameron Tudor!

In this metaphor, history—which is open to freedom because it is contingent—is represented as ideological and redemptive: circling back to the restoration of its originary moment, healing all rupture, repairing every violent breach through this return. This hope has become, for Caribbean people, condensed into a sort of foundational myth. It is, by any standards, a great vision. Its power—even in the modern world—to move mountains can never be underestimated.

It is, of course, a closed conception of "tribe," diaspora, and homeland. To have a cultural identity in this sense is to be primordially in touch with an unchanging essential core, which is timeless, binding future and present to past in an unbroken line. This umbilical cord is what we call "tradition," the test of which is its truth to its origins, its self-presence to itself, its "authenticity." It is, of course, a myth—with all the real power that our governing myths carry to shape our imaginaries, influence our actions, give meaning to our lives, and make sense of our history.

Foundational myths are, by definition, transhistorical: not only outside history, but fundamentally ahistorical. They are anachronistic and have the structure of a double inscription. Their redemptive power lies in the future, which is yet to come. But they work by ascribing what they predict will happen to their description of what has already happened, of what it was like in the beginning. History, however, like Time's arrow, is, if not linear, then successive. The narrative structure of myths is cyclical. But within history, their meaning is often transformed. It is, after all, precisely this exclusive conception of "homeland" that led the Serbs to refuse to share their territory—as they have done for centuries—with their Muslim neighbors in Bosnia and justified ethnic cleansing in Kosovo. It is a version of this conception of the Jewish diaspora, and its prophesied "return" to Israel, that is the source of Israel's quarrel with its Middle Eastern neighbors, for which the Palestinian people have paid so dearly and, paradoxically, by expulsion from what is also, after all, their homeland.

Here, then, is the paradox. Now, our troubles begin. A people cannot live without hope. But there is a problem when we take our metaphors too literally. Questions of cultural identity in diasporas cannot be "thought" in this way.[7] They have proved so troubling and perplexing for Caribbean people precisely because, with us, identity is irredeemably a historical question. Our societies are composed, not of one, but of many peoples. Their origins are not singular but diverse. Those to whom the land originally belonged have long since, largely, perished—decimated by hard labor and disease. The land cannot be "sacral" because it was "violated"—not empty but emptied. Everyone who is here originally belonged somewhere else. Far from being continuous with our pasts, our relation to that history is marked by the most horrendous, violent, abrupt, ruptural breaks. Instead of the slowly evolving pact of civil association so central to the liberal discourse of Western modernity, our "civil association" was inaugurated by an act of imperial will. What we now call *the* Caribbean was reborn in and through violence. The pathway to our modernity is marked out by conquest, expropriation, genocide, slavery, the plantation system, and the long tutelage of colonial dependency. No wonder in van der Straet's famous engraving of Europe encountering America (c. 1600), Amerigo Vespucci is the commanding male figure, surrounded by the insignia of power, science, knowledge, and religion: and "America" is, as often, allegorized as a woman, naked, in a hammock, surrounded by the emblems of an—as yet unviolated—exotic landscape.[8]

Our peoples have their roots in—or, more accurately, can trace their "routes" from—the four corners of the globe, from Europe, Africa, Asia, and forced together in the fourth corner is the "primal scene" of the New World. Their "routes" are anything but "pure." The great majorities are "African" in descent—but, as Shakespeare would have said, "north-by-north-west." We know this term "Africa" is, in any event, a modern construction, referring to a variety of peoples, tribes, cultures, and languages whose principal common point of origin lay in the confluence of the slave trade. In the Caribbean, "Africa" has since been joined by the East Indians and the Chinese: indenture enters alongside slavery. The distinctiveness of our culture is manifestly the outcome of the most complex interweaving and fusion in the furnace of colonial society, of different African, Asian, and European cultural elements.

This hybrid outcome can no longer be easily disaggregated into its original "authentic" elements. The fear that, somehow, this makes Caribbean culture nothing but a simulacrum or cheap imitation of the cultures of the colonizers need not detain us, for this is so obviously not the case. But the cultural logic at work here is manifestly a "creolizing" or transcultural one, as Mary Louise Pratt uses the term, following in the tradition of some of the best cultural theoretical writing of the region. Through transculturation, "subordinated or marginal groups select and invent from materials transmitted to them by a dominant metropolitan culture." It is a process of the "contact zone," a term that invokes "the spatial and temporal co-presence of subjects previously separated by geographic and historical disjunctions, whose trajectories now intersect." This perspective is dialogic since it is as interested in how the colonized produce the colonizer as the other way around: the "co-presence, interaction, interlocking of understandings and practices, often[9] [in the Caribbean case, we must say always] within radically asymmetrical relations of power."[10] It is the disjunctive logic that colonization and Western modernity introduced into the world and its entry into history constituted the world after 1492 as a profoundly unequal but "global" enterprise and made Caribbean people what David Scott has recently described as "conscripts of modernity."[11]

In the early 1990s, I made a television series, called *Redemption Song*, for BBC2 about the different cultural tributaries within Caribbean culture.[12] In the visits I made in connection with the series, what amazed me was the presence of the same, basic trace elements (similarity), together with the ways these had been uniquely combined into different configurations in each place (difference). I felt "Africa" closest to the surface in Haiti and Jamaica. And yet, the way the African gods had been synthesized with Christian saints in the complex universe of Haitian vodun is a particular mix only to be found in the Caribbean and Latin America—though there are analogues wherever comparable syncretisms emerged in the wake of colonization. The style of

Haitian painting often described as "primitive" is in fact the most complex rendering—in visionary terms—of this religious "double-consciousness." The distinguished Haitian painter whom we filmed—Andre Pierre—said a prayer to both Christian and vodun gods before he commenced work. Like the Jamaican painter, Brother Everald Brown, Pierre saw painting as essentially a visionary and "spiritual" task. He sang us the "story" of his canvas—white-robed, tie-headed black "saints" and travelers crossing The River—as he painted.

I felt close to France in both Haiti and Martinique, but to different Frances: in Haiti, the "France" of the Old Empire, which the Haitian Revolution (the explosive fusion of African slave resistance and French Republican traditions in the demand for liberty under Toussaint L'Ouverture) brought to its knees; in Martinique, the "France" of the New Empire—of Republicanism, Gaullism, Parisian "chic" crossed by the transgressions of black "style" and the complex affiliations to "Frenchness" of Fanon and Césaire. In Barbados, as expected, I felt closer to England and its understated social discipline—as one once did, occasionally, but feels no longer in Jamaica. Nevertheless, the distinctive habits, customs, and social etiquette of Barbados are so clearly a translation, through African slavery, of that small-scale, intimate plantation culture that refigured the Barbadian landscape. In Trinidad, above all, the complex traditions of "the East" in "the West"—of Indian, Carnival Queens, roti stalls on the savannah and Diwali candles glittering in the San Fernando darkness, and the distinctively Spanish Catholic rhythm of sin-contrition-and-absolution (Shrove Tuesday's masque followed by Ash Wednesday mass) that is so close to the Trinidadian character. Everywhere, hybridity, différance.

The dosed conception of diaspora rests on a binary conception of difference. It is founded on the construction of an exclusionary frontier and depends on the construction of an "Other" and a fixed opposition between inside and outside. But the syncretized configurations of Caribbean cultural identity require Derrida's notion of différance—differences that do not work through binaries, veiled boundaries that do not finally separate but double up as *places de passage*, and meanings that are positional and relational, always on the slide along a spectrum without end or beginning. Difference, we know, is essential to meaning, and meaning is critical for culture. But in a profoundly counterintuitive move, modern linguistics after Saussure insists that meaning cannot be finally fixed. There is always the inevitable "slippage" of meaning in the open semiosis of a culture, as that which seems fixed continues to be dialogically reappropriated. The fantasy of a final meaning remains haunted by "lack" or "excess," but is never graspable in the plenitude of its presence to itself. As Volosinov argued,

> The social multiaccentuality of the ideological sign is a very crucial aspect. . . . It is thanks to this intersecting of accents that a sign maintains its vitality and dynamism and the capacity for further development. A sign which has been withdrawn from the pressures of the social struggle . . . inevitably loses its force, degenerating into allegory and becoming the object not of live social intelligibility but of philological Comprehension.[13]

In this conception, the binary poles of "sense" and "nonsense" are constantly undermined by the more open-ended and fluid process of "making sense in translation."

This cultural "logic" has been described by Kobena Mercer as a "diasporic aesthetic":

> Across a whole range of cultural forms there is a powerful syncretic dynamic which critically appropriates elements from the master-codes of the dominant cultures and creolizes them, disarticulating given signs and re-articulating their symbolic meaning otherwise. The subversive force of this hybridizing tendency is most apparent at the level of language itself (*including* visual language) where Creoles, patois and Black English decentre, destabilize and carnivalize the linguistic domination of "English"—the nation-language of master-discourse—through strategic inflections, reaccentuations and other performative moves in semantic, syntactic and lexical codes.[14]

Caribbean culture is essentially driven by a diasporic aesthetic. In anthropological terms, its cultures are irretrievably "impure." This impurity, so often constructed as burden and loss, is itself a necessary condition of their modernity. As the novelist Salman Rushdie once observed, "hybridity, impurity, intermingling, the transformation that comes of new and unexpected combinations of human beings, cultures, ideas, politics, movies, songs" is "how newness enters the world."[15] This is not to suggest that the different elements in a syncretic formation stand in a relation of equality to one another. They are always differently inscribed by relations of power—above all the relations of dependency and subordination sustained by colonialism itself. The independence and postcolonial moments, in which these imperial histories remain actively reworked, are therefore necessarily moments of cultural struggle, of revision and reappropriation. However, this reconfiguration cannot be represented as a "going back to where we were before" since, as Chambers reminds us, "there is always something else between."[16] This "something else between" is what makes the Caribbean itself, preeminently, the case of a modern diaspora.

The relationship between Caribbean cultures and their diaspora cannot therefore be adequately conceptualized in terms of origin to copy, primary source to pale reflection. It has to be understood as one diaspora to another. Here, the national frame is not very helpful. Nation-states impose rigid frontiers within which cultures are expected to flourish. That was the primary relationship between sovereign national polities and their "imagined communities" in the end of European nation-state dominance. It was also the frame adopted by the nationalist and nation-building politics after independence. The question is whether it still provides a useful framework for understanding the cultural exchanges between the black diasporas.

Globalization, of course, is not a new phenomenon. Its history is coterminous with the era of European exploration, conquest, and the formation of the capitalist world market. The earlier phases of this so-called global history were held together by the tension between these conflicting poles— the heterogeneity of the global market and the centripetal force of the nation-state—constituting between them one of the fundamental rhythms of early capitalist world systems.[17] The Caribbean was one of its key scenarios, across which the stabilization of the European nation-state system was fought through and accomplished in a series of imperial settlements. The apogee of imperialism at the end of the nineteenth century, two world wars and the national independence and decolonizing movements of the twentieth century marked the zenith, and the terminal point, of this phase.

It is now rapidly drawing to a close. Global developments above and below the level of the nation-state have undermined the nation's reach and scope of maneuver, and with that the scale and comprehensiveness—the panoptic assumptions—of its "imaginary." In any event, cultures have always refused to be so perfectly corralled within the national boundaries. They transgress political limits. Caribbean culture, in particular, has not been well served by the national frame. The imposition of national frontiers within the imperial system fragmented the region into separate and estranged national and linguistic entities from which it has never recovered. The alternative frame of "the Black Atlantic," proposed by Paul Gilroy, is a powerful counternarrative to the discursive insertion of the Caribbean into European national stories, bringing to the surface the lateral exchanges and "family resemblances" across the region as a whole which a nationalist history obscures.[18]

The new post-1970s phase of globalization is, of course, still deeply rooted in the structured disparities of wealth and power. But its forms, however uneven, are more "global" in their operation, planetary in perspective, with transnational corporate interests, the deregulation of world markets and the global flow of capital, technologies and communication systems transcending and sidelining the old nation-state framework. This new "transnational" phase of the system has as cultural "center" everywhere and nowhere. It is becoming "decentered." This does not mean that it lacks power, or indeed that nation-states have no role in it. But that role has been in many respects subordinated to larger global systemic operations. The rise of supranational formations, such as the European Union, is testimony to the ongoing erosion of national sovereignty. The undoubted hegemonic position of the US in this system is related not to its nation-state status but to its global and neo-imperial role and ambitions.

It is therefore important to see this diasporic perspective on culture as subversive of traditional nation-oriented cultural models. Like other globalizing processes cultural globalization is deterritorializing in its effects. Its space-time condensations, driven by new technologies, loosen the tie between culture and "place." Glaring disjunctures of time and space are abruptly convened, without obliterating their differential rhythms. Cultures, of course, have their locations. But it is no longer easy to say where they originate. In this perspective, black British identities are not just a pale reflection of a "true" Caribbeanness of origin, which is destined to be progressively weakened. They are the outcome of their own relatively autonomous formation. However, the logic that governs them involves the same processes of transplantation, syncretization, and diaspora-ization that once produced Caribbean identities, only now operating in a different space and time frame, a different chronotope—in the time of différance.

Thus dancehall music and subculture in Britain was of course inspired by, and takes much of its style and attitude from, the dancehall music and subculture of Jamaica. But it now has its own variant black British forms, and its own indigenous locations. The recent "dancehall" film *Babymother* is "authentically" located in the mixed-race inner-city zone of Harlesden, in the streets and clubs, the recording studios and live venues, the street life and danger zones of North London.[19] The three ragga girls, its heroines, shop for their exotic outfits in another suburb of London, Southall, which is familiarly known as Little India.

These différances are not without real effects. Unlike the classic representations of dancehall elsewhere, this film charts the struggles of three girls to become ragga dancehall DJs—thereby bringing the vexed issue of sexual politics in Jamaican popular culture dead center to the narrative, where other versions are still hiding it away behind a cultural nationalist screen. Isaac Julien's documentary film *The Darker Side of Black* has three locations—Kingston, New York, and London. Perhaps it is this relative "freedom of place" that enables him to confront the deep homophobia common to the different variants of gangsta rap without collapsing into the degraded language of "the innate violence of the black posses" that now disfigures British Sunday journalism.

Dancehall is now an indigenized diasporic musical form—one of several black musics winning the hearts and souls of some white London "wannabe" kids (that is, "wannabe black"!), who speak a mean mixture of Trench Town patois, New York hip-hop, and estuary English and for whom "black style" simply is the symbolic equivalent of modern street credibility. (Of course, they are not the only garden-variety of British youth. There are also the skinheads, swastika-tattooed denizens of abandoned white suburbs such as Eltham, who also practice their violent maneuvers "globally" at international football matches, five of whom stabbed the black teenager Stephen Lawrence to death at a South London bus stop, simply because he dared to change buses in their "territory.")[20] What is now known as jungle music in London is another "original" crossover (there have been many since British versions of ska, black soul, two-tone, and "roots" reggae) between Jamaican dub, Atlantic Avenue hip-hop and gangsta rap, and white techno (as *bhangra* and tabla-and-bass are crossover musics between rap, techno, and the Indian classical tradition).

In the vernacular cosmopolitan exchanges that allow "Third" and "First" World popular musical traditions to fertilize one another, and which have constructed a symbolic space where so-called advanced electronic technology meets the so-called primitive rhythms—where Harlesden becomes Trench Town—there is no traceable origin left, except along a circuitous and discontinuous chain of connections. The proliferation and dissemination of new hybrid and syncretic musical forms can no longer be captured in the center/periphery model or based simply on some nostalgic and eroticized notion of the recovery of ancient rhythms. It is the story of the production of culture, of new and thoroughly modern diaspora musics—of course, drawing on the materials and forms of many fragmented musical traditions.

Their modernity needs, above all, to be emphasized. In 1998, the Institute of International Visual Arts and the Whitechapel Gallery organized the first major retrospective of the work of a major Caribbean visual artist, Aubrey Williams (1926–1990). Williams was born and worked for many years as an agricultural officer in Guyana. He subsequently lived and painted, at different stages of his career, in England, Guyana, Jamaica, and the US. His paintings embrace a variety of twentieth-century styles, from the figurative and the iconographic to abstraction. His major work demonstrates a wide variety of formal influences and inspirational sources—Guyanese myths, artifacts, and landscapes; pre-Columbian and Mayan motifs; wildlife, birds, and animal figures; Mexican materialism; the symphonies of Shostakovich; and the abstract-expressionist forms characteristic of postwar British and European modernism. His paintings defy characterization, as simply either Caribbean or British. These vibrant, explosively colorful canvases, with their cosmic shapes and the indistinct traces of forms and figures faintly but suggestively embedded in the abstract surfaces, clearly belong to, but have never been officially recognized as part of, the essential story of "British modernism." No doubt his flirtation with European music and abstraction, in some minds, qualified his credentials as a "Caribbean" painter. Yet, it is the two impulses working together, his translation position between two worlds, several aesthetics, many languages, that establish him as an outstanding, original, and formidably modern artist.

In the catalogue produced for the Williams retrospective, the art critic Guy Brett comments:

> Of course, the subtlety of the matter—the complexity of the history that has yet to be written—is that Aubrey Williams' work would have to be considered in three different contexts: that of Guyana, that of the Guyanese and West Indian diaspora in Britain, and that of British society. These contexts would have to be considered to a degree separately, and in their complicated interrelationships, affected by the realities of power. And all would have to be adjusted in relation to Williams' own desire to be simply a modern, contemporary artist, the equal of any other. At one moment he could say, "I haven't wasted a lot of energy on this roots business. . . . I've paid attention to a hundred different things. . . . Why must I isolate one philosophy?"; at another, "the crux of the matter inherent in my work since I was a boy has been the human predicament, specifically with regard to the Guyanese situation."[21]

What, then, about all those efforts to reconstruct Caribbean identities by going back to their originary sources? Were these struggles of cultural recovery useless? Far from it. The reworking of Africa in the Caribbean weave has been the most powerful and subversive element in our cultural politics in the twentieth century. And *its* capacity to disrupt the postindependence nationalist "settlement" is certainly not over. But this is not primarily because we are connected to our African past and heritage by an unbreakable chain across which some singular African culture has flowed unchanged down the generations, but because of how we have gone about producing "Africa" again, within the Caribbean narrative. At every juncture—think of Garveyism, Hibbert, Rastafarianism, the new urban popular culture—it has been a matter of interpreting "Africa," rereading "Africa," of what "Africa" could mean to us now, after diaspora.

Anthropologically, this question has often been approached in terms of "survivals." The signs and traces of that presence are, of course, everywhere. "Africa" lives not only in the retention of African words and syntactic structures in language or rhythmic patterns in music but in the way African speech forms have permanently disrupted, inflected, and subverted the way Caribbean people speak, the way they appropriated "English," the master tongue. It "lives" in the way every Caribbean Christian congregation, familiar with every line of the Moody and Sankey hymnal, nonetheless drag and elongate the pace of "Onward Christian Soldiers" back down to a more grounded body-rhythm and vocal register. Africa is alive and well in the diaspora. But it is neither the Africa of those territories, now obscured by the postcolonial map maker, from which slaves were snatched for transportation, nor the Africa of today, which is at least four or five different "continents" rolled into one, its forms of subsistence destroyed, its peoples structurally adjusted into a devastating modern poverty.[22] The "Africa" that is alive and well in this part of the world is what Africa has become in the New World, in the violent vortex of colonial syncretism, reforged in the furnace of the colonial cook-pot.

Equally significant, then, is the way this "Africa" provides resources for survival today, alternative histories to those imposed by colonial rule, and the raw materials for reworking in new and distinctive cultural patterns and forms. In this perspective, "survivals" in their original form are massively outweighed by the process of cultural translation. As Sarat Maharaj reminds us:

Translation, as Derrida puts it, is quite unlike buying, selling, swapping—however much it has been conventionally pictured in those terms. It is not a matter of shipping over juicy chunks of meaning from one side of the language barrier to the other—as with fast-food packs at an over-the-counter take away outfit. Meaning is not a readymade, portable thing that can be "carried over" the divide. The translator is obliged to construct meaning in the source language and then to figure and fashion it a second time round in the materials of the language into which he or she is rendering it. The translator's loyalties are thus divided and split. He or she has to be faithful to the syntax, feel and structure of the source language and faithful to those of the language of translation. . . . We face a double writing, what might be described as a "perfidious fidelity." . . . We are drawn into Derrida's "Babel effect."[23]

In fact, every significant social movement and every creative development of the arts in the Caribbean in this century has begun with or included this translation-moment of the reencounter with Afro-Caribbean traditions. The reason is not that Africa is a fixed anthropological point of reference—the hyphenated reference already marks the diasporizing process at work, the way "Africa" was appropriated into and transformed by the plantation systems of the New World. The reason is that "Africa" is the signifier, the metaphor, for that dimension of our society and history that has been massively suppressed, systematically dishonored, and endlessly disavowed, and that, despite all that has happened, remains so. This dimension is what Frantz Fanon called "the fact of blackness."[24] Race remains, in spite of everything, the guilty secret, the hidden code, the unspeakable trauma, in the Caribbean. It is "Africa" that has made it "speakable," as a social and cultural condition of our existence.

In the Caribbean cultural formation, white, European, Western, colonizing traces were always positioned as the ascendant element, the voiced aspect: the black, "African," enslaved, and colonized traces, of which there were many, were always unvoiced, subterranean, and subversive, governed by a different logic, always positioned through subordination or marginalization. Identities formed within the matrix of colonial meanings were constructed so as to foreclose and disavow engagement with the real histories of our society or its cultural "routes." The huge efforts made, over many years, not only by academic scholars but by cultural practitioners themselves, to piece together these fragmentary, often illegal, "routes to the present" and to reconstruct their unspoken genealogies, are the necessary historical groundwork required to make sense of the interpretive matrix and self-images of our culture and to make the invisible visible. That is, the "work" of translation that the African signifier performs, and the work of "perfidious fidelity" that Caribbean artists in this post-nationalist moment are required to undertake.

The struggles to rediscover the African "routes" within the complex configurations of Caribbean culture, and to speak through that prism the ruptures of transportation, slavery, colonization, exploitation, and racialization, produced the only successful "revolution" in the Anglophone Caribbean in this century—the so-called cultural revolution of the 1960s—and the making of the black Caribbean subject. In Jamaica, for example, its traces are still to be found in a thousand unexamined places—in religious congregations of all sorts, formal and irregular; in the marginalized voices of popular street preachers and prophets, many of them declared insane; in folk stories and oral narrative forms; in ceremonial occasions and rites of passage; in the new language, music, and rhythm of urban popular culture as well as in political and intellectual traditions—in Garveyism, Ethiopianism, revivalism, and Rastafarianism. The latter, as we know, looked back to that mythic space, "Ethiopia," where black kings ruled for a thousand years, the site of a Christian congregation hundreds of years before the Christianization of western Europe. But, as a social movement, it was actually born, as we know, in that fateful but unlocatable "place" closer to home where Garvey's return met the Reverend Hibbert's preaching and Bedward's delusive fantasies, leading to the retreat to and the forced dispersal from Pinnacle. It was destined for that wider politicized space where it could speak for those—if the phrase is forgiven—"dispossessed by independence"!

Like all these movements, Rastafarianism represented itself as a "return." But what it "returned" us to was ourselves. In doing so, it produced "Africa again"—in the diaspora. Rastafarianism drew on many "lost sources" from the past. But its relevance was grounded in the extraordinarily contemporary practice of reading the Bible through its subversive tradition, through its unorthodoxies, its apocrypha: by reading against the grain, upside down, turning the text against itself. The "Babylon" of which it spoke, where its people were still "suffering," was not in Egypt but in Kingston—and later, as the name was syntagmatically extended to include the Metropolitan Police, in Brixton, Handsworth, Moss Side, and Notting Hill. Rastafarianism played a critical role in the modern movement that made Jamaica and other Caribbean societies, for the first time, and irrecoverably, "black." In a further translation, this strange doctrine and discourse "saved" the young black souls of second-generation Caribbean migrants in British cities in the 1960s and 1970s, and gave them pride and self-understanding. In Frantz Fanon's terms, it decolonized minds.

At the same time, it is worth recalling the awkward fact that the "naturalization" of the descriptive term "black" for the whole of the Caribbean, or the equivalent, "Afro-Caribbean" for all West Indian migrants abroad, performs its own kind of silencing in our new transnational world. The young Trinidadian artist Steve Ouditt has lived and worked in the US, England, and what he describes as the "Sucrotopia" of Trinidad. He describes himself as "a post-independence American/English educated Christian Indian Trinidadian West Indian Creole male artist," whose work—in written and installation form—"navigates the difficult terrain between the visual and the verbal." He addresses this issue head-on in one of his recent pieces for his online diary, "Enigma of Survival."

> Afro-Caribbean is the blanket term for any Caribbean in England. For real. It is as real as when many well educated people here say to me, 'You are from the Caribbean, how come, you are not even black, you look Asian.' . . . I do believe that the term 'Afro-Caribbean' is a British naming and perhaps it is supposed to represent the image of the majority of West Indian migrants who came here in the post-war period. And it is used to mark and remember in their past the politics and horrors of slavery, the European classification of Africans as ultrainferior. The fragmentation and loss of "culture" but with desires to negotiate a new 'Afroness' in this diasporic site. . . . In this specificity I can deal with 'Afro-Caribbean' . . . but not when it is used as the privileged index of horror to settle and centre all other subaltern Caribbean historiographies under an Afrophilia of the Caribbean here in Britain. . . . Trinidad has had a history of indentureship of Indians in labour camp apartheid for as long as it has had "organized" slavery.[25]

What these examples suggest is that culture is not just a voyage of rediscovery, a return journey. It is not an "archaeology." Culture is a production. It has its raw materials, its resources, its "work-of-production." It depends on a knowledge of tradition as "the changing same" and an effective set of genealogies.[26] But what this "detour through its pasts" does is to enable us, through culture, to produce ourselves anew, as new kinds of subjects. It is therefore not a question of what our traditions make of us so much as what we make of our traditions. Paradoxically, our cultural identities, in any finished form, lie ahead of us. We are always in the process of cultural formation. Culture is not a matter of ontology, of being, but of becoming.

In its present hectic and accentuated forms, globalization is busily disentangling and subverting further its own inherited essentializing and homogenizing cultural models, undoing the limits, and, in the process, unraveling the darkness of the West's own "Enlightenment." Identities thought of as settled and stable are coming to grief on the rocks of a proliferating differentiation. Across the globe, the processes of so-called free and forced migrations are changing the composition, diversifying the cultures, and pluralizing the cultural identities of the older dominant nation-states, the old imperial powers, and, indeed, of the globe itself.[27] The unregulated flows of peoples and cultures is as broad and as unstoppable as the sponsored flows of capital and technology. The former inaugurate a new process of "minoritization" within the old metropolitan societies whose cultural homogeneity has long been silently assumed. But these "minorities" are not effectively ghettoized; they do not long remain enclave settlements. They engage the dominant culture along a very broad front. They belong, in fact, to a transnational movement, and their connections are multiple and lateral. They mark the end of a "modernity" defined exclusively in Western terms.

In fact, there are two, opposed processes at work in contemporary forms of globalization, which is itself a fundamentally contradictory process. There are the dominant forces of cultural homogenization, by which, because of its ascendancy in the cultural marketplace and its domination of capital, technological and cultural "flows," Western culture, more specifically, American culture, threatens to overwhelm all comers, imposing a homogenizing cultural sameness—what has been called the "McDonald-ization" or "Nike-ization" of everything. Its effects are to be seen across the world, including the popular life of the Caribbean. But right alongside that are processes that are slowly and subtly decentering Western models, leading to a dissemination of cultural difference across the globe.

These "other" tendencies do not (yet) have the power, frontally, to confront and repel the former head-on. But they do have the capacity, everywhere, to subvert and "translate," to negotiate and indigenize the global cultural onslaught on weaker cultures. And since the new global consumer markets depend precisely on their becoming "localized" to be effective, there is certain leverage in what may appear at first to be merely "local." These days, the "merely" local and the global are locked together; not because the latter is the local working-through of essentially global effects, but because each is the condition of existence of the other. Once "modernity" was transmitted from a single center. Today, it has no such center. "Modernities" are everywhere, but they have taken on a vernacular accentuation. The fate and fortunes of the simplest and poorest farmer in the most remote corner of the world depends on the unregulated shifts of the global market—and, for that reason, he or she is now an essential element part of every global calculation. Politicians know the poor will not be cut out of, or be defined out of, this "modernity." They are not prepared to be immured forever in an immutable "tradition." They are determined to construct their own kinds of "vernacular modernities," and these are the signifiers of a new kind of transnational, even postnational, transcultural consciousness.

This "narrative" has no guaranteed happy ending. Many in the old nation-states, who are deeply attached to the purer forms of national self-understanding, are literally driven crazy by their erosion. They feel their whole universe threatened by change and coming down about their ears. "Cultural difference" of a rigid, ethnicized, and unnegotiable kind, has taken the place of sexual miscegenation as the primal postcolonial fantasy. A racially driven "fundamentalism" has surfaced in all these western European and North American societies, a new kind of defensive and racialized nationalism. Prejudice, injustice, discrimination, and violence toward "the Other," based on this hypostasized "cultural difference," has come to take its place—what Sarat Maharaj has called a sort of "spook look-alike of apartheid"—alongside the older racisms, founded on skin color and physiological difference, giving rise in response to a "politics of recognition," alongside the struggles against racism and for social justice.

These developments may at first seem remote from the concerns of new emerging nations and cultures of the "periphery." But as we suggested, the old center-periphery, nation-nationalist-culture model is exactly what is breaking down. Emerging cultures that feel threatened by the forces of globalization, diversity, and hybridization, or that have failed in the project of modernization, may feel tempted to close down around their nationalist inscriptions and construct defensive walls. The alternative is not to cling to closed, unitary, homogenous models of "cultural belonging" but to embrace the wider processes—the play of similarity and difference—that are transforming culture worldwide. This is the path of "diaspora," which is the pathway of a modern people and a modern culture. This may look, at first, just like—but is really very different from—the old "internationalism" of European modernism. Jean Fisher has argued that, until recently,

> internationalism has always referred exclusively to a European-European diasporan axis of political, military and economic affiliations. . . . This entrenched and dominant axis creates, in Mosquera's words, "zones of silence" elsewhere, making it difficult for lateral communications and other affiliations to take place. Araeen and Oguibe remind us that the present initiative to define a new internationalism in the arts and culture is only the most recent in a history of such attempts at cross-cultural dialogue which have been erased from "established narrations of cultural practice in Britain [and which failed] to overwhelm the deep-seated and firm structures which we interrogate" (Oguibe).[28]

What we have in mind here is something quite different—that "other" kind of modernity that led C. L. R. James to remark of Caribbean people: "Those people who are in western civilization, who have grown up in it, but made to feel and themselves feeling they are outside it, have a unique insight into their society."[29]

NOTES

This lecture was first given as part of the celebrations of the fiftieth anniversary of the founding of the University of the West Indies (UWI) held at the Cave Hill campus, Barbados, in November 1998. It appears here in a revised form with the permission of the UWI.

1 This is the subtitle of *Windrush*, by Mike Phillips and Trevor Phillips (London: HarperCollins, 1998), the volume that accompanied the BBC TV series.

2 Benedict Anderson, *Imagined Communities* (London: Verso, 1991).

3 Mary Chamberlain, *Narratives of Exile and Return* (Houndsmill: Macmillan, 1998).

4 See T. Modood, R. Berthoud, et al., *Ethnic Minorities in Britain* (London: Policy Studies Institute, 1997).

5 Chamberlain, *Narratives*, 132.

6 Iain Chambers, *Border Dialogues: Journeys in Post-Modernity* (London: Routledge, 1990), 104.

7 See Stuart Hall, "Cultural Identity and Diaspora," in *Identity: Community, Culture, Difference*, ed. Jonathan Rutherford (London: Lawrence and Wishart, 1990); and S. Hall and P. du Gay, eds., *Questions of Cultural Identity* (London: Sage, 1997), 222–237.

8 See Stuart Hall, "The West and the Rest: Discourse and Power," in this volume.

9 Mary Louise Pratt, *Imperial Eyes: Travel Writing and Transculturation* (London: Routledge, 1992). See, among others, Fernando Ortiz, *Cuban Counterpoint: Tobacco and Sugar* (New York: A. A. Knopf, 1947); Édouard Glissant, *Le discours antillais* (Paris: Editions du Seuil, 1981); and Edward Kamau Brathwaite, *The Development of Creole Society in Jamaica, 1770–1820* (Oxford: Oxford University Press, 1971).

10 Pratt, *Imperial Eyes*, 6–7.

11 David Scott, "Conscripts of Modernity" (unpublished paper).

12 *Redemption Song*. Seven programs made with Barraclough and Carey for BBC2 and transmitted 1989–90.

13 V. N. Volosinov, *Marxism and the Philosophy of Language* (New York: Seminar Press, 1973).

14 Kobena Mercer, "Diaspora Culture and the Dialogic Imagination," in *Welcome to the Jungle: New Positions in Black Cultural Studies* (London: Routledge, 1994), 63–64.

15 Salman Rushdie, *Imaginary Homelands* (London: Granta Books, 1990), 394.

16 Chambers, *Border Dialogues*, 104.

17 Immanuel Wallerstein, "The National and the Universal," in *Culture, Globalization and the World System*, ed. A. King (London: Macmillan, 1991), 91–106.

18 Paul Gilroy, *The Black Atlantic* (London: Verso, 1993).

19 *Babymother* was released in London, the US, and Jamaica in 1998. It was directed by Julian Henriques, the son of the distinguished Jamaican anthropologist who lives in London, and produced by his wife and partner, Parminder Vir, who is from the Punjab. They met, needless to say, from these two poles of empire, in London.

20 The official inquiry chaired by Sir William Macpherson into the death of Stephen Lawrence, convened after five years only as a result of the heroic efforts of his parents, Doreen and Neville Lawrence, and a small group of black supporters, was a public event and a cause célèbre in 1998, and a turning point in British race relations. It resulted in the judge finding the Metropolitan Police guilty of "institutional racism": Sir William Macpherson of Cluny, *The Stephen Lawrence Inquiry Report*, Cmnd. 4262–1 (1991).

21 Guy Brett, "A Tragic Excitement," in *Aubrey Williams* (London: Institute of International Visual Arts and Whitechapel Gallery, 1998), 24.

22 See David Scott, "That Event, This Memory: Notes on the Anthropology of African Diasporas in the New World," *Diaspora* 1, no. 3 (1991): 261–284.

23 Sarat Maharaj, "Perfidious Fidelity," in *Global Visions: Towards a New Internationalism in the Visual Arts*, ed. Jean Fisher (London: Institute of International Visual Arts, 1994), 31. The reference is to Jacques Derrida, "Des Tours des Babel," in *Difference in Translation* (Ithaca, NY: Cornell University Press, 1985).

24 The title of one of the most important chapters in Frantz Fanon, *Black Skin, White Masks* (London: Pluto Press, 1986).

25 Steve Ouditt, "Enigma of Survival," in *Annotations 4: Creole-in-Site*, ed. Gilane Tawadros (London: Institute of International Visual Arts, 1998), 8–9.

26 For "tradition as the changing same," see Gilroy, *The Black Atlantic*.

27 See, for example, Arjun Appadurai, *Modernity at Large* (Minneapolis: University of Minnesota Press, 1996).

28 Jean Fisher, "Editor's Note," in *Global Visions: Towards a New Internationalism in the Visual Arts*, ed. J. Fisher (London: Institute of International Visual Arts, 1994), xii.

29 C. L. R. James, "Africans and Afro-Caribbean: A Personal View," *Ten.8*, no. 16 (1984).

The interview with David Scott, conducted in March 1996, comes at a significant moment in Stuart's career. Around that time, in the context of his retirement from the Open University and his burgeoning involvement with the Black Arts movement focused on the Rivington Place Art Centre initiatives (which came to increasingly occupy his time), Stuart was also settling a number of intellectual accounts. Principal among these were the burden of his perceived responsibility for the development of Cultural Studies, in its newly globalized forms, and his political investment in Marxism (from the "Bandung" moment of 1955 to the point of the collapse of the Soviet empire and the resurgence of neoliberalism), and these are the themes that are explored in this interview. However, a further theme that runs through the interview involves a question that Scott raises at its beginning concerning the extent to which Stuart should be understood to be a specifically Jamaican or West Indian intellectual. Evidently, as Scott observes elsewhere, while he and Stuart share an origin in Jamaica, they were shaped by different generational experiences, in quite separate moments in Jamaica's modern political history—the decolonization of the 1940s and the socialism of the 1970s, respectively—and subsequently lived their respective displacements from Jamaica in different metropolitan locations.[1] Nonetheless, despite the contrasts in these specific histories, we have a fascinating dialogue between two diasporic intellectuals, discussing the intellectual significance not only of their shared Caribbean origins but also of a set of related issues concerning race, ethnicity, colonialism, and empire.

In relation to the question of Cultural Studies, what is perhaps most striking is that Stuart is at pains here to recognize the significance of his own oblique debt not just to literary studies in general but specifically to the work of F. R. Leavis and what he calls the "moral seriousness of . . . [the] . . . attention to culture" at the heart of Leavis's work. Later in the interview, in a different context, he talks of his intellectual concern to "always honour the moment that I am trying to surpass," and this is an exemplary instance of his practice in this respect. While he disagrees entirely with Leavis's politics, and while his object of study is entirely different, he nonetheless recognizes the significance of not only his but also Hoggart's debt to Leavis. Thus he goes on to explain that his own earliest work on film and television—"teaching *Dr Zhivago* to cut into the question of Stalinism"—and then writing on the social significance of film and television as the new media of the day with Paddy Whannel in *The Popular Arts* were powerfully enabled by their employment of methods of cultural analysis that had their origins in Leavis's work—however much Leavis himself might have disapproved politically of the uses to which his methods came to be appropriated.

In offering this account, Stuart also indicates the extent of the overlap between the very early New Left, which included important figures such as Raymond Williams, Edward Thompson, Peter Worsley, and John Rex, and the early concerns of Cultural Studies.[2] In then accounting for his own subsequent relation to Marxism, Stuart offers a clear explication of the origins of his distaste for the Hegelian theoreticism of Frankfurt School Marxism and goes on to explain, in more detail than he does elsewhere, what was involved for him not only in the reinvention of "a Marxism I can assent to" by Althusser (read through Gramsci) in the 1970s but also in CCCS's own subsequent reinvention of a "non-reductionist, non-Leninist Gramsci." Here Stuart also offers a detailed account of his own relation to the political project of the ex–Communist Party journal *Marxism Today*, which, under the inspired editorship of Stuart's close collaborator at that time, Martin Jacques, offered a very important site for the articulation of an effective political response to Thatcherite hegemony, as it emerged in the 1980s.[3]

As indicated in my discussion of these issues in the general introduction to this volume, the middle section of this interview is taken up with discussion both of the place of questions of race and ethnicity in Stuart's overall oeuvre and of his relation to the Caribbean. The interview's final section is important for its discussion of the strengths and weaknesses of essentialist (and ultimately biologically based) notions of race. On the one hand, Stuart is perfectly willing to concede that there are particular historical moments in which strategic essentialism becomes absolutely germane—if, for instance, you are in a situation where that is all that stands between you and "the fucking LA police." On the other hand, while he will not accept an antiracism that presumes its politics to be "guaranteed" by racial origins, neither will he support any kind of "post-modern nomadism" that presumes a voluntaristic fluidity in matters of identity. Returning to the question of his own identity, he ends by averring that while his work has not, on the whole, been done "from a specifically Caribbean position," it has all been done from the "position of those who are ex-centric to the Eurocentric system," as he has pursued a project of "polemicising the Eurocentric frontier."

The interview with Les Back (chapter 9) begins with commentary on Stuart's involvement with arts-based audiovisual organizations such as inIVA and Autograph (ABP) in his later years. As Stuart explains here, these initiatives returned him to his much earlier interests in documentary/photographic imagery, but this time with a specific focus on the representation of race and ethnicity.[4] He avers that, in his own view, the experience of people of the Caribbean diaspora in Britain has always been his subject, ever since it "discovered" him (as he puts it) coming out of Paddington station in the 1950s. In this account, Stuart also throws an interesting light on the significance of his early involvement with Henry James. He explains that despite the profound differences in the positions of a "black boy from Kingston" and this "highly refined sophisticated trans-Atlantic mind" writing about the wealthy, he came to see that this "bizarre encounter" nonetheless offered him a productive analogy. Although a lot of the content of James's writings was alien, he clearly had much to offer—insofar as they were both engaged in the construction of a perspective on how Europe looks if you come from the other side of the Atlantic. Henry James too had developed a diasporic way of seeing the world, and one that fit well with C. L. R. James's comments on the particular significance of the insights of people who are "in but not of" Europe. Throughout the interview, Stuart returns to the theme outlined in earlier chapters about always feeling doubly displaced. He had "ineradicable traces" of Jamaican experience in his memory but would make no claim on that as an authentic culture of blackness, never having been "a Kingston street boy" and having only learned to be "Caribbean" in the UK.

At various points in the interview, he revisits the theoretical and methodological basis of his own characteristic mode of conjunctural analysis, insisting on the need to specify the intermediate determinations on how structural
factors come into play in specific contexts. On this basis, he engages in a
brief history of why debates on race and ethnicity, in the US and the UK,
took very different forms at various stages (beginning with the specific forms
of their entanglements in slavery and empire). These levels of conjunctural
specification, he insists, are crucial if we are to escape the dead hand of essentializing abstractions in our analyses of these issues.[5] At various points, he
speaks biographically of the history of his own involvement in these debates,
right from the moment of publishing *The Young Englanders* (1967).[6] In this
context, he explains why, while the first generation of white Cultural Studies
scholars with whom he worked in the UK were all themselves supportive
of anti-imperialist politics, they were, from his own point of view, nonetheless unable to grasp the significance of the transformative nature of the black
presence within Britain.

In its later stages, the interview offers a highly condensed sociocultural
history of Britain in the postwar period, from the arrival of rock 'n' roll and
the hedonism of the 1960s to the crucial role of racist demagogues—Enoch
Powell prominent among them—and how this provided the unconscious
bedrock for spiraling fears of Otherness, as the 1970s progressed and the
postwar settlement based on the welfare state fell apart. However, despite
the breadth of this canvas, the discussion never loses sight of the central
questions of diaspora and displacement: Stuart's point, typically, is that these
are matters that can only be understood in the context of their sociocultural
locations. In its final part, the interview also offers Stuart the opportunity to
articulate his rationale for the particular historical periodizations with which,
toward the end of his life, he was most concerned. Thus he gives here a particularly clear account of Thatcherism—not so much as a UK phenomenon
but as the first installment of the global capitalist project of neoliberalism,
which New Labour then continued. He then explores the rise—and subsequent difficulties—of multiculturalism in the UK and its quite transformed
relation, in the post-9/11 period, to new forms of social conflict defined not so
much by race as by religion. Evidently, these are crucial issues, as we stumble
forward into a period of "multicultural drift," cultural racism, and Islamophobia, amid calls to revive policies of assimilationism, and, accompanied
by the return of forms of xenophobia that we might have hoped to have left
behind, now seemingly relegitimized by public referenda.

In another interview from this same period (2007), this time with Bill Schwarz as his interlocutor, Stuart returns to the question of the long gestation of his understanding of Thatcherism.[7] As he explains, this analysis—working outward from the media's racialized coverage of a particular crime in a Birmingham suburb—treated race as the prism through which that whole conjuncture could be read symptomatically. Speaking as he did in 2007, in the wake of the ill-considered Western invasions of various Middle Eastern countries (forms of adventurism for which we are all, of course, still paying the price), he describes this as an imperializing project involving the attempt to imprint Western values and ways of life across the face of the globe, disguised as a civilizing mission in which "the West" saves "the Rest" from its backward ways. All this necessarily brings him to the question of cultural difference—and to the processes of negotiation necessary if people with different histories and values are to be able to live together peaceably, without the culture of any one group having to be neutralized. As he goes on to argue later, the assimilationist model ultimately works on the basis of a solipsist form of narcissism in which alterity can never be fully recognized or accepted, whereas Stuart draws implicitly on the kind of model of democracy as a necessarily agonistic process of continuous debate ("a big, staged, continuous row").[8]

In opening up these questions of cultural difference, Stuart explains here, possibly more clearly than anywhere else, why it was that he came to feel that the arts had a particular role to play in these debates. Thus he argues that in order to understand cultural difference, you have to be prepared to make the detour through the language of the imaginary to the realm "where [people] fantasise, where they symbolise." Here he touches on vital issues that have perhaps now come more clearly into focus in the wake of the Brexit vote and of Donald Trump's presidential victory in the US. In both of these processes, virulent forms of xenophobia and racism clearly played a large part in garnering support for seemingly nonrational ("post-truth") forms of politics. In this connection, Stuart argues that the nature of people's visceral fears of those who "don't look or think like them" are not matters that you can "get to by reasoning with them." Indeed, he claims that they can only be explicated by something other than "the language of straight description" and can only find expression in the domain of the symbolic, or other discourses that recognize the existence of the complex (and often unconscious) dynamics of our cultural and political lives.

In his introduction to Stuart's Du Bois lectures at Harvard in 1994, Kobena Mercer insists that Stuart's later work on questions of race, ethnicity, and identity was not just "critically enlivened by his engagement with black British artists, filmmakers and photographers . . ." but that this "late period" commitment to the visual arts also "followed directly from his constructionist trajectory" in which, through his engagements with poststructuralism, he moved beyond the more sociologically oriented earlier work on these topics. He also refers to the aforementioned interview with Schwarz, in which Stuart insists on the specific importance of the arts as "the one sphere of culture where . . . fears and fantasies can be brought into discourse and rendered speakable." As Mercer notes, the aesthetic can often play a crucial role in opening up differences that authoritative cultural discourses strive to close down. It thus renders "imaginable" alternative rearticulations that—crucially—function to ensure that political dialogues concerning identities are kept open.[9]

NOTES

1 David Scott, *Stuart Hall's Voice: Intimations of an Ethics of Receptive Generosity* (Durham, NC: Duke University Press, 2017), 11.

2 This was before Perry Anderson's makeover of the *New Left Review* as a journal of continental Marxist theory.

3 Not least as the site of publication for important essays such as Stuart's own "The Great Moving Right Show" (Hall, *The Essential Essays, Volume 1*, ch. 13).

4 Stuart Hall, "The Social Eye of *Picture Post*," *Working Papers in Cultural Studies*, no. 2 (1972): 71–121. Far from understanding Stuart's activities with these organizations as some kind of "hobby" that he took up as a way of leaving behind the "serious" concerns of his earlier theoretical work, it is important to understand that his conceptualization of these arts practices was developed precisely on the basis of his earlier theorization of a variety of forms of cultural production.

5 In this respect, as noted in the general introduction to this volume, Stuart's mode of analysis bears close comparison with that of Barrington Moore Jr.'s emphasis on the political significance of the specific form in which surplus labor was extracted from subordinate groups in different types of society, particularly in his *The Social Origins of Dictatorship and Democracy* (Harmondsworth: Peregrine, 1969); and see also Stuart's comments in Hall, *The Essential Essays, Volume 1*, ch., 6, on his lack of interest in developing an analysis of racism "in general," as opposed to its specific forms in different historical contexts.

6 Stuart Hall, *The Young Englanders* (London: National Committee of Commonwealth Immigrants, 1967).

7 "Living with Difference: An Interview with Bill Schwarz," *Soundings*, no. 37 (2007): 148–158.

8 For anyone with personal memories of cccs itself under Stuart's directorship, this description will doubtless also ring bells at a microlevel, in relation to the characteristic mode of conduct of collective intellectual work in that setting.

9 Kobena Mercer, ed., introduction to *The Fateful Triangle: Race, Ethnicity, Nation* (Cambridge, MA: Harvard University Press, 2017), 8, 28–29. In establishing this genealogy, it is also important to recognize that Mercer was himself the editor of the book in which Stuart's essay titled "New Ethnicities" originally appeared: Kobena Mercer, ed., *Black Film, British Cinema*, ica Documents no. 7 (London: Institute of Contemporary Arts, 1988).

CHAPTER 8

Politics, Contingency, Strategy:
An Interview with David Scott

Stuart Hall's name is perhaps most centrally associated with "Cultural Studies." Under his leadership Cultural Studies became a major player in the contemporary rethinking of the humanities and social sciences. It constituted not a discipline so much as a critical mode of intervention grounded in the investigation of nonelite or "popular" forms of social practice.

It is perhaps too little remembered, however, that Stuart Hall is a Jamaican and a West Indian whose work has been informed by some of the journeys and debates that constitute this region as a zone of history, culture, and politics. In this interview, Stuart Hall reflects on his intellectual itinerary: his early connection to West Indian literary and political questions, the politics of the New Left, the making of Cultural Studies, critical theory, Marxism, and race, diaspora, and ethnicity. To my mind, one of the most instructive aspects of Hall's cultural-political thought is the centrality to it of a concept of strategy. Hall is preeminently a strategic intellectual. Because he has given up the epistemological preoccupation with First Principles, with the search for a Final Philosophical Ground of True Knowledge, his approach to political questions depends crucially on such concepts as "contingency" and "conjuncture." That is to say, it depends on reading, at any given historical moment, the play of social forces and discursive hegemonies, and on identifying the move that will produce a shift in the cognitive-political configuration.

DAVID SCOTT: The first question that I want to ask you, Stuart, is what do you think it is that prompted the international recognition of your work in the mid-1980s?

STUART HALL: I think there are probably two reasons. One is Cultural Studies. Cultural Studies certainly comes into its own in the '80s, especially outside of Britain, and not just as something which is limited to what was going on at the Birmingham Centre. I was identified with that because I was the director in the '70s, and it is the '70s work that people know. I think that was one of the reasons I came to have wide visibility. I think the second reason is that I was writing about Thatcherism, [and] making an intervention into this public political space. And also because Thatcherism itself was extremely new and novel, a break with the past, both Left and Right, a puzzling political formation. And I had a lot to say about it. The origins of why I had something to say is another story. So to give a deeper answer to the question, you have to ask why it is that Cultural Studies becomes so center stage, and with it me, and why it is that people have become so involved with debating the turn to the New Right.

DS: I want to come back to that, but I want us to retrace our steps a little bit. As you say, it is the '70s work—the work on Gramsci, on the media, on communications—that people know about. But it is not often remembered that before the founding of *New Left Review*, etc., etc., you published a number of things in *Bim*. On West Indian literature. This would have been in the mid-1950s. What was your connection to writing about West Indian literature?

SH: Yes. Well, when I went to England in 1951, I was fully intending to come back home and have a relation with the university. The people I knew were mainly. . . . I mean, I became a West Indian in London. Before that, I was a Jamaican. A kind of Jamaican nationalist. I was a young student at the time. Very young; I was only eighteen. The people I met in London were not only other Jamaicans studying abroad but a whole range of people, like Lloyd Best's generation, Willie Demas, the whole generation who went back into government. They were, in fact, young civil servants. So I became aware of West Indian culture, the West Indies as an entity, and my own West Indian identity. I knew more Trinidadians than I knew Jamaicans in Britain. So my first years [in England] as an undergraduate were mainly spent in relation to West Indian students there. There wasn't yet a big migration. The West Indians around were students involved in a debate about West Indian literature. We also knew [George] Lamming and knew [Samuel] Selvon and other Caribbean writers who were there. We all worked for the World Service [of the BBC], which was a sort of meeting point for young poets and writers. My own training was in literature. I have no training in sociology at all.

DS: So your undergraduate training was in literature.

SH: Yes, my undergraduate training and postgraduate was in literature. That's a long story. But just to truncate this very quickly, it is really the failure of Federation that clinches my decision not to come back [to Jamaica].

DS: I see. Tell me a little more about that.

SH: Well, you know, the dream was that we were all going back to make Federation work. We were all convinced that the individual [island] entities were not viable—politically or economically viable—in their own right. Only the wider market, the wider community could be viable. And that's what our intention was. We were partly fired by Guyana. You know this was in 1953. It was a tremendous moment with all the talk about the ending of colonialism. . . . So those were very heavy moments. That's all that I was focusing on in those days. So of course I was writing about and reading about Caribbean literature. The others [i.e., other students] were in a slightly different position to me because they were civil servants who had been sent to England to prepare themselves to go back and administer this new formation. I didn't have a clear path like that, so when it broke down I could say, well, maybe not me, not yet.

DS: But the breakup of Federation was . . .

SH: Quite late. I was talking about after I'd finished postgraduate work. I'd decided to stay on to do postgraduate work.

DS: This would have been in the mid-1950s.

SH: Yes.

DS: By the end of the 1950s, you are no longer writing in *Bim*, and one sees, perhaps, the making of a Marxist.

SH: Yes. The relation to Marxism is very long and tortuous and complicated. But I suppose what happened is that right after I graduated, a lot of people I was close to came back to the Caribbean. My immediate circle.

DS: Which comprised?

SH: Which comprised people like Willie Demas, Lloyd [Best], Lewis, and so on. So I decided to stay and do postgraduate work. But I became involved in the ferment that was going on in Britain—among the British student-Left—which crested in 1956. I was part of an organization which was then called the Socialist Club. The Socialist Club was a club which refused to join the Communist Party because we were opposed to Stalinism, and refused to just hook up with the Labour Party, which was in a very anticommunist mood. In this group there were a lot of Third World students, a lot of students from outside of Britain. And also people who went on to make the *New Left Review*. People from Surinam, from Egypt, the Sudan, and so on. [The year] 1956 is a double whammy. Because it's Suez and Hungary. And then the New Left emerges at that moment as a wedge.

DS: How did you come to be the first editor of the *New Left Review*?

SH: That's a long and complicated story. You see, we started a student Left journal called the *Universities and Left Review* immediately after March 1956, which included two of us who were not communists, never had been, never were, and two people who joined the Communist Party and who left because of '56. So we started this journal, but it then joined up with another journal called the *New Reasoner*, which was an older generation of communists who also left the [Communist] Party over Suez, over Hungary . . . mainly over Hungary and over the 20th Congress. And these two journals merged in 1961, and I was made the editor. And that's what included Raymond Williams, Edward Thompson, Peter Worsley, John Rex, and so on.

DS: It also included Orlando Patterson.

SH: Yes.

DS: What was his association with the Left at that time?

SH: Well, he was a student in London during that period. He was at LSE [London School of Economics], then teaching a little bit. And I think his linkage was much more to the generation that took over after I left *New Left Review*, that is to say, to Perry Anderson, and . . .

DS: And Robin Blackburn in particular?

SH: Yes. I knew them at Oxford—I'd been there—and am leaving when Perry and Robin start a junior version of the *Universities and Left Review*.

DS: When and why did you leave the *New Left Review*?

SH: That is too long a story. There is a kind of takeover, a succession. . . . I decided to go because really I'd been involved in everything— *Universities and Left Review*, then *New Left Review*—ever since 1956. I was really worn out. [*New Left Review*] was very badly funded, so there were real problems keeping the journal going. I was the only full-time person employed in the journal. But the old generation, Thompson and so on, they couldn't go on with the same degree of involvement as before. And at the point when I decided to go, it was a question of who was going to take over, and we all agreed that Perry Anderson was the most outstanding person.

DS: So this wasn't a matter of ideological "differences"?

SH: It wasn't a matter then, but it quickly became one because it emerged that Perry had a slightly different project for the journal . . .

DS: I sensed that from what he says in his *Arguments in English Marxism*.

SH: Yes. It was a very different project for the journal. But he didn't reveal that beforehand. It was tricky, you know, to know how to make the succession, who was going to own the assets of the journal, whether the old guard was going to have any editorial control. I'm not suggesting that it was easy and simple, but we didn't think at the time it would be quite the ideological shift it turned out to be. As soon as the shift was made, Perry more or less didn't go the editorial route, and decided that the editorial board was not his editorial board. He moved in new people. The journal became much more theoretical, much less involved in political practice, much less addressed to the British political conjuncture, very much more influenced by Parisian debates. Then they started translating, so a wave of Western Marxism is translated by them. So the journal now had a very different character from what Edward Thompson envisaged. He was a social historian but very suspicious of theory, as he expressed in his essay "The Poverty of Theory." So there is a cleavage. It's after the event that we realized that this had been an ideological shift as well as a generational transition. I dropped out then.

DS: This would have been . . . ?

SH: 1962 . . . the end of 1961, the beginning of 1962.

DS: I want to come in a moment to . . .

SH: This, of course, is not an answer to the question about my relation to Marxism.

DS: I know. Yes, I understand that completely, and I want to come to the question of Marxism in relation to Richard Hoggart in a minute. But before we get there, I want to ask you about your connections to West Indian intellectuals at this time. Your connection to C. L. R. James (I remember that obituary you wrote after his death). And your connection to the student-intellectuals around the Caribbean Artists Movement (CAM). Did you have any connections to them?

SH: Oh, yes. I had connections with both. We were all, of course, very much students of James's work. And when James came back from the States to live in Britain, lots of us went to visit him, talk with him. There was also a political movement around James—*Race Today*, with Darcus Howe—which had a specific Jamesian orientation. I was not a part of that. I thought that was a very specific reading of James in the British context. So a lot of people were influenced by James and had conversations with him over and above whether they were part of the Race Today Collective. Among other things, I did two very long interviews with James—there is a long interview for his eightieth birthday which was not transmitted by the BBC, and the tapes were wiped. It no longer exists.

DS: There's no copy of it?

SH: No. What they [the BBC] said was he'll soon be dead, so we'll transmit it as his obituary. And then when the producer who made it was leaving, he said, you [i.e., the BBC] aren't going to use it, so let me have it. And they said the tapes were finished. So we started again, now with Channel 4, and we made a second long interview, two programs with James when he was about eighty-four. And those were transmitted. But I am very, very sorry that the first interview wasn't transmitted because between eighty and eighty-four he had deteriorated. His memory was stronger about the earlier days. And at eighty he was still lecturing a bit; Busby had just brought out a new edition of some of his work; he was still going back and forth to the States. It was a moment of another recognition of James's work. And he was still very cogent, very lucid. So that was my relation to James. He was the master, an image of what it would be like to be an independent Left intellectual. James was a model. It was a different question whether you agreed with everything James said. Just how to be in the world. He was a very powerful figure.

DS: And the Caribbean Artists Movement?

SH: Yes. I was involved in the first meeting. I spoke at the first conference. Do you know the book about it?

DS: Yes, Anne Walmsley's book.[1]

SH: Yes, well, I helped her with the research. So through that [through CAM] I met Kamau [Brathwaite], the historians, and writers who were there at that time. I went to several of the meetings.

DS: But at least from where I come at things, and as I have read you, you do not appear as a very visible Caribbean intellectual in the early 1960s.

SH: Yes. Because I am not coming home. Because I have taken the decision not to come home. And once you have taken that decision, you are in a very difficult situation in terms of who . . . who do you represent? What do you speak for? You no longer speak from a situation for which you have a political and intellectual responsibility in a direct sense. I don't have to take the sticks out of my back if I make a political statement in England about the Caribbean. Who cares about that? You know what I mean? I had taken that decision by then, or rather by then I recognized that I had taken that decision. I'd probably taken the decision before that, but I had never said to myself, I am going, soon I'll go, I'll get over the disappointment that earlier conditions aren't there. I'll work my involvement in the New Left and all that out of my system, and then I'll go home. But actually, I wasn't.

DS: So that the . . .

SH: You want to know why I wasn't going home? I've written about this. I wasn't going back for very specific reasons. I'd come from the middle class, the aspiring colored middle class, who lived that culture throughout my childhood. I hated it. I loathed it. But I never felt at that moment that I could come back to Jamaica and live in another way. After the '60s, it was a different Jamaica. But by then I had taken the decision not to come. Before that, I thought if you go back into that familiar, colonial, aspiring—you know, Stuart has gone abroad, he's got a Rhodes Scholarship, he's educated in England, he's coming back to a family who hate everything that he's doing out there. Everything. How do you get out of that? In large societies you move to somewhere else. You don't have to talk to your mother or father every day. How was I supposed to come back to Kingston where they lived. . . . For those personal reasons I thought I'd die.

DS: Yes, but the upsurge of the late '60s around those intellectuals, Kamau [Brathwaite], [Walter] Rodney, Gordon Rohlehr, Richard Small—that whole possibility doesn't inspire you?

SH: That in itself didn't inspire me. What would have inspired me is if one could have seen into the '70s at that point in terms of the difference it made in ordinary life—you know, because one wasn't just coming back to an intellectual movement, but back to a life. So it's not until the '70s when the cultural revolution takes place. . . . I wouldn't have come back just to join the intellectuals who were trying to make it [the cultural revolution] happen. It may have been wrong not to do that, but that was the moment of my recoil from it rather than my advance towards it. When I'd come back in the '70s, people were speaking patois everywhere, you'd turn on the radio and people were speaking patois. I'd been prevented from speaking patois my entire life. This is a black Jamaica for the first time. Jamaica was not black before that. It became possible to be black in Jamaica at the end of the '6os. But by then, in a curious way, I had started to get involved in Cultural Studies, and I had another project going there. I sort of felt, well, that moment has passed you by.

DS: As Walcott might have put it, you were in the middle of "another life."

SH: Yes, I was.

DS: I want to come now to Cultural Studies. How did you come to form your association with Richard Hoggart? Had you by then read his *Uses of Literacy*?

SH: Oh, yes. *Uses of Literacy* was published in '57—so just after '56. And it was very much part of the excitement, of what was going on, being discussed in Left student circles. But Cultural Studies didn't come from that. I was involved in Cultural Studies before it had a name. You see, because of what I'd been interested in and debating about before in relation to that first generation of West Indian intellectuals who were my reference point when I went to England, there is one difference between me and them, and that is that I am not an economist. They are all economists. I am a student of literature. So I was always more interested in cultural questions. I was interested in politics, but not as a thing to study. I was not in economics, which was the master discipline. Even if you were a historian, what you had to know about was economics. Of course, because the question that was at issue was the question of development. I wasn't that. I was always more interested in cultural questions.

DS: But there were other people who were "in literature." They too are not returning—Naipaul, for example. Isn't there a similarity?

SH: I'm not sure about that. Because, you see, I was into cultural questions, but by then I had stopped being a creative writer. So I was a kind of cultural theorist or critic. Which is different than if you were writing about [culture]. They were writers and poets, which of course was a perfectly legitimate thing that you could understand. Or you were trying to change the economic situation. But to be interested in culture, you know, what was that? A kind of halfway house?

Now, there are two things about it. One is, there is therefore initiated from then onwards a conversation in my head between my interest in culture and orthodox Marxism. Even though the two don't fit? So even though I am extremely interested and go through many variations of an intimate inside conversation with Marxism, I was never an economic reductionist. Never. I was never an orthodox Marxist. I was always a heterodox Marxist. Sometimes I was closer [than others to Marxism]. In the time of Althusser in the '70s, I am very Marxist. But why? Because Althusser's problematic is a counterreductionist Marxism. So of course I'm an Althusserian. And I am a Gramscian because . . . You see, so I go to these bits of Marxism that are not a straight system of reading everything from the logic of capital. That has never been my relation to Marxism.

So, I'm interested in culture. And I am still interested in Caribbean culture. So instead of doing my PhD, I go to Rhodes House library [at Oxford University], and I read the whole of that debate with Herskovits on survivals, syncretism, etc. That's what I read.

DS: But you never wrote anything about that?

SH: No, I just read it. And my interest in culture as an object is partly in response to those questions.

DS: But there is another . . .

SH: Yes, I have another one. Which is, because of literature, I've come through the Leavis school. Now Leavis is a very interesting character. Leavis is a leading literary critic—hence his influence on Hoggart and [Raymond] Williams and so on. Leavis has an elitist and conservative view of education. Education is to train and refine the sensibility of the minority. This is a conservative social program which I am not interested in. But Leavis has the broadest understanding of culture. Interest in language because it takes you to the heart of the meaning of a culture . . . He addresses this complicated question which Marxism cannot unlock: how to understand the relation between the cultural text and its context in something other than a mechanistic way.

So these two things drive me to an interest in culture via indirect routes. I can't be a Leavisite because I don't believe, I am not interested, in saving canonical English culture. Leavis is interested in the five great minds he can train against the onrush of mass society. I'm interested in popular culture. So I have different objects from Leavis. But I am interested in the moral seriousness of an attention to culture which takes you to the heart of a social formation. And I am interested in that debate in the context of what I suppose we'd now call diaspora culture. How to understand what is going on in religious culture especially, in Latin America, in the Southern churches, and in Jamaica in Rastafarianism, and in Revivalism, in the conversation we now recognize as popular culture.

DS: But we are talking about the mid-1960s now, aren't we? You don't yet have a theoretical language . . .

SH: The reading for that is earlier than that, when I was a graduate student, '58, '59. The other interest in Cultural Studies as a broader program comes in the 1960s.

DS: Which is when you meet Richard Hoggart.

SH: Yes. It's because Hoggart's book *Uses of Literacy* does the same kind of thing. Trained in Leavisite methods, he doesn't use these methods to read high literature but reads working-class speech and asks, What is happening in working-class culture under the conditions of affluence, and the coming of television, Americanization, and so on? He takes a kind of cultural root to that question rather than a historical or an economic root. We were influenced by that debate.

DS: Stuart, a good deal of your writing around this time, late 1960s, early 1970s, turns on the problem of communication, media, broadcasting, etc. But even before that, I understand from Lloyd Best that you had written a paper on the Beatles. I have not seen this. When was that written? Was that part of your concern with the question of working-class culture? Was that prior to this?

SH: Yes, it's prior to this. I went to the Centre for Cultural Studies in '64. I stopped working for *New Left Review* in '62. I became a lecturer in a small London university college in film and television. I was the first person ever appointed to teach film and television.

DS: How did you come to that?

SH: Because nobody is teaching it. Television has only just arrived. Film has been there, but nobody studies it. I have a friend at the British Film Institute who begins to teach about these new media often in literature classes in adult education. We all teach in adult education, so we are all going to night classes. An old man once said to me, "Not a bad lecture; that's the fifteenth lecture I've heard on the middle class." But we're not teaching literature in a formalized way. We're using literature to . . . I'm teaching *Dr. Zhivago* to cut into the question of Stalinism. We're talking about wider questions through literature. And we use film a lot. And begin to look at television because of the impact of television. If you read Hoggart's book, you know, he says there is this new medium—is it going to change working-class culture, replace some of the old oral modes and even earlier popular forms of popular culture by another kind of imposed culture? So the question is, What is television going to do in the transition from a class culture to a mass culture? These are the things that nobody is studying, the television relationship which you don't see if you ask questions about books. But television reorganizes the relation between who is speaking and who is spoken to, and what a popular genre is and how you touch popular emotions. You know, all the popular culture questions are bang in front of you. So we started to write about it. I wrote about it. I wrote a book about it for use of teachers, mainly literature teachers, wanting to talk about film and television and popular music in the classroom. It's called *The Popular Arts*.[2] And that book is published in '64, before I go to the Centre. In fact, I go to the Centre because Hoggart knows I am interested in these questions and because I have worked on film and television he gets me to come to the Centre to try to teach, to do some graduate work on this big transition.

DS: How did the New Left (not *New Left Review*, but the New Left) meet this kind of interest? Were they hostile?

SH: Well, that depends on who you mean. By then the New Left is the Perry Anderson New Left. And they are not terribly interested. The people who are interested in it are the old New Left. Hoggart was on our editorial board when Williams was there. The beginning of Cultural Studies feels to us like the New Left politics in another place. We couldn't keep the New Left going, but exactly the kinds of questions— is the culture changing, what is happening to working-class culture, what is the nature of affluent capitalism—these are the questions which we posed in cultural terms. And that's the agenda for Cultural Studies. So Cultural Studies feels like an opportunity to come inside under the shelter of the university and be paid to do some of this work and to take some students and subvert them into this line.

I've written an essay called "The 'First' New Left: Life and Times," and it plots what is cognate between the interests of the early New Left.[3] Because the early New Left was very much concerned with the constitutive nature of culture. Absolutely central. I mean, take E. P. Thompson's work. It suddenly brings questions of religion, questions of art, organization. These become cultural questions. In Raymond Williams it's the same. It's probably the first sentence of the first editorial of *Universities and Left Review* that politics is more than politics, politics is everything, politics is . . . all human life is politics, including our culture, our meanings, the way in which we make sense of the world. What is called ideology and in classical Marxism given a subordinate and dependent status is for us constitutive. So the New Left is itself grounded on a kind of debate with the reductionist nature of Left thinking. I say "Left thinking" because a lot of social democrats were just as reductionist about culture and the economy as orthodox Marxists. They defined how the economy works differently, but they don't differ in thinking that in some way, as Althusser would say, His Majesty the Economy can detach itself from its political, ideological, and cultural conditions of existence and dictate on its own. In one way or another, everybody around the first New Left had problems with that way of thinking. So Cultural Studies had a political definition of this broad kind. It was not a question of having to sign up for this political party or that political party. But it was perfectly well understood by everybody that there was a political project. So we were treated like lepers.

DS: So in the late '60s and early '70s you are writing about the media, communications, etc. Simultaneously with this, you are rethinking Marx, the question of ideology. These moments are presumably internally linked—how you come at a rethinking of the question of ideology.

SH: Yes. In a way the question of ideology is for me simply another way of posing the cultural question. It just happened under the impact of Althusserian work that offers a reading of Marx which gives these different analytic elements a more equal weight in determining a particular conjuncture. It doesn't make ideology dependent on the economic. So it gives space to the things I am interested in. But it calls that instance the ideological instance rather than the cultural instance. Ideology in my work is still thinking about culture, and the work I do on ideology is to kind of bring it more in touch with how I understand culture. So I am less interested in formalized ideologies than I am in ideology in everyday life, ideology in popular culture, ideology in mass communication, etc. I am interested in the ideological element rather than ideology as a class-specific form of thought.

DS: One of the essays from this period that I always come back to is "The Problem of Ideology: Marxism without Guarantees."[4] This question of "without guarantees" seems to have been crucial to the way you have thought about Marx; for how in a certain sense you have both resisted the Althusserian turn while appropriating a number of the antimetaphysical moves.

SH: Yes. I suppose this is because, in my view, the orthodox structure of Marxism is very much teleological. And I think in part it is its Hegelian heritage that leads in that direction. Marx inverts and Althusser says he not only inverts but breaks with the Hegelian proposition. I don't think that break is ever made. So in resisting that notion of determination as it is fixed in orthodox Marxist thought, I am also resisting therefore the notion of teleology. When it comes therefore to thinking about and reading people who might have come this route but put ideas on the table that might help us get past this roadblock, the obvious place to go is to the Hegelian Marxists, to [Theodor] Adorno and the Frankfurt School. And I am never interested in that because of the Hegelian move.

DS: You mean you have never approached Marx through Hegel?

SH: No. I have approached Marx through Hegel, but I don't like the Hegelian trace.

DS: And by the late '60s, early '70s, that's already clear to you. That that's the wrong road.

sH: Yes. I am not a Lukácsian. Everybody asks the question, Why does the Centre become so obsessed by the French, by French thought in general, when there is an available critical theory in Germany which is much closer to Marxism than that? And I think this is the reason.

DS: So that also has enabled you to make an argument for keeping aspects of Marxism, keeping in focus, for example, the question of the circulation of capital, without reading that teleologically.

sH: No, no. You must remember that these are two quite different things. I am in contention with some aspects of Marxism. I am in contention with certain forms, certain paradigmatic forms of the theory at an ontological level. Which is very different from the question of whether you find important Marx's riveting attention to the history of capital and the impact of capital, or the constraints of economic life on everything. All those questions are real questions. I come to be more dubious about Marx's definition of class. Not because I don't think class exists, but because I think it becomes itself lodged in a certain historical image of what class is. When the working class no longer looks like it did in Engels's Manchester, Marxists don't know what to do with it. They take off their flat caps. They can't think flexibly enough about class. It's not because class has gone away. It's just absurd to try to think about a society of private appropriation which doesn't create economic differences which are a measure of importance in everybody's life which you call classes. So because I'm never an orthodox Marxist, I don't feel the whole edifice is put at issue by questioning this or that about it. I don't feel I have destroyed the whole.

DS: And you never have.

sH: I never have. To be honest with you—and some people think it is a problem with me, and some people think it is a great merit of mine. I don't think it's either; I think it's just how I am—I never have been wholly anything. I may be closer to being wholly a Gramscian than anything else, but that is because—as Terry Eagleton just pointed out in a review of the new book—we have reinvented Gramsci.[5] I have reinvented a kind of nonreductionist, non-Leninist Gramsci. I think there is lots in Gramsci which is about that. But I recognize quite clearly that I have reconstructed a Gramsci that is in touch with Marx's questions but gives culture more seriousness and thinks there is an independent road to socialism. So my attitude to theory is that theory is absolutely essential, absolutely essential, because appearances are wrong, largely wrong. We need theory to break up appearances so that you can begin to understand how things work. What theory will never do is to tell you either what you ought to have done or act as a guarantee that the choices that you've made are right.

DS: In a recent retelling of the story of Cultural Studies, you describe yourself as someone who has always been "within shouting distance of Marxism." Isn't that a slightly different self-description than one you would have given when you were involved in battles around Marxism in the '70s?

SH: Yes, I would have. But remember one of the points that I have made. That is because this Marxism of the '70s is really Marx as reread by Althusser and Gramsci. And that one could defend because it is already different from the orthodox reading. So even at my most Marxist moment, I still have questions, and I don't feel that the having of questions in any way undermines my commitment to those ideas that I believe work. To be absolutely crude about it, I think that Marx works much better about capital than about class. Marx on the world market is absolutely crucial, but Marx on the class struggle is much more deeply lodged in a very specific historical experience. And so extrapolations from that to the idea of the revolutionary subject is dubious. And certainly the master centrality that is given to the class contradiction as the one which unlocks all the others—I can say that I have never held that. So I can say I am a Marxist in the Althusserian moment because Althusser suggests that there is always an economic instance, a political instance, and an ideological instance, and the economic and the political is the condition of the ideological instance and the ideological is the condition for the operation of the political and economic. So he gives me a Marxism I can assent to. If that is Marxism, I can begin to live with it.

DS: So that there is something at play here which is not explicitly thematized, and that is that you have a very *strategic* relationship to Marx.

SH: I have a strategic relation to theory. I don't regard myself as a theorist in the sense that that is my work. I am interested always in going on theorizing about the world, about the concrete, but I am not interested in the production of theory as an object in its own right. And therefore I use theory in strategic ways. I am not afraid to borrow this idea and try to match it up with this idea borrowed from another paradigm. I am aware of all the dangers of eclecticism and lack of rigor, which there is in my work. My work is open to both those criticisms. But on the other hand, it's because I think my object is to think the concreteness of the object in its many different relations. And, in that sense, the most powerful Marxist theoretical text for me is the introduction to the *Grundrisse*. I have written a long piece on this.

DS: Stuart, how did you come to write for *Marxism Today*?

SH: Well, *Marxism Today* was technically the official theoretical journal of the British Communist Party. But the fact is that from about the '56 break and much more after about the early '70s, it became a much wider formation. It broke with a kind of Stalinist model of politics, it broke with Moscow, it broke with that kind of orthodox Leninism, etc. So curiously enough, it became the site of a great deal of reworking and post-Marxism and not very Marxist kinds of work. And it was very active during the '70s, in setting up what was called the Communist University of London, which was, though it was sponsored by *Marxism Today*, a very broad meeting together, sort of spontaneous university over the summer of anything to do with the new social movements, social change, the Third World, philosophical questions, Cultural Studies, etc. So by the time I start to write for them, it was a journal that had been extracted from the teeth of the whole communist apparatus and so on. I mean, it still got some money from the Party. But I wasn't at all involved in that side of it. I simply knew Martin Jacques, who ran it. We got this title and ran with it and started to use it as a way of thinking the position of the Left. And of critiquing the existing position of the old Left, especially the old labor Left. The funny thing is that in 1989—we called it [the journal] MT, and I don't think anyone remembered it was *Marxism Today*—in '89, when the wall came down, people said "*Marxism Today*? What is Marxism today?" And we didn't know what Marxism today was, so it folded. We couldn't believe in the project under that title anymore. But for a long time, it acted just as an acronym for new thinking on the Left. I mean, a lot of people would tell you that it was not only not Marxist [but] was quite far to toying with elements of Thatcherism. Because we were quite excited by the fact that Thatcherism, from an opposite political position, had actually been able to change the bloody society in a very profound way. And as good Gramscians, we were interested in change whether it comes from the Right or the Left because we thought we had something to learn about how you constitute a hegemony. So people thought that this was breaking the old Right/Left barriers, the good manner of the Left, etc. We polemicized heavily about the old Labour Party and the old English working-class culture tradition, which was often very racist, very homophobic, very sexist, not a new modern kind of socialism at all. So it was our vehicle, really, which had little to do with its formal orthodox political location.

DS: How do you position yourself in relation to the work of Michel Foucault?

SH: This is not a short question. You know that I have made a critique of Foucault, which is really that I like very much the antiessentialist, the discursive way of thinking, and the historical specificity which is in Foucault. I made the critique that Foucault talks about a kind of endless proliferation of positionalities and antagonisms and never speaks about the moment when these are articulated together into a formation. Now I don't mean by that [that] we should just go back to the old totality. Articulations are not given, they don't last forever, and there is nothing necessary about their correspondences. But that is a very different thing from saying that nothing can ever be connected with anything. So I think in his vigorous attack against invoking the state as a class instrument, as a moment of unification of the economic, the political, and the cultural, he took it too far. But I must say that in more recent times, though I would still make that criticism, it stands between my work and Foucault's work less. I give it less weight.

DS: Right across the '80s, there is this engagement with Marx through Gramsci. But cutting across it and into it, there is this concern with a thematization of the popular, and with it the question of resistance, subculture, and also toward the mid- or late '80s the question of race. What is going on here?

SH: What is going on here? You see, I think that the moment you take this many-determined definition of a conjuncture you realize that the object of your strategy is not best expressed by the term "exploitation" but by the term "power." This is not to deny economic exploitation but to think about economic exploitation as the effect of a certain kind of economic power. Power is, for me, the larger concept, and I think in Gramsci it is too. Because power is something you can see operating at all these levels, whereas "exploitation" takes you right to the economy immediately. This is not a denial that people are exploited in the capitalist relation or anything like that. It's just that I don't think of it as ended if I have unlocked the question of exploitation. Now, the moment you think of power . . . you know, long before Foucault says power always constitutes its opposite, I have come to a pragmatic formulation of the same kind. Because if you think of power in terms of hegemony, since a hegemony is never a total obliteration of everything but only a formation where the balance of forces has those forces more powerful than that in a whole range of different sites. Well there is a lot left there. Which is precisely what you call history. No conjuncture will ever wrap history up. So how is that going to be unlocked? Well, these elements that are now constrained within the formation are going to begin to unlock themselves. And then you are into resistance, of course. And if you give culture not a primary but a constitutive role in this analysis, then you look at questions of cultural politics, cultural resistance, disaffiliation, etc., as the seeds or signs or symptoms of what is not resolved within the conjuncture. That over which power cannot exercise its totalizing force. And if you go to some of the new cultural movements which are being cited precisely as evidence of the end of conflict, the end of ideology, and we are saying that if you have a narrow conception of how these things work you might say that the '50s and '60s were a period when not much counterideology is around (I'm talking about before '68), but if you start to take soundings in other areas to which Gramsci directs your attention— civil society, the church, the school, education, the family, sexuality— you hear something else going on. Suddenly I started to go out onto the streets. So it's partly because of the nature of what you think the conjuncture is that all these apparently nonpolitical things have some bearing on how resistance is being lived and developed, especially when some of the formal channels of counterhegemony are locked up by social democracy.

DS: Around this time, too, Stuart, the mid-1980s, the question of race also enters your work. What has prompted this?

SH: Yes . . . I know why you say that. And lots of people say that. In fact, it's not quite true, you know. I begin writing about race in the late '60s again. What you really mean is I don't write about the Caribbean. But even that is not quite true. Because I wrote a long piece—two pieces, for UNESCO. One piece which I think most people don't know, which is a critique of the plural society model,[6] and the other is "Race, Articulation and Societies Structured in Dominance,"[7] and that was the result of work which I did throughout the time when I was at the Centre, for UNESCO's division of human rights . . .

DS: Was that the same time that you did the piece on Rastafari?

SH: That was the time that I gave the human rights lecture at UNESCO. Which was the anniversary of the signing of the Human Rights Charter. At which I played Bob [Marley] in extenso and made this interpretation of the importance of Marley and the, as it were, Africanization of Jamaican culture through Rastafarianism.

I think what you have to think of is what I said earlier, which is that I can't any longer write about the Caribbean because it's not the community in which I am embedded. But then the Caribbean comes to meet me; it comes to England. And all of a sudden there is a black community in whose politics I begin to get involved, so I begin to pick up again the question of race but now in the context of migration, immigration, etc. I wrote a very early pamphlet about second-generation black kids in Britain called "The Young Englanders,"[8] which raises this question of divided identity, of young blacks of the second generation feeling themselves British but being refused. So the reading of Rastafarianism is important in the British context. This is what saves the second generation from a kind of social suicide. Refused by British society, unable to go back home, they save themselves by at last hearing through the transistor, Bob [Marley], and roots reggae. And this is absolutely profound. I really think that that generation was in deep, deep, deep trouble in a way that this generation of blacks are not. This doesn't mean that they are not unemployed. They are. But they are not in trouble about who they are. They [i.e., the second generation] were in trouble about who they are. So I am writing about those questions and through UNESCO writing a bit about race in the Caribbean context. From time to time. The difference is that it's not something that I'm writing about in the context of Cultural Studies. So people who know my work through Cultural Studies don't very much know that I am also writing these other things.

DS: The work on the Caribbean, on race and social stratification, on Rastafari. What prompts that work? You said earlier that there was work you did in the archives in the late '50s and '60s that you didn't write up.

SH: Well, it's not a lot that I didn't write about, but I am much more involved in the early stages of antiracist politics in Britain. The New Left Club in '58 is one of the organizations that is escorting black people back from Notting Hill station. It's helping to set up black and white tenants' organizations in Notting Hill. So in the meetings around policing, "sus" laws, imprisonment, etc., I am quite active, speaking, and so on. More that than writing in a way. All that I mean is that the interest never goes away, the interest in the Caribbean and the interest in race doesn't go away, although it's not the most prominent and visible part of my work.

DS: But certainly in the '70s, there is a period: '76, '77, '78 . . .

SH: No, '72. The Centre starts a research project on black crime . . .

DS: No, no. I want to come back to those pieces, the Rastafari piece, the race and articulation piece, the one on pluralism, etc. Clearly, there you are thinking about the Caribbean. This is the mid-to-late '70s, yes. What is prompting that rethinking of the Caribbean?

SH: Well, I suppose what is prompting it is the sense that all that was bubbling up in the '60s has had a very profound impact on Caribbean societies. It's a very different place. And it's a place that I can reground in my own mind in a way that I'd sort of decided that I couldn't reground the old Caribbean like that. By the '70s, I start to come back more often. Mainly to visit family. I don't come back for official purposes. There is a long period in the '60s when having taken the decision, I don't come very much.

DS: Do you lecture here when you come back in the '70s?

SH: Hardly ever.

DS: Is your work known among intellectuals here?

SH: No, no. Not very much. And it doesn't feel relevant to me to tell them about it.

DS: No, sure, that I can understand. But certainly the way . . .

SH: They still don't . . .

DS: I know they still don't . . .

SH: I am not complaining about it.

DS: Yes, but I am.

SH: Yes, but they don't know about Cultural Studies.

DS: No, no, I am not even talking about Cultural Studies. I mean the question of how you think from a position that refuses to simply throw away Marxism, throw away Marx entirely. How do you try to think a relationship with a nonteleological Marx? Which is clearly one of the things you were trying to do.

SH: Yes, I was trying to do that. And I was trying to introduce race as a relatively autonomous element in all that.

DS: So that work certainly is relevant to what is going on here.

SH: Yes. That work is relevant.

DS: One of the essays that has become crucial to the whole question of rethinking diaspora, black identity, etc., is the essay "New Ethnicities," which appeared in 1988.[9] Again the question is, What is going on there? What are you trying to locate yourself among, to urge?

SH: Well, what is going on there is an awareness of an essentialist notion of race, especially of a kind of essentialist notion that, though it doesn't itself recognize it, is in fact ultimately discursively underpinned by a biological notion of race. And I am struck by the fact that antiracists often share the same premise, in the sense that they too want their politics guaranteed by their color, by their race. Racists want them discredited for their race and antiracists want them validated for their race, and I don't think race can do that job. So it's part of backing away from a teleological conception of the central contradiction. I am working on all these contradictions. And I am also very influenced by feminism, to rethink the primacy of class, and very influenced by sexuality, to think about subjectivity. And trying to work on race to get it not subsumed within class. And I'm trying to not lose class simply because one doesn't want it functioning as a master category.

And specifically with race, what I'm trying to do is not then slide from polemicizing against an essentialist conception of race to the point where difference doesn't make any difference. What I call a kind of postmodern nomadism where we are all a different identity every time you wake up. I want to hold on to specificity but where specificity is not reducible to an essence. It's more diverse than that; it's a set of positionalities rather than one position. So that's really what "New Ethnicities" is about—to rescue what is specific in the notion of an ethnicity. I use the discursive notion, that is, ethnicity is what enables us to enunciate ourselves, our identities. And everybody needs that, including the British. The British have an ethnicity like everyone else. Everybody comes through a set of specific cultural roots, which makes possible what they can and aren't going to say in a particular moment. And their roots are different from the set of roots that produce somebody else. So there is specificity there, but it's not one specificity which is reducible to an essence or expressible in terms of a kind of fellow traveling biologistic or genetic notion of race. That's really what I am trying to talk about.

And I suppose I've been on that line ever since. People sometimes misunderstand what I'm saying. They don't think they disagree with me as much as they do. And this is because I don't polarize; I'm trying not to think in a binary way. So of course I always recognize the moment of specificity, the moment of naming the African unsaid. It's absolutely critical. When I say that people say, "Oh, I know where he's coming from." I'm not really coming from quite that place. But I'm not from the point of view that we're all a smorgasbord, you know, the mix, the fruit cocktail, you're a bit of this and a bit of that. I am very much opposed to that notion of pluralism.

DS: And that is one of the things that I like about the way you set it up. But how do you prevent reading history as error? If in a certain sense the end of the essential black subject is now, and it appears as though the grasp of the discursive construction of ethnic identity ought to hold a privileged theoretical position now, how do you prevent yourself from reading Garvey or Du Bois as having made errors? That their understanding of race was essentialist and therefore . . .

SH: I understand exactly what you are saying. I can tell you what the strategy is, but it won't please or satisfy you because you are asking me a philosophical question. My strategy is what I have just described to you. I honor the moment that I am trying to surpass. I recognize, you see, that because there is no politics that is ever correct I don't claim for my particular version of a nonessentialist notion of race correctness for all time. I can claim for it only a certain conjunctural specificity. So I can understand the moment, historical moment, in which a strategic essentialism became absolutely germane. You know, I can understand the moment when feminism had to say to men, "Fucking shut up!" This is what I call "arbitrary," you see. It's arbitrary. It's not correct, but it's correct in the moment. It only begins to be troubling when you settle down in that position forever, when you don't see exactly that that is a frontier position, a frontier effect of having taken that position, and then how you then have to move yourself to dismantle what it has constituted as your constitutive outside. That's what the danger is. So I'm not afraid of positionalities. I'm afraid of taking positionalities too seriously.

DS: So again I hear you as saying that the question at the end of the essential black subject is a strategic, not a philosophic, question. So then one isn't reading in terms of the correctness or incorrectness of a cognitive or philosophical position. That then allows one to read, in a certain sense, the problem-space in which Garvey deployed race or Du Bois deployed race.

SH: Oh, absolutely. And to take it seriously.

DS: . . . And to take that very seriously.

SH: I mean I would actually go even further than that. I would say that, because we don't understand what it would be yet to constitute a politics of the end of the essential black subject, in a way we kind of just have to shut up because we can't defend communities. You can't defend South Central [Los Angeles] because you don't have anything to put in place of an essential notion of the black subject. An essential notion of the black subject is what's standing between them and the fucking LA police. If I have something better, then okay. If not, then I have to say I think you're theoretically wrong, and I think there are traps, and I think you're creating dangers, but what I can I do—you have to politicize. You know, I think that a lot of this comes from the notion that there will be a moment when theory will inform practice—not inform but adjudicate practice. And I don't think theory will ever adjudicate practice. Theory informs practice, but it never stands outside it and says, "You were right, and if only you understood me you could have been righter for longer."

DS: But Stuart, this is what I was trying to say earlier about my problem with Ernesto Laclau. One gets the sense that there is a moment . . .

SH: Oh yes, I agree with you. That's what I call his theoreticism. There is a belief that if he goes on thinking about Heidegger and Derrida long enough, he will come to a moment when all will be transparent, and that will hold. I don't believe that. But as I say, I don't believe it, but I know it is a strong temptation among political intellectuals to talk in that way. You know, I take what you're saying strategically, although they take it foundationally.

DS: I want now to come back to the Caribbean. You mentioned earlier that you begin to travel to Jamaica a lot more in the '70s, and perhaps even more recently. Is that the beginnings of a theoretical reengagement with what's going on here in the Caribbean rather than the Caribbean there [in England]?

SH: It's not the beginnings of a very systematic reengagement. I'm telling you this as a matter of fact. It's not that I'm proud of it. The reengagement is more fitful. I mean I keep up with particular things, but I wouldn't say that I have an overall map of how the debates have broken and developed in the last seven or eight years in a very detailed way. I have impressions about what is happening generally, but not more than that.

DS: What are those impressions? Can you share them with me?

SH: Well, I don't know that they're worth sharing. They're too fragmentary for that.

DS: Let me repose the question. The way I look at it is that one of the things that marks the present in a place like Jamaica is, on the one hand, the collapse of the Bandung project, the unraveling of the socialist project here [in Jamaica] as well as elsewhere, the dismantling of Soviet and East European communism that provided the block to US encroachment, and the return with a vengeance of liberalism, of neoliberalism. And what a lot of people now seem to recognize is that the neoliberal tinkering with the economy doesn't seem to be getting us out of the bankruptcy that we're in. So there is a sense in which now, what do we do? How do we rebuild oppositional criticism? Where do we begin is my question to you. What are the openings? What are the possibilities?

SH: Well, what you've said is my impression too. And I get the sense that people are much more questioning, and they have a sense of coming to the end of a range of ideologies, whatever they were, which have unraveled to the point where they can't stitch them together again. But, as I said earlier, I don't follow the debates in detail. I don't know where I would put my finger on within current work to say, "Now this is where I think there is beginning to be a coming together of new conceptions and new ideas which really might form an alternative current of thinking in the present conjuncture in the Caribbean." I think you have to know that literature in more depth than I do. So what I know are things from afar. And things from afar suggest that the Caribbean is, with all its specificities, emerging into the full light of the crisis of late modernity. You know it is in exactly the same relation as all nation-states are—at different levels of development, different histories—to the bewildering onslaught of globalization, which is a partner to a certain kind of neoliberalism. So I think it is a moment for the opening of a kind of dialogue across frontiers (ethnic, racial, regional frontiers). You know because I am not suggesting that the answer that might be found in the developed welfare states is the same as you are going to find in Jamaica, which has never had a welfare state. But some of the problems (or the ideas behind them) are really quite similar. We're not talking about completely different things. And I think you can see that in the participation in this conference. A lot of people who have come to the conference, I think, are not here because they're the next generation of North American intellectuals who have fallen in love with the Caribbean. They are people working on contemporary problems—postcolonial questions, for example, globalization issues—of which the Caribbean is a particularly interesting paradigm example. So I think it is a time for confluence with a lot of debates which up to now have been defined as "First World business," etc.

You know, some of the things we have been talking about are things which I wouldn't have talked about here because there has been the sense that they are completely irrelevant. Who the hell here cares about the constitutive outside, or the nature of the conjuncture. I don't feel that anymore. I feel that these things which have largely occupied my mind in a very different context because . . . The context hasn't been, of course, all that different because I have been thinking those things as an outsider over there. So I have not been thinking them inside a European . . . I have been polemicizing the Eurocentric frontier. So although I have not done that from a specifically Caribbean position, it is the position of those who are ex-centric to the Eurocentric system. And that's a lot of places.

So I don't know where to start, but I know that in conducting the debate about it we could let the wind of new theoretical and other ideas flow through in a much more open and welcoming way and not feel that that was going to simply result in the imposition of some foreign models.

DS: One of the things that strikes me as particularly interesting today in Jamaica is the sense of frustration, profound frustration, with the political system as such.

SH: I think there is deep disillusionment. And among the political class too. I think they themselves are disillusioned with the system. But I think it's also much wider than that.

DS: And one possible site for theorizing might be something like a public sphere in Jamaica. How would you respond to that?

SH: Yes, I suppose what I was trying to say earlier on about there being an opportunity for a much wider kind of frontierless exchange and dialogue is to reconstitute a public sphere, which was, after all, insofar as it existed, the product of a very specific set of historical and political circumstances. And was very narrow. And I think that a very different public sphere which is less grounded in a traditional conception of the disciplines and the professions and the institutions; which is more open to a kind of porous notion of civil society, more open to the organic intellectual function; which is responsive to a kind of Lloyd Best call for nondisciplinary, extradisciplinary disciplinary thinking. A lot of those things are to constitute a new space of dialogue in which, of course, people would harangue one another till the cows come home. But in which a different set of frameworks or parameters would be sketched. What I feel about the current one is that people are disillusioned because, although they think it doesn't work, they still feel imprisoned by the old parameters. They still feel they're required to think those problems in the way in which they have been magisterially defined over the '60s and '70s, which was a very important period for us. So it's a question of acknowledging what happened then and its importance, and showing the connections and lines of thought and influence, but really to think now the reconstitution of the public sphere.

NOTES

The interview took place at the University of the West Indies, Kingston, Jamaica, on March 6, 1996.

1 The reference is to Anne Walmsley, *The Caribbean Artists' Movement, 1966–1972: A Literary and Cultural History* (London: New Beacon Books, 1992).

2 Stuart Hall and Paddy Whannel, *The Popular Arts* (London: Hutchinson, 1964).

3 "The 'First' New Left: Life and Times," in *Out of Apathy: Voices of the New Left 30 Years On*, ed. Oxford University Socialist Discussion Group (London: Verso, 1989).

4 Stuart Hall, "The Problem of Ideology: Marxism without Guarantees," *Journal of Communication Inquiry* 10, no. 2 (1986): 28–43.

5 See Terry Eagleton, "The Hippest," *London Review of Books*, March 7, 1996, 3. This is a review of David Morley and Kuan-Hsing Chen, eds., *Stuart Hall: Critical Dialogues in Cultural Studies* (New York: Routledge, 1996).

6 "Pluralism, Race and Class in Caribbean Society," in *Race and Class in Postcolonial Society* (Paris: UNESCO, 1978).

7 "Race, Articulation and Societies Structured in Dominance," in *Sociological Theories: Race and Colonialism* (Paris: UNESCO, 1980).

8 Stuart Hall, *The Young Englanders* (London: National Committee of Commonwealth Immigrants, 1967).

9 Stuart Hall, "New Ethnicities," *ICA Documents*, no. 7 (1988): 27–31.

CHAPTER 9

At Home and Not at Home: Stuart Hall
in Conversation with Les Back

The opening of Rivington Place, new home of the Institute of International Visual Arts (InIVA) and Autograph ABP (Association of Black Photographers), in east London is a landmark not only for the Black Arts movement in Britain, but is also a testament to Stuart Hall's enduring contribution and relevance to its intellectual and political life. As chair of both InIVA and Autograph ABP, Stuart played an integral role in realizing this vision of a public space dedicated to creativity and diversity. The £3 million building, designed by architect David Adjaye, offers a place to exhibit art, but it also provides a home for ideas, thought, and reflection on the relevance of difference to the visual arts. A few weeks after its doors were opened officially, Rivington Place hosted the launch of Paul Gilroy's *Black Britain: A Photographic History* (2007). The book, planned initially to be a collaboration with Stuart Hall, portrays and documents the position of black people within British society through photographs drawn from the Getty Collection. Stuart's health prevented him from playing a full role in its completion, but he contributed a preface, and at the launch he discussed the project with Paul Gilroy in front of an audience gathered to celebrate its publication.

Stuart's attentiveness to the present through his notion of the conjuncture always involves an acute historical sensibility. So, it is entirely in keeping that one of the first events of the new artistic enterprise should be concerned with rethinking ways of telling and showing the history of black Britain. The return of the "documentary impulse" for Stuart also necessitates a reassessment of the form. "The photograph appears to have a more easy access to the truth," commented Stuart. "The 'being-there-ness' of the photograph gives it this quality, and yet, the photographs can't deliver the whole truth. The truth moves on them and the truth moves on us." The images also contain the concerns and priorities of the white photographers who took them. For this reason, reading the photographs involves animating them and noticing other things within their depth of field. This Stuart refers to as their "incidental documentary features." "Putting black people in the frame is not just a figural practice. It is what is going on around the figure being photographed and the situation in which it is placed, even though the photographer is not really focusing on these aspects. In these photographs the body language, for example, is extremely eloquent." The result is an extraordinary historical document but also a different model of historical and sociological analysis. It invites the reader's involvement not only as a consumer but also as a producer.

A member of the audience asks Paul Gilroy if there is not something a little romantic about producing a book like this now. "I am quite attracted to the idea that black history might be modeled on the kiss," he says, responding with a wry smile. "I've received lots of emails from people who are either in the photographs or who recognize friends or relatives. There is a lot of love in the photographs, or I should say, love circulates in that history." Gilroy's essay, that accompanies the photographic sequence, asks searching questions of the reader that prohibit the book becoming a coffee table accessory with a cozy relationship to the past. The photographs seem to look back at us in an inquiring way. They beg questions of our present and its compromises and accommodations with a society that remains haunted by the legacy of empire and racism.

As the proceedings come to a close, Paul stands and thanks the audience, his publisher, and the hosts of this evening's event. Then, finally, he turns to Stuart, who is sitting close to him, and says, "I also want to thank you, Stuart." He pauses for a moment, then, leaning forward, he says, softly, "Thank you." Furnished in the spaces between those words was something more than an individual debt of gratitude. Perhaps without realizing it, Paul spoke for many of us in the audience who have been helped—directly or indirectly—by the generosity of Stuart Hall's thought. David Scott wrote, "thinking for Stuart is a way of changing himself" (2005, 4). Yet this transformation is always sociable, a collective activity that happens in dialogue with others, forming part of a larger conversation that also transforms those around him. His work contains the rare compound of critique without dogma, acute insight coupled with humility, grave political seriousness that also retains its sense of humor.

A few weeks after the event at Rivington Place, I met Stuart at his home in North London and talked with him about his life and work over several pots of tea. Subjects ranged from his love of Henry James to the contemporary state of black politics. What is hard to represent is how much laughter that conversation contained. Sometimes it was simply a joyous way of punctuating thought; at other moments the mirth was sardonic and satirical. I hope the conviviality of Stuart's style of listening and talking is not muted in the transposition of his words to the page. What follows is a transcription of the entire conversation, which lasted over two hours without a break. It not only contains insight into the key questions of our time but also demonstrates what David Scott calls Stuart's "mode of practicing generosity" (2005, 12). This is expressed as much in the ways he speaks as in the content of what he says. We started by talking about the library at Rivington Place that is named in his honor.

LES BACK: The first thing I wanted to ask you about, Stuart, is the library at Rivington Place—it is called the Stuart Hall Library.

STUART HALL: Yes, it is a very nice gesture of theirs, really, to name it after me, a very nice gesture. So I'm very pleased. Have you been into it?

LB: I have.

SH: It's a wonderful room. It's one of the best rooms in the building. All those windows—it really is spectacular. And it's a very good library for its size and so on, so I'm very, very pleased with that association, and it's very nice of them. The only other people who are named are Barclays Bank, who gave them one million, one hundred thousand pounds. [*Laughter*] So I'm in good company.

LB: They're in good company, we should say. I've always thought of libraries as a kind of place of refuge, really.

SH: Well, I'll tell you another thing about it. I was going to say my move to the visual arts is very late in life, but it's not true. I've always been interested in painting but didn't know very much about it. And then I got involved with InIVA and Autograph as the chair of two boards, etc. Two things about that. One is that the director, the artists around them, are half my age. They really are in their forties; lots of them were active, emerged in the 1980s, so they're in their early forties now, so they just kind of rejuvenated me. It was like a dose of monkey gland. [*Laughter*]

Come alive again. There's lots of people out there who want to talk to you, whose work you are going to have to facilitate. I write a bit in relation to them, as I always do. I always write *a bit in relation to* whatever I'm doing, rather than any longer plan of work. So that act of generosity mattered a very great deal. But the one thing I will say about them is that they're not really very much into books. They think writing is sort of passé. [*Laughs*] They're also not very into academic writing. This is only a mild criticism—it's not true of all of them. So it's not a hostility, but it's just not quite in their universe in the way in which it is in mine. So what I'm very glad about is that there's this subversive thing called an old-style library with a lot of books in this visual arts space. [*Laughter*] Sitting there at the heart of this visual arts building, wonderful building, etc., quietly throbbing away.

LB: What a fantastic thing. Many people have said that your work has been enabling, and I certainly feel that very strongly. A lot of the books in that library are written by people that your work has touched indirectly or directly.

SH: That's true, yeah. It's not at all surprising or out of order that it should be so. On the other hand, the library represents all those things I don't really know about but would like to. I would really like to know more about art and the history of art, and especially the history of modern art. I'd like to be able to write with more authority about that than I feel really confident in doing, though I've written recently much more about that subject than anything else, especially in the last seven or eight years. But it's not an area which I feel is mine in the way in which other areas were. My work was not unrelated to it, but actually, more surprisingly, many people say now, including artists, how formative that work was in some ways for them. And I don't quite understand it. I did an interview with Hans Obrist, who's now at the Serpentine Gallery.[1] He published this interview in a book of discussions with artists, and he mainly wanted to know how many artists were at the Centre for Cultural Studies and what were they interested in? Well, unfortunately, there were only ever one or two. There were a few people interested in photography after a while, but generally it just wasn't like that. So it's partly because Cultural Studies has now become a much broader stream of influences, and then visual Cultural Studies is a kind of illegitimate child of that, challenging art history as a discipline and "infecting" the field, etc. So I quite understand why people like Hans Obrist imagine that this is where Cultural Studies began, although it wasn't. The same thing used to happen about film. We were passionately interested in film, and film is, for me, in some ways the visual medium that I most respond to, directly respond to and emotionally respond to, but at the Centre we didn't have the money to work on film, to show film, to get extracts, get copies. You can't work without the primary medium to look at all the time, so we sort of decided we couldn't do much research on film. But people imagine that Cultural Studies was falling down with film. [*Laughs*] And the same a bit about the visual arts now.

LB: You've said in the past how much there was at stake in the artistic work of a whole range of artists, I guess, who were coming of age in the 1980s.

SH: Well, I think that is the key moment in a sense, in that it's the big creative explosion in the visual arts and photography, amongst second-generation black people. It was born out of British racism and anti-racism, rather than the colonial context or slavery. It's born out of that direct experience of the metropolis. And by then I was writing about that issue quite consistently and in a sense more consistently than I ever had before. And also, it's very much a mutual, reciprocal influence. I could see that second-generation black people were deeply concerned about identity and their relation to the present and the past, but their relationship could not be accurately expressed in terms of a return to roots. Paul Gilroy said not "roots" but "routes," and so I wrote about that; I wrote about cultural identity in those terms. Well, black and Asian artists were some of the people I was looking at, so not surprisingly they found the way in which I tried to explore the question of identity in some of those essays sympathetic. So it was a double movement, really. I mean that's not the first time that's happened. I don't want to go into this, please, but I left the Caribbean, in flight from the Caribbean; I felt I couldn't fulfil my potential there, and I couldn't work out my relationship to Jamaican culture. I just couldn't. Because of my middle-class formation, because my parents are not only brown but thought the world would disappear with the departure of the British, etc., coming departure of the British. Okay, so I was in flight. Then I "discovered" my subject, or, rather, it discovered me. My subject was coming out of the station at Paddington. It was Caribbeans but over here; it was the *Windrush* journey to here. That has been my subject ever since: the diaspora. So this is what I had to explain when I did the conference "The Thought of Stuart Hall" at the University of the West Indies. "Are you a Caribbean intellectual?" Yes, but it's not the Caribbean you should have in mind. I unfortunately have not participated in the building of the nation there, so I have always had a bit of distance from the national movement which set fire to their imagination in Kingston. But Caribbean people have been my continuous subject. Lots of things that I've written about which don't appear to be about that are seen through the prism of trying to work out who the people of the diaspora are, who they think they are, where they want to go, where have they come from, what's their relation to the past, what's their memory, and so on, and how they express their creativity, how they express where they want to go to next. That's what has been, in a sense, my subject. So that is really where Cultural Studies began for me. It didn't begin with Raymond Williams; it began with my struggle to come to terms with that experience, which is when I first discovered I was a black intellectual. I'd never called myself black ever in my life, nor did most Jamaican people. Many, many people in Jamaica, including lots of people who were black, did not think of themselves in the way in which people after the late 1960s came to think of themselves as black. So it was a discovery for me, a rediscovery of the Caribbean in new terms, and a rediscovery of my thinking about culture, and a rediscovery of the black subject. So it's not surprising that people who are then painting out of the invisibility, the marginalization of the black body, figuring the black subject, the black experience, should hear something of that question resonating in my writing. And it's not just a sort of chosen intellectual project, if you know what I mean. I didn't choose that. I had no alternative.

LB: I think that's one of the things that's so powerful about your work—you're trying to make sense of those private, understood and not understood, both estranged and knowing, close-up experiences and the wider social, cultural, political forces.

SH: Yeah. Well, I know what you are saying, and it's again not something I tried to do, but it's just how I write or how I think. But I sort of know what that comes out of. It comes out of this horrendous family experience that I had, in which I came to understand that my family were living out in the interstices of the family, the most private domestic space, this huge colonial drama. That is what it was about. So the meaning of colonization was internalized into the intimate and the emotionally charged theater of the family; it was same thing on another terrain. And ever since then, I've really not been good at thinking about the distinction between private and public, the inside and outside, subjective interior and objective social relations; I don't quite buy how that is usually written about or thought about.

LB: You've mentioned in passing the idea of an intellectual vocation. And I just wanted to ask you a little bit about how you do the practice of thinking and criticism and writing. Or is it something that's so habitual to you now that it's hard to think about "how do I do the craft of an intellectual vocation?"

SH: I must show you the Caribbean book,[2] because I do respond to the conference by saying, "What is this strange object called 'The Thought of Stuart Hall,' which is the unbelievable title that they gave this conference. I said, 'Who is this person that we've been discussing for two days? I sort of see him every now and again; I recognize some of him. I recognize some quotes, but I don't recognize them all, and indeed I hope people will give me the references!'" [*Laughter*]

And when we had the launch in London, I went back to that question, because it's not something planned, it's not something conscious, and perhaps I should say that it's very limited. There's lots of things it can't do. I'm very admiring of all sorts of people who do things and write and think in ways that I think are much richer, much more insightful than I do. At a certain point, round about the point where the cultural terrain went into high theory, I was nearly lost in a species of ventriloquism, and I suddenly saw through this at the point where people kept making French puns in English. [*Laughter*]

They only worked in French. And I thought, "This is a crazy way to think." So it's not that one rejected the concepts, but . . . after that, I just sort of had to think in my own way. However you think is how you're going to think, so you'd better be satisfied with it. And that's also how you write, so write like that. Don't hanker after writing like Foucault; you don't write like Foucault, you know? I don't have the philosophical training—I just couldn't do it. I'm not that sort of person. So write like you write, [and] accept your own voice. Having done that, I'm not very good at talking about what that process is. I think about it, and I have some thoughts now about it, and there are things which other people have said which help me reflect on it. David Scott says he doesn't read me because of cultural theory; he reads me because of my political interventions.[3] And I realized that almost everything I write is a kind of political intervention. It may not be about politics explicitly, but it is trying to shift the terms of the debate, intervene on one side or another, clarify something, wipe some other distorting views out of place so that something else can come through. I suppose that's critique or criticism or whatever it is, but I'm aware that it is a kind of political intervention. I think that accounts for why (a) I've never written a big book, except for *Policing the Crisis*,[4] which is not all mine by any means, and secondly, why I write about so many different things. I write mainly because people ask me to, you know, "Will you write a piece about this? Will you come to a conference and write it up afterwards?" I don't sit in my study and think, "I ought to write a piece now about this and publish it here." If you look at the stuff I've written on identity, the first piece was given at the first film conference in the Caribbean. They're all occasional pieces. That's why they're not in serious sociological journals. One of the big pieces on identity and the diaspora is in this little collection that Jonathan Rutherford called *Identity*.[5] Do you understand what I mean?

LB: I do, yes.

SH: So they are interventions in a field, rather than autonomous scholarly works. And the other thing I know about it is that I am interested in the conjuncture. I am a sort of writer about the "history of the present," but also I think the past is understood in that way too. Now people say, "What is this 'conjuncture'"? I used to pass it off and say it's what Gramsci is interested in, because Gramsci does write about historical specificity and the difference between the conjuncture and the long term, etc. But people have pointed out to me that Gramsci thought the conjuncture was more superficial, and I don't think that at all. I don't deny that there are longer-term, deeper structural movements of society and economy which mark out different phases, for instance, in capitalism. But I think a conjunctural understanding of what is specific about each of those phases, what is specific about merchant capital that is not specific about, not the same as, industrial capital—what's interesting about Fordist capital that is not the same as global capital? Of course, the reason why I refer to capital is because this is something that I learned from Marx: surprisingly not the Marx most people think about, because they assume that Marx unfolded the laws of movement of capitalism, which are going to be always the same. In some ways yes, and in some ways no. At that level of generality, capitalism in the fifteenth century, merchant capital, was the same as global capitalism. But at the level of the conjuncture, they are not the same. I don't know if you've ever seen an essay of mine on Marx's 1857 "Introduction" to the *Grundrisse*?[6]

LB: No, I haven't seen that.

SH: In this essay Marx says, first of all, you can't just reflect the empirical in order to analyze it, because if you look at society it's full of people, so you begin with population. But people are divided into capital and labor, slave and slaveholder, and that division, that difference, is more important than just the fact that they're people. He calls beginning with population a chaotic abstraction, and that abstractions which arise from the differences are more worked through. That accounts for why he says you need theory, not to produce more theory, excuse me, but because you can't do without it. You need to change the scale of magnification. You have to break into the confusing fabric that "the real" apparently presents and find another way in. So it's like a microscope, and until you look at the evidence through the microscope, you can't see the hidden relations. And he describes this process as depending on adding more and more levels of determination. The basic laws may be the same, but you have to add more levels of determination before you—and this is another phrase of his—produce "the concrete in thought." And so my notion of the conjunctural is more like that than it's like Gramsci. I really believe that the work is done by historical specificity, by understanding what is specific about certain moments, and how those moments come together, how different tendencies fuse and form a kind of configuration—never one that's going to last forever, hegemony never does; it always has unruly elements, and it's always struggling to master a terrain, etc. And those forces are going to produce a shift to another conjuncture. In Britain, the late 1970s is a conjunctural shift of that kind—absolutely. What I thought was that Thatcherism was really the end of one configuration—the postwar settlement—and the beginning of something else. We're not going to go back to what was before it, so that's why I'm interested in thinking the values that we hold in terms of the present. But about my sense of that break, people do ask me, "How do you know of that?" I can't tell them that. It's not a precise methodology; it's not something which I apply outside to it. It's interpretive and historical. I have to feel the kind of accumulation of different things coming together to make a new moment: this is a different rhythm. We've lived with one configuration and this is another one. Now let us try to say what that transition means, what this new one is, what the forces in it are, what the contradictory things are. That's the "history of the present." So I think conjuncturally. I'm what Larry Grossberg calls a radical contextualist.[7] I think that's about as far as I can go in reflecting on my own way of thinking. [*Laughs*]

LB: I remember hearing you say in the radio interview for *Desert Island Discs* if you could take only one book with you, it would be Henry James's *The Portrait of a Lady . . .*

SH: I did my PhD on James, but I didn't finish it.

LB: I'd like to ask you about the other books you would choose to take to that "desert island," but before I do that, what was it about Henry James that caught your imagination?

SH: My undergraduate training is in literature. I never had a training in anything else to be absolutely honest. [*Laughter*] So when the vice chancellor of the Open University said, "But you've been in literature, you've been in Cultural Studies—are you willing to profess sociology?" I said, "I'm willing to profess anything if you'll only give me a job." [*Laughter*]

So my training is in literature. I was very disappointed with the Oxford course because it's so lodged in the past. I had to do so much Anglo-Saxon, [and] I was never very good at languages—I hated it. I was interested in medieval literature, but I was interested in it in a critical way, not in a scholarly way, and so on. So I pushed toward the modern. So when I thought of staying on and doing my PhD, I thought, "What would you like to write about?" Well, what I wanted to write about was the social realist literature, American literature of the 1930s, and they said, "Well, you can't do that because most of these people are still living. Even Dos Passos is still alive." [*Laughter*]

So in any case, I'd been reading a lot of American literature, and American literature was, for me, a kind of escape from the constraints of Oxford English in those days. And so I began to read Melville and Hawthorne, and Hawthorne led me back to James, and so on. So I got interested in James. And I was aware of the fact that this was a pretty bizarre encounter—this black boy from Kingston and this highly refined, sophisticated transatlantic mind. So I never confused myself with Henry James. But two things interested me about him. One was the international theme, the fact that the novels are often . . . a few are not, but many of his works, early and late, are framed around this contrast between Europe and America, between one place and another: Europe and somewhere else. And although the other place is not at all the same as my own, I'm aware of the fact that that is a kind diasporic way of seeing the world, a diasporic question. James's is a kind diasporic imagination, though most people wouldn't dream of using that concept about his work. So I wanted to write about the international theme. And he goes over it three times. Once in the very early novels: *Daisy Miller*, *The American*, *The Europeans*, etc. Then again in the big novels: *The Ambassadors*, *The Golden Bowl*, *The Wings of the Dove*, and then a wonderful unfinished work at the end, one in particular where he goes back to America and encounters the self, a successful businessman, that he would have been if he'd stayed. And it's the source of T. S. Eliot's line about the first turn of the winding stair; there's an ivory tower in which he encounters this other self—he sees the other self across the space. I just thought it was incredible stuff, and a way of thinking about James that I hadn't seen before. So that's what I wanted to write about. And then I was, of course, interested; if you're interested in James, you're interested in a statement that he made: "I want to be someone on whom nothing is lost." I wanted to be a consciousness that could respond to everything in the world, not universal but specific and deep. James said, you can tell that from five minutes of somebody's story at dinner that this is the source of your next novel. I don't want to hear any more. I don't want the literal detail. I want to explore the lives and conflicts

that come out of that, but it must be to the full extent of my consciousness. Now the funny thing about that is that there is no full extent of
one's consciousness because there's always the unconscious that one
can't think about. And there was in James, too, very profoundly—the
wonderful things that James didn't, couldn't know, which Colm Tóibín
has written about in *The Master*—I think it's a fantastic novel.[8] There's
a lot of unconsciousness in James, but he wanted to take the conscious
as far as he could in each situation. Well, I didn't care about the fact
that he mainly wrote about rich people. Shakespeare mainly wrote
about kings and queens—so what? It doesn't work at that literal level.
If you want to find out about kings and queens, you go and read some
history; you read *King Lear* for something else. And in the same way
I feel about James. I didn't mind about the fact that lots of the content of his material was alien to me. I'll say one more thing which has
just occurred to me, which is that his "other" was different from mine,
but his other was America, and America has played a very important,
but ambivalent, role in my thinking. America was the site of imaginative escape for me when I was in Kingston, although I didn't go there.
I came to England because the lines of connection were still to the
mother country. Now all the intellectuals from the Caribbean go and
are teaching and writing in the US. But although my connection was
to the UK, my imaginative escape was cinema—I went to films every
Monday or every Saturday throughout my teenage life, and a very rich
period it was. Bogart, Bette Davis, film noir, melodrama—incredible
cinema, American cinema, and of course American music and jazz.
And then once one came to England, America continued to stand as
that which is modern, which is not weighed down by the English social class system. It's a source of that ambivalence, the ambivalence
one feels about America, though I feel very distant from it now: I can't
stand it at the moment, I wouldn't go there, I don't go there. I'm sure
they wouldn't let me in, but I really don't want to go there. And it's not
just because of Bush. It's about the culture and the politics in a much
wider sense. But at one point, America was a source of liberation for us
all. Jazz liberated my soul, and the coming of rock 'n' roll transformed
English popular culture. So it wasn't James's "other"; he wasn't writing
about that bit either. He wasn't writing about the black experience. I
could go to Ralph Ellison and to James Baldwin and so on for that, but
still America was not as foreign as it might have sounded. Sitting in

Oxford reading about James writing about New England and Florence was not quite as absurd as it has seemed to many people since.

LB: No, it's not absurd. But the idea of encountering the life that you may have had, as you said that, it reminded me of a few comments you made about sometimes you think about the life you would have had had you stayed in Jamaica.

SH: Yes. I think about that very much because my school generation was in the thick of independence. I left. People don't remember, [but] I came to England in 1951. Jamaica wasn't independent until 1962. So the people who became the political and intellectual leadership of independence, the political class defining the nation after decolonization, were all people I knew and had been to school with, yet I wasn't there. I followed it from afar. My hopes and fears were invested in it. I often went back; I sort of debated with them. I tried at one point to bring a sort of reconciliation between the Black Power people and the Marxists. So I wanted to be part of it. But I had always the sense that that could have been me, and I know many people who were like me. They went to the big secondary schools like me; they were in my class at Jamaica College. They're judges and political leaders and senior civil servants and so on, many of them retiring now or retired. So there always was another life, and there's also the long period in which I wasn't sure whether I was going home or not. After I gave up my thesis and moved to London, I was going home anytime now. Perhaps I'm still going home anytime now . . . [*Laughter*]

It wasn't true. I wasn't going back. I knew to go back at that point for me was psychic death—it would have enclosed itself around me; I could feel it waiting for me. So I was right not to go back. But it was a loss. One has to say that. Diaspora is a loss. It's not forever; it doesn't mean that you can't do something about it, or that other places can't fill the gap, the void, but the void is always the regretful moment that wasn't realized. History is full of what is not realized, and I feel that about it. Whenever I go back, I think I'm at home, but still I'm not at home.

LB: It reminded me as you were talking there of the beautiful George Lamming book *The Pleasures of Exile*,[9] on the one hand the pleasure, the freedom of exile, [and] at the same time, the loss which you are describing.

SH: Wonderful book. It's a very, very important book for me. You asked me about important books—that is one. Of course, I knew George in London. He used to work for the Caribbean World Service, which a lot of writers did, and indeed the Caribbean novel was written in London. And what's more, we became consciously West Indian in London. I came as a Jamaican. I'd never been to anywhere else in the Caribbean. I remember at one point in the sixth form, a Latin master came from Barbados to teach us. Well, I'd been taught by the Scots, by the British, by the Irish, but I'd never been taught by a Caribbean, and I thought his accent was the funniest thing I'd ever heard; I thought he was from outer space. We used to have this joke with him: of course Barbados produces good cricketers because it's so small; the whole island is the pitch. You have to hit the ball into the sea to get a six. [*Laughter*]

So very strange. And then suddenly we discovered what was common between Caribbean people. In spite of the fact that the islands are all different, nevertheless there's a kind of core commonness. So I discovered myself as a West Indian at that point. That was a very liberating moment for me. I mean, there's a dark moment in that as well because what that meant was that politically the idea of West Indian Federation became the focus of all of our hopes. We thought, "We can't do this without each other." It works in London. It produces wonderful literature. Each place is too small to sustain independently. And I suppose if eventually a West Indian Federation had come off, I might well have gone home.

LB: Really?

SH: I don't know when I took the decision not to go back, but by then it was sort of already made, really. So *The Pleasures of Exile*. I feel my experience has been close to two books. One is Lamming's *The Pleasures of Exile*, [and] the other is Edward Said's *Out of Place*.[10] Though it's from the other side of the world, in relation to a different set of histories and cultures, etc., I just find myself "read" into the center of Edward's book. I felt out of place in Jamaica, and when I came to England I felt out of place in Merton College, Oxford, and I feel out of place even now. I feel out of place in relation to the British, which might sound a very strange thing because I've lived here for fifty-something years. I know the different kinds of English, the British people; I know how the society works from the inside. I love parts of the landscape. I feel at one with it. It is my home in a certain kind of way. But I will never be English—never. I can't be, because traces in my life, and the traces in my memory, and the traces in my history of another place are just ineradicable. I can't get them out of my head. I don't want to have a fight about it, but that's just how one is. So being displaced, or out of place, is a characteristic experience of mine. It's been all throughout my life. I even felt displaced in relation to black culture in Jamaica. I was a kind of nationalist from the very beginning, lots of my friends were. We were anti-imperialist; we wanted Jamaica to be free. But in relation to black culture and the life of ordinary black people, I really didn't know what it was about in any depth, and I couldn't get to it. I was a middle-class brown schoolboy with middle-class parents; I couldn't reach it. I could sort of imagine it and relate to it by empathy, but I couldn't be of it. I was never a Kingston street boy. I can't pretend to have been, because I wasn't. So even out of place in relation then to what became black in England. Black people sometimes talk about things like slavery as if they know it in their genes. They don't need to find out about it because if you're black you know it. Well, first of all, I don't believe that. I think, unfortunately, a lot of black people don't know enough about their own history to begin with and aren't passing it on to their kids and so on. That's a separate question, but that is what I feel. But I've always felt that there's no kind of automatic relationship to one's belonging. It's forged. Jamaica became consciously black in the 1960s and early 1970s. I don't care what Jamaican people look like—and remember that people don't always look like people here imagine them to be. Most people who go to the Caribbean are surprised at the range of colors that people are, and the more we know about it, the more we know a lot of people who look black are not in any sense genetically "African." It's a very mixed, very hybrid society. Black is important historically, because it's the bit that was never named, never spoken, couldn't speak its history until it was released, and that was not until after independence. So all of us in different ways learn to be black. All of us are out of place in relation to slavery. How can we think about slavery? How can we think about ancestors of mine being enslaved in chains to somebody else, particularly to the English and the Scots? It's kind of unthinkable. So I think out-of-place-ness is inevitably a condition of the diaspora but is strangely enough a condition of the Caribbean too, which is, of course, a diaspora too, because everybody who is there came from somewhere else. The indigenous people who belonged there were wiped out within one hundred years, and after that everybody comes from somewhere else. The Spanish, the Dutch, the French, the British, the Africans, the Indians, the Chinese, the Portuguese—they're all from somewhere else. We are one of the first diaspora societies. So I don't think "out-of-place-ness" is just because of my peculiar biographical history.

LB: I wonder whether part of that sense of dislocation, out-of-place-ness, also enables a kind of insight?

SH: Well, I suppose it does. I used to comfort myself, I think, with that thought. You know the German sociologist Simmel said the stranger has insights into where he or she is, which the people who live it instinctively, live their culture instinctively, can't possibly have. You need the shock of translation, etc. So I think that may be true. I thought you were going to say something else, which is that really a lot of people who are diasporic also have that. C. L. R. James called it the insights of the people who "are in but not of Europe."

LB: One of the lessons is the mutual implications of all of these stories of being out of place are about, to use Said's words, "overlapping territories, intertwined histories."

SH: Yes. Contrapuntal. There's a little piece of mine called "Minimal Selves."[11] I don't know if you know it?

LB: Yes, of course.

SH: And this was given at a conference at the Institute for Contemporary Arts, at which myself, Homi Bhabha, Salman Rushdie, and I can't remember who else, spoke. It was about identity. And I looked out into the hall, and I saw a lot of white faces, and, one after another, everybody stood up and said, "Well, actually I'm not really English because my parents come from 'Australia' or 'from the North' or 'from Scotland' or 'from Wales' or 'from the working class,'" and I suddenly got this feeling that everybody was becoming diasporic. There wasn't an English person in the room! And I met a friend in the loo, and I said, "Speak up for England." I had always thought of him as a kind of quintessential English person. So I went back into the room, and I said, "Welcome to the diaspora." Something about modern experience is the experience of dislocation, which I associated very much with my own experience and with living in the diaspora.

LB: Could we go back a little to your early days in London? I've read that you worked for a time as a teacher in south London, is that right?

SH: Yes, when I left university, I came to London. I was editing *Universities and Left Review*, which had an office in Soho. I lived in south London in Clapham in the house of a wonderful old Trotskyist called Jock Haston, and I wanted to stay in London until I went home—still not quite deciding when I'm going. So I thought, "Well, what can you do?" Practically, nothing! I couldn't then drive, so I couldn't drive a milk float. You can teach. So I got a job in a secondary school as a supply teacher, and you're sent round to different schools, but my school was unable to retain any of its supply teachers, or indeed its teachers. So once I'd got in there, they never let me go. I was a supply teacher in a school at the Kennington Oval for quite a while, about three or four years, and I used to leave there, get on a train, go to Soho, edit the journal, and go back on the night bus—try to wake up in time to get to the Oval for the opening of class. I've written a bit about that. There's an essay which has never been republished, in *Universities and Left Review*, called "Absolute Beginnings," which is sort of a nod to an old friend, because I got to know Colin MacInnes well, but it's about my experiences in secondary school.[12]

LB: I love those books as well. Those were very important to me.

SH: Me too.

LB: I read that some of the kids you took home afterwards because of the intensity of street racism at that time?

SH: No, I followed them. I was going to edit the journal, and all of a sudden these kids, who were bedded down in south London—I wasn't sure they'd ever even been to Piccadilly Circus—were actually on a train. And I said, "Where you going?" "Oh sir, we're going across town." I said, "What do you mean 'across town'?" "We're going to Notting Hill, Shepherd's Bush." I said, "What's going on?" "A bit of argy-bargy," they said meaningfully. And so then I began to get interested in what was happening over there. And a lot of people then working in Notting Hill came to the *Universities and Left Review* club, and people got involved in the Notting Hill riots and their aftermath. One of them was Michael X. I used to go down there to see where on earth these kids were, and they were on the street corners, and the adults were in the pubs behind them shouting through the doors; they were harassing black women who were walking home from work, going in to the multi-occupation flats in Powys Terrace and the terraces behind. So that's one thing. Then I got involved in the politics of Notting Hill through the club. Do you know Michael de Freitas?

LB: Yes, Michael X.[13]

SH: Well, Michael came to the New Left club, and I got to know him. First of all, we talked about jazz, because Michael was passionate about jazz, and he used to go to Stockholm [on] the weekends to hear American jazz bands. But after a bit he said, "Well, you know, a lot's going on round my place." Well, Michael was a thrower of black families out of their homes for . . . what's the name of the rack-renting landlord? Rachman.

LB: Of course, the notorious profiteer Peter Rachman.

SH: He [Michael] was a sort of strong-arm man on the street, putting the belongings of people who couldn't pay rent on the pavement. On the other hand, he had all these local connections, [and] he didn't like what was going on. He said, "We must do something about this." This is why I think Michael X is a tragedy, because he had exactly the same formation as Malcolm X, who was from exactly the same hustling background, and Malcolm became something and Michael lost his way. Anyhow, all that is irrelevant. It's just that we got involved in Notting Hill, but my first awareness that something was happening in Notting Hill was before the riots, by kids in my school alerting me. So when we got back to school, I said, "What are you doing up there?" "Oh, you know." I said, "Why are you shouting at them?" "Well, they're taking our women." I said, "What do you mean? If only you had had any women!" [*Laughter*] "They're taking our things," etc. So I said, "Do you mean these?" And I pointed to several black kids in the class, and they looked at them as if they'd never seen them. "No sir."

LB: He's one of us.

SH: "They're one of us." So I said, "What about me?" "No sir. Not you. Them." It was a very important experience for me.

LB: Incredible. What an incredible scene, actually, and also I guess in that one moment a whole conjuncture, really.

SH: That's the conjuncture. There's no doubt, yes. That's when a great deal of racism which has been simmering underneath finally gets spoken, finally erupts in the straightforward, open aggression and violence. It's a moment like Powellism in 1968, when people can say and do on the street what they've been careful not to say and do until that moment.

LB: They're being taught by Stuart Hall, who they don't count as being in the "them," and their black friends, who they're walking home from school with, maybe not, but certainly on the playground with, they don't count as being "them" either.

SH: Exactly. Funny. Complicated. I became aware of how complicated local allegiances and images of the people outside are. I think you've written about this. I became aware of that really then. I loved teaching, though it was a completely harrowing experience for me. First of all, I couldn't keep discipline. I was very young still and had no experience of teaching. I'd never been taught to teach, so I just walked in. I was given a class, which was 4FX. This was a secondary modern school, so everybody in it had already failed their 11 Plus.[14] The classes started at 1A, 1B, 1C, and at about 1E they fade into 1FX. So these are kids right at the bottom of the pile. What was I to do with them? So I said, "What are you going to do when you leave school?" "Oh sir, we're going into the print." Their fathers all worked then in the print; that was the only route into the print. You couldn't get into the print industry by knocking on the door and filling out a form. So they didn't see any reason why they should ever study anything again. Well, I'd teach them—I tried to teach them English grammar. Can you imagine? Gerunds, commas, and semicolons. [*Laughter*] I had to teach them geography, and one day the geography master came in and said, "This is interesting. You're teaching them about the trade wind, except that you've got the southeast and northwest the wrong way round on the blackboard." [*Laughter*]

I was so naive, I'd left it there. I tried to get them to act *Romeo and Juliet*. Craziness—just completely crazy and made up out of my head, really. But I also had to take them swimming and do lifesaving. I'd never life-saved anything in my life, so I was terrified. I said, "Before we go to the pool, we're going to practice lifesaving in the hall upstairs." [*Laughter*] These kids, all lying in the hall, saving one another, while I read the book. Eventually, of course, I had to take them to the pool. I was sure one of them was going to drown; I was absolutely certain, but they didn't. My only problem was when, coming back from school on a Friday afternoon from the pool, I was supposed to bring them back to school to be dismissed. Well, they were passing their homes—it was completely ridiculous nonsense. They were not going back to school for anything, least of all my bringing them to school to dismiss them. So of course they used to peel off, just disappear. So I'd start out with thirty, and by the end I had about fifteen stragglers. It was a very rich experience, but not for very long.

LB: I often teach the "Culture Is Ordinary" essay by Raymond Williams. Well, every time I teach a first-year undergraduate class, I start off with that. There's something about what you were saying about being out of place, the library figuring within that essay too, and the tea shop and all that stuff, but I did my spiel on this particular year on Williams, and I showed some images of him, showed the signal box and all those images. And then there's this black student at the back of the class—puts his hand up and says, "Les, but you know, I read this essay and I really loved it, but I felt sure that Williams was black." [*Stuart laughs wryly.*] And he just assumed, because what he was describing was that sense of out-of-place-ness, I suppose.

SH: Yes, of course.

LB: And I know that some people have criticized you for not writing about issues of racism and the black experience until quite late in your career. I wanted to ask you a little bit about what was possible in terms of making the connection between that Kennington school and the drama, the theater of race and racism that's unfolding there, and then the intellectual, political circles.

SH: Well, I also became a socialist and part of the Left at Oxford. *Universities and Left Review* was started in Oxford in response to 1956. So if you're out of place, the Left becomes a kind of home. And so for a time, lots of people like Raphael Samuel, Peter Sedgwick, Chuck Taylor, and all of those people were my interlocutors. In that period, I'd read a bit of Marx before, but I read Marx for the first time, and I used to go to . . . I was one of the few people, there was myself and a Scot called Alan Hall, who were permitted to go to Communist Party meetings and not be communists, because they thought, "We'll get them soon." I had no intention of becoming a communist, but I used to go. And I'd argue with them and argue with Raphael about class. So, of course, I got involved in those debates and in British socialist politics. So before the critique of the exclusiveness of the politics of class arises, and it doesn't arrive until the social movements of the 1970s, really, until that moment, everything was organized through the perspective of class and its politics. The black people in Britain who came in the early 1950s, were they members of the working class? Yeah, lots of them were. Did they have the same kind of class consciousness? Clearly not. If you're a conjuncturalist like me, the difference between Raymond Williams's class consciousness as the son of a railwayman in Wales and the boy who comes from the back streets of Kingston is very evident. The black cause, the politics that arises from race, is not an autonomous political arena to which you could relate, until, I would say, the mid-1960s. It doesn't surface in that way. So it's not that one didn't think about that. Let me put it personally. It's not that I didn't think about that, but I thought partly one is a subordinate element of the other—really this is a question about capitalism and imperialism and the poverty of Jamaica, the situation in which black men and women find themselves in urban deprivation and class politics are really a slightly differentiated part of one whole thing. I'm not defending this, you know. I'm just telling you, this is the consciousness you're inside. It's not a moment of autonomous black politics, and that debate doesn't happen until later, and it happens in relation to the arrival on the scene of a black presence, and that happens kind of in response to racism which is very . . . as we said, in the Notting Hill period, is just coming to the surface as a conscious political movement and issue. The response to that, in terms of anti-racism, doesn't come until a bit later than that. So there wasn't really yet what people mean by "black politics." You couldn't get writing about black politics in the way in which you could in the US, because the black presence has been there forever. It's written into part of what America is, and what it means to be American. It wasn't written into part of what to be British was. Of course, imperialism was, but it all happened so far away. To try to indigenize race in relation to Britain and find a way of identifying the importance of race in relation to class politics. So it isn't a surprise to me that I didn't write very much about that at this stage, though my first pamphlet when I went to Birmingham in 1964 was about the second generation, prophetically titled "The Young Englanders"! *The Birmingham Post* said it was much too pessimistic. It's not so much of a surprise to me, but a regret, that people who were older and more sophisticated at that stage than I was, like Raymond [Williams] and Edward Thompson, couldn't see that the whole political terrain was changing. They couldn't see what the emergence of a black politics was going to mean. Well, people say it's because they're too English or British. They were too English, or British, no question about that. I was the only black person on the editorial board of *New Left Review*, the only black person. My symbolic fathers, Edward Thompson, Raymond Williams, Ralph Miliband, Peter Worsley, John Rex—these were very experienced people. They were interested in imperialism, they were committed to the anti-imperialist struggle as part of Left politics, but they didn't understand that the black presence within Britain would be a transformatory social and political presence, that it was going to expand, that it was part of the first tip of a wave which was going to follow in much-expanded numbers after. They didn't see it was a change of conjuncture. I know you can't imagine yourself to that time, but it really was like that. I mean, it may have been that I could have been more articulate about it. You have to remember also that having just taken the decision to stay, I was thinking about something else, really. I was thinking about, well, you're going to be here, what's your accommodation with "here"? What is your relation to British politics? What is it in relation to British class questions, and so on? So my mind was slightly somewhere else. And I guess people can't now imagine a black intellectual whose mind was somewhere else, until you think about C. L. R. James. C. L. R. was always conscious of race. He wasn't articulating indigenous and authentic independent black politics in relation to Britain. He was a Trotskyist, [and] he was one of the finest speakers. Jock Haston, who I used to live with, told me he'd never heard anybody speak in public like C. L. R. James, on the hustings for the ILP.[15] He wasn't addressing a crowd of black people. Do you know what I mean?

LB: I do, yeah.

SH: And now, having discovered the degree to which James was always thinking about that, the fact that he was a Marxist has got lost. Nobody wants to talk about that anymore. So I just think that it's a mess, really, to be absolutely honest. I think there's so much that needs disentangling, and I suppose the most important thing I would say about it is, if you have a historical imagination, you have to transport yourself to the moment you're writing about and what it is like to be interior to it, to live inside it. There's no point asking, "Why wasn't she a feminist in the seventeenth century?"—excuse me. It has nothing to do with whether women weren't oppressed and exploited, or whether there wasn't, as there was in the seventeenth century already, a small consciousness of women who thought they would have to struggle to be independent. There was a large number of women who talked about marriage as a form of slavery, even by the time you get to Wollstonecraft. But you can't just say, "Why weren't they feminist?" in the same way you can't really say about British politics in the 1950s, "Why wasn't it black?"

Now I want to separate that from the question, "Was I at fault?" Was I not sufficiently involved and committed? Couldn't I carry the argument with those people? Were they blind to it? All of those things are true.

LB: For Williams, that border landscape is such a primal kind of place to think, not unlike your Kennington classroom.

SH: And for Hoggart, I mean Yorkshire, Hunslet is the same. That kind of respectable, industrial, working-class landscape is at the back of his head all the time, all the time, no matter how elevated he eventually became.

LB: Yes, indeed, though, on the one hand, that furnishes a kind of imagination, but it also forecloses.

SH: Yes, it always does. It does both. It makes possible insights that you can't really get any other way, because it takes you deep and close, and it frames you emotionally as well as analytically, and it takes you subjectively as well as objectively. So there's certain kinds of insights you can't gain without that. But it means the furniture of your mind is sort of set. What can you do about that? You have to try to expand it.

LB: That's a beautiful way of putting it. You also wrote that race was the modality through which class was being experienced, which was a very suggestive and powerful idea to me.

SH: Yes, and I know other people for whom it is. That comes out of the work on *Policing the Crisis* in the 1970s, and it was a way of rethinking what in the 1950s would have been seen as two quite separate things: race and class. Would I say it now? Well, I would also want to remind people that class is the way in which race is lived. Once you get into globalization and the working classes, people earning one dollar a day in Calcutta, class is lived through race and race is lived through class. So they're two interdependent, not exactly the same. The mistake earlier was to try to collapse them together. If you solve the class question, you would of course solve the other question. So when Edward Thompson responded to *Policing the Crisis* by saying, "What's all this stuff about race?," he didn't mean that race was not important, but he meant that once you get rid of capitalism, the race question will of course solve itself, because of course we all are against imperialism. "My father was a friend of Tagore's, my house was full of Indian nationalism," as indeed it was. It didn't figure as a political question which somebody involved in British class politics could ask directly. That was a limitation, a severe limitation. But that is what consciousness is like. So now we are in another conjuncture. We're through the conjuncture, to that extremely important moment when race, class, and gender emerged as overlapping but distinct formations.

LB: I was struck by that comment that Orwell made about the British working class, most of whom don't live in Britain.

SH: Yes.

LB: I wanted to ask you about *Policing the Crisis* because just reading it again and thinking about it again, it's so much a book about the damage that fear does in a society like this one. And it made me think about how enduring those fears have become—and shifting at the same time. I know that you wrote about that specifically.

SH: Yeah, I think it was particularly acute in the 1970s, because one could see an unconscious or subconscious set of feelings being released in relation to race, which is not released in relation to anything else. I mean, of course, some people might have hated the working class, or hated the organized labor movement, etc., but the hatred about race was visceral and it had to do with things like that "otherness." People think about race in terms of skin color, and I don't think that's really the right way to think about it, though skin color matters. In that period, it mattered profoundly. It mattered as a line of difference inscribed by nature: these are other than us; they don't belong to "us"; they don't come out of ourselves. It was massive historical denial of Britain's responsibility in relation to imperialism over four hundred years, but nevertheless it was there. I think of Mary Douglas, you know. What is "dirt" but "matter out of place." This is what Enoch Powell thought: "matter out of place." And they felt black people were dirty because they were "fouling up our space." I said to somebody who was making a radio program about Powell, Powell adored India. He's almost a sort of classic Orientalist. He thought it was a wonderful, rich civilization. He just thought none of them should be *here*—not here, not in my backyard, not living in our houses, disporting their picaninnies in my street, but in Delhi, etc., of course, wonderful city, wonderful people. So I guess we wrote about fear in *Policing the Crisis* because we were aware of these unconscious feelings—the unrequited roots of racism in British culture. It doesn't mean everybody is racist; it doesn't mean there are no anti-racist white people; it doesn't mean any of those things, but this culture does partly live off a reservoir of unconscious feelings about race, and in particular those feelings remain unconscious because they're about race. It's difficult for them to get expressed somehow. So of course you need equal opportunities, of course you need legal defense of people's rights, of course you need people to be punished if they incite violence, but how you get to the core of the subconscious roots of English racism, which is the legacy of colonization, I don't know. But what we were aware of in the 1970s is that this was a spiraling up of a kind of fear. And remember that in this period they began to be afraid about all sorts of other things—afraid about young people, about hedonism, about the explosion of sexuality on the streets, about drugs and "turn on, tune in, and drop out," about student riots, about the anti–Vietnam war protests, you know—the hydra-headed other was stalking the fields of Britain. [*Laughter*]

And a lot of people [who] we were reading in the press, and political spokespeople, really spoke about it like that. Lord Hailsham spoke about it. We think it's just one thing, but it's not. Everything is sort of out of control, and you can move from one thing to another. It's a kind of symptomatic reading of the crisis, because the race problem is only symptomatic of the violence problem, which is only symptomatic of the drug problem . . . You know, everything is symptomatic of something else. That is why in *Policing the Crisis* we felt justified in calling it a crisis because it was experienced as a crisis, that's a breakdown of the whole society and you don't really . . . you don't understand Powell's speech until you understand that it comes out of that vision.

LB: I think sometimes people forget actually how concerned you were with the different aspects of that hydra, if you like, and in particular the book you edited, *Resistance through Rituals*.[16]

SH: Yes. In some ways, the break in English culture begins there. It begins in television; it begins with youth culture; it does begin with "Rock around the Clock" in a funny kind of way. [*Laughter*] Those of us who listened to "Rock around the Clock" just knew that something was happening here that, if it gets loose, if it leaves the Odeon and starts to take root out there, will unhinge the British stoicism, the tight-arsed, stiff-upper-lip class, whatever that is, repression. It will just unpack that from the inside. And so it has done, so it has done.

LB: I also wanted to ask you, I know that you've written about a skepticism about revolutionary movements that move everything in a few days. But I also wanted to ask you about your notion of multicultural drift.

SH: I know there have been revolutions. I know that there are circumstances in which there is nothing to do but have a revolution. If only one could have a revolution tomorrow in Burma—it needs it—it owes itself a major rupture. So that's not my concern, although I've never myself been into revolutionary politics very much. And that's because the Caribbean became independent without an anti-imperial struggle, whereas Kenya, Burma, and so on did not. And I came and got involved in British class politics. Well, British class politics just, I'm sorry friends, is not a revolutionary formation. Would that it were in some respects.

LB: If only that were the case.

SH: But it ain't. So one has a more difficult task of understanding how class politics really work and how class reconciliation works and how class enmity . . . it's not without questions of class, but it's not pointing towards a single explosive moment. Well, is that just because of the milieu in which I've had to think? Well, not only. It is because of the two revolutionary moments to which my politics are very much related. One is the Russian Revolution and the other is the Cuban Revolution. And the Russian Revolution I knew was not the beginning of Year One . . . It was not start again from the beginning. You've only to look at what happened under Stalinism to see the vengeance which the past wreaked on the present. Just to see things which could not be undone, the drastic attempt to drive society in some other direction simply could not get away from the grip of the long authoritarian political culture, for instance. And the Cuban Revolution, well, of course I was more excited about the Cuban Revolution. I went to Cuba a year after it happened, and I thought it was incredible. Coming down the steps of that plane into a tropical airport of a Caribbean island which had just had a revolution. This could be Jamaica; it just happened to be there. And also I think that there are many achievements of that revolution which have to be defended, but what it isn't is a start again from the beginning. I just think if you have a sort of historical cast of mind . . . I'm not a historian, but the notion of conjuncture and historical specificity gives my thinking and writing a certain ever-present historical cast, and if you have a historical cast of mind, you just aren't persuaded that everything can start again from the beginning. Year One. Socialist Man . . . I don't really believe in origins of that kind. I don't believe in origins culturally; I don't believe in them in terms of identity; and I don't believe in them in terms of history and politics.

LB: You said at the beginning when we were talking that the dynamism of black British life has been one of your touchstones, and, in a sense, your writing life, your intellectual life has run parallel with that.

SH: It's what I've been thinking about. It is my subject. It's not the only topic that I've written about, but it is my subject insofar as I've written with these lives and experiences in mind, written to a kind of imaginary audience; insofar as new questions are seen through the prism of an experience which arises from that, it's my subject. It's not what I've always written about. I don't know what to call it. It's not my topic, but it is my subject in a way.

LB: It's a really profound way to describe it, actually, I think, but when you use that notion of "multicultural drift."

SH: Ah, yes. Don't misunderstand the term. I don't mean that there's nothing to multiculturalism but its drift. Without antiracist politics, without the resistance to racism at the local level, without a change of consciousness among black people, there's no multiculturalism of any kind. Multicultural drift is really an idea from the other side. Things are not going so well, really. There hasn't been a profound change in British society. We haven't got to the deep level of racism in the culture that I think throbs on. Well, has nothing changed? Yes, something has changed. What has changed is, you go into the street—and I came here in 1951—and it just looks different. Britain will never go back to being a culturally homogenous society ever again. It can't. I mean, it can have purges, it can throw people out into the sea, it can enforce assimilation, but it can't go back to being stable and steady on its own monocultural foundations. It can't happen. So I want to say multicultural drift is sort of what we've had to be getting on with. At least this is the thing that's not in their control. It doesn't, unfortunately, lead to or underpin a very active black politics, which, as you know, has sort of declined since the 1980s in a way. [The years] 1980 and 1985 were the last moments of a really big black conscious political movement.

LB: Why do you think some people react against the idea of multicultural drift?

SH: It's because people don't like the word "drift," you see. They think politics must be conscious and so on, and I think that too, but if you don't succeed in making a movement, do things stop? Do they not change? They continue to change incrementally. And that is the raw materials out of which another politics will emerge at some later moment, so you'd better attend to it. It's not Bob Marley; it's not kids in the street with afros; it's not Rastafarianism; it's not black consciousness; it's not black is beautiful; it's a much more ambiguous world. But does that mean the impact of the black presence on the wider society has halted? It has not. They've not been able to halt it. It goes on unraveling, very slowly unraveling, and Gramsci called it a passive revolution. Multicultural drift is a passive revolution, but passive revolutions happen. Only they happen more incrementally.

LB: What I like and admire about it is the idea that they are small, incremental, cumulative, no-going-back kind of change.

SH: I think that is so. That's exactly what I was trying to capture in the term "drift." So it wasn't by any means a recommendation that you should work for drift. You should work for something more serious, and more wide-ranging and far-reaching, than that.

LB: Some of my friends have said, "Well, there are things that make the current move faster, and that's what you have to focus on."

SH: Of course, absolutely, but when that is not around, what Marx called the old mole, the old black mole, is still working along, weaving its way through in the bowels of society, looking for another way out.

LB: I suppose as well the thing I wanted to ask you about was several times in your writing you talk about how important it is for that black presence in Britain or there to be understandings and representations that are recognizable, that in some ways make sense of that conjuncture, of that predicament, if you like, of those people.

SH: Yeah, I think that's very important, and in some ways it's because if you move towards . . . if your analysis moves towards the level of the conjunctural, you have to take a much wider range of phenomena into account. You can't just rest with the underlying structural logic. And so you think about what is likely to awaken identification. There's no politics without identification. People have to invest something of themselves, something that they recognize is of them or speaks to their condition, and without that moment of recognition . . . Politics also has a drift, so politics will go on, but you won't have a political movement without that moment of identification. So, of course, it matters to me profoundly what strikes the popular imaginary. What is not necessarily a political theory or a political doctrine, but what appeals to the imaginary and in the imaginary unlocks something which isn't usually unlocked elsewhere. I once said about popular culture, which, as you know, I've been an aficionado and still am (I must be the only academic viewer of *Neighbours*[17] left on earth!), that often the first sign of a deeper political and social rupture we have is in the culture of everyday life. [*Laughter*]

So I'm still addicted to parts of popular culture, but I said once about it, it's only what is at stake in the popular that makes it worthwhile. Otherwise, who gives a shit about it? Otherwise, it's of no importance. And also it's just an inventory. This is popular culture, that is high culture, and this is a bit of popular culture moving into high culture . . . who cares about that? What matters is where the popular imaginary gets itself expressed and how its meanings are struggled over, and it does not always get expressed in high culture. It gets expressed in the dirty, compromised, commercialized, overridden world of popular culture, which is never an uncontradictory space, never an uncontested space. So one must attend to it.

LB: And I guess as well there's no sense of what British popular culture is in this context without a black presence?

SH: Of course that is so, and it's so politically. That's why I said, today, class is lived through the modality of race in the same way that race is lived through the modality of class. That's what has happened. So that is true of any kind of politics you can think of, but even if you didn't, the signs of the black presence are all around us. So there isn't a . . . there may be less of a black movement, less of an affirmation of black consciousness. But it's there. How could you look at popular culture, popular lives, how could you look at the cities, how could you look at football, how could you look at popular music, how could you look at any of those spheres, how could you look at the NHS? For goodness' sake, I go to dialysis three times a week; it's like a cross-section of multicultural drift. If you want to see multicultural drift, come with me on a Thursday to the dialysis unit of St. Charles Hospital—you will see it. You will see it, I tell you.

LB: It's very alive in my mind, too, Stuart—the hospital is an incredibly important place to think about issues of multiculture.

SH: The hospital, absolutely. I do a lot of my thinking there. So what sustains the black presence? Well, it's sustained in all sorts of ways, and there's no reason to give up hope because it's not at the high political pitch that it was in the 1980s, not at the high level of political consciousness. The problem is really not so much going back to that but trying to imagine what that might be in the next decade, in the next conjuncture. How will these informal presences which are so important come together in another moment to create another kind of black, or whatever, multicultural politics? We don't have the capacity to imagine that yet, but still, that is the question. So the sustainers of that black presence and what is happening in them, including a lot of contradictory things, you know. I mean what is happening to black young people, young boys especially, is completely horrendous, completely horrendous, and I have to confess to you that one of the reasons for it, or one of the things which contains it, is precisely some of the deformations of black popular culture. As an aficionado of black popular culture, it gives me deep pain to have to say it, but black popular culture gives young black people an alternative point of recognition, which they're not going to find in the everyday world; they're not going to find through academic success. Some of them have, of course, that's one of the things that's happened in multicultural drift—some people have made it. Some black people make it much more than they ever had before, and some by dint of very hard work—for instance, a lot of women at the bottom of the social work and medical professions, etc., have studied, brought up their children on their own, they've really lived a heroic life in this period, but not everybody can do that. And an alternative has been offered to them in certain aspects of what we used to be quite romantic about—drop out; yeah, that's cool. But lives are being lost, lives are being sacrificed.

LB: There's no easy way to speak about it, is there?

SH: I find it almost impossible to speak about it. The terrain of the dialogue is so horrendously skewed that one can hardly talk about it at all, but I mourn it every day.

LB: I think of those young lives damaging themselves, actually damaging people who are the mirror image of themselves.

SH: Damaging themselves and damaging other people just like them.

LB: I wanted to ask you, to end with really, about our current conjuncture. Do you think that our current conjuncture begins, as so many say, with September 11th? There's been an awful lot of talk about the death of multiculture and death of multiculturalism.

SH: Well, in pure conjunctural terms—but this is just speculation—I think the present conjuncture begins in the mid-1970s, with Thatcherism as the first installment of it. It's really about globalization: so all the things to do with this world and that world, with the other here, with asylum, with waves of migration, with people thrown out of their homes, with people living in transit camps, all of that stuff is the underside of globalization, in my view. Globalization is how capital saved itself from the welfare state. Once it realized it couldn't directly roll back the welfare state, it had to go somewhere else and increase its capacity to exploit labor, and "global" is where it went, to the new division of labor between the office in Manhattan and the dollar-a-day worker in Indonesia. And I happen to think that the present phase of Muslim extremism, or really, of the politicization of Islam, is part of that phenomenon too, which is not to say it doesn't have religious roots and not to say it doesn't take another step up to get to the moment of the suicide bomber and terrorism and all that. September 11th did make a profound change in explicitly making cultural difference and multiculturalism dangerous. On the other hand, it takes us a step right backwards in terms of occupying other people's countries, which is so old and ancient that apparently the Brits and the Americans don't even recognize it to be what it is. They can't imagine why they're seen in that way. They came to save them! This is the oldest imperialist story there ever has been. "We're here to discharge the white man's burden." I think about Islam; I think about the possibility of Islamic nationalism; I think about the moment of Islamic socialism. All of them exhausted, one after another, in the Cold War and in the period after that. What is left as a way of identifying yourself but religion? Unfortunately, this is a move to the regressive side of the political spectrum, but it's performing a lot of the same functions as these other movements performed at an earlier stage. And I happen to think that, as they say, it's really being driven by young people, young people on the street. Why are they as poor as they are? Why do they feel boxed in by so many constraints? Why is it that they can't recognize themselves in the modern world? Well, because of the way in which the division of labor in global capitalist society does make them the objects, rather than the subjects, of economic, social, and cultural development. So I think there are these underlying factors. That's why I hesitate to say 9/11 came out of the blue; we don't know where it came from, [but] suddenly everything has changed. It didn't come out of the blue. There has been a long colonial history between Iraq and Britain. It's not very long ago since we were there. We colluded in the formation of a religiously exclusive state in Palestine at the expense of driving Palestinians into camps. Nothing in the Middle East is from the day before yesterday—nothing. Of course, that's not to say it remains the same. This is a new phase, and it's a phase particularly difficult for people on the Left, because of religion, the ambiguous situation of religion, and because we've never understood religion, and because our secular sociological selves thought religion was going to go away, and because communism and the socialist movements were all secular movements. Culture has taken its revenge on our failure to understand history. So, of course, in one sort of way I feel we'll never be the same again, and I think we may never be, but I wouldn't myself identify the conjunctural shift there [September 11, 2001]. I identify it at another place.

LB: I suppose in a way identifying it there enables an easy forgetting or an erasure of what's gone before.

SH: Yes, I think it involves precisely that, and I think it allows Americans precisely to absolve themselves of a long historical responsibility, which has been going on since the end of the nineteenth century.

LB: You've said many times that New Labour has been a historic missed opportunity.

SH: I think it's a missed opportunity, yes, but it is the second phase of Thatcherism really—really, that's what it is. So it's a missed opportunity only because it would have had to do something just as dramatic as Thatcherism to have found a counterpolitics. And that's what those of us on the Left kept saying—you aren't going back to the nationalization of everything in sight; you aren't going back to the old-style labor movement. It has been decentered and distributed around the world by global capitalism. The way is not to go back; the way is to go forward.

And it is to try to redefine what your hopes were of that forward movement and of that kind of equality in the new conditions. That requires a lot of hard thought, not sentimentality. And the thinking never happened. The thought was, since there is no alternative, how do we accommodate to it? That's what Anthony Giddens taught them. Globalization is irreversible—what we can do is accommodate to it, improve the supply side, build up the entrepreneurial skills, make Britain more competitive, marketize society, open the doorway to trade, lower the barriers, deregulate and privatize, make globalization work. And the surprise to me is, of course, that social democracy in its New Labour form has been more successful than Thatcherism was because, in addition to the fact that it attends to the poor, it attends to those who are residually left out. Whereas Thatcherism didn't give a damn about anybody, it was just driving the new managerialism and marketization through society. And the end of Thatcherism is really an interesting moment for me, because nobody quite explained why it happened. The conservatives adore Mrs. Thatcher; they think she's the most wonderful leader they've had since Churchill. Why did they get rid of her? There was some sense that you can't fundamentally remodel society just like that, that the costs, that's what's falling apart as a consequence of this, have to be dealt with as well. So they moved more to the middle terrain, a bit of good governance, etc. If you're talking about a long-term political project, essentially the neoliberal global capitalist project, New Labour is a more successful installment of it than the first installment, which was Thatcherism. And, as you know, I wrote a lot about Thatcherism—much of it was to try to persuade the Left to take it seriously. I argued, it's not just a turn of the electoral screw; it's a much deeper movement going on here. The call to drink deeply didn't catch fire, but actually some people heard it. The wrong side heard it! The Blairites heard it and thought, "Oh yes. This is inevitable. We've got to adapt it."

But what I was going to say was that, at the time, I was preoccupied with the impact of all that on Britain. I sort of saw the relationship to Reaganism abroad, but I didn't see its global dimensions. It was a global moment, not a national moment. It paraded under the nationalist guise—British values, the flag, the Falklands, send the gunboat—but that's just the Marxist notion that the future comes masquerading like the past. It was a masquerade. What was happening underneath was much deeper, more transformatory than that. The rise of a new, more planetary phase of global modernity.

LB: On occasion, Stuart, you have referred to Althusser's idea of the importance of bending the twig. I just wondered how you think we need to bend the twig now in terms of what you've described, in which direction do we need to bend it, and what kind of things do we need to bend the twig towards and away from?

SH: [Pauses] No, I mean if I were more certain, I would have written more about it, so this is a very tentative answer, and it will reveal how old-fashioned I am. We need to bend the twig in the direction of understanding the full outcome of the new phase of global capitalism. And that is about difference, it's about why the question of difference is so much on the table; it's why religion has made a return; it's why half the world feels as if it's become the proletariat of the other half; it's why so many people are left out; it's why Africa is in such a terrible disastrous state, on and on and on. So that is not enough. Lots of things follow on from that. But if you ask me in terms of how I would intervene in any discussion, I'd intervene to remind them of the global dimensions of what is going on. So whereas twenty years ago I would intervene in relation to questions of blackness in terms of race, I would intervene now not forgetting race at all but intervene in the direction of questions of difference.

LB: Under New Labour, there has been a hardening of the border, the open hand being shown those people seemed to speak to something that you're pointing towards and at the same time talk of cohesion and integration?

SH: You asked me earlier on, and I didn't reply to you, whether I think that's what's going on, and I do. I think the so-called declared death of multiculturalism is a route back to assimilationism. And assimilationism is a new way of dealing with difference, by way of erasing it. It might say, "only some of you can belong," but "if you're here, you must look and behave like us." You must, in other words, liquidate all those differences that meant anything to you—erase them and become like us. And if you become deeply black English, yes, some of you can stay. That's the new accommodation. It's not quite the Powell moment, when I guess they did think they could send us all home. The agents of global capitalism didn't understand that global capitalism is not going to send anybody home. I do think that the crises that are appearing now appear in very different forms. You talked about the closure [of] borders, I'm transfixed by people displaced from their homes, millions of people across the world who are living in transit camps or in UNICEF camps, who are the objects of humanitarian aid, who are being fed from the air. This is Agamben's bare life. This is a way in which the system has simply ground half of civilized life into nothingness, into just relying on its bare bones, operating on its flesh and its body and nothing more to give. People stowing away on the undercarriages of airplanes to get out of it, setting sail in leaky boats when they know they probably won't arrive, boats that are already leaking before they leave, but they must leave the horrors that they are now obliged to live in. I don't recognize this world in the way in which most people describe it at all. I know perfectly well that at the other end two-bed flats in Mayfair can go for £2 million. I know that. Of course, markets have always done that, always created the very rich and the very poor. But global capitalism at the moment creates such a gap between the wealthy and the deeply immiserated people and societies. And so some of that will surface in terms of black people in terms of Africa, where the people we're talking about are black. But in the Middle East, the people are brown, and in China they're something else; I don't know what they are in China. China is a complete mystery to me, but you understand what I'm saying? Race alone, the line along which the field was divided, will no longer on its own sustain the strong sense of difference around which contemporary struggles polarize. You have to expand it in some way to see how difference plays into the way in which rich and poor now have to negotiate a common space, a common life. That's the "multicultural question"!

NOTES

1 See http://www.serpentinegallery.org/.
2 Brian Meeks, ed., *Culture, Politics, Race and Diaspora: The Thought of Stuart Hall* (London: Lawrence and Wishart, 2007).
3 David Scott, "Stuart Hall's Ethics," *Small Axe* 17 (2005): 3.
4 Stuart Hall, C. Critcher, T. Jefferson, J. Clarke, and B. Roberts, *Policing the Crisis: Mugging, the State and Law and Order* (London: Macmillan, 1978).

5 Stuart Hall, "Cultural Identity and Diaspora," in *Identity*, ed. J. Rutherford, 222–237 (London: Lawrence and Wishart, 1990).

6 Stuart Hall, "Marx's Notes on Method: A 'Reading' of the '1857 Introduction,'" *Cultural Studies*, no. 6 (1974).

7 Lawrence Grossberg, "Stuart Hall on Race and Racism: Cultural Studies and the Practice of Contextualism," in *Culture, Politics, Race and Diaspora: The Thought of Stuart Hall*, ed. Brian Meeks (London: Lawrence and Wishart, 2007).

8 Colm Tóibín, *The Master* (London: Picador, 2004).

9 George Lamming, *The Pleasures of Exile* (Ann Arbor: University of Michigan Press, 1992).

10 Edward W. Said, *Out of Place: A Memoir* (London: Granta Books, 1999).

11 Stuart Hall, "Minimal Selves," in *Identity: The Real Me*, ed. L. Appignanesi (London: ICA Document 6, 1988).

12 Stuart Hall, "Absolute Beginnings," *Universities and Left Review* 7 (1959): 17–25.

13 Michael de Freitas emigrated to London in 1957 from Trinidad. He renamed himself Michael X, styling his politics on the "Black Power" movement in the US. In 1969, he founded the Racial Adjustment Action Society and became the self-appointed leader of a Black Power commune on Holloway Road, North London, called the "Black House."

14 These exams, taken by children at eleven, determined whether they went to selective "grammar schools" or the second tier of secondary modern schools. Secondary modern schools became synonymous with working-class schooling.

15 Independent Labour Party.

16 Stuart Hall and Tony Jefferson, *Resistance through Rituals: Youth Subcultures in Postwar Britain* (London: Hutchinson, 1976).

17 An Australian soap opera.

REFERENCES

Gilroy, Paul. 2007. *Black Britain: A Photographic History*. London: Saqi.

Grossberg, Lawrence. 2007. "Stuart Hall on Race and Racism: Cultural Studies and the Practice of Contextualism." In *Culture, Politics, Race and Diaspora: The Thought of Stuart Hall*, edited by Brian Meeks. London: Lawrence and Wishart.

Hall, Stuart. 1959. "Absolute Beginnings." *Universities and Left Review* 7:17–25.

Hall, Stuart. 1974. "Marx's Notes on Method: A 'Reading' of the '1857 Introduction.'" *Cultural Studies*, no. 6.

Hall, Stuart. 1988. "Minimal Selves." In *Identity: The Real Me*, edited by L. Appignanesi. London: ICA Document 6.

Hall, Stuart. 1990. "Cultural Identity and Diaspora." In *Identity*, edited by J. Rutherford, 222–237. London: Lawrence and Wishart.

Hall, Stuart, and Tony Jefferson. 1976. *Resistance through Rituals: Youth Subcultures in Postwar Britain*. London: Hutchinson.

Hall, S., C. Critcher, T. Jefferson, J. Clarke, and B. Roberts. 1978. *Policing the Crisis: Mugging, the State and Law and Order*. London: Macmillan.

Lamming, George. 1992. *The Pleasures of Exile*. Ann Arbor: University of Michigan Press.

Meeks, Brian, ed. 2007. *Culture, Politics, Race and Diaspora: The Thought of Stuart Hall*. London: Lawrence and Wishart.

Said, Edward W. 1999. *Out of Place: A Memoir*. London: Granta Books.

Scott, David. 2005. "Stuart Hall's Ethics." *Small Axe* 17:1–16.

Tóibín, Colm. 2004. *The Master*. London: Picador.

Caribbean and Other Perspectives

This final chapter began life as the closing address at a conference on Stuart's work held at the Centre for Caribbean Thought at the University of the West Indies in Mona, Jamaica, in 2004.[1] Here Stuart offers his response to the various commentaries on his work that had been presented at the conference over the previous days. Even by his own high standards, it is an extraordinarily wide-ranging tour de force in which he speaks both autobiographically and politically, addressing with a remarkable freshness of perspective a series of key analytical, disciplinary, and methodological issues in the life of this "critical intellectual," to use the self-definition with which he ends.

As is self-evident, up until this point, these introductions to the various parts of this volume, besides providing some commentary on the relevant contexts of each text's production and pointing to links between them, have also functioned to install my own preferred readings (to use Stuart's own terminology) of the various pieces selected. I am very conscious, as I said in the general introduction, that other selections would have been possible. Moreover, the selections having been made, readers may very well nonetheless choose to decode any individual piece in ways different from (and quite possibly at odds with) the implicit interpretations offered by my own highlighting of specific points in my introductions. It is almost certain that Stuart himself would have done so, in his inimitably good-natured but critical manner. If we consider the principal example we have in which he offers a metacommentary on the decoding of his own work (in the interview with Justin Lewis and his colleagues on the encoding/decoding model itself, referred to in part III of the first volume), we see him quite prepared to insist on the need to define (and argue evidentially for) what constitutes a more (or less) adequate reading of any given text (his own quite definitely included) rather than resigning himself to any merely relativist position in matters of interpretation.[2]

That being so, it is appropriate to leave the last word to Stuart himself, without the further interposition of an editorial voice, so that the final framing of this material is of his own choosing.

NOTES

1 For the conference proceedings, see Brian Meeks, ed., *Culture, Politics and Diaspora: The Thought of Stuart Hall* (Kingston: Ian Randle, 2007).
2 He does this rather in the manner of Derrida's insistence on the fact that his opponents have, in his view, misread him, in his dispute with John Searle about the definition of deconstruction. For a good account of this debate, see Christopher Norris, *Deconstruction: Theory and Practice* (London: Routledge, 1991), 156.

CHAPTER 10

Through the Prism of an Intellectual Life

Thinking about Thinking

I cannot begin at this point to try to reply or respond in any detail to the many papers which have been presented, the important ideas which have been circulated, and the points which have been raised.[1] Since I cannot respond in detail, what on earth can I do? Perhaps I can start by trying to invoke a certain way of experiencing myself over the past two days of the conference. I keep looking around trying to discover this person "Stuart Hall" that everybody is talking about. Occasionally I recognize him. I sort of know him. He has a certain familiarity every now and again. I am familiar with a lot of the ideas people are referring to. I recognize some of the quotes, though, I have to confess, not all! There are one or two I am very grateful to have rediscovered, and I hope to get the references. But this experience of, as it were, experiencing oneself as both subject and object, of encountering oneself from the outside, as another—an *other*—sort of person next door, is uncanny. It is like being exposed to a serialized set of embarrassments. And I want just to draw from that experience a first thought about thought. I think theory—thinking, theorizing—is rather like that, in the sense that one confronts the absolute unknowingness, the opacity, the density, of reality, of the subject one is trying to understand. It presents itself, first, as both too multifarious and too complicated, with its patterns too hidden, its interconnections unrevealed. One needs the act of distancing oneself—as Lacan would say—"from the place of the other." Marx once suggested that one should use concepts like a scientist uses a microscope, to change the magnification, in order to "see differently"—to penetrate the disorderly surface of things to another level of understanding. There is a sense in which one has to stand back, outside of oneself, in order to make *the detour through thought*, to approach what it is one is trying to think about indirectly, obliquely, in another way, another mode. I think the world is fundamentally resistant to thought, I think it is resistant to "theory." I do not think it likes to be thought. I do not think it wants to be understood. So, inevitably, thinking is hard work, a kind of labor. It is not something that simply flows naturally from inside oneself. Thus, one of the perplexities about doing intellectual work is that, of course, to be any sort of intellectual is to attempt to raise one's self-reflexiveness to the highest maximum point of intensity. Someone—I think Mike Rustin[2] earlier on—referred to my early work, the subject of my putative DPhil, on the novels of Henry James, and what a bizarre thing it is that this is where my academic career started. One of the things about James was, of course, his attempt to gain the maximum intensity of self-consciousness, to be as self-aware as possible about the finest movements of his own conscious thinking—as he said, "to be someone on whom nothing is lost." Yet to do that is to become instantly aware of the enormous *unconsciousness* of thinking, of thought; one simply cannot and will never be able to fully recuperate one's own processes of thought or creativity self-reflexively.

These provisional thoughts about thinking come from being present at a conference at which I am, somehow, both being discussed and also discussing! If I distance myself, see myself "from the place of the other," I can see what James, in one of his finest short stories, called "the figure in the carpet" that I could not see before. I was often tempted during these past two days to join in and speak of me in the third person! Now what I wanted to say about this strategy is that, of course, by taking the "detour through thought," one sees all sorts of things about one's self and one's own thinking, connections in one's work, the patterns behind the patterns, which one could not possibly see for oneself in any other way. In that sense, one is always unconsciously escaping the attempt to self-knowledge, the attempt to become identical with oneself. That is not possible. I cannot become identical with myself. That is the paradox of identity which I have tried to write about elsewhere—one can only think identity through difference. To think is to construct that inevitable distance between the subject that is thinking and the subject that is being thought about. That is just a condition of intellectual work.

Caribbean Formation

The second thought about thinking and about the "thought" that we have been discussing these two days was my response to the invitation from Brian Meeks, Tony Bogues, and Rupert Lewis to, as it were, become, at this very late stage in my life, a Caribbean intellectual. In what sense could I possibly claim to be a Caribbean intellectual? Certainly, not in the most obvious sense of the term. My work has not been largely about the Caribbean. I have not been actively present in the enormously important work of trying to *write* the history of the Caribbean and Caribbean societies in the period of independence, including writing its past from the perspective of an independent nation. Of course, my hopes have been caught up with the fate of the nations of the region since decolonization. However, I have not been party in that deep way to the project of "nationhood." I am Caribbean in the most banal sense, in the sense that I was born here. But that accident of birth is not enough to justify owning up to the title. I have to confess, although they do not know it, that I did seriously think of saying to them, "I am sorry, but I am not a Caribbean intellectual in the sense in which I think the Centre ought to be honoring people." The reason I decided not to do that was because, reflecting on my own life and practice, I have to say that, although in many moments of my life I have been thinking about what many people in the Caribbean would think of as other problems, other places, other dilemmas, it seems to me I have always been doing so through what I can only call "the prism of my Caribbean formation." In that sense I am committed to the idea of a politics of location. This does not mean all thought is necessarily limited and self-interested because of where it comes from, or anything like that. I mean something rather looser—that all thought is shaped by where it comes from, that knowledge is always to some degree "positional." One can never escape the way in which one's formation lays a kind of imprint on or template over what one is interested in, what kind of take one would have on any topic, what linkages one wants to make, and so on. This is true even about so-called Cultural Studies, the field with which, inevitably, my work and my career have been identified, and for which I feel a certain responsibility. I have tried as far as possible to evade this "burden of representation," and I sometimes make rude noises about it so people think "oh well, it does not really belong to him after all." I deny paternity. Cultural Studies had many origins, many "fathers," but nevertheless, one feels a certain responsibility for it.

Well, Cultural Studies has its own internal history as a discipline, but when I think about why I ever got into it, I know it was because, before what is called Cultural Studies ever began at Birmingham in the early 1960s, I had to confront the problem of trying to understand what Caribbean culture was and what my relationship was to it. I put it that way because my relationship to it, in terms of a naturalistic logic—"He was born here, so he must be a Caribbean intellectual"—does not work. My relationship to the Caribbean was one of dislocation, of displacement, literally and figuratively. My life as a young person, as a child, as an adolescent, was spent there. I left when I was eighteen years old. Though I have never ceased to think of myself as in some way Jamaican, I have never lived for long periods in the Caribbean since then. A relationship then—a negative relationship, you would think—of displacement and dislocation. Dislocation in a deeper sense, too. The reason why I was so committed to leaving the Caribbean when I finished school at the end of the 1950s and the reason why in some ways I never returned to live here had to do with my colonial formation, my formation and experience as *a colonial subject*. Because there are so many young people in the audience, I want to remind you that I am talking about something very specific, now more or less lost as an immediate experience to those who are not of or nearly my age. Most of you are children of the "postcolonial." I am talking about experiencing oneself, thinking about one's society and one's future, from the position of a colonial subject. I left for England twelve years before independence. My whole formation had been as a child of colored middle-class Jamaican society. That is to experience oneself as "colonized"— that is, fundamentally displaced from the center of the world, which was always represented to me as "elsewhere" and at the same time dislocated from the people and conditions around me. My relationship to that background, which I do not want to go into in a personal sense, was to make me feel (in the eloquent term which the great critic of Orientalism, Edward Said, used as the title of his memoir of a strikingly similar childhood halfway around the world in another colonized space) "out of place," both in relation to my family and my personal formation, and in relation to the society into which I had been born. I hope it is not necessary to add that colonization, class, race, and color were intrinsic to that troubled story.

Up to the point where I left Jamaica in 1951, I did not understand what the source of that dislocation was. I thought it was a largely personal one. It was not until much later that I discovered that this was a feeling of dislocation experienced by a whole generation of intellectual Caribbean people at the end of empire. When I went to London, there they all were, hiding out: all of them making some kind of escape attempt from colonial society. All of them in search of a way to become modern subjects, but with the bizarre thought that in order to do so, you had to leave the place of your birth—to go somewhere else—to become, borrowing the title of one of George Lamming's novels, "a native of my person." Not anywhere else, of course, but right to the heart of the dislocation itself, to that which had, at a distance, dis-placed, un-homed you. And when I say "dislocated," I am talking about serious stuff. I am talking about never feeling at one with the expectations my family had for me, of the sort of person I should become, of what I should do with my life. And of dislocation from the people themselves—from the mass of the Jamaican people: not at home "in the castle of my skin." Not being able to find myself "at home" in the context in which I was born, brought up, and lived. And I thought, "This is a recipe for disaster." The thing to do, I felt, is get out of there. There is a wonderful passage in Lamming's *The Pleasures of Exile*—a book which I strongly recommend to you if you are interested in this period of Caribbean intellectual history, and especially if you can appreciate and enjoy the ironies of the word "pleasures"—in which Lamming, speaking of the West Indian writers who all found themselves living in London between 1948 and 1958, says, "They simply wanted *to get out* of the place where they were born."[3] This is the decade which, as he says, "witnessed the 'emergence' of the novel as an imaginative interpretation of West Indian society by West Indians. And every one of them: Mittelholzer, Reid, Mais, Selvon, Hearne, Carew, Naipaul, Andrew Salkey, Neville Dawes, everyone has felt the need *to get out*."[4] As an aspiring young writer, get out I did. However, what I soon discovered was that I had not and could never really "get out" or be fully part of this "elsewhere" that had simultaneously made and unmade me. To make the return journey: not literally, because for many, "you can't go home again," but symbolically, in my head. I had no alternative but to come to terms with and try to understand the very culture from which I had felt distanced and, unsuccessfully, engineered an impossible escape. And when in the mid-1950s, after the *Empire Windrush* and the beginning of mass migration to England from the Caribbean, I met black Caribbean men and women looking for work and a place to live in the gray, wet, and inhospitable London streets—one more turn in the story of the Middle Passage and a critical moment in the formation of another displaced black diaspora—I resolved to go back, to read, read about, try to understand and to make a part of me the culture which had made me and from which I could never—and no longer wished—to escape. The central theme of *Pleasures of Exile*, Richard Drayton says in the preface to the new edition, is "the recovery of self"—even if it can only be recovered on the other side of the Black Atlantic.[5] That was the personal origins, for me, of my own "making" as a black intellectual (like many Jamaicans of my generation and class background, I had never until then thought of myself as "black"); and also the first encounter with what later came to be called Cultural Studies. All this no doubt explains how my perspective on "being a Caribbean intellectual" and my conceptualization of "culture" acquired from its earliest point so disrupted and *diasporic* an inflexion.

Subjectivity and Culture

What we think of as our individuality—something given before culture, which we possess as a subject just by being born, after which we learn to use the tools of culture—is quite the reverse. This is part of what I meant by saying that identity is not settled in the past but always also oriented toward the future. We enter culture, and by doing so appropriate a language, a culture, which someone else—many other people—created for us, and only in that way gradually become subjects. Men and women make history, not on conditions of their own making, but with elements which are provided for them from the past, and which in some sense are their conditions of existence, and they shape and form them in ways that they have to live subjectively but for which they cannot be directly responsible. It is one of Michel Foucault's greatest insights that in order to become "subjects" we must be "subjected" to discourses which speak us, and without which we cannot speak. Of course, culture is also enabling as well as constraining, disciplining. Within culture, we can form intentions, make purposes, create the most extraordinary intuitions into life. We can produce great works of philosophy, of painting, of literature, but only because we have already subjected ourselves to the laws and conventions and meanings of a language, the circumstances of history and culture, without which we could not have made ourselves. This process is called "the decentering of the subject." It represents the dislocation of the subject from the position of authorship and authority. It is the dislocation from that humanist dream which, I think, is really a humanist fantasy, that actually man [*sic*] is the center of the universe; it all proceeds from us and we are the origin. I could say more about how that figure of the displacement from the position of origin and identity has recurred in my own thinking, but this is not the place or the time. However, it represents the end of a certain fantasy of romantic individualism to which I once subscribed (I went to England, after all, as a Romantic poet manqué) and the starting point in my thinking of a profound belief that "the social" is more than the sum of individuals: it is what the early sociologists—Marx, Weber, Durkheim—called "society *sui generis.*" My critics would say this is how I fell prey to structuralism, but it really preceded all that. It came in part from thinking about my own formation, my own subjecthood. I do not apply this insight substantively. It is not what I think about but rather what I think *with*. When I think about a problem, I realize retrospectively that I have done so by making this "detour." I am sure this "methodological presupposition" of my thinking has something to do with my own personal "displacement," but this is a connection I cannot spend time reflecting on—it is part of the unconsciousness of thought about which I was speaking earlier.

Transdisciplinary Thought and Intellectual Activism

I am trying to now respond or refer to things which have been said in the last couple of days without actually being able to take on directly arguments which have been made. I am trying to share with you my thoughts, prompted by the last few days, about this strange object/subject—"the thought of Stuart Hall." I have been describing a kind of "thinking under erasure." What I mean by that is simply that in intellectual thought there are rarely absolutely new paradigms, which nobody has ever attended to before. We think within traditions and paradigms of thought—they think us—even when our intention is to break with and transcend them. But there are moments when the paradigms shift, when what David Scott calls "the problem space" changes. We do live in a period when many of the existing paradigms established and developed within traditional intellectual disciplines either no longer in themselves adequately correspond to the problems that we have to resolve, or require supplementing from other disciplines with which they have not historically been directly connected. These are the openings for what is called a transdisciplinary field of inquiry. And I speak about it because I have—once again, somewhat unconsciously—found myself in a transdisciplinary field. I have never been able to be satisfied with working from within a single discipline. It has nothing to do with not respecting what has gone on in the work of developing intellectual disciplines, but I am at the same time aware of the fact that the organization of modern knowledge into the disciplinary framework occurred at a specific historical moment. That historical moment may have passed, or may be passing, or may be "on the wane," or that particular way of organizing knowledge may no longer be adequate to the reality it is trying to analyze and describe. I feel a disjuncture between the disciplines, on the one hand, and the rapidly shifting and changing fragments of reality which confront us today. Again, I am not recommending to you an antidisciplinary pathway; I am simply saying that I have not found it possible to think simply within the framework of the given disciplines. I started in literature and literary criticism, but I never became a writer or a critic. I was a professor of sociology, but I have no formal academic training in the field. Cultural Studies is a transdisciplinary field of inquiry, not a discipline.

Now, that has had profound costs on my own thought. First of all, I really am not an academic in the traditional sense at all. I mean Barry Chevannes was very kind to refer to me as a "scholar," but I am not really in the true sense of the word a "scholar."[6] That is not what I am. I have lived an academic life and earned my living—not terribly well—from doing academic work. I love to teach. I wanted to teach from the earliest point that I can remember. And teaching goes on in academic worlds. I respect and defend the academy to the hilt and the capacity it gives to transmit knowledge to future generations and to pursue knowledge for its own sake. One has to defend this arena of critical thought—especially these days, when it is under such attack from so many quarters—with one's life. But it does not mean that I want to be or think of myself as having been an academic. I would claim, I would insist on, my right to the title of having done intellectual work. I am an intellectual. I am an intellectual in Gramsci's sense because I believe in the power and necessity of ideas. Of course, as a sort of materialist, I do not believe ideas alone make the world go round. And I certainly do not mean that I think my task is to produce theory. I would do without theory if I could! The problem is, I cannot. You cannot. Because the world presents itself in the chaos of appearances, and the only way in which one can understand, break down, analyze, grasp, in order to do something about the present conjuncture that confronts one, is to break into that series of congealed and opaque appearances with the only tools you have: concepts, ideas, and thoughts. To break into it and to come back to the surface of a situation or conjuncture one is trying to explain, having made "the detour through theory." Marx, in his "1857 Introduction," which is a wonderful methodological text about which I have written, as Larry Grossberg remarked the other day, describes exactly this process. I am talking here about a working method of Marx.[7] I am not talking about whether one subscribes to all the theories of Marxism or not. That is a different question. And what Marx says is you begin with an obvious fact: a social system is composed of people, and this gives us our first, what he calls "chaotic," conception—the category of "population." How far can you take this category of population? Well, you can take it quite far. But really, you have to break with that descriptive approach at the moment when you understand that every population is always divided—it is not a homogeneous or multifarious single object. Always within that population are relations between capitalists and labor, men and women, masters and slaves. Relations of difference are what matters. The social categories into which people are inserted are more important than the sum of the humanity—the fact "that we are all human under the skin"—which they constitute. And to make the move of analyzing the population, as it were, into its particular categories, and the relations of similarity and difference between them, seems an abstract movement: the necessary moment of abstraction. However, as Marx says, you cannot stop there—which a great deal of theory does. You know, it is pleased to produce the categories and it proceeds to refine the abstractions, but, Marx says, far from it. You need to return then to the problem you really wanted to solve, but now understanding that it is the product of "many determinations," not of one: not of a singular logic unfolding through history; not of a teleology, a deterministic circle which has its own end already inscribed in its beginning. Not Hegel's fantasy of the "resolution of reason," the subsumption of the real and the rational, the dialectical resolution which is some moment when Thought and the Real—theory and historical reality— could be identically the same. None of that. Instead, you return to a world of many determinations, where the attempts to explain and understand are open and never eliding—because the historical reality to be explained has no known or determined end. Well, some of the things that people have remarked on in my work arise from this method of thinking, which I am only addressing because you selected the absurd notion of spending two days thinking about the thought of Stuart Hall!

Studying the Conjuncture

So I have been thinking about the thought of Stuart Hall too, and I am telling you what I seem to have found out! Certain habits of thinking, certain ways of addressing a problem. If you are not interested in the disciplines, and if your subject is not given by the discipline, what is it you are trying to find out about? What is the object of your inquiry, what methods can you use, and most important of all, when does your object of inquiry—and thus the questions demanding answers—change, opening a new paradigm moment, a new "problem space"? David Scott has done much, especially in his challenging new reading of C. L. R. James's *The Black Jacobins*, to make me think about this idea of a problem space and to relate it to what Althusser called "a problematic" and Gramsci called "the conjuncture." Does this cluster of concepts refer to aspects of the same thing? (Incidentally, I nearly said when David had finished his wonderful paper that we can go home now, because we now know all we ever need to know about the thought of Stuart Hall!)[8] David said that the question I am addressing is what he called the "contingency of the present." Now, actually, I would not quite put it that way myself, although I understand perfectly well why he did. I would say that the object of my intellectual work is "the present conjuncture." It is what Foucault called "the history of the present." It is, "What are the circumstances in which we now find ourselves, how did they arise, what forces are sustaining them, and what forces are available to us to change them?" The "history of the present," which is a kind of Foucauldian way of talking, brings together two rather contradictory ideas: history and the present. The present sounds as if it is very "presentist" in its implication: right now, what is happening to us right now. What confronts us immediately now, which is certainly what he describes as "dangerous and difficult times." Yet the history of the present commits us to thinking of its anterior conditions of existence, what Foucault might have called its "genealogies." So the present, of course, is a force we have to now transform, but in the light of the conditions under which it came into existence: the history of the present. The question of the contingency of the history of the present is critically important because this is what I want to say about the present—that it is the product of "many determinations" but that it remains an open horizon, fundamentally unresolved, and in that sense open to "the play of contingency."

Contingency and Identity

Here I am simply going to try to identify a number of ideas or themes which have emerged over the course of the past few days and make a few brief remarks about them before I pass on. Why contingency? What is it that I have been wanting to say about contingency? I do not want to say, of course, that the world has no pattern, no structure, no determinate shape, no determinacy. But I do want to say that its future is not already wrapped up in its past, that it is not part of an unfolding teleological narrative whose end is known and given in its beginning. I do not believe, in that sense, in "the laws of history." There is no closure yet written into it. And to be absolutely honest, if you do not agree that there is a degree of openness or contingency to every historical conjuncture, you do not believe in politics, because you do not believe that anything can be done about it. If everything is already given, what is the point of exercising yourself or of trying to change it in a particular direction? This is a paradox which lies, of course, right at the heart of classical Marxism. If the laws of history are certain to unfold, who cares about the practice of the class struggle? Why not just let them unfold? There are a whole series of Marxisms which were precisely mechanistic and reductionist in that "scientistic" way. Let the laws of capital unfold! Contingency does require you to say, "Of course, there are social forces at work here." History is not infinitely open, without structure or pattern. The social forces at work in any particular conjuncture are not random. They are formed up out of history. They are quite particular and specific, and you have to understand what they are, how they work, what their limits and possibilities are, what they can and cannot accomplish. As Gramsci said, "Pessimism of the intellect, optimism of the will." But the outcome of the struggle between those different contending relations or forces is not "given," known, predictable. It has everything to do with social practice, with how a particular contest or struggle is conducted. Even Marx, who was too inclined to subscribe to nineteenth-century scientific historical laws, thought the triumph of socialism which was supposed to be written in "the logic of history" was not inevitable. He saw another alternative—one which unfortunately seems much closer in the days of the New World Order. "Socialism or barbarism," he predicted, "the ruin of the contending classes."

My task has been to try to think what determinacy means—what I once called "the contradictory, stony ground of the present conjuncture"—but without falling into absolute determinacy. I do not believe history is already determined. But I do believe that all the forces at work in a particular historical conjuncture or a situation one is trying to analyze, or a phase of history or development one is trying to unravel, are *determinate*. They do not arise out of nowhere. They have their own specific conditions of existence. So the conceptual issue is, is there a way of thinking determinateness which is not a closed determinacy? And contingency is the sign of this effort to think determinacy without a closed form of determination. In the same way, people say, "You are a conjuncturalist. You want to analyze, not long epochal sweeps of history, but specific conjunctures." Why the emphasis on the conjunctures? Why the emphasis on what is historically specific? Well, it has exactly to do with the conception of a conjuncture. The fact that very dissimilar currents, some of a long duration, some of a relatively short duration, tend to fuse or condense at particular moments, into a particular configuration. It is that configuration, with its balance of forces, which is the object of one's analysis or intellectual inquiry. The important thing about thinking conjuncturally is its historical specificity. So, for example, to put it very crudely, I am not as interested in racism as a single phenomenon marching unchanged through time, but in different racisms that arise in specific historical circumstances, and their effectiveness, their ways of operation. I am less interested in capital or capitalism from the seventeenth century to now than I am in different forms of capitalism. I am interested particularly, just now, in the enormously important shift in global capitalism which occurs in the 1970s. That represents the end of what I would call one conjuncture: the conjuncture of the period of postwar settlement, dominated largely—especially in Europe—by a social-democratic balance of forces and the welfare state, and the beginning of the rise of neoliberalism, of global capitalism, and the dominance of "market forces," which constitutes the contradictory ground on which new interrelationships and interdependencies are being created across the boundaries of nationhood and region, with all the forms of transnational globalization that have come to dominate the contemporary world. This is what is stamping a new rhythm on politics, in different ways, across the face of the globe. Nation-states, national cultures, national economies remain important, but these "differences" are being condensed into a new, contradictory "world system," which is what the term "global" actually stands for. This is radically different from the world of decolonization—what David Scott has called "the Bandung moment"—into which new nations, like Jamaica, emerged. This is a radically new historical moment and sets us radically new questions, radically new political questions. That is all that is entailed in the move from one conjuncture to another. And the task of—as I once put it—"turning your face violently towards things as they really are" is what is required by "thinking conjuncturally."

I have also emphasized the question "Why identity?" I am interested in identity because identity is a source of agency in action. It is impossible for people to work and move and struggle and survive without investing something of themselves, of who they are, in their practices and activities, and building some shared project with others, around which collective social identities can cohere. This is precisely because, historically, there has been an enormous waning and weakening in the given collective identities of the past—of class and tribe and race and ethnic group and so on, precisely because the world has now become more pluralistic, more open-ended, though of course those collective identities have not disappeared in any sense. So those constraints are still on any identity formation. But to me there is a relatively greater degree of openness in the balance between the "givenness" of an identity and the capacity to construct it or make it. That is all that I was trying to register in the new work on identity. I thought the greater global interdependence and interconnectedness would undermine strongly centered but exclusive identities and open the possibility of more complex ways of individuals and groups positioning themselves in their own narratives. And I believed that the complexities of the black and "creole" cultures of the Caribbean and the complexities of the "hybrid" diaspora identities emerging in the wake of global migration had a great deal to teach us about the dynamics of this new process of identity formation. Paradoxically, you might think that the revival of fundamentalisms of all lands runs counter to this thesis. Actually, I believe that the pull of fundamentalism and all types of exclusive identities is a reaction to being marginalized or left out of the process of "vernacular modernization"—the search everywhere for all peoples to have equal access to the means of becoming "modern persons" and to live the technological possibilities of modern life, in their own ways, to the fullest, as it were, "from the inside," which I think is, hesitantly, also going on across the world: in the very teeth of the struggle by global capital to master and hegemonize historically constituted differences.

However, though I wrote a lot about "identity," I always refused the notion that a whole politics could be identified with any single identity position. I have tried to say that identity is always the product of a process of identification. It is the product of taking a position, of staking a place in a certain discourse or practice. In other words, of saying, "This is, for the moment where I am, who I am and where I stand." This positional notion of identity enables one then to speak from that place, to act from that place, although sometime later in another set of conditions, one may want to modify oneself or who it is that is speaking. So in that sense, identity is not a closed book any more than history is a closed book, any more than subjectivity is a closed book, any more than culture is a closed book. It is always, as they say, in process. It is in the making. It is moving from a determinate past toward the horizon of a possible future, which is not yet fully known.

Globalization and Diaspora

I want to think of one more set of terms, which has arisen during the course of our discussion. These are around the terms "diaspora" and "globalization." I was, as you can imagine, absolutely astonished to discover that the Jamaican government is this week having the very first conference on the diaspora. Since the *Empire Windrush* landed in 1948, there has been a massive black diaspora in Britain, and I am not only thinking about the numbers of people from the Caribbean, Africa, India, and elsewhere from the former colonial world who have landed up in Britain and the other postcolonial metropolises since World War II. What is happening to the nation, here, cannot be insulated from the process of globalization and from the formation of diasporas elsewhere—which is, indeed, in my view, the "dark side" of the globalization process. I do not have time to unravel this problem, but I do want to say one or two things, rather dogmatically, about it. In this new awareness of "the diasporic" dimension, something very important is happening to the idea of nations and nationhood, to nationalism, which was the driving force of decolonization and to social identities. The nation cannot be taken unproblematically as the "given" entity which social and historical explanation takes for granted. What's more, the nation cannot be any longer identified with its territorial boundaries. Further, the nation is a territorial entity and a political power, but it is also an "imagined community," and so the questions about how the nation is constructed culturally and represented are part of its contemporary reality. These three dimensions interact, but they are not the same and do not always coincide. Now, the thinking so far in Jamaica about its diaspora is, of course, really just emerging—I think it is a sign of how slowly but irreversibly globalization is decentering the experience of nation-building which focused our minds in the first stage of decolonization. I do think you largely think of Jamaicans living abroad as just like you, as belonging to you. I think you largely think, these are really *us*—only, over there. When they come back, they will come back and rediscover their "us-ness." This is, of course, partly true: of course, those connections are deep and long-lasting and are constantly reforged. But don't you think about how they made any connections with there as well as with here? Do you think people live a whole life, survive in strange conditions, often of poverty, discrimination, and certainly of institutional and informal racism in Britain—brought up children, schooled them, watched them grow up in the multicultural metropolis—and it does not rub off in any way on them? Do you imagine their culture—their Jamaicanness—which they took with them just goes on throbbing, unchanged, untransformed, preserving their culture as a fixed umbilical cord? Of course, they have roots, but don't you think they also had to put down new roots? How otherwise did they survive? For Caribbean people—part of a colonial and Pan-African diaspora who, having emigrated again, have been twice "diasporized," who go on being "translated"—their "routes" are as critical to their identities as their "roots." Oh, they certainly survived by thinking about home. They planned from the beginning to go back home. They are a little disturbed when they return that everybody says, "But you been in 'foreign'!" Something about the way you stand, walk, talk, shift around, or, as somebody said, can't move the hips, marks out the difference!

The problem of the diaspora is to think of it always and only in terms of its continuity, its persistence, the return to its place of origin, and not always and at the same time in terms of its scattering, its further going out, its dissemination. The impossibility of ever going home in exactly the same way as you left it. The diaspora is always going to be, in a certain way, lost to you. It has to be lost to you, because "they" have a double stake, an investment in both here and elsewhere. It is not because they love us or because elsewhere has been good to them, but because the material conditions, the historical necessity, of having to "make a life" means that they have to have ideas, investments, relationships with somewhere else as well. Now, my writing about the notion of the diaspora, about identity, even about the necessary "hybridity" or creolization of all culture, has been shaped profoundly by reflecting on the Caribbean experience, even when I have not directly written about it. I have been trying to think about these very complicated processes of continuity and rupture, of the return to the old, of the imaginary recuperation or reconfiguring of the old, as well as the becoming—the opening to the new, to the future—and what is happening, concretely, on the ground, in everyday life, in changing the culture of those people who have been "diasporized." That is certainly one dimension of the work that I have been trying to do on the diaspora.

The second one is to remember that in the particular circumstances of the Caribbean, the people are themselves "a diaspora." We are ourselves the effect of the dislocation and displacement, of the dissemination from somewhere else, and of what then happens, culturally, as, out of the cauldron of colonization, enslavement and plantation society, something new, something genuinely novel, emerges. Does that mean that we do not have any connection with what went before? How could it possibly mean that? But it does mean that that connection is not something which can now be naturally summoned up as if it exists in all of us, somewhere down there, in our bodies, in our genes, as a force of nature. It has to be re-created, has to be sustained in the culture, reconfigured, in the new historical circumstances which confront us. It has to be sustained in the mind, or the connection cannot be made. We would be wrong to adopt a notion of tradition as something which does not change, which protects us against change. As I have had to say to people before, "Africa is alive and well in the diaspora," but the Africa we left four hundred years ago under the conditions of slavery, transportation, and the Middle Passage has not been waiting unchanged—to go back to, either in our heads or in our bodies. That Africa, far from being just the ancestral home, is the subject of the most brutal and devastating modern forms of exploitation. It is the subject and the object of the most vicious forms of contemporary neoliberalism, victim of the strategies of the new forms of geopolitical power, as well as ravaged by civil war, poverty, hunger, the rivalry of competing gangs, and corrupt governing powers and elites. Long after we left it, even after the war, Africa was first of all inserted into a relationship with the West in the very moment of decolonization, in the relations of neocolonial subordination. In the second phase of the Cold War, all the difficulties of creating independent polities and independent national economies were overridden by the Cold War struggle between two competing world systems. All the difficulties of the emerging societies and the nascent postcolonial states were overridden by the struggle between the two world powers: a struggle which was then, paradoxically, fought out on postcolonial terrain. When next we invoke the problem of "failed states" in Africa, let us remember the distortions that the Cold War imposed on the problems of the emerging postcolonial states. Remember who is implicated in the failure of the capacity of those states. Since the mid-1970s, those already-failing states, states with the enormous difficulty—never resolved—of becoming postcolonial, like the Caribbean and elsewhere in the so-called Third World, have been enmeshed in new constitutive relations of geopolitical, economic, cultural, and symbolic global power: the new system, the New World Order. That is what the signifier "Africa," so often bandied about in Western media and political discourse, means today. I do not need to unpack that story for you. Now, of course, there is the most profound connection between the African diasporas of the Caribbean, the US, of Brazil, and Latin America and the diasporas of London or Paris, but these different "Africas," though deeply interconnected, historically, cannot be "the same" any longer. They are not the same. There are, of course, strong and deep persistent threads which connect them. At the same time, each has negotiated its relation to the West, to the surrounding world, differently. This is the complicated dialectic of "sameness" and "difference" which confronts us in today's globalizing world. So when one talks about the way in which identities of this kind have been ruptured by the different conjunctural breaks in postwar history, reorganized and reordered by them, yielding deep and concretely specific, differentiated formations, we know we have to, not discover, but *rediscover* what our connection now is with Africa. I believe this is the difference between a "cultural nationalist" approach to our African connection and the Pan-African imaginary, which has done so much over the years to keep these connections alive. The concept of "diaspora" is—for me—central to that imaginary.

So diaspora led me to think, first of all, about what is happening, and the complicated cultural processes going on, in the black diasporas of the metropole. Second, it led me to think about what exactly is meant by the "diasporic" nature of Caribbean society and Caribbean culture. What exactly do we mean by that? And that led me to think about the diasporic nature of cultures themselves. I became aware of the fact that, discursively, cultures always represent themselves as fixed, exclusive, originary, and unchanging, but, historically, when you look at them, that cannot be the case. Some change very slowly, some more rapidly: but they all change. They are all interrupted by movement, by conquest, by colonization, by trade, by migration, free and forced. They are disrupted by external influences, as well as evolving internally. Culture—the forms through which individuals and societies make sense of themselves and represent their real conditions of life, symbolically, to themselves—cannot be outside of history. Cultures are changed within and changed by history. So the broadly diasporic nature of culture itself is a kind of conceptual model that I have derived, analogically, from, thinking about a specific diaspora and reflecting on the diasporic nature of the culture which I thought I had left behind and had to rediscover in myself and come to terms with in a different way. This is my very long way of trying to answer the question, "In what sense can I be 'a Caribbean intellectual'"?

Just a final twist to that: under globalization, everywhere is becoming more diasporic. It is not because people like to travel. It is because the very conditions under which the world now operates create what one can only call the astonishing late twentieth-century, early twenty-first-century movement of dispersed peoples. From that perspective, I go back and look at my own movement in 1951, the black migration, and the migration from the Asian subcontinent to Britain in the 1950s and 1960s as the beginning of an enormous historical tide. The disruption of people from their settled places, from their homes, from their familiar surroundings, their roots in the land and landscape, from their traditional ways of life, from their religions, from their familial connections—the uprooting that has become the history of modern "global society." The fact of the homeless, of what Negri and Hardt, in their book *Empire* call "the multitudes"; of people who only survive by buying a ticket from some person who is trading in bodies; hanging out on the bottom of a train, crossing boundaries in the depth of night, running the gauntlet of surveillance cameras and border patrols, and disappearing into the depths of the cities.[9] The economic migrants and the asylum seekers, the illegal immigrants, the "*sans papiers*," the ones without proper papers. The ones driven into the camps across the borders by famine, civil war, environmental devastation, or pandemic. A movement of people trying never to be "there" crossing every boundary in the world. And think, though we did not know it at the time, we were the forerunners! Since then, into the UK alone, there have been—how many? Seven waves? Caribbean, Indians, Pakistanis, people from Bangladesh, West Africans, Cypriots, Chinese, then the people displaced from North Africa and the Middle East—from Afghanistan, Iraq, the people displaced from ethnic cleansing in the Balkans, now the people from Eastern Europe, from the former Soviet empire. Wave after wave after wave of people living in the new multicultural metropole, presenting the question of "How is it possible to make a life where people from very different historical backgrounds and bearing different cultural values and religious traditions are required to make some kind of common life?" People attempting to negotiate the terms of some kind of tolerant life without either eating one another, shooting one another, or separating out into warring tribal enmity.

That is what I call the multicultural question of modern times. And this globalization from below is occurring in the context of the globalization from above, which is of course the movement of every single thing apart from people. The movement of capital, of technologies, the "flow" of messages and images, the "flow" of investment, the movement of entrepreneurs, of the executive corporate global class. Everybody is "on the move" according to the logic of globalization, except the poor. Labor—ordinary folks—is the only factor which is not supposed to move. Why? Because how can you take competitive advantage of the translocation of production and consumption if the one-dollar-a-day laborer in Latin America is going to be "free" to move to the West Coast and claim advanced salaries? The function of the dispersal of capital around the globe of the decentralization of capital in the modern global system depends on the capacity to exploit labor, cheap labor, where it is! So the control on the movement of how many people are allowed to cross borders is absolutely central to the new, constituent logic of contemporary globalization. The movement of peoples for economic purposes—escaping poverty, escaping ill health, escaping ecological devastation, escaping civil war, escaping ethnic cleansing, escaping rural depopulation, escaping overurbanization, escaping a thousand and one problems—has become illegal. This is the underbelly of the contemporary globalization system. Therefore, our new diasporas are simply one part of this huge new historic movement, of a huge new geopolitical formation, which is creating the mixtures of cultures and peoples and histories and backgrounds and religions, which is the contemporary problem of the modern world.

Speaking Truth to Power

So though I started with a question of diaspora in a rather limited empirical way, it has—here's my last reflection on the thought of Stuart Hall—in its usual way, undergone enormous conceptual expansion. It has illuminated something else of vital significance to the Caribbean. The idea of the diaspora now is obliterating, not nations and nationhood, but the moment of the nation-state, the moment of nationalism. It is quietly subverting it. It is quietly transcending the project of one life in one nation, in one nation-state, located in one national economy, and superintended by one national culture, attached to one national identity, which was for decades the driving vision of nationalism.

What the ultimate balance might be between globalization from above and globalization from below, whether there is any way of transforming that system, it is not my purpose at this stage to discuss. I am trying to suggest what it might mean to be riveted throughout my life by the present conjuncture, by being disturbed by, and trying to analyze so as to transform, systems and structures of power, of injustice, of inequality, which are generated by forces that one does not fully understand and whose consequences one therefore cannot fully estimate and whom one cannot therefore effectively resist. Well, I commend to you what I have to call the politics of intellectual life. David Scott quite rightly said that, though he would not subscribe to everything that Edward Said has said about the nature of intellectual life, there is a kind of vocation there which is similar to my own. I am honored by the comparison, for Edward Said's life and practice have been exemplary for me, and I mourn deeply and personally his recent death. I do think it is a requirement of intellectuals to speak a kind of truth. Maybe not truth with a capital *T* but, anyway, some kind of truth, the best truth they know or can discover—to speak that truth to power. To take responsibility, which can be unpleasant and is no recipe for success, for having spoken it. To take responsibility for speaking it to wider groups of people than are simply involved in the professional life of ideas. To speak it beyond the confines of the academy. To speak it, however, in its full complexity. Never to speak it in too simple a way, because "the folks won't understand." Because then they will understand, but they will get it wrong, which is much worse! So, to speak it in its full complexity, but to try to speak it in terms in which other people who, after all, can think and do have ideas in their heads, though they are not paid or paid-up intellectuals, need it. They need it like you and I need food. They need it in order to survive. I commend the vocation of the intellectual life in this sense to you. I remind you that the academy is one of the places in which it takes root. It is not the only place, and I do plead with you not to overestimate its role or to get entrammeled in its internal rituals. Simply because one is on the site, you might be led to think that somehow, because you are there, you are therefore thinking. It does not absolutely follow, believe me! But I commend to you the duty to defend it and the other sites of critical thought. I commend you to defend it as a space of critical intellectual work, and that will always mean subverting the settled forms of knowledge, interrogating the disciplines in which you are trained, interrogating and questioning the paradigms in which you have to go on thinking. That is what I mean by borrowing Jacques Derrida's phrase "thinking under erasure." No new language or theory is going to drop from the skies. There is no prophet who is going to deliver the sacred books so that you can stop entirely thinking in the old way and start from year one. Remember that revolutionary dream? "Year One"? "From now on, socialist man"? This is when the new history begins! Today, the dawn of the realm of freedom! I am afraid the realm of freedom will look mostly like the old realm of servitude, with just a little opening here and there toward the horizon of freedom, justice, and equality. It will not be all that different from the past; nevertheless, something will have happened. Something will have moved. You will be in a new moment, a new conjuncture, and there will be new relations of forces there to work with. There will be a new conjuncture to understand. There will be work for critical intellectuals to do. I commend that vocation to you, if you can manage to find it. I do not claim to have honored that vocation fully in my life, but I say to you: that is kind of what I have been trying to do all this while.

NOTES

1 This essay was first presented to the conference titled "Culture, Politics, Race and Diaspora: The Thought of Stuart Hall," held at the Centre for Caribbean Thought, Department of Government, University of the West Indies, Mona, Jamaica, in June 2004. I want to thank Brian Meeks, Anthony Bogues, Rupert Lewis, directors of the Centre for Caribbean Thought, University of the West Indies, Mona, for the enormous work which has gone into organizing and presenting this conference, and Rex Nettleford for his generosity. I also want to thank Adlyn Smith, Sonjah Stanley Niaah, and others who worked with me to prepare for this conference and the University Library for its tremendous work of research and discovery.

2 See Michael Rustin, "Working from the Symptom: Stuart Hall's Political Writing," in *Culture, Politics, Race and Diaspora: The Thought of Stuart Hall*, ed. Brian Meeks (Kingston: Ian Randle, 2007).

3 See George Lamming, *The Pleasures of Exile* (London: Alison and Busby, 1984).

4 Lamming, *Pleasures of Exile*, 41; emphasis in original.

5 Richard Drayton in George Lamming, *The Pleasures of Exile* (London: Pluto Press, 2005).

6 Barrington Chevannes, Dean of Social Sciences at the University of the West Indies, Mona, 2004, and chair of Stuart Hall's address.

7 See Larry Grossberg, "Stuart Hall on Race and Racism: Cultural Studies and the Practice of Contextualism," in *Culture, Politics, Race and Diaspora: The Thought of Stuart Hall*, ed. Brian Meeks (Kingston: Ian Randle, 2007).

8 David Scott's paper, which opened the conference, was titled "Stuart Hall's Ethics." It was published in *Small Axe* 17 (2005).

9 See Michael Hardt and Antonio Negri, *Empire* (Cambridge, MA: Harvard University Press, 2000).

blacks, 57, 75–79, 81, 89–90, 92, 186, 197, 203, 216, 254, 263–264, 267, 268, 273, 277, 280, 283–285, 287, 290, 293, 298; black churches, 193; black consciousness, 19, 90, 192, 291–292; black crime, 8, 9, 255; black diasporas, 73, 84, 89, 93, 138, 193–194, 204, 206, 214, 307, 316, 319 (*see also* blacks, British; African Americans; Afro-Caribbeans); black experience, 76, 78, 90, 92, 93, 268, 275, 282; black film-makers, 57, 203; black identity, 56, 76, 77, 256; black Marxists, 203; black mascu-linities, 78, 92–93; black nationalists, 203; blackness, 5, 56, 78, 80, 93, 107, 110, 127, 219, 229, 297; black photographers, 12, 203, 263; black politics, 76, 91, 93, 197, 265, 283–284, 290; black popular culture, 56, 59, 83–85, 87–93, 293; black society, 8, 138, 192, 203; black students, 135, 203, 282; black subject, 9, 17, 57, 78, 93, 257–258, 268; black women, 78, 93, 280; black youth, 12, 56, 111, 115, 254, 293. *See also* Africa; Africans; African slaves; African Americans; Afro-Asians; Afro-Caribbeans; black arts initiatives; blacks, British; race; racism

blacks, British, 115, 126, 213, 215, 290; *Black Britain* (Gilroy and Hall), 263

Black Sea, 153

Blair, Tony: Blairite positions, 127, 296

Bogart, Humphrey, 274

Bogues, Tony, 305

Bosnia, 96, 100, 111, 210

Bougainville, Louis Antoine de, 162, 166, 174

bourgeoisie, 34, 179, 187; bourgeois state, 36

Bradford, England, 106

Brathwaite, Edward Kamau, 241–242

Brazil, 150, 318

Brecht, Bertolt, 19n4

Brett, Guy, 217

Brexit referendum, 60, 231

Bristol, 194

Britain, 25, 56–57, 59–60, 73–74, 76–77, 80, 104–105, 107–109, 111, 115–117, 126–127, 197–199, 206–207, 229–230, 240, 254, 257, 268, 276–278, 283–284, 287, 290–291, 295–297, 316; "being British," 117; black-and-British, 115, 126; British cities, 108,

221; British class politics, 284, 286, 289; British colonies, 151, 173; British culture, 55–57, 64, 109, 117, 196, 287; British diaspora, 91; British documentary move-ment, 196, 201; British empire, 2; British explorers, 151; British law, 119; British Marxists, 195; British multiculturalism, 112, 119, 126; Britishness, 12, 59, 104, 109, 116–117, 126; British people, 104, 105, 195, 277, 294; British politics, 6, 8–9, 64, 196, 284–285; British popular culture, 216, 292; British race relations, 48, 225, 267; British socialist politics, 283; British society, 12, 48, 95, 107, 117, 204, 217, 254, 263, 290, 297; British stoicism, 288; Brit-ish working class, 286; British writers, 81; British youth, 216; Cool Britannia, 108. *See also* England; Scotland; United Kingdom

British Communist Party, 251

British East India Company, 151

British Film Institute (BFI), 3, 201, 246

Brixton, 106, 196, 220

broadcasting, 136, 245

Brown, Brother Everald, 212

Bukharin, Nikolai, 30, 31

Burke, Edmund, 175–176

Burma, 288–289

Bush, George W., 274

business, 106, 152, 189, 273

Butler, Judith, 128n17

Byron, Commodore John, 164

Byzantium, 154

Cabot, John, 151

Cabral, Pedro, 150

Calcutta, 84, 286

Cambridge School Certificate, 188

Cambridge University, 199

Campaign for Nuclear Disarmament (CND), 3, 197, 199

Canada, 96, 129, 151, 188, 206

cannibalism, 166, 168, 169–170, 173; cannibals, 137, 170–172

canon, traditional Western artistic, 59, 79, 87

Cape Bojador, 149

Cape of Good Hope, 149

capital, 24–25, 36–37, 48–50, 88, 189, 215, 222, 244, 249–250, 271, 294, 314, 320–322; cultural, 89; Fordist, 271; global, 101, 271, 315; industrial, 36, 271; international, 36; merchant, 271; moral, 196. *See also* capitalism

capitalism, 26, 36, 66, 142, 148, 178–180, 247, 271, 283, 286, 311, 314; capitalist economies, 39, 49, 50; capitalist relations, 253; capitalist world market, 214; development of, 24, 138, 179; global, 271, 296–298, 314. *See also* capital

Carby, Hazel, 8, 127n3

Carew, Jan, 307

Caribbean Artists Movement, 240–241

Caribbean federation, 194, 203

Caribbean islands, 2, 104, 165, 168, 194, 211, 218, 255, 269, 305, 317, 167, 289, 229, 261; artists from, 220; black settlements in, 206; Caribbean culture, 201, 211–214, 219–220, 244, 306, 319; Caribbean history, 188, 206, 221, 307; Caribbean music, 193; Caribbean nationhood, 188, 206, 207, 215, 218; Caribbean people, 206, 208–211, 215, 218, 224, 268, 276, 306, 317; Caribbean societies, 109, 193, 220, 255, 305, 319; Caribbean writers, 189, 237; Caribs, 170–171; Hall as a Caribbean intellectual, 305–308, 319; migrants from, 58, 105, 127, 206, 207, 221, 229; returnees to, 105, 207. *See also* Afro-Caribbeans; Haiti; Jamaica; Martinique; Trinidad; West Indies

Caribbean World Service, 276

Caribs, 170–171

carnivalesque, the, 87, 94

Carnival Queens, 212

Carolinas, 150, 167

Cathay, myth of, 163

Catholicism, 45, 150, 153–154; Catholic majesties, 158, 166; Celtic-Catholic element, 104

Catholicism, popular, 45, 52

cccs. *See* Centre for Contemporary Cultural Studies

center and periphery, 223

Central America, 150, 165, 167. *See also* Latin America

Central Asia, 100, 152, 153

Central Europe, 98

Centre for Caribbean Thought, 301, 323n1

Centre for Contemporary Cultural Studies (cccs), 3–4, 8, 19, 135, 228, 233n8, 245, 266; Race and Politics Group, 8. *See also* Cultural Studies

Césaire, Aimé, 212

Ceuta, battle of (1415), 148

Ceylon (Sri Lanka), 70, 148

Chamberlain, Mary, 207

Chambers, Iain, 208

Charles X, 173

Chelsea College, 201–202

Chen, Kuan-Hsing, 5, 137, 185

Chevannes, Barry, 310

China, 36, 102, 106, 109, 139, 141, 146–147, 149–150, 152–153, 160, 163, 176, 178, 203, 211, 278, 298, 320; Canton, 149; "Cathay" myth, 163; Chinese culture, 102; Chinese silk, 152; Ming dynasty, 153; Quinsay, 141, 150

Christianity, 139, 149, 150, 153, 158, 193, 212; Christ, 154; Christendom, 153–154, 156; Christianization, 220; Christian saints, 211; Christmas story, 209; Orthodox churches, 154. *See also* churches; Church of England

churches, 40, 52, 153, 172–173, 220, 253. *See also* Christianity; Church of England

Churchill, Winston, 296

Church of England, 173

cinema, 3, 196, 274; American, 274; emerging work in, 55. *See also* films

civil rights movement, 75

civil society, 19, 38–39, 41–42, 52, 165–166, 176, 253, 261; institutions of, 40, 42, 47

Clapham, 279

class, 5–9, 34, 36–38, 48–51, 55, 57, 66–68, 116–117, 195, 198, 249–250, 256–257, 281–283, 286, 292; anticlassism, 78; class interests, 158, 160; class politics, 2, 283–284, 289; class relationships, 27, 48; class structures, 11, 17, 46; class struggle, 10, 178, 180, 250, 313; English social class system, 274; English working-class family, 197; lower-middle class, 185, 186; middle-class homes, 186; social, 34, 36;

subaltern, 37, 79. *See also* middle class; working class

Codrington College, 188

Cold War, 2, 100, 189, 195, 198, 294, 318

colonialism, 40, 105, 180, 190, 192, 218; British colonies, 151, 173; colonial India, 98; colonial subject, 116, 306; colonial world, 187, 316; colonies, 104, 148, 152; colonized cultures, 113; colonizers, 12, 139, 166, 186, 211

Columbus, Christopher, 141, 149–150, 159, 161–163, 165–166, 168, 170; voyages of, 147

commodities, 173, 175

The Communist Manifesto (Marx and Engels), 189

Communist Party, 195–196, 199–200, 228, 238, 283; Italian, 27

Communist University of London, 251

communitarianism, 125, 126; communitarians, 96, 115, 120, 123

communities: cultural, 96, 106; ethnic, 107–109, 119; migrant, 105, 120; multiethnic, 96, 117

Cook, Captain James, 165, 167; biographer, 166; crew of, 168; death of, 168, 174; voyages of, 148

Cool Britannia, 108

Cortés, Hernán, 151

cosmopolitans, 124, 127, 139

counterhegemony, 253

counterideology, 253

counterpolitics, 63, 74, 78, 295

Creoles, 213; creolization, 12, 128, 139, 211, 317

cricketers, 276

Crusades, 148, 153

Cuba, 36, 165; Cuban Revolution, 289

Cultural Studies, 4, 6, 11–13, 135–136, 227–228, 235–236, 243, 245–247, 250–251, 255–256, 266–268, 272, 305–306, 308, 310; academic, 7; implications of, 202. *See also* Centre for Contemporary Cultural Studies

culture, 44–45, 83–90, 104, 106–108, 112–116, 120–123, 127–128, 139, 143–146, 193–194, 211–216, 220–224, 242–249, 307–308, 317–319; black, 277; creole, 315; cultural difference, 85, 97, 109–112, 120, 125–126, 222–223, 231; cultural diversity, 4, 98, 121; cultural forms, 139, 213; cultural identity, 67, 85, 122, 185, 204, 207–210, 222, 267; cultural models, 187, 222; cultural politics, 44, 63–64, 73, 76, 79, 83–84, 86–87, 89, 91, 93, 203, 218, 253; cultural trauma, 8; high, 83–85, 87, 292; mass, 246; non-European, 145

cultures, precolonial, 113

Cypriots, 320

Daisy Miller (James), 273

dancehall music, 115, 215, 216

Dark Ages, 162

da Vinci, Leonardo, 147

Davis, Bette, 274

Dawes, Neville, 307

de Bry, Theodor, 164, 168

decolonization, 75, 84, 105, 227, 275, 305, 314, 316, 318

de las Casas, Bartolomé, 173

Delhi, 287

Demas, Willie, 236, 238

democracy, 39, 115, 124–125, 231

deracination, 193

Derrida, Jacques, 4, 55, 71–72, 102, 127, 212, 219, 259, 302, 322; différance, 71; politics of, 72

Desert Island Discs, 272

dialectic, cultural, 87

Dialogic: The Dialogic Imagination (Bakhtin), 194

dialogue, cross-cultural, 224

Dias, Bartolomeu, 149

diaspora, 89, 108, 114, 137, 185, 193, 203, 215, 227, 229, 279, 317; Caribbean, in Britain, 229; diaspora communities, 107, 245; diaspora formation and experience, 207–208; diaspora-ization, 215, 216; "diaspora of the diaspora" (Hall), 139; diasporic aesthetic, 213; diasporic cultures, 113, 319; diasporic populations, 139; Hall's diasporic perspective, 2, 9; marginalized, 5; modern, 214, 321; thinking and rethinking the, 138, 256

Diderot, Denis, 174, 176. *See also* immigrants and immigrant culture; migrants difference: ethnic, 57, 85; gender, 106; racial, 50, 85, 92, 109; religious, 109; sexual, 71, 85; shared racialized, 111

disasters, natural, 98

disciplines, 164, 235, 261, 267, 281, 306, 309–311, 322

discourse: authoritative cultural, 232; ideological, 45, 53

Dos Passos, John, 273

Douglas, Mary, 287

Dr. Zhivago, 228, 246

Drake, Sir Francis, 150

Drayton, Richard, 308

Dryden, John, 173

Du Bois Lectures (Harvard University), 17, 231

Durkheim, Émile, 22, 309

Dutch East India Company, 151

Eagleton, Terry, 249

East Africa, 76, 105; East African Asians, 106. *See also* Africa

Eastern Europe, 26, 100, 142, 153, 320; Eastern Europeans, 145, 260; underdeveloped societies in, 100

East Indies, 139, 148–149, 151; East Indians, 185–186, 211

East London, 12, 263

economy, 9, 17, 31, 67, 71, 247, 253, 260, 271; economists, 189, 195, 243

Ecuador, 151. *See also* Latin America; South America

Eden, Garden of, 162

Edinburgh Festival, 80

education: British academic, 188; classical, 188; political, 44

Egypt, 2, 8, 146, 193, 209, 220, 238

El Dorado, 162

elephants, 154, 163

Eliot, T. S., 188, 273

Ellison, Ralph, 274

Empire Windrush, 2, 58, 60, 105, 126, 206, 268, 307, 316

Encyclopédie (Diderot), 174

Engels, Friedrich, 22, 25, 249; *The Communist Manifesto*, 189

England, 5, 7–8, 74–76, 80–81, 137–138, 150, 152, 186, 191–192, 194–195, 221, 236–237,

241–243, 274–277, 306–307; "being English," 144; English culture, 1, 245, 279, 288; English history, 70, 188; English literature, 188; English slave trade, 173; Englishness, 80, 109, 117, 138, 194, 197; Little England, 126; Marxism in, 239; public school system in, 188; racism in, 287; social class system in, 274; as Spain's rival, 150. *See also* Britain; Thatcher, Margaret; United Kingdom

engravings of New World, 164, 174

Enlightenment, 66, 97, 102, 112, 137, 144, 175–178, 181, 222; post-Enlightenment, 137; Enlightenment modernity, 58; French, 176; post-Enlightenment, 115

Equal Opportunities Act, 127

Eratosthenes, 161

Ethiopia, 163, 220

ethnicity, 4–6, 8–9, 11–12, 17–19, 21, 26, 29, 52, 55–56, 58–59, 84–86, 108–112, 121–122, 228–231, 257; ethnic class struggles, 51; ethnic minorities, 60, 77, 106, 207

Eurocentrism, 2, 11, 53, 55, 122, 145, 229, 261

Europe, 25, 27, 60, 83–84, 88, 117, 119, 141–142, 144, 146–147, 149–150, 152–156, 158–159, 161, 164, 166–168, 170, 174–176, 202–203, 210–211, 219, 221, 261, 273; central, 98; cultures, 146, 160–161; eastern and western, 39, 145; high culture, 84–85; industrial, 50; nation-state system, 214; slave-masters, 186; western, 39, 56, 84, 105, 142, 145, 147, 154, 178, 180–181, 220. *See also* Eurocentrism; European Union

European Union, 215

exile, 192, 193, 207, 276, 307–308

expatriates, 194. *See also* diaspora; exile

exploitation, 44, 49–50, 97, 99, 109, 137–138, 148, 220, 252–253, 318

explorers: British, 151–152; Dutch, 151–152; Portuguese, 148–150; Spanish, 149–152. *See also* imperialism

Falkland Islands, 150, 297

Fanon, Frantz, 70, 84, 128, 219, 212, 221

Far East, 146, 151, 160, 189

fascism, 25–26, 28, 52

feminism, 4, 69, 81, 86, 118, 199, 203, 257, 258, 285; feminist critiques, 55; feminist history, 79; feminist writers, 71

Ferdinand (king of Spain), 149, 158, 172
Ferguson, Adam: *Essay on the History of Civil Society*, 176
Fernando, San, 212
feudalism, 142, 147, 178–179
films: film charts, 216; "Free Cinema" movement, 201; filmmakers, 232; film noir, 274; film studies, 201. *See also* Akomfrah, John; British Film Institute; cinema
First World, 100, 216, 261
Fisher, Jean, 224
Fordism, 271. *See also* capital
Foster, Hal, 85
Foucault, Michel, 4, 122, 136, 155–157, 159–161, 169, 252–253, 270, 308, 312; Foucauldian, 5, 115, 136, 312. *See also* power
France, 96, 105, 147, 152–153, 212; French Enlightenment, 176; French explorers, 151; Frenchness, 212; French Pacific, 162, 174; French philosophers, 173–174; French Republican traditions, 212; French thought, 72, 84, 155, 249; Gaullism, 212
Frankfurt School, 228, 248
Frears, Stephen, 56, 80
"Free Cinema" movement, 201
freedom, 209, 276, 322
Freedom Ride, 209
Freitas, Michael de (Michael X), 280, 299n13
Freud, Sigmund, 4, 65, 93, 100, 188. *See also* psychoanalysis

Galilean revolution, 147
Gama, Vasco da, 149, 158
Garvey, Marcus, 220, 258; Garveyism, 218, 220
gay and lesbian identity and politics, 4, 5, 81, 86, 93, 126. *See also* queer politics
gender, 4, 8, 29, 40, 56–57, 66, 78, 91–92, 104, 107, 116–117, 286
Genovese, Eugene, 10
Geographia (Ptolemy), 161
Germany, 105, 189, 249
Getty Collection, 263
Giddens, Anthony, 101, 127, 296
Gilman, Sander, 172
Gilroy, Paul, 8, 91, 125, 128, 214, 263–264, 267; *Black Atlantic* (Gilroy), 194; *Black Britain* (Gilroy), 263

Glissant, Edouard, 109
globalization, 100, 103, 206, 260, 297, 314, 316; contemporary, 101–102, 321; cultural, 84, 215; global culture, 84, 88, 102; global postmodern, 84–87; global postmodernism, 85–86
gold, 148, 150–151, 158–159, 162, 168
Golden Age, 161, 165–166, 187
The Golden Bowl (James), 273
government, 120, 166–167, 174, 177, 195, 236
Gramsci, Antonio, 4, 6, 11, 17–19, 21–49, 50–53, 78–79, 87–88, 101, 127, 228, 236, 244, 249–250, 252–253, 270–271, 310, 312–313; Istituto Gramsci (Rome), 23; as non-Leninist, 228, 249. *See also* hegemony
Great Exodus, 209
Great Khan, 141, 153
Great Moving Right, 6
Great Powers, 98
Greece, 58, 98, 105, 162; ancient Greeks, 174; Greek philosophers, 172
Grossberg, Larry, 272, 310
Grundrisse (Marx), 10–11, 18, 24, 178, 251, 271. *See also* Marx, Karl
Gunder Frank, Andre, 10
Guyana, 194, 217, 237. *See also* Latin America

Habermas, Jürgen, 119, 129
Hailsham, Lord, 288
Haiti, 139, 211–212; Haitian Revolution, 212. *See also* Caribbean islands
Hall, Alan, 195–196, 283
Hall, Catherine, 3, 202–203
Hall, Stuart, 13n1; anti-essentialist analysis of race and ethnicity, 7, 57; and Black Arts movement, 12; career, 6, 227; as a Caribbean intellectual, 305–308, 319; commentary on Marx's methodology, 10; directorship of cccs, 3, 233n8; education, 1–5, 195; as "familiar stranger" in Jamaica, 192; health, 263; Jamaican family, 1, 185, 186, 191–192; as "Negro," 5; at Oxford, 194–195; postgraduate work, 237–238; and questions of race, class, and≈ethnicity, 9, 12; style, 265
Hamlet (Shakespeare), 65
Handsworth, 106, 220

Mayfair, 298
McLennan, Gregor, 19
Mediterranean and Black Sea, 153
Meek, Ronald, 175–177
Meeks, Brian, 305
Melville, Herman, 273
Mercer, Kobena, 17, 19, 90, 213, 231, 232
Merleau-Ponty, Maurice, 200
metacommentary, 301
metaphors, 38, 193
methodology, 6, 9, 18, 272
Mexico, 151, 167
Michael X (Michael de Freitas), 280, 299n13
Middle Ages, 142, 147, 152, 162–163
middle class, 1, 76, 185–186, 190, 242, 246, 267, 277; colored, 242
Middle East, 98, 146, 160, 179, 210, 231, 295, 298, 320
Middle Passage, 307, 318
migrants, 8, 58–59, 105; mass migration, 307; migration, 12, 76, 98, 103, 105, 193, 206, 254, 294, 319–320
Miliband, Ralph, 284
Millar, John, 176
Ming dynasty, 153. See also China
minorities, 107, 113–114, 120, 126; minoritization, 222
modernism, 27, 84–85; British, 217; European, 217
modernity, 19, 55, 66, 97, 102–103, 112–114, 121, 135–137, 139, 177–178, 180–181, 210, 213, 217, 222–224; capitalist, 100, 138; global, 98, 297; late, 121, 193, 260; modern world, 22, 26, 37, 42, 66, 68, 88, 118, 182, 209, 295, 321
"The Modern Prince" (Gramsci), 29, 32
Moluccas, 149
Mona, Jamaica, 301
money, 175, 202–203, 251, 267
Mongols, 153
Montaigne, Michel de, 173
Montesquieu, 176
Moors, 148
More, Thomas, 147
Moscow, 30, 251
Moses, 194, 209
Mouffe, Chantal, 59, 103, 110, 118, 122, 124
Mozambique, 99

mugging, 8
multiaccentuality, 5, 47, 194; social, 213. See also multiculturalism
multiculturalism, 56–58, 60, 77, 87, 95–99, 111, 119, 124–125, 127, 230, 288, 290–294, 298; boutique, 97; Liberal, 96; "multiculturalism" vs. "multicultural," 95–98; multicultural diasporas, 113; multicultural metropole, 320; pluralist, 96. See also multiaccentuality; Report on the Future of Multi-Ethnic Britain
music, 89, 218, 220; American, 274; Beatles, 245; bhangra, 216; dancehall, 115, 215, 216; gangsta rap, 216; jazz, 274, 280; jungle, 115, 216; new, 90; ragga dancehall DJs, 216; reggae, 8, 193–194; tabla-and-bass, 216
Mussolini, Benito, 23, 28
My Beautiful Laundrette (film), 56, 80–81
myths, 65, 141, 159, 162–163, 209–210; classical, 162

naiads, 165, 169
Naipaul, V. S., 243, 307
Namibia, 99
narcissism, 231; "the narcissism of minor differences" (Ignatieff), 100
National Health Service, 104
nationalism, 59, 75, 117, 214, 277; postindependence, 218; racialized, 223
nation-states, 66, 98, 104, 214–215, 260, 314, 321
native peoples, 163, 167
Negri, Antonio, 320
neoliberalism, 227, 230, 260, 314
neutrality, cultural, 116, 129
Newby, Eric, 148, 163, 167
New England, 151, 275
New Labour, 108, 119, 125, 129, 230, 295–297; Blair/New Labour/Third Way position, 127
New Left, 2–3, 7–8, 12, 138, 194–201, 203, 235, 238, 242, 246–247; early, 203, 228, 247; first British, 196; old, 246; work on race, 197. See also New Left Clubs; New Left Review
New Left Clubs, 197, 198, 255, 280
New Left Review, 2, 197–198, 199–203, 232n2, 236, 238–239, 245–246, 284; club, 197. See also Universities and Left Review

University of London, 201
University of the West Indies (UWI), 206, 209
Utopia, 164–165; *Utopia* (More), 147

value, surplus, 14n16. *See also* labor
values: political, 103; traditional, 108
Venezuela, 162
Venice, 151, 152; Marco Polo, 153. *See also* Italy
Versailles Palace, 174
Vespucci, Amerigo, 150, 166, 169, 210
Vietnam, 36, 127
Vietnam War, 288
violence, 110, 125, 169, 209–210, 223, 281, 288
Vir, Parminder, 225n19
Virginia, 164
Volosinov, V. N., 5, 97, 213
Voltaire, 176

Walcott, Derek, 243
Wales, 104, 278, 283
Wallace, Michele, 85, 98
Walmsley, Anne, 241
Walpole, Horace, 175
Walzer, Michael, 118, 119, 129n25
war, 38, 40, 98, 105, 169, 188–189, 318; civil, 98, 318, 320–321
wealth, 152, 179, 215
Weber, Max, 22, 178–180, 309
welfare state, 104, 119, 230, 260, 294, 314
Werbner, Pnina, 128
West, Cornel, 83, 90
West, the, 25–26, 39–40, 139, 141–145, 154–157, 212, 222, 231; capitalism in, 113, 180, 189; civilization in, 59, 87, 97, 150, 224; culture in, 115, 181, 222; Enlightenment in, 177; expansion of, 181; media discourse in, 318; modernity in, 136, 210–211; nation-states in, 96, 101; non-Western societies, 141, 143–144, 155; political tradition in, 115; societies in, 101, 104, 143; "the West and the Rest," 141, 145–146, 148, 155–156, 159–161, 165, 171–172, 175–179, 182; westernization, 66, 102; women in, 145

West Indian federation, 194, 276. *See also* Caribbean islands; West Indies
West Indies, 5, 138, 150, 194–195, 206–207, 217, 221, 227, 235–237, 240, 243, 268, 276, 301, 307; black West Indians, 191; West Indian culture, 236; West Indian identity, 236, 276; West Indian literature, 7, 236–237; West Indian students, 194–195, 237. *See also* Afro-Caribbeans; West Indian Federation
Whannel, Paddy, 3, 13, 201, 228
White, Allon, 88
White, John, 164
Whitechapel Gallery, 217
white population, 107
Wieviorka, M., 111, 128n15
Williams, Aubrey, 217
Williams, Raymond, 3, 67, 195, 198, 199–202, 228, 238, 244, 246, 247, 268, 282–285
Windrush. See Empire Windrush
Wolpe, Harold, 9
women, 65, 106–107, 115, 118, 120, 122, 129–130, 165–166, 169, 172, 280, 283, 285, 307–308, 311
work: cultural, 80; graduate, 195–196, 202, 246
working class, 26, 27, 34, 50, 53, 195, 199, 249, 278, 283, 285–287; English working class, 197, 252; white, 37, 78; working-class backgrounds, 198; working-class culture, 129, 245–246; working-class history, 79; working-class speech, 245. *See also* class
world market, 66, 101, 215, 250
World War I, 27, 148
World War II, 98, 105, 316; Holocaust, 209
world wars, 214. *See also* World War I; World War II
Worsley, Peter, 228, 238, 284

xenophobia, 59, 230–231

York, 167; Yorkshire, 285
Young, Robert, 128n21
The Young Englanders (Hall), 7, 230, 254, 284
Young Soul Rebels (film), 93